What it was was Rockabilly

To Herb Merrill, Jr.,
Keypon Rockin

What it was was Rockabilly

A History and Discography
1927-1994

by
Richard E. Jandrow

Boxcar Publishing
Worcester, Massachusetts

LIBRARY OF CONGRESS CATALOG CARD NUMBER
95-75534

SUGGESTED AREA
Main entry under title:
What it was was Rockabilly,

(Music in American life)
Includes discographies and index.

1. Rock musicians — United States — Biography
I. Jandrow, Richard E., 1942-

ISBN
1-886791-01-5

1st Printing
Edited by Nancy DeFalco

Contents

Introduction

To say that this book is a mere compilation of information would be the same as saying that Elvis was just another singer and the Beatles were just another rock group.

When a historian compiles a history of a topic for the benefit of people in the future, he or she ordinarily does so out of an *interest* in the aspects of history presented and the times involved, in the hopes of sparking that same interest in the reader. My interest is one of pure feeling: Having loved the sound and the emotions of the times, but never really understanding what was happening, I can only relate this feeling to the similar feeling of those who attended Woodstock or to those who were ripe during the emergence of the Beatles.

To have been there during the beginning of rock and roll: to have experienced its uniqueness, but to have been too ignorant and too young to realize what was happening is something that I regret.

Jerry Lee Lewis, Elvis Presley, Hank Williams, Chuck Berry, Jimmie Rodgers (the original), Bill Haley, Gene Vincent, Carl Perkins, Bob Wills, Buddy Holly, Eddie Cochran — whether white or black, good or bad, smooth or rough --- all have something in common. They were associated with the beginnings of rock and roll. At the root of these beginnings was the creation and development of rockabilly music.

Rockabilly began in an era of despair and hunger, using an instrument that was assumed to be unsophisticated and simple, to create a background sound for the rhythm section only. The guitar, which was the basic instrument of the rockabilly sound, took many, many years to develop from the background, strictly rhythm sounds of the big bands, through the ranks of Negro blues and country pickin', and into the electric era of the 1950s and 1960s. It Went along with the early development of Negro blues and later into the white sounds of Jimmie Rodgers and the Carter Family.

In the beginning, there were various types of ethnic music, peculiar to the different areas of the country. Whether it be Kentucky bluegrass, Louisiana Cajun, Texas swing, Chicago blues, Tennessee country music, New York bop, 42nd Street breakdance music, or 16th Avenue country and western, the United States is unequaled in the variety of its musical forms and styles.

This book attempts to recreate one small aspect of the development of American popular music, through a form that was born in the late 1940s and early 1950s and went into seclusion in the 1960s, only to be resurrected in the 1980s. This type of music was called rockabilly, and the artists mentioned here were creators of this genre of rock 'n roll.

What It Was Was Rockabilly

Rockabilly: A Definition

The sounds of rockabilly began in the mountains of the South, and those that blocked the passage to the West, stopping at mid-country to merge with the inner-city sounds of the blacks and their roots in the older, more dated sounds of the African music that came to America during the early years of slavery. These sounds began to merge somewhere near the end of the 1940s and the beginning of the 1950s. Rockabilly was a reflection of the restlessness of youth, coupled with the desire for something that was theirs, and only theirs. It starts with the driving beat of an electric guitar, and sometimes, with a pumping piano, accented with heavy drums, or rhythm guitar. It grabs the energy of its youthful creators and propels itself through the sounds of the day, reflecting the rebelliousness of the time. It is a full sound, in that three musicians can sound like a full band; it is a very sexy sound, driven by the beat of a heart, projecting love on its audience: It is the fulfill-ment of years of musical development in this country that, somehow, refuses to die.

Epigraph

The fifties were the time of contentment and innocence... Even though we were at war, it seemed far away and non existent... The country was flourish-ing; people were travelling; and jobs were plenty... Everything was written for us in black and white and was good . A cheerleader could sleep with every member of the football team after the big game, and the next day she would be renewed as a virgin. There was magic in the air, and music in our hearts.. Then, it happened!!! On a nice quiet day in July, of 1954, in Memphis, Tennessee, a young hillbilly entered a recording studio and created a sound that would change the course of history.

What It Was Was Rockabilly

CHAPTER 1

THE CONCEPT

The late '40's and early '50's ushered in a state of flux that was to have a uniquely dramatic effect on every diminutive aspect of life as we knew it. It was during this period of time, after the development of the Atomic Bomb, and the Second World War, that the isolationism of the United States, which ended during the war, would be changed into a type of protectionism which would spread the culture of America throughout the world in a dramatic and hurried way.

In music, this movement started as an isolated segment of the American culture, and rose dramatically to engulf the imagination of the whole world. It began in the remotest parts of our country, in the hills, as far back as the '20's and '30's, and paralleled the development of the guitar as a main musical instrument, rather than a strictly background rhythm instrument. The big bands were beginning to disappear, and the singers of the bands began to become stars in their own right, but the war babies would reject this adult music, and search for a medium of their own.

> The year 1954, however, saw the emergence of a new musical force which completely engulfed the other musical forms, dominated American popular music for several years, and shattered the existing conception of what a popular song should be. *[Malone, 1985, p. 246]*

Thus, the innocence of the '40's, with the distinct divisions of styles and sounds, on a few music charts, would soon cause the development of new charts and subcharts, black mixed white. The merging of the cultures of our society would son develop into a tremendous force to be unleashed upon the world. With the advent of the '50's came a musical void: There were no songs for the teenagers. Popular music was comprised of show tunes, ballads, and sing-along novelty songs by such performers as Frank Sinatra, Perry Como, Johnny Ray, and Frankie Laine. It wasn't until 1953 that we began to hear the likes of Bill Haley, or "House of Blue Lights," and other sounds of the new rebellion.

Until the 50's, there were basically six major record companies: Columbia and Victor, which managed to survive since the beginning of recording in the late 1800's; Decca which was founded as the American division of British Decca, in 1932; Capitol which was founded in 1942, as the first major record company on the west coast; MGM which was established by the motion picture company in 1946; and Mercury Records which was formed in 1946 in Chicago.

It was the age of style. The youth of the day were desperately searching for something different—crew cuts, Balboas, DA's, Mohegan Cuts, Flattops, Pegged Pants, extra large suit coats (black leather jackets came a little later). Undershirts were worn as clothing with the sleeves rolled up (perhaps with a cigarette pack and matches in the sleeve). Fast cars, especially 32 Fords, were in, and so was Marlon Brando.

For teenagers, the void was not solely in the types of available music. There was also a void in movies suited to teenagers; movies were either for adults or for children. Thus teenagers were faced with the problem of having too much money and nothing to spend it on.

The world was boring to the teenagers of the day. Regardless of the rise of television, there was just nothing to do. Therefor teenagers began to hang around various locations, just looking for some form of action to fill up their time and create some excitement. Hanging out on a street corner, usually at a Spa or corner drug or candy store became popular. Local gangs began to form throughout the country, segmenting the teenage population even further.

Teenagers across the country began to search for and demand their own music, switching the dials as fast as they could to find music that they liked. In order to survive in the market, most radio stations at the time were generally required to play popular music. There were, however, many predominantly black stations cropping up all over the country, and many smaller independent stations in the smaller southern communities. The music that these stations played was the rhythm and blues of the north, and country and western of the South. Eventually these two types of music would merge.

The earliest sounds of rock and roll emerged from rhythm and blues, but the subject matter concerned the new tastes and style of the new teenage population that was developing across the country. The black musical hits contained disguised sexual innuendos, hidden in the lyrics, which were understood only by the subculture of blacks within the musical sphere. It would take most of the white population a number of years to understand the hidden meanings, although some would comprehend them immediately. Those who understood would become the artists or producers of the period.

The teenagers of the day, the white jukebox players, were seeking out and listening to the black singers and musicians for a different sound than they could find in their white world. These black artists were the legendary rhythm and blues artists who heretofore were known only in the black world. It was the time to break down the barriers that existed between the worlds, and to mesh together the primary sounds of each to create a third.

The early rock hits were merely cover songs -- songs recorded by white artists that had been hits by black artists in Rhythm and Blues, or hillbilly songs made popular in the country and western style. Until 1954 the cover versions of rhythm and blues records, done by white artists, or groups, generally outsold the independent black releases. For the most part, the deejays were forced to play the white versions, because whites controlled most of the radio stations in the country. The cover artists such as Pat Boone, The Diamonds, The Hilltopers, and others were brought in to record these songs simply to attract the white audience to the black sound. The major labels of the day — Columbia, RCA, Decca, Mercury, and Capitol — were too "respectable" even to consider having black artists on their label. This situation later led to the speedy growth of the smaller black labels.

In some cases, these white cover artists copied the music and style exactly as it was on the black records, but in other cases, they didn't even bother. When Pat Boone was placed before the teenagers instead of Little Richard, or Fats Domino, it didn't take too long for teenagers to realize that they were being fooled. To complete the picture, the large record companies were convinced that the teenagers were satisfied with the cover versions of the songs, since they, the owners, and producers, were satisfied.

> In 1955, the music industry started booming, beginning a climb in sales that kept going till 1959, by which time sales were almost treble what they had been in 1954. *[Gillitt, 1983,p.39]*

The major part of this increase in sales was due to the enormous amount of small independent labels that arose during this period. Some of these labels later became large in themselves, thus changing the industry's method of doing business and the content of the sound emanating from the recording studios.

> The vintage year for rock 'n' roll was 1956. Only nineteen rock 'n' roll records made the top ten that year, but they included many of the best records in that style. *[Gillitt, 1983, p. 40]*

As it happened, the majority of the hits for 1956 were in the typical previous top 40 pop type style, which obviously indicated that rock and roll did no yet totally dominate the market. The percentage of rock hits would increase every year, until rock would basically dominate the charts, and a new chart for middle of the road, or MOR, hits would be created.

CHAPTER 2

Beginnings

The new forms of music took many years to develop and did not arise overnight. The rhythm and blues and new country music sounds themselves took several years,while the new sounds of rock took even longer. This music would start in the hills and the open spaces of the country and blend with the current sounds of the time and the environments of its originators long before it would be classified as a new sound.

Jimmie C. Rodgers

Jimmie Rodgers was Born in Meridian, Mississippi, on September 8, 1897. and died in New York on May 26, 1933. He was the son of Aaron W. Rodgers, and Eliza Bozeman Rodgers. His mother died of tuberculosis when Jimmie was four years old: He grew up a sickly child.

Jimmie Rodgers has often been called the father of modern country and western music, and in this case, he was also one of the fathers of rockabilly — not a bad achievement for someone who lived a very brief life, in a relatively obscure area of the country.

He grew up surrounded by the sounds of country music, and the country Blues sounds of the Negro field workers singing of the pain and hardship of working in the fields. When he was a teenager he spent some time as a cowboy, but he quit to work on the railroad, his first real love.

For nearly ten years, he was a brakeman on the railroad, spending both his free time and his work time entertaining his fellow railroad workers with his guitar and songs. His compositions reflected his environmental background, and stressed the hard times of work and the fun of play.

Jimmie was well known when he met Carrie Williams, whom he married on April 7, 1920. At the time of their marriage, he contracted pneumonia, from which he never really recovered. Somewhere along the line, he had also contracted tuberculosis, and by 1923, he was no longer fit for railroading. Since he and Carrie had a daughter by this time, they found it tough to survive.

Carrie worked in a store, while Jimmie tried entertaining as a black faced musician in a travelling medicine show. Later, he worked white face in a tent show, and managed to scrape together enough money to buy out the owners of the show. In 1925, the tent, and all the equipment was wiped out by a tornado. Jimmie turned, once again, to railroading.

With the help of a friend, he travelled to Asheville, North Carolina, to work as a city detective; his wife and daughter would join him later. He soon got bored, however, and formed a group with three instrumentalists — Jack Pierce, on guitar; Jack Grant, on mandolin, and banjo; Claude Grant, on tenor banjo, and Jimmie, on tenor banjo. He called the group The Jimmie Rodgers Entertainers. He worked locally with the group, and soon convinced them to go north on a summer tour, to Baltimore. He later changed his mind when he found out that Ralph Peer, who was with the Victor Recording Company, was holding auditions in Virginia.

For some reason, the band decided to dessert him, and convinced Ralph Peer to record them separately as the Tenneva Ramblers. Peer was not that anxious to record Jimmie, but Jimmie convinced him to record two songs, for which Jimmie received twenty dollars. The recorded songs were "The Soldiers Sweetheart" and "Sleep Baby Sleep." After the recording, Jimmie moved on to Washington, D.C., where he worked odd jobs, basically forgetting about the recording business, for the time being..

However, having heard word of the moderate success of his recordings, he decided to further his musical career. He went to New

York, to convince Peer to let him record more songs. In November of 1927, Victor released "Away Out on the Mountain" and a song which was temporarily called "T For Texas" (complete with the Jimmie Rodgers yodel). This song was later released as "Blue Yodel No. 1." The concept of using the "Blue Yodel" titles would soon expand to include many tunes. Within six months, Jimmie was receiving upwards of $2000 a month in royalties.

In 1928, he recorded "Blue Yodel No. 2 (My Loving Girl Lucille)," "Blue Yodel No. 3 (The Evening Sun Yodel)," "Memphis Yodel," "My Little Home Town Down In New Orleans," and "Ben Dewberry's Final Ride." Almost every one of them sold a million copies within a short period of time, basically to the rural farmers of the day. Crowds began to follow Jimmie wherever he was playing, but it was the rural farmers and workers who purchased the records and made him successful. As he continued to tour the country, the crowds began to get larger and larger, and his songs became more and more successful. By 1933, he would sell close to 20 million records.

In 1928, the record company experimented with four songs and a corny backing of guitar, steel guitar, cornet, clarinet, and string bass. One of the songs to come out of this session was "Waiting For A Train," one of his most famous and most popular songs.

Jimmie began to appear on many radio programs, and in many movie shorts. With the money just pouring in, he moved his family to Kerrville, Texas. Unfortunately, he spent his money as quickly as he earned it, helping anyone along the way who showed any kind of need.

In 1929, Jimmie began to capture the Hawaiian-style music phase sweeping the country by including steel guitar, as well as the ukulele in many of his recordings, This certainly helped to sell more recordings. In September of that year, he made his only film, *The Singing Brakeman*, a Columbia-Victor short lasting about 10 minutes.

In the winter of 1932, with his health beginning to deteriorate, he sold his meagre holdings in Kerrville, and moved to San Antonio to receive the proper medical treatment for his ailment. Soon the bills began to pile up and he decided, that since he felt better, he would do an enormous amount of recordings, so he headed north. Unfortunately, his improved health was only temporary. In New York, his health soon deteriorated further, and he was constantly resting in his Cadillac, and being propped up in the recording studio. His original intention was to record 24 songs, but this number was soon changed to 12, the last of which was completed on May 24. He spent his last days in the Taft Hotel, in New York City.

On May 25, he went to Coney Island with his private nurse, but he began to hemorrhage. He was put to bed in his room, where he went into a comma, from which he never regained consciousness . He died early on May 26, at the age of 35.

In all, he recorded a total of 113 songs, during a period of three years, all of which may still be available on RCA Records. He had a greater influence on future musicians, up to the advent of Elvis, than any other singer in history, and many of his songs are still recorded today. His unique method of playing the guitar using half tones, and picking the base notes was similar to the methods of the Carter Family. To this day every musician or music lover has somehow been touched by the hand of Jimmie Rodgers, his music, his songs, or his style of playing.

The Carter Family

Alvin Pleasant "A.P." Carter was born in Maces Spring, Virginia, on December 15, 1889, and died on November 7, 1960. Sara Carter was born in Wise County, Virginia on July 21, 1899, and died on January 8, 1979. "Mama" Maybelle Carter was born in Nickelsville, Virginia on May 10, 1879, and died on October 23, 1978.

A.P. Carter was the oldest of eight children. His father, too, was musically inclined, but gave up his musical intentions, after the marriage, to further his religious convictions. His wife, however, continued to teach the children all the songs handed down by their families, through the years.

Starting at an early age, A.P. sang in the local church and was a member of a singing quartet with two uncles and his oldest sister, Vergie. The quartet was very popular in the area. He also learned to play fiddle, but he was never allowed to play jigs around the house

A.P. constantly wrote songs about his mountain home area. He met his wife Sara Daugherty on one of his many trips selling fruit trees, She was singing and playing the autoharp. She lived over the mountain in Copper Creek, near Nickelsville. Her uncle, Milburn Nickles, played fiddle, and she had learned to play banjo, guitar, and autoharp. On June 18, 1915, A.P. and Sara were married and went to live in Maces Springs. They were offered a recording contract with Brunswick Records, for which they sang "Log Cabin by the Sea," and "The Poor Orphan Child," with a few fiddle tunes thrown in for good measure. Maybelle Addington was added when she married A. P.'s brother Ezra, in 1926. She too had learned to play the Autoharp as a child.

In August, 1927, the Carter Family first recorded for the Victor Talking Machine Company in Bristol, Tennessee: Jimmie Rodgers was recorded at the same sessions. Ralph Peer. was impressed with their music and recorded six of their songs: "Bury Me Under the Weeping Willow," "Little Log Cabin by the Sea," "The Poor Orphan Child," "The Storms Are on the Ocean," "Single Girl, Married Girl," and "The Wandering Boy." Ralph did the same thing with A. P as he did with Jimmie Rodgers: He had A. P. copyright the songs in his name, and Peer's Southern Music Publishing Company published them. Although many of the songs were folk songs in the public domain, and A. P. never really wrote them, it became a universal practice to redo them in your own name..

The Carter style blended harmony with the music, which was unusual for its day. The songs they recorded for Ralph Peer were successful, so they journeyed to Camden, New Jersey, in 1928, in order to record eleven more songs, and again, in February of 1929, to record twelve others. Meanwhile their fame was growing throughout the country.

A. P. was being called on to produce more and more songs, but he was running out of ideas. So on several occasions, he went on song searching trips to find new songs. He followed the practice of buying the songs for a few dollars from the poor people he came across in his travels.

> In addition to furnishing a rich legacy of songs for American folk and country music, the Carters introduced a new stylistic and rhythmic content to the music, and it was perhaps this that was to prove their greatest legacy. [Malone & McCulloh, 1975, p. 64]

Sara Carter played either second guitar or autoharp on the records, with Maybelle in the lead. A.P. seldom played an instrument on the recordings.

In 1931 Ralph Peer united the Carter Family and Jimmie Rodgers on record in Louisville, Kentucky. This was the first time that the artists had ever met. Some of the recordings they made together were: "The wonderful City" and "Why There's a Tear in My Eye," duets with Jimmie and Sara; others were skits, part of the humor that went with the shows in which they performed .

In June of 1936, the Carter Family began recording for Decca Records. This period is considered by many to be their most productive period. The guitar picking and harmonies were at their best.

In 1938, they went to Del Rio, Texas to begin a series of broadcasts on the border stations. In 1938, Maybelle's three daughters, Helen, June, and Anita were added to the group. The radio broadcasts, from the border states, expanded their music much further than the south, and they began to become known throughout the country.

In 1941, they went to New York City to record for Victor, the last recordings that they would ever make. After 14 years, and nearly 300 recordings they would finally stop.

In 1943, the original Carter Family disbanded.. Mama Maybelle and the girls continued throughout the years, not only in the family tradition, but with a certain amount of success for each of the girls, and as a group backing up Johnny Cash, as part of "The Johnny Cash show."

Roy Claxton Acuff

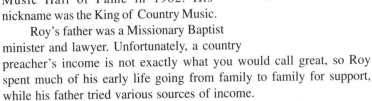

Roy was born in Maynardsville, Tennessee on September 15, 1903. He became the first member of the Country Music Hall of Fame in 1962. His nickname was the King of Country Music.

Roy's father was a Missionary Baptist minister and lawyer. Unfortunately, a country preacher's income is not exactly what you would call great, so Roy spent much of his early life going from family to family for support, while his father tried various sources of income.

Until his late 20's, Roy's interest was primarily athletics, not music, and he earned 13 letters in high school sports. He also showed great interest in the theater, in high school, where he acted in every play that he could. He played semi-pro baseball, but his tryout for a major league team met with disaster. He suffered a sunstroke and collapsed while playing a game in Knoxville, Tennessee, on July 7, 1929. He would continue to have fainting spells for several years after this incident.

Roy spent his idle time at home listening to his father's country music recordings, and learning to play his father's fiddle. He continued to strengthen the voice that had matured from his choirboy days, by taking some lessons from a sister, as well as from listening to the artists on his father's recordings.

In 1932, he joined a neighbor selling Moc-A-Tan Compound in Doc Hauer's medicine show, entertaining the audience with music and acting. He gained his style of singing from his boyhood choir days, and by being forced to raise his voice, so that the people were able to hear his singing.

In 1933, he founded a band called the Tennessee Crackerjacks and played in the Knoxville area at shows, and on radio station WROL, and WNOX. This work led to the band being approached by the American Record Company. The band changed its names to the Crazy Tennesseans and in 1936 the band recorded "The Great Speckled Bird." The song was actually "I'm Thinking Tonight of My Blue Eyes," but at some point during the years, different words were added, and the song grew in length.

After yearning to join the Grand Ole Opry for many years, Roy's chance came in 1938, when a fiddler on the Opry was fired in an argument, and Roy convinced the powers that be to let him take the fiddler's place. On the show, Roy and his band performed "The Great Speckled Bird." He was so nervous that he felt that he was terrible, and that he would never be invited back. At that time, however, the Opry was basically a barn dance type of program and any singer would probably have been accepted.

Two weeks after his appearance on the show, Roy received a telegram from David Stone asking him if he would like to be a regular at the Opry -- the mail had come in by the thousands, asking who he was, and if he would be on again. From there, he began to make his mark in the world, setting attendance records accross the country. He soon become the top rated act at the Opry, surpassing Uncle Dave Macon.

In 1939, when NBC started broadcasting it's 30 minute segment of The Opry, no one but he was even considered for the roll of host, and he became the first real singer on the show. It was then that he changed the name of the band to its final name, the Smokey Mountain Boys. The band held together for several years, without changing; with Howard "Howdy" Forrester on harmonica, Jimmy Riddle on accordion, and Peter Kirby (Bashfull Brother Oswald) on dobro, banjo, and vocals. Later members of the band would be: Lonnie "Pop" Wilson, Jess Easterday, and Tommy Magness.

Roy lacked the confidence he needed to play the fiddle, even though he was quite good, and tended to let the band do the playing. He later used it to do tricks, like balancing the bow on his nose. He preferred the natural acoustic sounds to the new electrified sounds, and for many years he resisted the temptation to electrify his group.

When the band sang on gospel numbers with him , there was no attempt to sing true harmony; instead their music represented the looseness of a choir, and the naturalness of a mountain grown singing group. While the rest of the country acts tended toward western sounds, Roy and his band remained true to mountain music.

In 1940, he wrote 16 songs for Gene Autry, including the popular "Be Honest With Me," which was his first venture in country-style music with the western touch. In the years to come, he would write hundreds of songs, both for himself, and for other country performers.

> "In 1942, he put up $25,000 to form Acuff-Rose Publications with Fred Rose, and that soon became the most successful publishing house in Nashville." *[Stambler&Landon, 1983,p.3]*

Acuff-Rose Publishing would become the center of country music in the years ahead, as Nashville slowly became the haven for country musicians and songs throughout the country. In 1945, Fred Rose turned over the business portion of the publishing company to his son Wesley and began a tradition of helping to develop the career of young singers and writers. The most important of these artists, of course, was Hank Williams.

Some of Roy's greatest songs of the period were "Wreck on the Highway," "Fireball Mail," "Night Train to Memphis," "Low and Lonely," and "Pins And Needles (In My Heart)." This was wartime; the war was a mystery to uneducated Southerners, and the songs, such as "Smoke on the Water", "I'll Be True While You're Gone," "We'll Meet Again, Sweetheart," and most important of all, "The Soldier's Last

Letter," reflected the times.

In the 1940's Roy was a major force in country music, and in 1948, he ran for governor of Tennessee, as the Just Plain Country Candidate, but he could not convince the voters of his sincerity. It was during the war that a friend of his nicknamed him the King of Country Music, and it stuck. His music, however, began to fade in the 50's and 60's, and he does not record anymore.

> A Japanese banzai charge is reported to have yelled, when attacking a Marine Corps position on Okinawa, *To Hell with President Roosevelt, to hell with Babe Ruth, to hell with Roy Acuff! [Malone & McCulloh, 1975, p. 199]*

In 1961, Roy won entrance to The County Music Hall of Fame. In 1962, he became its first living member. Roy died on November 23, 1992, after a short illness. As he requested, he was burried only four hours later, thus preventing "a circus type of atmosphere".

James Robert Wills

Bob Wills was born on March 6, 1905, near Kosse, in Limestone County, Texas. He was the first of 10 children born to John And Emmaline Foley Wills. Both families were musically inclined and most of them had a preference to play fiddle. In spite of this, Bob favored the mandolin, at an early age, but his interests were not geared toward music.

In 1913, the family moved to Hall County, Texas. It was after the move that Bob began to show an interest in the fiddle. This change of instruments supposedly occurred because one of his cousins played the fiddle terribly, and Bob challenged the cousin to a contest and won.

In 1915, 10-year-old Bob had to replace his father, who was drunk at the time, in playing the fiddle at a dance. He was so impressed with the way people were dancing to his music that he vowed to play only danceable music from then on.

Although there were many influences in Bob's life, his future music would reflect his surroundings, including the black influences.

Jim Rob lived around blacks so much in his formative years that not only his music and style but his personality and speech as well were permanently marked by their culture. *[Malone & McCulloh,1975,p.174]*

The black influence is more than evident in Bob's older songs. His most precious memories were of seeing Bessie Smith perform. His attempt to recreate the blues on his fiddle in the same way that jazz tries to recreate the voice gave him a much different sound than the other artists.

In 1929, he formed the Wills Fiddle Band, consisting of himself as fiddler, and Herman Arnspiger as guitarist. They played for many of the home dances in the area. In November, they travelled to Dallas to cut two songs for the Brunswick Record Company: "Gulf Coast Blues" and "Wills Breakdown." However, there was very little positive reaction to the recordings.

In 1930, Bob decided to add Milton Brown as a vocalist, his brother Durwood on guitar and Clifton "Sleepy" Johnson as tenor banjoist. Together they studied and played pop, blues, New Orleans jazz, folk, and race music in order to be able to play any style which may be requested.

In January, 1931, he began to perform on KFTZ radio, and his show became one of the most popular shows in the Southwest. They started advertising for Light Crust Flour, and so they called themselves the Light Crust Doughboys. The show soon began to broadcast over several stations in the area, and it remained on the air until the early '50's.

Because of the popularity of the show, the band was invited to record for Victor, and on February 9, 1932, they recorded "Nancy Jane" and "Sunbonnet Sue." Just as before, nothing much came of the recordings.

Troubled times soon hit the band, when arguments broke out between Milton Brown and the others, so Bob advertised for a new singer. He auditioned about 67 singers before he finally decided on Thomas Elmer Duncan. Also, because of their fights, and Bob's drinking habits, the band was fired from the radio program.

The band needed a new name, so in 1933, while it was broadcasting over WACO, Bob changed the band's name to Bob Wills and the Playboys. At this time, the band consisted of: Bob Wills, on fiddle; Tommy Duncan, vocals and piano; Kermit Whalin, on bass and steel guitar; Johnny Lee Wills, tenor banjo, and June Whalin, on rhythm guitar. The band soon headed for the greater glory and the wide open spaces of Oklahoma. The band members settled in Tulsa, and joined KVOO on which they bought their own radio time, and advertised Play Boy flour for General Mills. In one form or another, the program would remain on the air for 24 years. During this period, Bob would develop his final dance schedules as well as his greatest band.

In September of 1935, he took the band to Dallas for his second try with Brunswick Records. In all, there were 13 musicians in the session; this group became the basis of the new groups he would develop in the years ahead. Among the musicians were Bob, on fiddle; Tommy Duncan, vocals; Johnnie Lee Wills, on tenor banjo; Son Lansford, bass; Everett Stover, on trumpet; Robert Zeb McNally, on saxophone and clarinet; Herman Arnspiger, on guitar; Art Haines, on trombone and violin; Jesse Ashlock, on violin; Clifton Johnson, on guitar and tenor banjo; William Eschol Smokey Dacus, on drums; Leon McAuliffe, on steel Guitar; and Alton Stricklin, on piano.

Although he was constantly warned, by those that know, that horns and strings didn't mix, Bob paid no attention to the warnings, because he thought they sounded good together. He would constantly react to each musician's playing, and when one of them would play some good "licks" he would let out with a musical "moan" to show his appreciation for the music.

By 1940, he had put together what he referred to as a band, but what everyone else would probably refer to as an orchestra. The reason being that he used upwards of 18 instruments: 4-6 saxophones; 2-3 clarinets; 2-3 trumpets; a trombone, piano, bass drum, tenor banjo, steel guitar, electric guitar, and 3 fiddles.

Shortly after they recorded "The New San Antonio Rose," Bob and the band began to make movies — the real shoot 'em up, cowboy type of movies. This, naturally, spread their music throughout the country.

Between 1935 and 1942, he was married and divorced 5 times. When World War II broke out, most of the band went off to fight, even Bob. Unfortunately, at 38 years old, he could not take the rigors or the service, and he was discharged the following year. He headed for

California, and the San Fernando Valley.

During the war, he married Betty Anderson, with whom he had three children. As he grew fonder of his family, he wanted to return home every night to see them, so the territory where the band performed became closer and closer to his home. However, in 1949, he moved to Oklahoma City, and his management company, MCA, booked him on a tour of Texas and the Southwest.

Bob suffered his first heart attack in 1962, and his second in 1964, while on a national tour. By this time, his manager, Sam Gibbs, was booking him as a single, and making him more money than he used to make as a group. Besides all the appearances in the '60's, he recorded nearly 100 songs between 1963 and 1969.

Although he would never believe that he was a country artist, he was elected to the Country Music Hall of Fame on October 18, 1968. The following year, on May 31, 1969, he had a major stroke, and for months he showed no interest in music, whatsoever.

In 1971, he started getting better, and in the following year, he began attending award shows, in his honor. On one of the award shows, in Nashville, for ASCAP, he contacted United Artists Records, and arraigned for a recording date to be held in Dallas, on December 3-4, 1973. He contacted all his old friends and fellow musicians to ask them to attend.

All the Texas Playboys arrived the day before for a jam session at Bob's home. The group included: Smokey Dacus, Leon McAuliffe, Al Stricklin, Eldon Shamblin, Keith Coleman, Johnny Gimble and Leon Rauech, and a special guest star Merle Haggard. Merle had driven down from Chicago to fulfill one of his dreams, to play with Bob Wills.

Merle had joined the members of the band, previous to this, in April of 1970, when they recorded together to help him create a concept album based on the life of Bob Wills, entitled *A Tribute to the Best Damn Fiddle Player in the World.*

In the 2 day session, they recorded 27 selections. The last night, Bob Wills had a stroke and never regained consciousness. He died 17 months later, on May 13, 1975. His career ended where it began, in Dallas.

It would be impossible to discuss in this brief essay the numerous tributes that have been made to Wills by admiring country-and-western artists. His legacy, however, is not limited to country-and-western. He was an important link in western music between the race music of the 20's, thirties, and forties and the rockabillies of the 50's.... Bob Wills was one of the stars of country-and-western music, but his role went beyond that: he was the creator of western swing in the Southwest and on the West Coast, a founding father of country-and-western in Nashville, a transitional figure in rock, an idol of musicians in Bakersfield, and now an influence on country music in Austin. *[Malone & McCulloh, 1975, p. 176]*

With the creation and development of a new genre referred to as western swing, Bob Wills influenced popular music, as well as country music musicians throughout the world for years to come. His influence is still felt today with the music of Willie Nelson, and other country musicians building on his Texas swing style, and using it to form their own special sound.

King Hiram "Hank" Williams

Hank Williams was born on September 17, 1923, in Mount Olive, Alabama. His family moved to Georgiana when he was five. His father was a part-time farmer and log train engineer for a lumber company, until sickness forced him to retire. He had little contact with his father, but Hank presented his father to the world in his song entitled, "The Log Train," recorded on a home tape recorder before Hank died.

Hank's mother influenced his singing of gospel music in early childhood, and developed his presentation of music and his style at an early age, but he was forced basically to raise himself after his father became ill.

He was the leader of his own country music band by the time he was 14. He admitted to his being influenced by such artists of the time as Ernest Tubb, and Roy Acuff. His style became a mixture of gospel and honky tonk music, affected by the sounds of the black men of the south. He followed many of the black artists of the day in order to observe their style and presentation. His most popular black idol at that time was Rufus Payne (also known as Tee-Tot), and though little is known about his influence on Hank , one song can be directly attributed to him, that is "My Bucket's Got a Hole In It."

Hank entered and won an amateur night contest during this period, and was so impressed by the acceptance of his audience that from then on, he was driven to succeed in the music business. In 1937, he formed the Drifting Cowboys, and began wearing the cowboy attire that would later become one of his trademarks. The band soon began appearing on radio shows and at medicine shows and parties throughout the area. At this time Hank began to develop the alcoholic tendencies which would eventually destroy him.

In 1942, Hank temporarily gave up music and moved to Mobile, Alabama, to work in the shipyards as a welder. After the war, however, he regained his interest in music and soon began playing in honky tonks throughout Alabama. His marriage to Audrey Sheppard in this year would end in divorce, and help to inspire some of his greatest songs.

In September of 1946, he and Audrey made an unscheduled call on Fred and Wesley Rose in Nashville. He auditioned a few songs for them, and they, in turn, issued a songwriting contract to him. Several of his songs, "When God Comes and Gathers His Jewels," "Six More Miles to the Graveyard," and "I Don't Care If Tomorrow Never Comes" were recorded by Molly O'Day, who was also being helped by them.

In December of 1946, Hank signed his first recording contract with a New York record company, Sterling Records, which was just getting into the country field. His first recordings for the label , Sterling 201, came out in January of 1947: "Calling You" and "Never Again (Will I Knock on Your Door)." The next releases on the label were "When God Comes and Gathers His Jewels" and "Wealth Won't Save Your Soul". All were received poorly by the trade papers, but Fred Rose was impressed with Hank's style of singing, and soon helped him get a contract with a brand new record company, MGM Records.

Hank's first recordings for MGM, in 1947, "Move It On Over," and "I Heard You Crying In Your Sleep," were greatly received by his peers, as well as the public. His association with MGM would remain throughout his career, and later would continue with his son, Hank Williams, Jr.

The public's acceptance of his style and songs was enormous as well as strange. Here was a totally country boy, singing totally country songs, that were accepted by the city folk more than any other singer of his type in history. Even Elvis, who began in the country music genre, would soon change his style to a more sophisticated one in order to attract and maintain his group of city fans.

On August 7, 1948, only four months after it began, the Louisiana Hayride Show invited Hank to become a regular. This invitation was largely due to the popularity of his "Lovesick Blues." The song was one of the top country and western songs of the year, and the first million seller for Hank. It was written way back in 1922, by Irving Mills and Cliff Friend. In the same year, 1948, MGM released "My Bucket's Got a Hole in It," which became the second million seller for Hank.

Hank soon became the headliner on the Louisiana Hayride Show, and began to reach many more people through other radio shows and personal appearances. In the next four years he would become the most popular, most copied, and most followed entertainer in the United States. This accomplishment earned him a position on the Grand Ole Opry, which he joined on June 11, 1949.

In November of that year, he left the Hayride, and moved on to The Grand Ole Opry, as would many new artists, such as Faron Young and Webb Pierce, in the years to come.

The Drifting Cowboys was the band he had formed while at the Hayride, and he continued to use the name wherever he could. During the glory years, the band consisted of Jerry Rivers, on fiddle; Don Helms, on steel guitar; Bob McNett and later Sammy Pruet, on lead guitar; Hillous Butrum and later Cedric Rainwater, on bass. When the band was formed, they were young and inexperienced, but they worked very hard and eventually became the most sought after band in the country.

In 1950, he had two more million sellers, "Long Gone Lonesome Blues," and "Moanin' The Blues," both of which he wrote. Because of his enormous popularity in the country music field, he was beginning to come to the notice of the popular music producers in the country. They began to copy his songs, using the most popular singers of the day, in order to take advantage of Hank's popularity. Many of his songs became "crossover hits," being as popular in the pop field as in the country field. In 1951, three more million sellers hit the charts: "Hey, Good Lookin'," "Cold, Cold Heart," and "Ramblin' Man."

Early in his career, he developed the habit of singing his preaching type songs under the name of "Luke the Drifter." Thus, he not only was able to release more songs, at the same time, but it allowed him a second character to develop in the public image. He was creating the image of Hank Williams, the drunkard, who cheated on women, and was cheated on by them, and that of Luke the Drifter, who went across the country preaching the gospel, and doing good deeds.

Hank's career was now guaranteed to be successful, and he continued to have one hit after another. His battle with the bottle, however, also continued, and he was fired from the Opry, in August of 1952, because of his heavy drinking. He immediately rejoined the Louisiana Hayride, where he was graciously accepted.

But good things happened during the year, as well: Four of his songs became million sellers: "Jambalaya," "Your Cheatin' Heart," "Honky Tonk Blues," and "I'll Never Get Out of This World Alive."

He started divorce proceedings against Audrey and quickly married a beautiful model and singer named Billie Jones, who was the daughter of the Bossier City, Louisiana police chief. He actually married her three times: once before a justice of the peace, and twice before a paid-admission audience at New Orlean's Municipal Auditorium. The only problem was that the divorce from Audrey was not finalized at the time.

Hank died in his car in Oak Hill, West Virginia, at the age of 29, while on the way to a scheduled performance on New Years Day, 1953, in Canton, Ohio. Immediately after his death many songs commemorating his life and his death were written and released as records; among these were, "The Death of Hank Williams," "Singing Teacher in Heaven," and "Hank, It Will Never Be the Same Without You."

In 1961, both Hank Williams and Fred Rose were named to the Country Music Hall of Fame. No other singer in the history of country music had as popular a following in the urban areas of the country, and among the more famous people of these areas than Hank Williams. His songs were covered by all country singers, and by most popular singers, at one time or other. His influence on future artists would be tremendous. He should be considered the first natural rockabilly artist in history.

The following codes and classifications are used in the discography.

R	Reissue of a previous release
Rx	Additional Reissue of previous release
1	The first recording of the song.
2	The second recording... etc.
33	A 33 1/3 speed single release
S	Stereo (noted only on early singles and EP's)
ACM	Academy of Country Music
OH	Old Homestead
SM	Suffolk Marketing
ASVEA	ASV Living ERA
CMF	Country Music Foundation
PSP	Polygram Special Products
Philips Int	Philips International
Hickory/M	Hickory/MGM
Western Hrtage	Western Heritage

Recordings are listed chronologically under each artist's heading.
Most CD listings are available on tape with similar numbers
Most LP Records are no longer available
Artists are arranged alphabetically.

Roy Acuff-

Singles

Crazy Worried Mind	-Decca 28748	(1953)
Goodbye Mister Brown	-Decca 28835	(1953)
Swamp Lily	-Capitol 2642	(1953)
It's Hard to Love	-Decca 30141	(1954)
I'm Planting a Rose/Streamline Heartbreaker	-Capitol F-2901	(1954)
Don't Judge Your Neighbor	-Capitol 3062	(1954)
The Night Spots	-Capitol 3115	(1954)
The Great Speckled Bird/Wabash Cannonball	-Capitol 6047	(1955)
Night Train to Memphis/Wreck on the Highway	-Capitol 6163	(1955)
The Great Speckled Bird/Wabash Cannonball	-Columbia 33057	(1955)
Once More	-Hickory 1073	(1957)
The One I Love	-Hickory 1081	(1957)
So Many Times	-Hickory 1090	(1958)
Come and Knock	-Hickory 1097	(1959)
Don't Know Why	-Hickory 1113	(1960)
The Streamlined Cannonball/Time Will Make You Pay	-Hickory 1142	(1961)
Lost John He's Gone	-Hickory 1149	(1961)
Things That Might Have Been	-Hickory 1271	(1965)
Freight Train Blues	-Hickory 1291	(1965)
Life to Go	-Hickory 1316	(1965)
Tennessee Central No. 9	-Hickory 1331	(1965)
Baby Just Said Goodbye	-Hickory 1348	(1965)
I Couldn't Believe It Was True/Kaw-liga	-Hickory 1424	(1965)
I'm Movin' On	-Hickory 1479	(1967)
Uncle Pen	-Hickory 1497	(1968)
Don't Be Angry/The Nearest Thing to Heaven	-Hickory 1519	(1968)
Somebody Touched Me	-Hickory 1627	(1972)
Back in the Country	-Hickory 314	(1974)
Old Time Sunshine	-Hickory 319	(1974)
Don't Worry 'Bout the Mule/Precious Memories	-Hickory 331	(1974)
Most Remarkable Guy	-Hickory 336	(1974)
I Can't Find a Train	-Hickory 348	(1975)

Albums

Songs of the Smokey Mountains	-Columbia HL-9004	(1949)
Old Time Barn Music	-Columbia HL-9010	(1949)
Songs of the Saddle	-Columbia HL-9013	(1949)
Songs of the Smokey Mountains	-Capitol T-617	(1955)
Old Time Barn Dance	(R)-Columbia HL-9010	(1958)
Favorite Hymns	-MGM E-3707	(1958)
The Great Speckled Bird	-Harmony HL-7082	(1958)
Once More	-Hickory LPM-101	(1961)
Hymn Time	-MGM SE-4044	(1962)
All Time Greatest Hits	-Hickory LPM-109	(1962)
Star of the Grand Ole Opry	-Hickory LPM-113	(1963)
The World Is His Stage	-Hickory LPM-114	(1963)

-Roy Acuff Cont'd-

Hand Clapping Gospel Songs	-Hickory LPM-117	(1963)
Country Music Hall of Fame	(R)-Capitol T-1870	(1963)
The Great Roy Acuff	-Capitol T-2103	(1964)
Country Music Hall of Fame	-Hickory LPM-119	(1964)
Great Train Songs	-Hickory LPS-125	(1965)
Sacred Songs	-Metro M-508	(1965)
How Beautiful Heaven Must Be	-Pickwick JS-6028	(1965)
Voice of Country Music	-Capitol T-2276	(1965)
The Great Roy Acuff	-Harmony HL-7342	(1965)
Waitin' for My Call to Glory	-Harmony HL-7376	(1966)
Roy Acuff Sings Hank Williams	-Hickory LPS-134	(1966)
Famous Opry Favorites	-Hickory LPS-139	(1967)
Songs of the Smokey Mountains	-Columbia HL-9004	(1967)
Living Legend	-Hickory LPS-145	(1968)
Treasury of Country Hits	-Hickory LPS-147	(1969)
Roy Acuff Country	-Pickwick JS-6090	(1969)
Waitin' for My Call to Glory	(R)-Harmony HS-11334	(1969)
Night Train to Memphis	-Harmony HS-11403	(1970)
Roy Acuff Time	-Hickory LPS-156	(1970)
Greatest Hits	-Columbia CS1034E	(1970)
Greatest Hits	(R)-Columbia PC-1034	(1970)
Country & Western Classics	-Time/Life TLCW09	(197?)
I Saw the Light	-Hickory LPS-158	(1970)
The Great Speckled Bird	-Harmony HS-12289	(1973)
Who Is Roy Acuff (2 LP)	-Hickory LPS-162	(1973)
The King of Country Music	-Hickory/M HR4504	(1974)
Back in the Country	-Hickory/M HR4507	(1974)
Smokey Mountain Memories	-Hickory/M HG4517	(1974)
That's Country	-Hickory/M HG4521	(1975)
Interview with Roy Acuff	-Elektra E-C	(1978)
Greatest Hits, Vol. 1 (2 LP)	-ELektra 9E-302	(1978)
Greatest Hits, Vol. 2 (2 LP)	-Electra 9E-303	(1979)
Country Music Hall of Fame	(R)-Capitol SM1870	(1979)
Sings Hank Williams	-Elektra 6E-287	(1980)
Back in the Country	-Elektra El-60012	(1982)
Columbia Historic Edition (1936-62) (CD)	-Columbia CK-39998	(1985)
Greatest Hits(1936-39) (CD)	-Rounder SS-23	(1985)
Roy Acuff & His Smokey Mountain Boys (1939-41)(CD)	-Rounder SS-24	(1985)
The Best of Roy Acuff (CD)	(R)-Capitol C41C-91621	(1989)
Greatest Hits (CD)	(R)-Columbia PCT01034	(1990)
The Best of Roy Acuff (CD)	(R)-Curb DK21K-77454	(1991)
Wabash Cannonball (CD)	-Intersound CDA5008	(1992)
The Essential Roy Acuff (CD)	-Columbia CK-48956	(1992)

Extended Play Mini Albums

EP Revival Time	-Columbia H-1514	(1951)
EP Revival Time	-Columbia H-1514	(1951)
EP Great Speckle Bird	-Columbia H-2070	(1954)

-Roy Acuff Cont'd-

EP Songs of the Smokey Mountains, Vol. 3	-Capitol EAP3-617	(1955)
EP Songs of the Smokey Mountains, Vol. 1	-Capitol EAP1-617	(1955)
EP Songs of the Smokey Mountains, Vol. 2	-Capitol EAP2-617	(1955)
EP Roy Acuff and the Smokey Mountain Boys	-Columbia B-2803	(1957)
EP Roy Acuff	-Columbia B-2825	(1958)
EP Songs of the Smokey Mountains	-Columbia HL-9004	(1967)
EP Living Legend	-Hickory LPS-145	(1968)
EP Treasury of Country Hits	-Hickory LPS-147	(1969)

*Elektra releases are basically re-releases of Hickory recordings

The Carter Family-

Singles

The Poor Orphan Child	-Victor 20877	(1927)
Storms are on the Ocean	-Victor 20937	(1927)
Little Log Cabin by the Sea	-Victor 21074	(1927)
Keep on the Sunny Side	-Victor 21434	
Chewing Gum	-Victor 21517	
Will You Miss Me When I'm Gone?	-Victor 21638	
On the Rock	-Victor 23513	
Where Shall I Be?	-Victor 23523	
Lonesome Valley	-Victor 23541	
There's Someone a Waiting for Me	-Victor 23554	
Can't Feel at Home	-Victor 23569	
Jimmie Rodgers Visits the Carter Family	-Victor 23574	
Sow 'Em on the Mountain	-Victor 23585	
My Old Cottage Home	-Victor 23599	
Let the Church Roll On	-Victor 23618	
Weary Prodigal Son	-Victor 23626	
Dying Soldier	-Victor 23641	
I Have Never Loved But One	-Victor 23656	
Where We'll Never Grow Old	-Victor 23672	
Mid the Green Fields of Virginia	-Victor 23686	
Amber Tresses	-Victor 23701	
Carter's Blues	-Victor 23716	
Wabash Cannon Ball	-Victor 23731	
Will the Roses Bloom in Heaven?	-Victor 23748	
Sweet As the Flowers in May Time	-Victor 23761	
The Church in the Wildwood	-Victor 23776	
Two Sweet Hearts	-Victor 23791	
I Wouldn't Mind Dying	-Victor 23807	
Gold Watch and Chain	-Victor 23821	
I Loved You Better Than I Know	-Victor 23835	
On the Sea of Galilee	-Victor 23845	
Wildwood Flower	-Victor 40000	
I Have No One	-Victor 40036	
Foggy Mountain Top	-Victor 40058	

-The Carter Family Cont'd-

Engine One-Forty-Three	-Victor 40089
Little Moses	-Victor 40110
Sweet Fern	-Victor 40126
Diamonds in the Rough	-Victor 40150
Bring Back My Blue-eyed Boy	-Victor 40190
The Homestead on the Farm	-Victor 40207
When the Roses Bloom in Dixieland	-Victor 40229
Western Hobo	-Victor 40255
Lover's Farewell	-Victor 40277
When the World's on Fire	-Victor 40293
Worried Man Blues	-Victor 40317
Don't Forget This Song	-Victor 40328
Keep on the Sunny Side	-Bluebird 5006
Where We'll Never Grow Old	-Bluebird 5058
Meet Me by the Moonlight Alone	-Bluebird 5096
When the Springtime Comes Again	-Bluebird 5122
Will the Roses Bloom in Heaven?	(R)-Bluebird 5161
Amber Tresses	(R)-Bluebird 5185
Mid The Green Fields of Virginia	(R)-Bluebird 5243
God Gave Noah the Rainbow Sign	-Bluebird 5272
My Clinch Mountain Home	-Bluebird 5301
Wildwood Flower	(R)-Bluebird 5356
Anchored in Love	-Bluebird 5406
Sow 'Em on the Mountain	(R)-Bluebird 5468
I'll Be All Smiles Tonight	-Bluebird 5529
A Distant Land to Roam	-Bluebird 5543
Darling Daisies	-Bluebird 5586
The East Virginia Blues	-Bluebird 5650
I'm Working on a Building	-Bluebird 5716
One Little Word	-Bluebird 5771
I'll Aggravate Your Soul	-Bluebird 5817
Longing for Old Virginia	-Bluebird 5856
My Heart's Tonight in Texas	-Bluebird 5908
I'll Be Home Some Day	-Bluebird 5911
Little Moses	-Bluebird 5924
Lulu Wall	-Bluebird 5927
The Mountains of Tennessee	-Bluebird 5956
On a Hill Lone and Gray	-Bluebird 5961
Sailor Boy	-Bluebird 5974
Kitty Waltz	-Bluebird 5990
The Church in the Wildwood	(R)-Bluebird 5993
Lonesome for You	-Bluebird 6000
Worried Man Blues	(R)-Bluebird 6020
Diamonds in the Rough	(R)-Bluebird 6033
Carter's Blues	-Bluebird 6036
When I'm Gone	-Bluebird 6053
Where Shall I Be?	-Bluebird 6055

-The Carter Family Cont'd-

Two Sweet Hearts	(R)-Bluebird 6106	
Lonesome Valley	(R)-Bluebird 6117	
Fond Affection	-Bluebird 6176	
Engine One-Forty-Three	(R)-Bluebird 6223	
I Have Never Loved But One	(R)-Bluebird 6257	
Little Log Cabin by the Sea	(R)-Bluebird 6271	
The Carter Family & Jimmie Rodgers in Texas	-Bluebird 6762	
Wabash Cannon Ball	-Bluebird 8350	
Dark And Stormy Weather	-Bluebird 8368	
My Dixie Darling	-Decca 5240	(1936)
My Native Home	-Decca 5241	(1936)
No Depression	-Decca 5242	(1936)
Just Another Broken Heart	-Decca 5254	(1936)
My Honey Lou	-Decca 5263	
You've Been a Friend to Me	-Decca 5283	
Bonnie Blue Eyes	-Decca 5304	
Sweet Heaven in My View	-Decca 5318	
In the Shadow of the Pines	-Decca 5359	
The Last Move for Me	-Decca 5386	
The Only Girl	-Decca 5441	
Lover's Lane	-Decca 5430	
He Never Came Back	-Decca 5447	
Honey in the Rock	-Decca 5452	
Jim Blake's Message	-Decca 5467	
Hello Stranger	-Decca 5479	
Lord I'm in Your Care	-Decca 5494	
Broken Down Tramp	-Decca 5518	
Goodbye to the Plains	-Decca 5532	
Stern Old Bachelor	-Decca 5565	
Happy in the Prison	-Decca 5579	
Coal Miner's Blues	-Decca 5596	
Who's That Knockin' on my Window	-Decca 5612	
Little Joe	-Decca 5632	
Bring Back My Boy	-Decca 5649	
Cuban Soldiers	-Decca 5662	
Farewell Nellie	-Decca 5677	
You Are My Flower	-Decca 5692	
Charlie And Nellie	-Decca 5702	
Reckless Motorman	-Decca 5722	

(most titles on Montgomery Ward as well)

Broken Hearted Lover	-Vocalion 02990	
Can the Circle Be Unbroken	-Vocalion 03027	
Lonesome Valley	-Vocalion 03112	
The Storms Are on the Ocean	-Vocalion 03160	
Don't Forget Me Little Darling	-Vocalion 04390	
Wildwood Flower	(2)-Acme 102	(195?)

-The Carter Family Cont'd-
Albums

All Time Favorites	-Acme LP-1	(195?)
In Memory of A.P.Carter	-Acme LP-2	(195?)
The Carter Family	-Decca DL-4404	(1960)
The Famous Carter Family	-Harmony HL-7280	(1961)
Great Original Recordings by the Carter Family	-Harmony HL-7300	(1962)
The Carter Family Album	-Liberty LST-7230	(1962)
Original and Great	-Camden CAL-586	(1962)
The Carter Family (Original Recordings)	-Harmony HL-7300	(1963)
The Carter Family (Collection of Favorites)	-Decca DL-4404	(1963)
Echoes of the Carter Family	-Starday SLP-248	(1963)
Mid the Green Fields of Virginia	-RCA LPM-2772	(1963)
Keep on the Sunny Side (With Johnny Cash)	-Columbia CS-2152	(1964)
Best of the Carter Family	-Columbia CS-2319	(1965)
Home Among the Hills	-Harmony HL-7344	(1965)
More Favorites by the Carter Family	-Decca DL-4557	(1965)
Great Sacred Songs	-Harmony HL-7396	(1966)
The Carter Family Country Favorites	-Sunset SUS-5153	(1967)
The Country Album	-Columbia CS-2517	(1967)
Country Sounds of the Original Carter Family	-Harmony HL-7422	(1967)
The Famous Carter Family	-Harmony HS-11332	(1969)
I Walk the Line	-Harmony HS-11392	(1970)
Lonesome Pine Special	-Camden CAS-2473	(1971)
More Golden Gems from the Carter Family	-Camden CAS-2554	(1972)
Travelin' Minstrel Band	-Columbia KC-31454	(1972)
My Old Cottage Home	-Camden ACL1-0047	(1973)
Three Generations	-Columbia KC-33084	(1974)
The Happiest Days of All	-Camden ACL1-0501	(1974)
The Original and Great Carter Family	(R)-Pickwick CAS-586	(1975)
Lonesome Pine Special	(R)-Pickwick CAS-2473	(1975)
Look! A.P.Carter and the Carter Family	-OTC 6001	
Mid the Green Fields of Virginia	-RCA ANL1-1107	(1975)
Original Carter Family (Early Classics)	-ACM ACM-1	
Country's First Family	-Columbia KC-34266	(1976)
The Original Carter Family (1936 Radio Transcripts)	-OH OHS-90045	
The Original Carter Family (Legendary Performers)	-RCA CPM1-2763	(1978)
The Original Carter Family (Sacred Collection)	-ACM Acm-8	
Original Carter Family on Border Radio	-J.E.M.F. 101	
The Carter Family	-Audgrph Alve 025	(1982)
Carter Family in Texas, Vol. 1	-OH 111	
Carter Family in Texas, Vol. 2	-OH 112	
Carter Family in Texas, Vol. 3	-OH 116	
Carter Family in Texas, Vol. 4	-OH 117	
Carter Family in Texas, Vol. 5	-OH 130	
Carter Family in Texas, Vol. 6	-OH 136	
Carter Family in Texas, Vol. 7	-OH 139	
Country's First Family (With Johnny Cash)	-SM P14911	(1979)

-The Carter Family Cont'd-

Their Last Recordings		-Pine Mountain 207
The Original and Great Carter Family	(CD)	(R)-Camden CAK-586 (198?)
On Border Radio	(CD)	-JEMF-101 (198?)
The Carter Family	(CD)	(R)-Camden CAK-2473 (198?)
EP A.P. Carter Memorial Album		-Acme DF-100
EP The Carter Family		-Decca ED-2788 (1965)
EP Beyond the River		-Acme DF-101
EP The Titanic		-Acme DF-102
EP Beautiful Home		-Acme DF-103

Jimmie Rodgers-

Singles

Soldier's Sweetheart/Sleep Baby Sleep	-Victor 20684	(1926)
Away Out on the Mountain/Blue Yodel #1	-Victor 21142	(1927)
Ben Dewberry's Final Run	-Victor 21245	(1927)
Blue Yodel No. 2	-Victor 21291	(1928)
Treasures Untold	-Victor 21433	(1928)
Blue Yodel No. 3	-Victor 21531	(1928)
Dear Old Sunny South by the Sea	-Victor 21574	(1928)
Memphis Yodel	-Victor 21636	(1928)
Daddy And Home	-Victor 21757	
Blue Yodel No. 5	-Victor 22072	
Frankie and Johnny	-Victor 22143	
My Rough and Rowdy Ways	-Victor 22220	
Blue Yodel No. 6	-Victor 22271	
The Drunkard's Child	-Victor 22319	
Train Whistle Blues	-Victor 22379	
Hobo Bill's Last Ride	-Victor 22421	
Any Old Time	-Victor 22488	
High Powered Mama	-Victor 22523	
Pistol Pakin' Papa	-Victor 22554	
Blue Yodel No. 8	-Victor 22503	
Nobody Knows But Me	-Victor 23518	
T.B.Blues	-Victor 23535	
Jimmie, The Kid	-Victor 23549	
I'm Lonesome, Too	-Victor 23564	
Moonlight and Skies	-Victor 23574	
Blue Yodel No. 9	-Victor 23580	
What's It	-Victor 23609	
Rodgers' Puzzle Record	-Victor 23621	
Gambling Polka Dot Blues	-Victor 23636	
Roll Along Kentucky Moon	-Victor 23651	
My Time Ain't Long	-Victor 23669	
Home Call	-Victor 23681	
Blue Yodel No. 10	-Victor 23696	

-Jimmie Rodgers Cont'd-

Hobo's Meditation	-Victor 23711
Mother, The Queen of My Heart	-Victor 23721
Miss the Mississippi and You	-Victor 23736
Whippin' That Old T.B.	-Victor 23751
Gambling Bar Room Blues	-Victor 23766
Peach Pickin' Time in Georgia	-Victor 23781
Blue Yodel No. 11	-Victor 23796
The Southern Cannon Ball	-Victor 23811
Mississippi Delta Blues	-Victor 23816
The Yodeling Ranger	-Victor 23830
Old Love Letters	-Victor 23840
Blue Yodel No. 12	-Victor 24456
Blue Yodel No. 14	-Victor 40014
The Sailor's Plea	-Victor 40054
My Little Lady	-Victor 40072
My Carolina Sunshine Girl	-Victor 40096
Blue Yodel No. 12 (picture record)	-Victor 18-6000
Moonlight and Skis	-Bluebird 5000
Gambling Bar Room Blues	-Bluebird 5037
Happy Til She Met You	-Bluebird 5057
You've Got Me Crying Again	-Bluebird 5061
Prairie Lullaby	-Bluebird 5076
Mother, The Queen of My Heart	(2) -Bluebird 5080
Down the Old Road to Home	-Bluebird 5081
Roll Along, Kentucky Moon	-Bluebird 5082
My Time Ain't Long	-Bluebird 5083
What's It	-Bluebird 5084
Blue Yodel	-Bluebird 5085
Mississippi Moon	-Bluebird 5136
Waiting For a Train	-Bluebird 5163
When It's Harvest Time	-Bluebird 5199
In the Jailhouse Now	-Bluebird 5223
Jimmie Rodgers' Last Blue Yodel	-Bluebird 5281
My Blue-eyed Jane	-Bluebird 5393
Ben Dewberry's Final Run	-Bluebird 5482
Yodeling Ranger	-Bluebird 5556
My Old Pal	-Bluebird 5609
Any Old Time	-Bluebird 5664
I'm Lonesome Too	-Bluebird 5739
In the Hills of Tennessee	-Bluebird 5784
Treasures Untold	-Bluebird 5838
Why Did You Give Me Your Love	-Bluebird 5892
My Good Gal's Gone	-Bluebird 5942
Daddy And Home	-Bluebird 5991
Old Love Letters	-Bluebird 6198
Sleep, Baby, Sleep	-Bluebird 6225
The Sailor's Plea	-Bluebird 6246

-Jimmie Rodgers Cont'd-

Mule Skinner Blues	-Bluebird 6275
Why There's a Tear in My Eye	-Bluebird 6698
The Carter Family & Jimmie Rodgers In Texas	-Bluebird 6792
I've Only Loved Three Women	-Bluebird 6810
Yodeling My Way Back Home	-Bluebird 7280
Take Me Back Again	-Bluebird 7600

(Same Titles On Montgomery Ward)

Blue Yodel No. 9	(R)-Montgomery Ward 4209
My Good Gal's Gone Blues	-Montgomery Ward 5014
Pistol Packin' Mama	(R)-RCA 47-0027
Prairie Lullabye	(R)-RCA 47-0028
Old Pal Of My Heart	(R)-RCA 47-0029
Blue Yodel	(R)-RCA 47-0098
Never No Mo' Blues	(R)-RCA 47-0099
Frankie and Johnny	(R)-RCA 47-0100
Desert Blues	(R)-RCA 47-0102
Sleep, Baby, Sleep	(R)-RCA 47-0104
Blue Yodel No. 2	(R)-RCA 47-0105
Blue Yodel No. 6	(R)-RCA 47-0106
Milk Cow Blues	(R)-RCA 47-6430

Albums

Jimmie Rodgers Memorial Album, Vol. 1	-RCA LPT-3037	(1952)
Jimmie Rodgers Memorial Album, Vol. 2	-RCA LPT-3038	(1952)
Jimmie Rodgers Memorial Album, Vol. 3	-RCA LPT-3039	(1952)
Travelin' Blues	-RCA LPT-3073	(1952)
Never No Mo' Blues/Memorial Album	-RCA LPM-1232	(1955)
Train Whistle Blues	-RCA LPM-1640	(1957)
My Rough And Rowdy Ways	-RCA LPM-2112	(1960)
Jimmie the Kid	-RCA LPM-2213	(1961)
Country Music Hall of Fame	-RCA LPM-2531	(1962)
Short But Brilliant Life of Jimmie Rodgers	-RCA LPM-2634	(1963)
My Time Ain't Long Enough	-RCA LPM-2865	(1964)
Best of The Legendary Jimmie Rodgers	-RCA LSP-3315	(1965)
Country Music	-DOT 3710	(1966)
Jimmie Rodgers Sings & Plays 12 Immortal Hits	-Hamilton HLP-148	(1965)
The Legendary Jimmie Rodgers, Vol. 1 (2 LP)	-RCA DPL2-0075	(1974)
My Rough and Rowdy Ways	-RCA ANL1-1209	(1975)
Jimmie Rodgers Memorial Album	-Pickwick ACL7 029	(1976)
Jimmie Rodgers- A Legendary Performer	-RCA CPL1-2504	(1978)
This Is Jimmie Rodgers (2 LP)	-RCA VPS-6091	(1983)
Unissued Jimmie Rodgers	-ACM ACM-11	(1983)
Never No Mo' Blues	(R)-RCA AHM1-1232	(1983)
Train Whistle Blues	(R)-RCA AHM1-1640	(1983)
My Rough and Rowdy Ways	(R)-RCA AHM1-2112	(1983)
Jimmie the Kid	(R)-RCA AHM1-2213	(1983)
Country Music Hall of Fame	(R)-RCA AHM1-2531	(1983)
Short But Brilliant Life of Jimmie Rodgers	(R)-RCA AHM1-2634	(1983)

-Jimmie Rodgers Cont'd-

My Time Ain't Long		(R)-RCA AHM1-2865	(1984)
Best Of The Legendary Jimmie Rodgers		(R)-RCA AHL1-3315	(1984)
The Best of Jimmie Rodgers	(CD)	-MCA MCAD31086	(1985)
The Best of Jimmie Rodgers	(4 CD)	-Rhino 70942	(1990)
First Sessions (1927-28)	(CD)	-Rounder CD-1056	(1990)
The Early Years (1928-29)	(CD)	-Rounder CD-1057	(1990)
On The Way Up (1929)	(CD)	-Rounder CD-1058	(1990)
Riding High (1929-30)	(CD)	-Rounder CD-1059	(1990)
America's Blue Yodeler (1930-31)	(CD)	-Rounder CD-1060	(1990)
Down The Old Road (1931-32)	(CD)	-Rounder CD-1061	(1990)
No Hard Times (1932)	(CD)	-Rounder CD-1062	(1990)
Last Sessions (1933)	(CD)	-Rounder CD-1963	(1990)
A Country Legacy	(CD)	-Pair PDC2-1248	
Jimmie Rodgers	(CD)	(R)-Camden 2717	(1984)
The Best of Jimmie Rodgers	(CD)	-Curb/CEMA 77442	(1991)
Train Whistle Blues	(CD)	-ASVLE AJA-5042	(1992)
My Old Pal	(CD)	-ASVLE AJA-5058	(1992)

Extended Play Mini Albums

EP Immortal Performances		-RCA WPT-6	(1950)
EP Jimmie Rodgers, Vol. 1		-RCA EPAT-10	(1950)
EP Jimmie Rodgers, Vol. 2		-RCA EPAT-11	(1950)
EP Jimmie Rodgers Memorial Album, Vol. 1		-RCA EPAT-21	(1951)
EP Jimmie Rodgers Memorial Album, Vol. 2		-RCA EPAT-22	(1951)
EP Jimmie Rodgers Memorial Album, Vol. 3		-RCA EPAT-23	(1951)
EP Jimmie Rodgers Memorial Album, Vol. 4		-RCA EPAT-409	(1951)
EP Jimmie Rodgers Memorial Album, Vol. 5		-RCA EPAT-410	(1951)
EP Jimmie Rodgers Memorial Album, Vol. 6		-RCA EPAT-411	(1951)
EP Jimmie Rodgers Memorial Album, Vol. 1		-RCA WPT-21	(1951)
EP Jimmie Rodgers Memorial (Yodeling Yours).Vol. 2		-RCA WPT-22	(1951)
EP Jimmie Rodgers Memorial (Yodeling Yours), Vol. 3		-RCA WPT-23	(1951)
EP Travelin' Blues	(2 LP)	-RCA EPBT-3073	(1952)
EP Never No Mo' Blues	(2 LP)	-RCA EPB-1232	(1955)
EP Never No Mo' Blues		-RCA EPA-793	(1956)
EP Legendary Jimmie Rodgers		-RCA EPA-5097	(1958)

Hank Williams-

Singles

Calling You/Never Again (Will I Knock on Your Door)	-Sterling 201	(1947)
Wealth Won't Save Your Soul/When God Comes & Gathers His Jw	-Sterling 204	(1947)
I Don't Care (If Tomorrow Never Comes)	-Sterling 208	(1947)
Pan American	-Sterling 210	(1947)
Move It on Over/I Heard You Crying in Your Sleep	-MGM	(1948)
Rootie Tootie	-MGM 10124	(1948)
I'm a Long Gone Daddy	-MGM 10212	(1948)
Lovesick Blues	-MGM 10352	(1949)

-Hank Williams Cont'd-

Wedding Bells	-MGM 10401	(1949)
Mind Your Own Business	-MGM 10461	(1949)
Lost Highway/You're Gonna Change	-MGM 10506	(1949)
My Bucket's Got a Hole In It	-MGM 10560	(1949)
I Just Don't Like This Kind of Livin'	-MGM 10609	(1950)
Long Gone Lonesome Blues	-MGM 10645	(1950)
Why Don't You Love Me	-MGM 10696	(1950)
Why Should We Try Anymore	-MGM 10760	(1950)
Moaning the Blues	-MGM 10832	(1950)
Dear John	-MGM 10904	(1950)
I Can't Help It/Howlin' at the Moon	-MGM 10961	(1951)
Hey, Good Lookin'	-MGM 11000	(1951)
Crazy Heart/Lonesome Whistle	-MGM 11054	(1951)
Baby We're Really In Love	-MGM 11100	(1951)
Cold, Cold Heart/Dear John	-MGM 10904	(1951)
Honky Tonk Blues	-MGM 11162	(1952)
Half As Much	-MGM 11202	(1952)
Jambalaya (On the Bayou)	-MGM 11283	(1952)
Settin' the Woods on Fire	-MGM 11318	(1952)
I'll Never Get Out of This World Alive	-MGM 11366	(1952)
Kaw-liga/Your Cheatin' Heart	(1) -MGM 11416	(1953)
Take These Chains From My Heart/Ramblin' Man	-MGM 11479	(1953)
I Won't Be Home No More/My Love For You	-MGM 11533	(1953)
Weary Blues From Waitin'	-MGM 11574	(1953)
Low Down Blues	-MGM 11675	(1953)
House Of Gold	-MGM 11707	(1953)
I Ain't Got Nothin' But	-MGM 11768	(1954)
The Angel of Death	-MGM 11861	(1954)
A Teardrop on a Rose	-MGM 12029	(1954)
The Battle of Armageddon	-MGM 12127	(1955)
California Zephyr	-MGM 12185	(1955)
I Wish I Had a Nickel	-MGM 12244	(1956)
The Pale Horse And His Rider	-MGM 12394	(1956)
Ready To Go Home	-MGM 12438	(1957)
Leave Me Alone with the Blues	-MGM 12484	(1957)
No One Will Ever Know	-MGM 12535	(1957)
My Bucket's Got a Hole in It	(R)-MGM 12635	(1958)
Roly Poly	-MGM 12727	(1959)
Lovesick Blues/Your Cheatin' Heart	(R)-MGM 107	
Half As Much/Honky Tonk Blues	(R)-MGM 109	
Jambalaya (On the Bayou)/ I'll Never Get Out of This World Alive	-MGM 110	
Kaw-liga/Ramblin' Man	(R)-MGM 111	
Moaning The Blues/You Win Again	(R)-MGM 112	
Cold, Cold Heart/I'm So Lonesome I Could Cry	(R)-MGM 113	
I Can't Help It/House Of Gold	(R)-MGM 128	
Roly Poly/Just Waiting	(R)-MGM 142	

-Hank Williams Cont'd-

Cold, Cold Heart/I'm So Lonesome I Could Cry	(R)-MGM 514	(1965)
Your Cheatin' Heart/Hey Good Lookin'	(R)-MGM 515	(1965)
Lovesick Blues/Ramblin' Man	(R)-MGM 516	(1965)
Jambalaya (On the Bayou)/Honky Tonk Blues	(R)-MGM 517	(1965)
Lovesick Blues/Your Cheatin' Heart	(2)-MGM 13305	(1965)
The Pale Horse and His Rider	(R)-MGM 13359	(1965)
(Sung with Audrey Williams)		
I'm So Lonesome I Could Cry/You Win Again	(2)-MGM 13489	(1966)
Kaw-liga	(2)-MGM 13542	(1966)
There'll Be No Teardrops Tonight	-MGM 13630	(1966)
Long Gone Lonesome Blues/Dear John	(2)-MGM 13717	(1966)
Ramblin' Man/Why Don't You Love Me	(2)-MGM 14849	(1972)

Albums

Hank Williams Sings	-MGM E-107	(1952)
Moanin' the Blues	-MGM E-168	(1952)
Hank Williams Memorial Album	-MGM E-202	(1953)
Hank Williams As Luke the Drifter	-MGM E-203	(1953)
Honky Tonkin'	-MGM E-242	(1954)
I Saw The Light	-MGM E-243	(1954)
Ramblin' Man	-MGM E-291	(1954)
Ramblin' Man	(R)-MGM E-3219*	(1955)
Hank Williams As Luke the Drifter	(R)-MGM E-3267*	(1955)
Hank Williams Memorial Album	(R)-MGM E-3272*	(1955)
Moanin' the Blues	(R)-MGM E-3330*	(1956)
I Saw the Light	(R)-MGM E-3331*	(1956)
Honky Tonkin'	(R)-MGM E-3412*	(1957)
36 of Hank Williams' Greatest Hits (3 LP)	-MGM 3E2*	(1957)
Sing Me A Blue Song	-MGM E-3560*	(1958)
Immortal Hank William	-MGM E-3605*	(1958)
36 More of Hank Williams' Greatest Hits (3 LP)	-MGM 3E4*	(1958)
The Unforgettable Hank Williams	-MGM E-3733	(1959)
I Saw the Light (Church release)	(R)-MGM E-3331	(1959)
The Lonesome of Hank Williams	-MGM E-3803	(1960)
Wait for the Light to Shine	-MGM E-3850	(1960)
Hank Williams Greatest Hits	-MGM E-3918	(1961)
Hank Williams Lives Again	-MGM E-3923	(1961)
Let Me Sing a Blue Song	-MGM E-3924	(1961)
Wanderin' Around	-MGM E-3925	(1961)
I'm Blue Inside	-MGM E-3926	(1961)
Hank Williams As Luke the Drifter	(R)-MGM E-3927	(1961)
First, Last and Always	-MGM E-3928	(1961)
(Repackaging of 3605)		
Spirit of Hank Williams	-MGM E-3955	(1961)
On Stage! Hank Williams Recorded Live	-MGM E-3999	(1962)
14 More of Hank Williams' Greatest Hits, Vol. 2	-MGM E-4040	(1962)
Hank Williams on Stage 2	-MGM E-4109	(1963)
Beyond the Sunset	-MGM E-4138	(1963)

-Hank Williams Cont'd-

14 More of Hank Williams' Greatest Hits, Vol. 1		-MGM E-4140	(1963)
The Very Best of Hank Williams		-MGM SE-4168	(1963)
The Very Best of Hank Williams, Vol. 2		-MGM SE-4227	(1964)
Lost highway		-MGM SE-4254	(1964)
Hank Williams		-METRO M-509	(1965)
The Hank Williams Story	(4 LP)	-MGM E-4267	(1965)
Hank Williams, Sr., and Hank Williams, Jr.		-MGM E-4276	(1965)
Kaw-Liga and Other Humorous Songs		-MGM SE-4300	(1965)
Mr. and Mrs. Hank Williams		-Metro M-547	(1965)
Hank Williams with Strings		-MGM SE-4377	(1966)
(Hank Williams, Sr., and Hank Williams, Jr.) Again		-MGM SE-43788	(1966)
Movin' On-Luke the Drifter		-MGM E-4380	(1966)
More Hank Williams and Strings		-MGM SE-4429	(1966)
The Immortal Hank Williams	(R)	-Metro M-602	(1967)
I Won't Be Home No more		-MGM SE-4481	(1967)
Hank Williams with Strings, Vol. 3		-MGM SE-4529	(1968)
In The Beginning		-MGM SE-4576	(1968)
24 Karat Hits-Hank Williams (2 LP)		-MGM SE-240-2	(1968)
Essential Hank Williams		-MGM SE-4651	(1969)
Life to Legend		-MGM SE-4680	(1970)
24 of Hank Williams' Greatest Hits	(2 LP)	-MGM SE-4755	(1971)
The Last Picture Show		-MGM SE-33ST	(1971)
The Unforgettable Hank Williams		(R)-MGM SE-3733	(1972)
The Hank Williams Treasury	(4 LP)	-Columbia P4S-5616	(197?)
The Great Hits of Hank Williams, Vol. 1	(2 LP)	(R)-Blaine House	(1972)
Archetypes-Hank Williams		(R)-MGM SE-4954	(1974)
Reflections of Those Who Loved Him	(3 LP)	(DJ)-MGM PRO-912	(1975)
(Promotional set of various artists eulogizing Hank Williams)			
A Home in Heaven		-MGM M3G-4991	(1975)
Hank Williams on Stage		(R)-MGM CM-1042	(1976)
Hank Williams & the Original Drifting Cowboys Live		-Boll Weevil 111	(1976)
I Won't Be Home Nomore		(R)-MGM SE-4481	(1976)
(Strings added to above)			
Hank Williams Live at the Grand Ole Opry		-MGM MG1-5019	(1976)
Hank Williams Treasury	(4 LP)	-MGM MG1-5616	(1978)
History of Country Music, Vol. 1		-Sunrise Media 3001	(1981)
History of Country Music, Vol. 2		-Sunrise Media 3002	(1981)
History of Country Music, Vol. 3		-Sunrise Media 3003	(1981)
History of Country Music, Vol. 4		-Sunrise Media 3011	(1981)
Hank Williams- A Collection of His Greatest Hits		-Sunrise Media	(1981)
Hank Williams-Country Western Classics (CD)		-Time-Life	(1982)
Early Country Live, Vol. 1	(CD)	-ACM 3	(1983)
Early Country Live, Vol. 2	(CD)	(R)-ACM 10	(1983)
Moanin' the Blues	(CD)	(R)-Polydor SE-3330	(1983)
I Saw the Light	(CD)	(R)-Polydor SE-3331	(1983)
Honky Tonkin'	(CD)	(R)-Polydor E-3412	(1983)
Hank Williams Greatest Hits	(CD)	(R)-Polydor SE-3918	(1983)

-Hank Williams Cont'd-

The Very Best of Hank Williams	(CD)	-Polydor E-4168	(1983)
Moanin' the Blues	(CD)	(Rx)-Polydor 811899	(1984)
I Saw the Light	(CD)	(Rx)-Polydor 811900	(1984)
40 Greatest Hits 2LP	(2 CD)	-Polydor 821233	(1984)
Hank Williams' Greatest Hits	(CD)	(Rx)-Polydor 82329	(1984)
The Very Best Of Hank Williams	(CD)	(R)-Polydor 823292	(1984)
24 Greatest Hits	(2 CD)	(R)-Polydor 823293	(1984)
24 Greatest Hits, Vol. 2	(2 CD)	(R)-Polydor 823294	(1984)
Fare Takes and Radio Cuts	(CD)	-Polydor 823695	(1984)
I Ain't Got Nothin' But Time (12/46-8/47)	(2 CD)	-Polydor 825548	(1985)
Lovesick Blues (8/47-12/48)	(2 CD)	-Polydor 825551	(1985)
Lost Highway (12/48-3/49)	(2 CD)	-Polydor 825554	(1986)
I'm So Lonesome I Could Cry (March-August 1949)(CD)		-Polydor 825557	(1986)
On the Air (Radio 1949-52)	(CD)	-Polydor 827531	(1986)
Hank Williams Memorial Album	(CD)	(Rx)-Polydor 827568	(1986)
I'm So Lonesome I Could Cry (3/49-7/49)	(2 CD)	-Polydor 830557	(1986)
Beyond the Sunset	(CD)	(Rx)-Polydor 831574	(1987)
Hey Good Lookin (12/50-7/51)	(2 CD)	-Polydor 831634	(1987)
Long Gone Lonesome Blues (8/49-12/50)	(2 CD)	-Polydor 831633	(1987)
Wait for the Light to Shine	(CD)	(Rx)-Polydor 833071	(1987)
Wanderin' Around	(CD)	(Rx)-Polydor 833072	(1987)
Let's Turn Back The Years (7/51-6/52)	(2 CD)	-Polydor 833749	(1988)
I Won't Be Home Nomore (6/52-9/52)	(2 CD)	-Polydor 833752	(1988)
Just Me & My Guitar	(CD)	-CMF-006	
The First Recordings	(CD)	-CMF-007	
Grand Ole Country Classics	(2 CD)	-Pair PDK2-1165	
Health & Happiness Shows Chronicles Series	(CD)	-Mercury 517862	(1993)
I Saw The Light	(CD)	(R)-Mercury 811900	(1993)
24 Greatest Hits	(2 CD)	(R)-Mercury 823293	(1993)
24 Greatest Hits, Vol. 2	(2 CD)	(R)-Mercury 823294	(1993)
The Original Singles Collection	(3 CD)	-Mercury 847194	(1993)

Extended Play Mini Albums

EP Moanin' the Blues	(2 EP)	-MGM X-168	(1952)
EP Hank Williams Memorial Album	(2 EP)	-MGM X-202	(1953)
EP Honky Tonkin'	(2 EP)	-MGM X-242	(1954)
EP I Saw the Light	(2 EP)	-MGM X-243	(1954)
EP Ramblin' Man	(2 EP)	-MGM X-291	(1954)
EP Crazy Heart		-MGM X-1014	(1955)
EP Hank Williams as Luke the drifter		-MGM X-1047	(1955)
EP Move It on Over		-MGM X-1076	(1955)
EP There'll Be No Teardrops Tonight		-MGM X-1082	(1955)
EP Hank Williams Sings		-MGM X-1101-02	(1955)
EP Ramblin' Man		(R)-MGM X-1135-36)	(1955)
EP Hank Williams As Luke the Drifter		-MGM X-1165	(1956)
EP Moanin' the Blues		(R)-MGM X-1215-17	(1956)
EP I Saw the Light		-MGM X-1218	(1956)
EP Honky Tonkin'		(R)-MGM X-1317-19	(1957)

-Hank Williams Cont'd-

EP Sing Me a Blue Song	-MGM X-1491-93	(1958)
EP Immortal Hank Williams	-MGM X-1554-56	(1958)
EP Hank Williams Memorial Album	(R)-MGM X-1612-13	(1959)
EP Hank Williams Memorial Album	(R)-MGM X-1636	(1959)
EP Unforgettable Hank Williams	-MGM X-1637-39	(1959)
EP Hank Williams As Luke the Drifter	(R)-MGM X-1643-44	(1959)
EP I Saw the Light	(R)-MGM X-1648-49	(1959)
EP Ramblin' Man	(R)-MGM X-1650	(1959)
EP Lonesome Sound of Hank Williams	-MGM X-1698-1700	(1960)
EP The Very Best of Hank Williams	-MGM SE-4168	(1966)
EP Legend Lives on (Juke Box)	-MGM SE-4377	(1966)
EP Crazy Heart	-MGM X-1014	(1980)
EP Hank Williams and His Guitar	-Arhoolie 45-548	(1983)

*These albums were re-released in 1960, and many times after
E000 series is special promotional series of 1976
4900-5400 series released 1975-1977
reissued on Polydor 1983-1984
All early albums were reissued several times with the same number)

Bob Wills (& His Texas Playboys)-

Singles

Have I Stayed Away Too Long	-The Antones 501
St. Louis Blues	-Vocalion 03076
Mexicali Rose	-Vocalion 03086
Osage Stomp	-Vocalion 03096
Black and Blue Rag	-Vocalion 03139
Wang Wang Blues	-Vocalion 03173
I Ain't Got Nobody	-Vocalion 03206
Blue River	-Vocalion 03230
Never No More Blues	-Vocalion 03264
Oklahoma Rag	-Vocalion 03295
Trouble in Mind	-Vocalion 03343
Basin Street Blues	-Vocalion 03344
Fan It	-Vocalion 03361
Steel Guitar Rag	-Vocalion 03394
She's Killing Me	-Vocalion 03424
Right or Wrong	-Vocalion 03451
Mean Mama Blues	-Vocalion 03492
Too Busy	-Vocalion 03537
Swing Blues No.2	-Vocalion 03578
Bleeding Hearted Blues	-Vocalion 03597
White Heat	-Vocalion 03614
Rosetta	-Vocalion 03659
The New St. Louis Blues	-Vocalion 03693
Maiden's Prayer	-Vocalion 03924

-Bob Wills Cont'd-

Sunbonnet Sue	-Vocalion 03997	
Black Rider	-Vocalion 04132	
Empty Bed Blues	-Vocalion 04184	
Gambling Polka Dot Blues	-Vocalion 04275	
Tulsa Stomp	-Vocalion 04325	
Loveless Love	-Vocalion 04387	
Moonlight and Roses	-Vocalion 04439	
Oh, Lady Be Good	-Vocalion 04515	
That's What I Like 'Bout the South	-Vocalion 04566	
Whoa, Babe	-Vocalion 04625	
Don't Keep It a Secret	-Decca 29453	
That's the Bottle Talking	-Decca 30165	
Texas Blues	-MGM 11767	(1953)
So Long I'll See You Later	-MGM 11985	(1954)
Square Dance	-MGM 12142	(1955)
San Antonio Rose	(R)-Kapp 116	(1968)
South of the Border/In My Adobe Hacienda	(R)-Kapp 117	(1968)
San Antonio Rose/Across the Alley From Alamo	(R)-MCA 60085	(1973)
In My Adobe Hacienda/South of the Border	(R)-MCA 60086	(1973)
Deep in the Heart of Texas	(R)-MCA 60087	(1973)

Albums

Bob Wills Roundup	-Columbia HL-9003	(1949)
Ranch House Favorites	-MGM E-91	(1951)
Texas Playboys	-The Antones 6000	(195?)
Old Time Favorites By Bob Wills	-The Antones 6010	(195?)
Dance-O-Rama #2	-Decca DL-5562	(1955)
Ranch House Favorites	-MGM E-3352	(1956)
Bob Wills Special	-Harmony HL-7036	(1957)
Bob Wills and His Texas Playboys	-Decca DL-8727	(1957)
Bob Wills String Band Hits	-Kapp KS-3601	(1960)
Together Again-Bob Wills and Tommy Duncan	-Liberty LST-7173	(1960)
A Living Legend-Bob Wills	-Liberty LST-7182	(1961)
Mr. Words and Music	-Liberty LST-7194	(1961)
Bob Wills and Tommy Duncan	-Liberty LSX-1912	(1961)
Bob Wills Sings and Plays	-Liberty LST-7303	(1963)
The Best of Bob Wills	-Harmony HL-7304	(1963)
The Great Bob Wills	-Harmony HL-7345	(1965)
Western Swing Along	-Vocalion VL-3735	(1965)
Bob Wills Keepsake Album No. 1	-Longhorn LP-001	(1965)
Bob Wills Keepsake Album No. 1	(R)-Club of Spade 001	(1965)
San Antonio Rose-Steel Guitar	-Starday SLP-375	(1965)
Together Again-Bob Wills & Tommy Duncan	-Sunset SUS-5108	(1966)
Bob Wills and His Texas Playboys	(R)-Decca DL7-8727	(1966)
From the Heart of Texas Bob Wills & the Playboys		
Featuring Leon Raush	-Kapp KS-3506	(1966)
Bob Wills Collectors Series	-Longhorn 007	(1967)
Bob Wills	-Metro M-594	(1967)

-Bob Wills Cont'd-

King of Western Swing	-Kapp KS-3523	(1967)
Here's That Man Again	-Kapp KS-3542	(1968)
Bob Wills Special	(R)-Harmony HS-11358	(1969)
Time Changes Everything	-Kapp KS-3569	(1969)
The Living Legend	-Kapp KS-3587	(1969)
Bob Wills Plays the Greatest String Band Hits	-Kapp KS-3601	(1969)
San Antonio Rose	-Vocalion VL7-3922	(1967)
Bob Wills	-Texas Rose 2709	
The Voice and Band of Bob Wills	-Pickwick SPC-3592	
A Country Walk	-Sunset SUS-5248	(1969)
For the Last Time (2 LP)	-UA UALA216J2	
The Bob Wills Story	-Starday SLP-469	(1970)
In Person	(R)-Kapp KS-3639	(1970)
The Best of Bob Wills	-Kapp KS-3641	(1971)
Legendary Masters-Bob Wills and Tommy Duncan	-UA UAS-9962	(1971)
A Tribute to Bob Wills	-MGM GAS-141	(1971)
24 Great Hits By Bob Wills (2 LP)	-MGM MG2-5303	(1977)
Bob Wills Anthology (2 LP)	-Columbia KG-32416	(1973)
Bob Wills Plays the Greatest String Band Hit	(R)-MCA 152	(1973)
The Best of Bob Wills	(R)-MCA 153	(1973)
The History of Bob Wills and His Texas Playboys	-MGM E-4866	(1973)
Western Swing Along	(R)-Coral CB-20109	(1973)
The Best of Bob Wills (2 LP)	(R)-MCA 2-4092	(1975)
Bob Wills and His Texas Playboys In Concert (2 LP)	-Capitol SKBB11550	(1976)
Remembering the Greatest Hits of Bob Wills	-Columbia KC34108	(1976)
Bob Wills 'I Love the People'	-Western Hrtage 176	(1976)
The Tiffany Transcriptions	-Lariat 1	(1977)
Bob Wills: The Tiffany Transcriptions 1945-1948		
on the West Coast	-Tishomingo BW01	(1978)
Lone Star Rag	-Columbia P-14390	(1979)
Bob Wills Special	(R)-Columbia P-15813	(1981)
Country Music-Bob Wills	-Time-Life P-15836	(1981)
Faded Love	-Delta DLP-1124	(1981)
The San Antonio Rose Story	-Delta DLP-1138	(1982)
Bob Wills Is Still the King	-Delta DLP-1140	(1982)
Texas Fiddle and Milk Cow Blues	-Delta DLP-1141	(1982)
Bob Wills (Columbia Historic Collection)	-Columbia FC-37468	(1982)
For the Last Time (2 LP)	-Liberty LXB-216	(1982)
The Best of Bob Wills	(R)-MCA MCA-5917E	(1982)
The Best of Bob Wills, Vol. 2 (2 LP)	-MCA MCA2-4092	(1982)
Heaven, Hell or Houston	-Delta DLP-1142	(1983)
Tiffany Transcriptions, Vol. 1	-Kleidoscope KLD16	(1983)
Best of the Tiffanys, Vol. 2	-Kleidoscope KLD19	(1983)
Basin Street Blues, Vol. 3	-Kleidoscope KLD20	(1983)
Your From Texas, Vol. 4	-Kleidoscope KLD21	(1983)
(Unknown title), Vol. 5	-Kleidoscope KLD25	(1984)
Sally Goodin', Vol. 6	-Kleidoscope KLD27	(1984)

-Bob Wills Cont'd-

Keep Knockin', Vol. 7		-Kleidoscope KLD29	(1984)
Bob Wills on Stage		-Delta DLP-1149	(1984)
King of Western Swing Bob Wills & the Texas Playboys (2 CD)		-MCA 2-8019	(1984)
The Greatest String Band/Bob Wills/Mel Tillis	(2 CD)	-MCA -2-8020	(1984)
Bob Wills & His Texas Playboys	(CD)	(R)-MCA 526	(1985)
Time Changes Everything	(CD)	(R)-MCA 545	(1985)
The Living Legend	(CD)	(R)-MCA 546	(1985)
In Person	(CD)	(R)-MCA 550	(1985)
Bob Wills Keepsake Album #1	(CD)	-Longhorn 001	(1986)
24 Greatest Hits	(CD)	-Polydor 827573	(1986)
Bob Wills and His Texas Playboys	(CD)	-Texas Rose 2709	(1987)
The Golden Era (50th Anniversary)	(2 CD)	-Columbia C-240149	(1987)
Bob Wills Fiddle	(CD)	-CMF 010	
King of Western Swing	(2 CD)	-MCA 2-38019	
21 Golden Hits	(CD)	-Hollywood 411	
The Best of Bob Wills	(CD)	(R)-MCA 153	
Bob Wills Greatest Hits	(CD)	-Curb 77389	(1990)
Bob Wills (& His Texas Playboys) (1935-37)	(2 CD)	-Rhino 70744	(1991)
Bob Wills (Columbia Historic Collection)	(CD)	(R)-Columbia FC-37468	(1991)
The Essential Bob Wills and His Texas Playboys	(CD)	-Columbia 48958	(1992)
Anthology: 24 Greatest Hits	(CD)	-Sony 32416	(199?)
The Best of Bob Wills	(CD)	(R)-MCA 5917	(199?)
The Best of Bob Wills	(CD)	-Camden CBK-3023	(199?)

Extended Play Mini Albums

EP Bob Wills (San Antonio Rose)	-Columbia B-2805	(1957)
EP Dance-O-Rama	-Decca ED-2223-24	(1955)
EP Ranch House Favorites	-MGM X-1237-39	(1956)

Bob Wills & Tommy Duncan

Singles

Bob Wills and Tommy Duncan	-Liberty LSX-1912	(196?)
Together Again	-Liberty LST-7173	(1960)
Legendary Masters-Bob Wills and Tommy Duncan	-UA UAS-9962	(1971)

CHAPTER 3

THE PRIMARY SET

With black sound being integrated into white music came a unique recognition by the American people that a great amount of prejudice was running rampant in the country. The early music was banned from the airwaves of white stations all over the country. Even when Elvis arrived, his music was banned, because many stations believed that he was black.

The major record companies would never dream of having a black artist playing or singing black music. It took many years for someone like Nat King Cole to be accepted, and he only sang white music. Questions like "What would become of our society if this were to remain?" became dominant throughout the country and the music industry.

The giants of the record business were actually convinced that this type of music was a minor trend, and they had no intention of adding this type of music to their libraries. By 1957, the black labels were eagerly searching for more and more white rockabilly sounds and black artists were being squeezed out.

> The first rock record is the original version of Sh-Boom by the Chords. Issued on the Cat label, a subsidiary of Atlantic. Sh Boom occupies a unique position in the history of popular music: It not only heralded the style of the new music, but the history of its success established the pattern followed by nearly all of the successful rock records between 1954 and 1956. *[Belz, 1972, p. 25-26]*

The first really white rock and roll record is considered to be "Black Denim Trousers and Motorcycle Boots," by the Cheers in 1955.

The power of early rock and roll was enormous, as indicated by the resurgence of Golden Oldies sounds on both recordings and in live shows in every decade since the concept was introduced. Every generation would try to enlarge upon the sound, yet the basic, original sound would continue to return and thrive in the music world. The creation of rock and roll was similar, in effect, to the creation of the Frankenstein monster, in that it would continue to survive and endure, all by itself, through the decades ahead.

> The advent of rock disturbed the security of the music business: instead of domination of the charts by the top labels, and top established artists, lingering for upwards of twenty weeks at a time, we now had a surge of new acts (not only single artists, but groups) from unknown record labels, who dominated the charts for several weeks, and were no longer heard from again.[Belz, 1972, p. 10]

The independent labels were, of course, eager to expand to this new sound. It was a lot easier for them to do so than it was for the major labels. They had less overhead, fewer employees and less fat. They needed fewer sales to make a profit, and they were more apt to try something new, as they had a closer awareness to the local sounds.

The medium would generate more dances than any particular music in history: the duck, the pony, the fly, the popeye, the Madison, the monkey, the stroll, the twist, the swim, the mashed potato, the Watusi, the limbo, the hully gully, the hitchhiker, the boogaloo, the freddie, the frug, the jerk, the chicken — and many, many more.

The sounds of rock would take many forms in the years ahead, among them the surfer sound, folk music, folk rock, skiffle music, punk rock, heavy metal, rockabilly, rhythm & blues, swing, acid rock, and many more. This was the music of the future, and the future was now.

> In the years 1954 to 1956, there were five distinctive styles, developed almost completely independently of one another, that collectively became known as rock 'n' roll: northern band rock 'n' roll, whose most popular exemplar was Bill Haley; the New Orleans, dance blues; Memphis

country rock (also known as rockabillly); Chicago rhythm
and blues; and vocal group rock 'n' roll. All five styles, and
the variants associated with each of them, depended for their
dancing beat on contemporary Negro dance rhythms. *[Gillitt,
1983, p. 23]*

By the end of the '50's the small independent companies had just as
much chance, and perhaps more, as the major companies to have a hit.
The smaller companies, of course, because of their experiences with the
music, had a much better sound to their rhythm and blues, and rock and
roll records, than did the major ones.

William John Clifton Haley, Jr

Much of the early sounds of rock and roll
were merely covers of various hits from the
rhythm and blues genre until the advent of Bill
Haley and his Comets. It was Bill Haley, born in High-
land Park, Michigan, in March of 1927, who opened the doors to the
music that would allow Elvis Presley and others the chance to be heard.
He completed the connection between the white and black music of the
country, to make them both respectable.

At age 13, he toured with a country group, The Down Homers, and
at age 19, he became a disc jockey and music director of WPWA in Chester,
Pennsylvania.

His sound was originally country and western, but not being easily
satisfied, he kept constantly adding other sounds to his music, and soon
began to cover various rhythm and blues numbers, as well. With the release of his song "Dim Dim The Lights" (1954), he became the first white
artist to be popular on the rhythm and blues charts.

The original sound of Bill Haley & His Four Aces of Western Swing
was definitely that of the western genre. He began recording as early as
1949, but never really made an impact. Changing his sound and the name
of his group to Bill Haley & His Saddlemen during the early 50's, he
began to grow in stature, and gain a little recognition. In 1951 he recorded for Holiday Records, and started to experiment with the rhythm

and blues sounds of black music. He created a real "rocking" drive during the Holiday times, his first releases being "Rocket 88," a cover of a heavy rhythm and blues hit, and "Rock The Joint." He soon graduated to the company's main label, Essex, where the drive continued. The music he created was fun, loud, and rocking, a sound never expressed publicly before by any white musician. His first three releases, "Rock the Joint," "Rocking Chair on the Moon," and "Stop Beatin' Round the Mulberry Bush," were outstanding, and created quite a stir among the parents of the teenagers who purchased the records.

First hitting the charts in 1953, with his Essex Label release of "Crazy Man Crazy," he was destined to become the leader in the beginning of this era of rock and roll, and to a great extent of the rockabilly genre. In 1954, he moved up to a big label with his signing with Decca Records, and he released one of their biggest hits, "Shake, Rattle, and Roll," which was already a top ten rhythm and blues hit by Joe Turner. The record sold well over a million copies, and allowed him to start travelling all over the world on one tour after another.

In 1954, Decca released his most popular song, the largest hit he ever had, and the one that he is most noted for, "Rock Around The Clock." Although the song took over a year to catch on, in 1955 it was number one on the charts for seven weeks in a row, an achievement few artist have ever accomplished. The record was also the first to sell over one million copies in Great Britain alone, and was number one on the British charts for five weeks. The collective sales of the song have been estimated at over 22 million copies. It was on the bestseller list for 29 weeks. It was again on the charts for an additional fourteen weeks when it was re-released in 1974.

In 1956, he added another million seller to his repertoire with the release of "See You Later, Alligator," which became a synonym for goodbye among teenagers throughout the country for years.

In the beginning, he was the actual representation of the form of music known as rockabilly. The nonsense words, the heavy use of guitars and drums, a handful of musicians screaming, and playing loudly with background vocals and loud music gave the impression of having a huge room full of musicians creating an enormous sound. The saxophone was used as a screaming, crying sound to bring out the basic rhythm and blues sounds of black music.

Bill Haley never really knew what he was creating. He started with a sound, and kept adding to it, until it sounded great. He retained the early black sounds of the saxophone, bull fiddle, drums and such, and helped incorporate the rocking sounds of electric guitars and drums into it. By the mid-'50's, most of the successful white artists were almost all from the country music genre.

> "I'm the first to admit that I didn't invent that rocking train that just keeps a-rollin'- but I can lay claim to being it's first conductor. I got on board at the start and I had a darn good ride — Thank the Lord I got off safely ......*[Bill Haley, quoted in Belz, 1972, p. 37]*

Bill Haley led the young people of this country toward these new sounds of the city, and the new music of youth. The most ironic part, of course, was that he was not young, but obviously his age did not deter him in any way. By the end of 1956, he would be overshadowed by "the King" Elvis Aaron Presley. Bill Haley and his Comets (formerly his Saddlemen), were comprised of: John Grande, on accordion; Billy Williamson, on steel guitar; Rudy Pompelli, on saxophone; Al Rex, on bass; Francis Beecher, on Spanish guitar; and Don Raymond, on drums. Together, they were the first step in the creation of true rockabilly music. The second step was soon to come, in a small independent record company in Memphis, Tennessee. Bill Haley died of a heart attack in Harlingen, Texas, on February 9, 1981.

These early sounds of rock, country, and rockabilly contained nothing but the simplest chords and progressions. Later, in the '60's, the sound would constantly expand with the introduction of well-trained musicians and writers and with the introduction of advanced electronic music.

> As the word implies, rockabilly is hillbilly rock-and-roll. It was not a usurpation of black music by whites because its soul, its pneuma, was white, full of the redneck ethics ...... What made rockabilly such a drastic new music was its spirit, a thing hat bordered on mania. Elvis's "Good Rockin' To-night" was not merely a party song, but an invitation to a holocaust.*[Gillitt, 1983, p. 28]*

The music contained its own built-in energy source, exploding upon impact with the human ear — an impact that could destroy the very soul of its listeners. With all its seemingly uncontrollable energy, it demanded a unique and equal balance between the white and black sounds, and between the truth and fiction of life as presented by the artist. The music spoke of love, hate, truth, justice, and sex in such a way that was never before presented to the American people, and for that matter, the rest of the world. It was the simplest of melodies wrapped up in the most complicated package for its unveiling to the world.

> Rockabilly was a fast, aggressive music: simple, snappy drumming, sharp guitar licks, wild country boogie piano, the music of kids who came from all over the South to make records for Sam Phillips and his imitators. Rockabilly came and it went; there was never that much of it, and even including Elvis's first Sun singles, all the rockabilly hits put together sold less than Fats Domino's. But rockabilly fixed the crucial image of rock 'n' roll: the sexy, half-crazed fool standing on stage singing his heart out. *[Gillett, 1983, p. 135]*

In the beginning, the South was bursting with the talent of the new sound — the sound of the fields, the country, and the city — the black and white sound that would soon develop into the new music. The artists in the south had to go to Chicago, to record their blues sounds, to New York, to record their their country sounds. There was, however, no place to record the new sound that was seeping under the doorway to the future.

> ... Memphis,Tennessee. Musically this was where rock 'n' roll came from, sent rocketing on its way through the loud dance music of Bill Haley and the presence and power of Elvis. For if Haley was everyone's introduction to rock 'n' roll, Elvis was Chapter One all by himself. *[Miller, 1976, p. 62]*

Thus, the time was ripe for the coming of the savior of the modern sound — the man who would lead the world into the future with the connections of the past, the man who would set fire to the conservative voices of the giants, and unleash the harnessed power of the small independents, which would take over the music world.

Sam Cornelius Phillips

Sam Phillips was born near Florence, Alabama, on January 5, 1923. After quitting high school in 1941, he worked as a radio announcer, while studying engineering, podiatry, and embalming (obviously trying to be a success at something) at night. He kept on the move: in 1942 he became a deejay at WLAY, in Muscle Shoals, Alabama. In 1943 he went to WHSL in Decator, Georgia; in 1945 he joined WLAC in Nashville; 1946-1949 he was with WREC in Memphis, and began to promote shows on the side.

Sam purchased his studio at 706 Union Avenue in Memphis, Tennessee, in 1950 — the city's first permanent recording facility. He began to record various artists, and lease the records to other companies, such as: Chess, Modern, Meteor and Trumpet. In addition, he recorded weddings, Rotarian speeches, and anything for which he could charge money. The Sun label was founded in 1952, when Sam joined with his brother Judd, who would provide him with much help and knowledge in the future. Sun's first release was numbered 174 (it was common in those days for the smaller independents to begin with an uncommon number, usually one that had a personal meaning, and it also tended to fool distributors into thinking the company had been around for a long time). The label just about ceased producing anything meaningful by the early 60's

> In 1951 Sam Phillips was the owner of a shoe string operation that cut records by young black blues singers in Memphis, Tennessee. A few years later he would shape the careers of such founding rockers as Elvis Presley, Carl Perkins, Roy Orbison, and Jerry Lee Lewis; today, he counts his money. But at least one writer has stepped forward to call him "America's Real Uncle Sam", a title he might like. *[Stambler & Landon, 1983, P. 16]*

Sam Phillips main source of income was in recording local talent and charging them for it. Occasionally, he would sell or lease various recordings to other labels, in other parts of the country; labels such as Chess in Chicago, and Modern in Los Angeles, that were capable of supporting such artists. Eventually, his Sun record label would be released as well, and he developed a strong regional following.

Many of the artists which he recorded would only reach local or minute stardom: Jackie Boy and Little Walter, Johnny London, Walter Bradford and the Big City Four, Handy Jackson, Joe Hill Louis, Jimmy and Walter, among others.

Some of the artist would reach a higher degree of stardom, not necessarily at the time, but in later years. including Rufus Thomas, Jr.; Little Milton; Billy (The Kid) Emerson; James Cotton; Charlie Feathers; Warren Smith; Billy Riley; Edwin Bruce; Jack Clement; Dickey Lee; Ray Smith; David Houston; Bobby Bland; Sleepy John Estes; Howlin' Wolf; and B. B. King.

Although Sun originally started as a blues record company, Sam was constantly looking for a certain sound — a mixture of the religious zeal of gospel and the soul searching emotion of rhythm and blues. He began to seek this sound in the white youths of the south, and rather then create it, he tended to guide it to perfection. We can see his guiding hand in the likes of Elvis Presley, Johnny Cash, Carl Perkins, Roy Orbison, Jerry Lee Lewis, and the many other known and unknown artists who made up the roster of talent in this great company.

> "My Kind of Carryin' On" by Doug Poindexter and The Starlight Wranglers... It fluttered, shook like a creature flirting with madness. Sam must have slept well that night. *[Tosches, 1985, p. 44]*

Unfortunately, this was to be the only release by Poindexter on Sun, for in 1955 he retired from the music business after the breakup of his band. His lead guitarist, Scotty Moore, and his bass player, Bill Black, had joined with a new young singer by the name of Elvis Presley. On July 5, 1954 this young singer recorded "That's All Right, Mama" which would have a profound effect on the music industry, and on Sun Records. The style was raw, new, and exciting, and would, in a year or so he called rockabilly.

The fact that Elvis used only two backup artists, and later three would inspire many later singers to copy his lead. Among these would be Buddy Holly, Buddy Knox, and Johnny Cash.

Elvis Aaron Presley

Elvis Presley was born in Tupelo, Mississippi, on January 8, 1935, to a relatively poor lower class family. In September 1948, the family moved to Memphis, Tennessee, where they lived in a low-cost government sponsored housing complex while he attended Humes High School. In high school he developed the desire to become a singer, but had no idea how to accomplish such a feat. He would listen to the songs of the Carter Family, Jimmie Rodgers, Roy Acuff, Ernest Tubb, Bob Wills, Hank Williams, as well as to the many white gospel and black blues singers in the south. He imitated many of the popular singers of the day, but he was warned against singing the black blues, as it was "sinful" music.

After high school he took a job as a truck driver for the Crown Electric Company, where he would remain for several years. He would make extra money by selling his blood, by ushering in the local theaters, or in any way he could. He spent it both to help support his parents and to fulfill his desire for flashy clothes.

Like many parents with no possible future, Elvis's lived only for their son, so they pampered and spoiled him, and desired the best for him, so that he would fulfill their dreams. On Sundays they would attend their church, the Assembly of God and hear the minister proclaim the evils of the earth, in the great southern way.

Elvis's desire for a special birthday present for his mother would lead him to his destiny at Sun Records, where he would record a few songs for his mother. This led to a special meeting, and recording session with the label. It's been said that when Elvis was asked, over the phone, how soon he could get to the studio, he was there before Sam could hang up the phone.

There were four people there, when it happened; Scotty Moore, the great lead guitarist; Sam Phillips, in the background, just waiting for something to happen; Bill Black, playing his slap bass, and eating up every minute of it, and the young, wild kid, slapping his guitar, and making like he was the only one in the whole world. Then it finally happened, as Sam knew it would. They recorded a song called "That's All Right, Mama" which made everyone happy, Sam had to wonder who in the world would dare to play this "nigger" music sound. The whites wouldn't play it because it was black music, and the blacks wouldn't play it because it sounded like hillbilly music.

Elvis would be destined to play the circuit for years — the car dealerships, carnivals, political rallies, and so forth throughout the south — constantly improving his sound, and learning how to react to his audience (which consisted mainly of adoring teenage girls).

No one would have the same impact on the world, as Elvis did, until 1964 when the Beatles came to America, and began a new phase of rock and roll. His sincerity, his movements, and his honesty would carry him to the hearts of America and the world.

He recorded for Sun for only one year, but during that year Sun released ten songs, some from the blues genre and some just plain country. The amount of material that Elvis recorded in this period was unheard of in the industry.

"Baby Let's Play House" was his first record to reach the national charts, and it hit number 10 on the country and western charts in July 1955. In October of that year, a 19-year-old artist named Buddy Holly was the opening act for Elvis in Lubbock, Texas. It was now time for every rockabilly artist in the world to come out of the swamps, the farms, and the factories, in order to let the world know that they were around.

Elvis also had enough impact on the music world to cause many artists who would have been pure country and western musicians to turn to this new sound. Among these future stars were; Conway Twitty, Carl Perkins, Roy Orbison, Johnny Cash, Dorsey and Johnny Burnette, George Hamilton IV, Marty Robbins, the Everly Brothers, and Buddy Holly. Because of Elvis, there would soon be a tremendous void in the area of country and western music for many years to come.

By 1960, this sound would eventually be swallowed up by the flourishing rock format, and many of these artist would take a turn either toward country, or toward pure rock and pop music.

In 1955 Elvis met Colonel Tom Parker, who had originally been a carnival pitch man, and who had previously managed Eddy Arnold, and his world changed. Parker negotiated a contract with RCA, making it one of the first major labels of the day to jump on the bandwagon of the new rock sound. For approximately $40,000.00 RCA purchased the rights to Elvis Presley and his recordings, a relatively cheap price to pay for the enormous sums that would be made in the future. Soon Elvis would be on the lips of everyone in the world. His actions would cause havoc in the industry, and his success would be nothing less than phenomenal. No other single artist would ever achieve his success.

RCA was Elvis's biggest pusher, and promoted him with enthusiasm. They began by booking him on "The Tommy And Jimmy Dorsey Show" on national television, for six Saturday night appearances. The reactions were enormous, and so were the ratings. This reaction caused Ed Sullivan, who had previously called him "unfit" for his family audience, to offer Elvis $50,000 for three performances, rather than the normal scale paid to most of the artists who appeared on his show.

Shortly afterward, RCA released "Heartbreak Hotel" backed with "I Was The One," the first of over 50 records to sell one million copies, or more. The record immediately went to the top of the charts, and two million copies were sold. This first release on RCA was pure rockabilly, with echoes, heavy on guitars, and ridiculous loving lyrics — a song destined to go immediately to the top of the charts. RCA also re-released all of the Sun Records cuts at about the same time. Never before had anyone dominated the charts more than Elvis, and no one would ever touch him, although the Beatles came close. He was called everything from a "no talent bum" to a "sexabitionist," but nothing could stop him in his rise to the top.

Elvis had a rapport with his audience that very few entertainers ever acquire. He was hated, with jealousy by the males, and loved with uncontrollable desire by the females -- yet everyone learned to respect his ability, his sincerity, and his charms of innocence.

His singing was crude and unrestrained, as were his movements on stage, but he projected the hurt and emotions that every teenager has experienced at some time, thus making direct contact with his audience. He was the personification of pure sexual lust, and his audience loved it. By 1961, he had sold $76 million worth of records.

Of all the rockabilly singers who sprouted up after Elvis, few could compete with their own studio sound. The echo chambers; background singers; and the loud, yet stylish, guitar chords created in the studios were much too difficult to duplicate on the road. Elvis created his own action and his own motivation and projected his own image, exactly the way the records sounded.

Since other early rockabilly and rock and roll stars found it diffi-

cult to recreate the sound of the studio, they began to lip-synch the
lyrics to a recording to create the exact sound of the recording. Many
good artists, however, continued to sing their own sound, in front of the
audience.

It was the Colonel's desire to graduate Elvis from the low, sensual
sounds of poor trash to the more sophisticated sounds of large orches-
tras, complete with chorus. With each new recording session, Elvis grew
further and further away from the pure rockabilly sounds of his beginnings. By 1958, when he entered the army, his rockabilly days were
over, and the polished sounds were beginning to develop. His world,
however, was changing. He could go nowhere without being recognized,
and hounded. He soon developed his own world at Graceland Mansion,
he made the rest of the world stay out.

He continued to record hit after hit, even while he was in Germany, serving in the U. S. Army. From 1956, and 1962, he had 18 number one songs on the charts. In 1956, he signed a movie contract with
Hal Wallis, and made his film debut in the 20th Century-Fox movie
Love Me Tender. The movie made its entire investment back within
three days of its release — an unprecedented and unheard of act in film
history.

One movie after another followed: *Flaming Star; G. I. Blues; Wild
in the Country; Blue Hawaii; Follow That Dream; Kid Galahad; King
Creole; Girls, Girls, Girls,* and many more. Elvis continued to turn out
movie after movie and record after record, but it was different. He was
no longer the hottest thing in the world.

In 1968, all this would change. It would start quietly with the
release of Jerry Reed's "Guitar Man," and by 1970 would result in
a complete comeback -- the result of strategic planning by Elvis
and the Colonel.

Elvis's first national show, at The International Hotel in Las Vegas, was a great performance, and he agreed to return. NBC TV released his first TV specia., He staged performances at special locations
across the country. All of them were successful.

Regardless of how much money or fame came his way, Elvis always managed to retain the image of the lovable country boy. Elvis
Presley died on August 16,1977, as a result of obesity and the use of
drugs. To this day his hundreds of thousands of followers still remember
and cherish him. His death not only startled his fans, but created questions concerning the actual cause of his death. His doctor claimed he

died of a heart attack, but later his death was investigated because of the abnormally high amount of prescription drugs that were issued to Elvis. Traces of 13 types of drugs were found in his system.

RCA Records was swamped for years after Elvis's death, with requests for material, songs, records, pictures, and anything pertaining to Elvis. The world was flooded with memorabilia, and books. Elvis was the epitome of the fairy tale story of the poor pauper who comes into wealth and fame. His records continue to be released on a yearly basis.

The following codes and classifications are used in the discography.

R	Reissue of a previous release
Rx	Additional Reissue of previous release
1	The first recording of the song.
2	The second recording...etc.
33	A 33 1/3 speed single release
S	Stereo (noted only on early singles and EP's)
Decca/W	Decca/Webcor
Great NWM	Great North Western Music
GNP/Crscndo	GNP/Crescendo
RAG	Radio Active Gold
AOB	Association of Broadcasters
SMC	Special Music Company
Warner B	Warner Brothers (or Bros)

Recordings are listed chronologically under each artist's heading.
Most CD listings are available on tape with similar numbers
Most LP Records are no longer available
Artists are arranged alphabetically.

Bill Haley & His Four Aces Of Western Swing-

Singles

Candy Kisses/Tennessee Border	-Cowboy 1202	(1949)
Four Leaf Clover Blues/Too Many Parties	-Cowboy 1700	(1950)
My Sweet Lil Girl From Nevada/My Palomino and I	-Cowboy 1701	(1950)
Stand Up And Be Counted/Loveless Blues	-Center N/A	(1950)

Bill Haley and his ad dleMen-

Singles

Deal Me a Hand/Ten Gallon Stetson	-Keystone 5101	(1950)
Susan Van Dusen/I'm Not To Blame	-Keystone 5102	(1950)

Bill Haley and His Saddlemen-

Singles

Why Do I Cry Over You/I'm Gonna Dry Every Tear with a Kiss	-Atlantic 727	(1950)

Bill Haley and The Saddlemen-

Singles

Rocket 88/Tear Stains on My Heart	-Holiday 105	(1951)
Green Tree Boogie/Deep Down in My Heart	-Holiday 108	(1951)
Pretty Baby/I'm Crying	-Holiday 110	(1951)
A Year Ago This Christmas/I Don't Want To Be Alone This Christmas	-Holiday 111	(1951)
Jukebox Cannonball/Sundown Boogie	-Holiday 113	(1952)
(Duet with Loretta)		
Rock the Joint/Icy Heart	-Essex 303	(1952)
Rocking Chair on the Moon/ Dance with the Dolly (With the Hole in the Stocking)	-Essex 305	(1952)

Bill Haley and His Comets-

Singles

Stop Beatin' Around the Mulberry Bush/Real Rock Drive	-Essex 310	(1952)
Yes Indeed/Real Rock Drive	(R)-Transworld 718	(1953)
Crazy, Man, Crazy/Whatcha Gonna Do	-Essex 321	(1953)
Pat-a-cake/Fractured	-Essex 327	(1953)
Live It Up/Farewell, So Long, Goodbye	-Essex 332	(1954)
I'll Be True/Ten Little Indians	-Essex 340	(1954)
Rocket 88	(R)-Transworld 381	(1954)
Rock Around the Clock/Thirteen Women	-Decca 29124	(1954)
Shake, Rattle and Roll/A.B.C. Boogie	-Decca 29204	(1954)
Straight Jacket/Chattanooga Choo Choo	-Essex 348	(1954)
Dim, Dim the Lights/Happy Baby	-Decca 29317	(1954)

-Bill Haley And His Comets Cont'd-

Mambo Rock/Birth of the Boogie	-Decca 29418	(1955)
Jukebox Cannonball/Sundown Boogie	(R)-Essex 374	(1955)
Rocket 88/Green Tree Boogie	(R)-Essex 381	(1955)
Razzle-Dazzle/Two Hound Dogs	-Decca 29552	(1955)
Rock the Joint/Farewell, So Long, Goodby	-Essex 399	(1955)
Burn That Candle/Rock-a-beatin' Boogie	-Decca 29713	(1955)
See You Later Alligator/The Paper Boy	-Decca 29791	(1955)
R-O-C-K/The Saints' Rock and Roll	-Decca 29870	(1956)
Hot Dog Buddy Buddy/Rockin' Through the Rye	-Decca 29948	(1956)
Rip It Up/Teenager's Mother (Are You Right?)	-Decca 30028	(1956)
Rudy's Rock/Blue Comet Blues	-Decca 30085	(1956)
Don't Knock the Rock/Choo Choo Ch'boogie	-Decca 30148	(1957)
Forty Cups of Coffee/Hook, Line and Sinker	-Decca 30214	(1957)
(You Hit the Wrong Note) Billy Goat/Rockin' Rollin' Rover	-Decca 30314	(1957)
The Dipsy Doodle/Miss You	-Decca 30394	(1957)
Rock the Joint/How Many (Broken Hearts)?	-Decca 30461	(1958)
Mary, Mary Lou/It's a Sin	-Decca 30530	(1958)
Skinny Minnie/Sway with Me	-Decca 30592	(1958)
Lean Jean/Don't Nobody Move	-Decca 30681	(1958)
Chiquita Linda/Whoa Mabel	-Decca 30741	(1958)
B.B. Betty/Corrine, Corrina	-Decca 30781	(1959)
I Got a Woman/Charmaine	-Decca 30844	(1959)
A Fool Such As I/Where'd You Go Last Night?	-Decca 30873	(1959)
Caldonia/Shaky	-Decca 30926	(1959)
Joey's Song/Ooh! Look-A-There Ain't She Pretty	-Decca 30956	(1959)
Skokiaan/Puerto Rican Peddler	-Decca 31030	(1960)
Strictly Instrumental/Music, Music, Music!	-Decca 31080	(1960)
Candy Kisses/Tamiani	-Warner Bros 5145	(1960)
Chick Safari/Hawk	-Warner Bros 5154	(1960)
So Right Tonight/Let the Good Times Roll	-Warner Bros 5171	(1960)
Flip Flop and Fly/Honky Tonk	-Warner Bros 5228	(1961)
The Spanish Twist/My Kind Of Woman	-Gone 5111	(1961)
Rock Around the Clock/Shake, Rattle and Roll	-Warner Bros 7124	(1961)
Riviera/War Paint	-Gone 5116	(1961)
Yakety Sax/Boot's Blues	-Logo 7005	(1961)
A B C Boogie/(Flip side by someone else)	-Kasey 7006	(1961)
Florida Twist/Negra Consentida	-Orfeon 1047	(1961)
Pue De Papas/Anoche	-Orfeon 1195	(1962)
Tenor Man/Up Goes My Love	-Newtown 5013	(1963)
Midnight in Washington/Whit Parakeet	-Newtown 5014	(1963)
Dance Around the Clock/What Can I Say	-Newtown 5024	(1964)
Tandy/You Call Everybody Darling	-Newtown 5025	(1964)
The Green Door/Yeah! She's Evil	-Decca 31650	(1964)
Skinny Minnie/Lean Jean	(R)-Decca 31677	(1964)
Burn That Candle/Stop, Look, and Listen	(2) -Apt 25081	(1965)
Haley A Go Go/Tongue-Tied Tony	-Apt 25087	(1965)
Rock Around the Clock/Rock the Joint (live)	(2) -Buddah 45	(196?)

-Bill Haley And His Comets Cont'd-

Rock A-beatin' Boogie/Shake Rattle & Roll	(2) -Buddah 46	(196?)
Crazy Man Crazy	(2) -Buddah 50	(196?)
Rock Around The Clock/Shake, Rattle And Roll	(3) -Warner Bros 7124	(1967)
That's How I Got to Memphis/Ain't Love Funny Ha Ha Ha	-UA 50483	(1969)
The Green Door/Corrine, Corrina	-Decca 72751	(1969)
Rock Around the Clock/Rock the Joint	(R)-RAG 45	(1970)
Shake Rattle and Roll/Rock-A-Beatin' Boogie	(R)-RAG 46	(1970)
See You Later, Alligator/Rudy's Rock	(R)-RAG 47	(1970)
Skinnie Minnie/The Saints Rock and Roll	(R)-RAG 48	(1970)
Razzle Dazzle/Rip It Up	(R)-RAG 49	(1970)
Crazy Man Crazy/Framed	(R)-RAG 50	(1970)
Framed/Rock Around the Clock	(2) -Kama Sutra 508	(1970)
A Little Piece at a Time/Travelling Band	-Janus 162	(1971)
Rock Around the Clock/13 Women	(R)-MCA 60025	(1973)
See You Later Alligator/Shake Rattle and Roll	(R)-MCA 60067	(1973)
Kohoutek/Tony's Theme	-MGM 14688	(1974)
Rock Around the Clock/Crazy Man Crazy	-Essex 102	(1954)
(This is a '70's bootleg record)		
Within This Broken Heart of Mine/Yodel Your Blues Away	-Arzee 4677	(1977)
See Ya Later Alligator/Skinny Minnie	(3) -Scepter 21090	(197?)
Rock Around the Clock/13 Women	(R)-MCA 60025	(1980)
Rock Around the Clock/13 Women	(R)-Old Gold 9220	(1980)
Shake Rattle and Roll/See You Later, Alligator	(R)-Old Gold 9221	(1980)
Football Rock and Roll/ Six Year Old Rock and Roll	-Jukebox 1958	(1980)

Albums

Rock With Bill Haley and His Comets	-Essex ESLP-202	(1954)
Rock With Bill Haley and His Comets	(R)-Somerset P-4600	(1954)
Shake Rattle and Roll	-Decca DL-5560	(1954)
Rock Around the Clock	-Decca DL-8225	(1955)
Rock and Roll Dance Party (With various artists)	-Somerset P-1300	(1955)
Rock With Bill Haley and His Comets	(R)-Transworld 202	(1955)
Music for the Boyfriend	-Decca DL-8315	(1956)
Rock 'n' Roll Stage Show	-Decca DL-8345	(1956)
Rockin' the Oldies	-Decca DL-8569	(1957)
Let's Have a Party	-Decca DL-8655	(1957)
Rockin' Around the World	-Decca DL-8692	(1957)
Rockin' the Joint	-Decca DL-8775	(1958)
Bill Haley's Chicks	-Decca DL-8821	(1959)
Strictly Instrumental	-Decca DL-8964	(1959)
Bill Haley and His Comets	-Warner B W-1378	(1960)
Bill Haley's Jukebox	-Warner B W-1391	(1960)
Country and Western Bonanza	-Camay C-3001	(1962)
(with various artists)		
Rock Around the Clock	(R)-Decca DL78225	(1962)
Rock the Joint	(R)-Roller Coastr 2002	(1962)
Rockin' Around the World	(R)-Decca DL7-8692	(1962)
Twistin' Knights at the Roundtable (Live)	-Roulette SR-25174	(1962)

-Bill Haley And His Comets Cont'd-

Bill Haley and His Comets		(R)-Ambassador 1454	(1962)
Bill Haley and His Comets		(R)-Vocalion VL-3696	(1963)
Rock Around the Clock King		(R)-Guest Star 1454	(1964)
Ten Million Sellers		(R)-Guest Star 1474	(1964)
Trini Lopez/Scott Gregory (AKA Bill Haley)		-Guest Star 1499	(1964)
Discotheque (with various artists)		-Diplomat 2397	(1964)
Rock Around the Clock		(R)-Decca DL-78225	(1967)
Bill Haley's Greatest Hits		(R)-Decca DL-75027	(1968)
Bill Haley's Greatest Hits		(R)-MCA 161 *	(1968)
Rock 'n' Roll Revival		-Warner Bros 1831	(1969)
Bill Haley's Scrapbook		-Kama Sutra 2014	(1970)
Rock 'n Roll Revival	(with various artists)	-Kama Sutra 2015	(1970)
Rock 'N Roll Survival	(with various artists)	-Decca DL-75181	(1970)
Rock Around the Clock		(R)-MCA/Coral CP55	(1970)
Bill Haley and His Comets		(R)-Ambassador 98089	(1970)
King of Rock 'n Roll		(R)-Alshire 5202	(1970)
Rockin'		(R)-Pickwick 3256	(1970)
Rock 'n' Roll Revival		(R)-Valiant 1831	(1970)
Rock 'n' Roll Revival		(R)-Warner Bros 1831	(1971)
Rock 'n' Roll Revival		(R)-Pickwick 3280	(1971)
Razzle Dazzle (2 LP)		-Janus JX25-7003	(1971)
Travelin' Band		-Janus JLS-3035	(1970)
Rock Around the Clock		(R)-MCA DL78225	(1972)
Bill Haley's Golden Hits	(2 LP)	(R)-Decca DXSE-7211	(1972)
Bill Haley's Golden Hits	(2 LP)	(R)-MCA 2-4010 *	(1972)
Bill Haley's Greatest Hits		(R)-MCA 161*	(1973)
Rockin'		(R)-MCA/Corl 20015*	(1973)
Bill Haley King of Rock and Roll		(R)-Alshire 5313	(1974)
Rock and Roll (repackage of Essex 202)	(2 LP)	(R)-GNP/Crscndo 2077	(1974)
Rock Around the Country		(R)-GNP/Crscndo 2097	(1976)
The Bill Haley Collection	(2 LP)	-Pickwick 006D	(1976)
Greatest Hits Live in London		-Springboard 4066	(1977)
Rock Around the Clock		(R)-MCA DL78225*	(1978)
Rock Around the Clock		(R)-Koala AW14132	(1979)
King of Rock 'n' Roll		(R)-Exact 207	(1980)
R-O-C-K		(R)-Sun/SSS 143	(1980)
Rock Around the Clock		(R)-Joker SM3869	(1981)
Bill Haley Interview		-Great NWM4015	(1981)
Dedications, Vol 1		-Silhouette 10006	(1981)
Rockin' and Rollin		-Accord SN-7125	(1981)
Greatest Hits		-Phoenix 306	(1981)
Bill Haley and His Comets (German Import)	(5 LP)	-Bear Family	(1981)
Mr. Rock 'n' Roll		(R) -Accord SJA-7902	(1982)
Live from New York City		-Accord SN-7960	(1983)
		-51 West	(1983)
Bill Haley's Scrapbook		(R) -Buddah BDS69008	(1984)

-Bill Haley And His Comets Cont'd-

Rock and Roll	-GNP 2077	(1984)
Bill Haley's Golden Hits (2 LP)	-MCA MC2-4010 *	(1984)
Bill Haley's Golden Hits (2 LP)	(R)-MCA MCM-5004*	(1985)
Rock Around the Country	-GNP 2097	(1985)
From the Original Masters	-MCA MCA 5539*	(1985)
Rock and Roll Giant	-Pair MSM2-35069	(1986)
The Original Hits '54-'57	-Pickwick 3207	(1987)
Bill Haley's Rarities	-Ambassador A8100	(1987)
Bill Haley's Greatest Hits (2 LP)	-Connoisseur 116	(1988)
Bill Haley and the Comets	(R)-Everest 4110	(1988)
Bill Haley and His Comets	(R)-MCA MCL-1617*	(1988)
Rip It Up	(R)-Connoisseur 116	(1988)
Vintage Gold (3 inch disc)	-MCA 37294	(1988)
Bill Haley the Decca Years And More	-Bear Family 15506	(1990)

(German import   5 CD, all 104 songs)

Best of Bill Haley and His Comets	-Vogue 600072	
Bill Haley's Greatest Hits	-Evergreen 269051-2	
Bill Haley & His Comets.. The Holiday-Essex Recordings(CD)		(1995)

Extended Play Mini Albums

EP Bill Haley's Dance Party	-Essex EP 102	(1954)
EP Rock With Bill Haley and the Comets (Vols 1 - 3)	-Essex EP 117-19	(1954)
EP Dance Party	(R)-Transworld 102	(1955)
EP Shake, Rattle and Roll	-Decca EP 2168	(1955)
EP Dim, Dim the Lights	-Decca EP 2209	(1955)
EP Rock With Bill Haley and His Comets	-Somerset	(1955)
EP Rock With Bill Haley and His Comets	(R)-Transworld 117-19	(1955)
EP Rock and Roll	-Decca EP 2322	(1955)
EP He Digs Rock and Roll (Vols 1-3)	-Decca EP 2398	(1956)
EP Rock 'n' Roll Stage Show	-Decca EP 2416-18	(1956)
EP Rockin' the Oldies	-Decca EP 2532	(1957)
EP Rock and Roll Party	-Decca EP 2533	(1957)
EP Rockin' and Rollin'	-Decca EP 2534	(1957)
EP Rockin' Around the World	-Decca EP 2564	(1957)
EP Rockin' Around Europe	-Decca EP 2576	(1958)
EP Rockin' Around the Americas	-Decca EP 2577	(1958)
EP Rockin' the Joint, vol. 1	-Decca EP 2615	(1959)
EP Rockin' the Joint, vol. 2	-Decca EP 2616	(1959)
EP Bill Haley's Chicks	-Decca EP 2638	(1959)
EP Top Teen Hits	-Decca EP 2661	(1959)
EP Bill Haley and His Comets	-Decca EP 2670	(1960)
EP Strickly Instrumental	-Decca EP 2671	(1960)
EP Eloise (Various artists, 1 with Haley)	-Decca/W 4247	(1960)
EP Bill Haley Sings (2 Songs on Side 1)	-Arzee R2-137	(1979)
EP Rock Around the Clock (Selections from 1950)	-Claire 4779	(1979)

*(MCA titles are just repackages of Decca)

Jodimars (Members of The Comets)-

Singles

Let's Rock/Now Dig This   -Capitol 3285   (1955)

Kingsmen (Members of The Comets)-

Singles

Weekend/Better Believe It   -East West 115   (1958)
The Cat Walk/Conga Rock   -East West 120   (1958)

Lifeguards (Members Of The Comets)-

Singles

Everybody Out 'a the Pool/Teenage Tango   -ABC Par 10021   (1959)
Everybody Out 'a the Pool/Teenage Tango   (R)-Casa Blanca 5535 (1959)
Everybody Out 'a the Pool/Teenage Tango   (R)-Dr 69   (1965)

The Merri-Men (Members of The Comets)-

Singles

Big Daddy/St. Louis Blues   -Apt 25051   (1961)

Elvis Presley- (Rockabilly only)

Singles

That's All Right (Mama)/Blue Moon of Kentucky   -Sun 209   (1954)
Good Rockin' Tonight/I Don't Care If the Sun Don't Shine   -Sun 210   (1954)
Milkcow Blues Boogie/You're a Heartbreaker   -Sun 215   (1955)
I'm Left, You're Right, She's Gone/Baby Let's Play House   -Sun 217   (1955)
Mystery Train/I Forgot To Remember To Forget   -Sun 223   (1955)
Mystery Train/I Forgot To Remember To Forget   (R)-RCA 6357   (1955)
That's All Right (Mama)/Blue Moon of Kentucky   (R)-RCA 6380   (1955)
Good Rockin' Tonight/I Don't Care If the Sun Don't Shine   (R)-RCA 6381   (1955)
Milkcow Blues Boogie/You're a Heartbreaker   (R)-RCA 6382   (1955)
I'm Left, You're Right, She's Gone/Baby Let's Play House   (R)-RCA 6383   (1955)
Heartbreak Hotel/I Was the One   -RCA 6420   (1956)
I Want You, I Need You, I Love You/My Baby Left Me   -RCA 6540   (1956)
Hound Dog/Don't Be Cruel   -RCA 6604   (1956)
Blue Suede Shoes/Tutti Frutti   -RCA 6636   (1956)
I'm Counting on You/I Got a Woman   -RCA 6637   (1956)
I'll Never Let You Go/I'm Gonna Sit
                        Right Down and Cry Over You   -RCA 6638   (1956)
Tryin' To Get to You/I Love You Because   -RCA 6639   (1956)
Blue Moon/Just Because   -RCA 6640   (1956)
Money Honey/One-Sided Love Affair   -RCA 6641   (1956)
Shake, Rattle and Roll/Lawdy Miss Clawdy   -RCA 6642   (1956)

-Elvis Presley Cont'd-

Love Me Tender/Anyway You Want Me	-RCA 6643	(1956)
Old Shep	-RCA CR-15	(1956)
Too Much/Playing for Keeps	-RCA 6800	(1957)
All Shook Up/That's When Your Heartaches Begin	-RCA 6870	(1957)
(Let Me Be Your) Teddy Bear/Loving You	-RCA 7000	(1957)
Lover Doll/Young and Beautiful	(2) -RCA 47-9224	(1957)
Jailhouse Rock/Treat Me Nice	-RCA 7035	(1957)
Blue Christmas/Blue Christmas	(DJ)-RCA 0808	(1957)
Don't/I Beg of You	-RCA 7150	(1958)
Wear My Ring Around Your Neck/Doncha' Think It's Time?	-RCA 7240	(1958)
Hard-Headed Woman/Don't Ask Me Why	-RCA 7280	(1958)
I Got Stung/One Night	-RCA 7410	(1958)
A Fool Such As I/I Need Your Love Tonight	-RCA 7506	(1959)
A Big Hunk of Love/My Wish Came True	-RCA 7600	(1959)
Don't/Wear My Ring Around Your Neck	(DJ)-RCA 45-76	(1960)
Stuck on You/Fame and Fortune	-RCA 7740	(1960)
Stuck on You/Fame and Fortune	(S) -RCA 61-7740	(1960)
(First Stereo 45 Release)		
It's Now or Never/A Mess of Blues	-RCA 7777	(1960)
It's Now or Never/A Mess of Blues	(S) -RCA 61-7777	(1960)
King of the Whole Wide World/Home Is Where the Heart Is	-RCA 45-118 (DJ)	(1960)
Are You Lonesome Tonight?/I Gotta Know	-RCA 7810	(1960)
Are You Lonesome Tonight?/I Gotta Know	(S) -RCA 61-7810	(1960)
Surrender/Lonely Man	-RCA 7850	(1961)
Surrender/Lonely Man	(33) -RCA 37-7850	(1961)
Surrender/Lonely Man	(S) -RCA 61-7850	(1961)
Wooden Heart/Shoppin' Around	-RCA 7865	(1961)
I Feel So Bad/Wild in the Country	-RCA 7880	(1961)
I Feel So Bad/Wild in the Country	(33) -RCA 37-7880	(1961)
I Feel So Bad/Wild in the Country	(S) -RCA 61-7880	(1961)
(Marie's the Name of) His Latest Flame/Little Sister	-RCA 7908	(1961)
(Marie's the Name of) His Latest Flame/Little Sister	(33) -RCA 37-7908	(1961)
Can't Help Falling in Love/Rock-A-Hula Baby	-RCA 7968	(1961)
Good Luck Charm/Anything That's Part of You	-RCA 7992	(1962)
Good Luck Charm/Anything That's Part of You	(33) -RCA 37-7992	(1962)
She's Not You/Just Tell Her Jim Said Hello	-RCA 8041	(1962)
She's Not You/Just Tell Her Jim Said Hello	(33) -RCA 37-8041	(1962)
Return to Sender/Where Do You Come From?	-RCA 8100	(1962)
Return to Sender/Where Do You Come From?	(33) -RCA 37-8100	(1962)
One Broken Heart for Sale/They Remind Me Too Much of You	-RCA 8134	(1963)
Devil in Disguise/Please Don't Drag That String Around	-RCA 8188	(1963)
Such a Night/Never Ending	-RCA 8400	(1964)
Ain't That Loving You Baby?/Ask Me	-RCA 8440	(1964)
Blue Christmas/Wooden Heart (recorded in 1957)	-RCA 0720	(1964)
It Feels So Right/(It's Such an) Easy Question	-RCA 8585	(1964)
Mystery Train/I Forgot To Remember	(R)-RCA 447-0600	(1964)
That's All Right (Mama)/Blue Moon of Kentucky	(R)-RCA 447-0601	(1964)

-Elvis Presley Cont'd-

Good Rockin' Tonight/I Don't Care If The Sun Don't Shn		(R)-RCA 447-0602	(1964)
Milkcow Blues Boogie/You're a Heartbreaker		(R)-RCA 447-0603	(1964)
I'm Left, You're Right, She's Gone/Baby Let's Play House		(R)-RCA 447-0604	(1964)
Heartbreak Hotel/I Was the One		(R)-RCA 447-0605	(1964)
Heartbreak Hotel/I Was the One	(DJ)	(R)-RCA PB-11105	(1964)
I Want You, I Need You, I Love You/My Baby Left Me		(R)-RCA 447-0607	(1964)
Hound Dog/Don't Be Cruel		(R)-RCA 447-0609	(1964)
Hound Dog/Don't Be Cruel	(DJ)	(R)-RCA PB-11099	(1964)
Blue Suede Shoes/Tutti Frutti		(R)-RCA 447-0609	(1964)
Blue Suede Shoes/Tutti Frutti	(DJ)	(R)-RCA PB-11107	(1964)
I'm Counting on You/I Got a Woman		(R)-RCA 447-0610	(1964)
I'll Never Let You Go/I'm Gonna Sit Right Down and Cry Over You		(R)-RCA-447-0611	(1964)
Tryin' To Get to You/I Love You Because		(R)-RCA 447-0612	(1964)
Blue Moon/Just Because		(R)-RCA 447-0613	(1964)
Money Honey/One-Sided Love Affair		(R)-RCA 447-0614	(1964)
Shake, Rattle and Roll/Lawdy Miss Clawdy		(R)-RCA 447-0615	(1964)
Love Me Tender/Anyway You Want Me		(R)-RCA 447-0616	(1964)
Love Me Tender/Anyway You Want Me		(R)-RCA PB-11104	(1964)
Love Me Tender/Anyway You Want Me	(DJ)	(R)-RCA PB-11108	(1964)
Too Much/Playing for Keeps		(R)-RCA 447-0617	(1964)
All Shook Up/That's When Your Heartaches Begin		(R)-RCA 447-0618	(1964)
All Shook Up/That's When Your Heartaches Begin	(DJ)	(R)-RCA PB-11106	(1964)
Jailhouse Rock/Treat Me Nice		(R)-RCA 447-0619	(1964)
Jailhouse Rock/Treat Me Nice	(DJ)	(R)-RCA PB-1110	(1964)
(Let Me Be Your) Teddy Bear/Loving You		(R)-RCA 447-0620	(1964)
(Let Me Be Your) Teddy Bear/Loving You	(DJ)	(R)-RCA PB 11109	(1964)
(Let Me Be Your) Teddy Bear/Loving You	(DJ)	(2)-RCA PB-11320	(1964)
Don't/I Beg of You		(R)-RCA 447-0621	(1964)
Wear My Ring Around Your Neck/Doncha' Think It's Time?		(R)-RCA 447-0622	(1964)
Hard-Headed Woman/Don't Ask Me Why		(R)-RCA 447-0623	(1964)
I Got Stung/One Night		(R)-RCA 447-0624	(1964)
I Got Stung/One Night	(DJ)	(R)-RCA PB-11112	(1964)
A Fool Such As I/I Need Your Love Tonight		(R)-RCA 447-0625	(1964)
A Big Hunk of Love/My Wish Came True		(R)-RCA 447-0626	(1964)
Stuck on You/Fame and Fortune		(R)-RCA 447-0627	(1964)
It's Now or Never/A Mess of Blues		(R)-RCA 447-0628	(1964)
Are You Lonesome Tonight?/I Gotta Know		(R)-RCA 447-0629	(1964)
Surrender/Lonely Man		(R)-RCA 447-0630	(1964)
(Marie's the Name of) His Latest Flame/Little Sister		(R)-RCA 447-0634	(1964)
Can't Help Falling in Love/Rock-A-Hula Baby		(R)-RCA 447-0635	(1964)
Can't Help Falling in Love/Rock-A-Hula Baby	(DJ)	(R)-RCA PB-11102	(1964)
Good Luck Charm/Anything That's Part of You		(R)-RCA 447-0636	(1964)
Return to Sender/Where Do You Come From?		(R)-RCA 447-0638	(1964)
Suspicion/Kiss Me Quick		(R)-RCA 447-0639	(1964)
Such a Night/Never Ending		(R)-RCA 447-0646	(1964)

-Elvis Presley Cont'd-

Blue Christmas/Wooden Heart	(R)-RCA 447-0720	(1964)
Blue Christmas/Santa Claus Is Back In Town	(R)-RCA 447-0647	(1965)
Ain't That Loving You Baby?/Ask Me	(R)-RCA 447-0649	(1965)
Tell Me Why/Blue River (recorded in 1957)	-RCA 8740	(1966)
Big Boss Man/You Don't Know Me	-RCA 9341	(1967)
Guitar Man/High Heel Sneakers	-RCA 9425	(1968)
U.S. Male/Stay Away	-RCA 9465	(1968)
Suspicious Minds/You'll Think of Me	-RCA 9764	(1969)
Guitar Man/High Heel Sneakers	(R)-RCA 447-0663	(1970)
U.S. Male/Stay Away	(R)-RCA 447-0664	(1970)
Suspicious Minds/You'll Think of Me	(R)-RCA 447-0673	(1970)
Burning Love/It's a Matter of Time	-RCA 0769	(1972)
The Lady Loves Me	(R)-Sun 101	(1978)
Jailhouse Rock	(R)-Sun 102	(1978)
Let's Have a Party	(R)-Sun 103	(1978)
Mean Woman Blues	(R)-Sun 104	(1978)
Heartbreak Hotel/Shake, Rattle and Roll	(R)-Sun 227	(1978)
Tiger Man/Harbor Lights	-Sun 520	(1978)
Blue Suede Shoes/My Baby's Gone	(R)-Sun 521	(1978)
Money Honey/Blue Moon	(R)-Sun 522	(1978)
Tutti Frutti/	(R)-Sun 523	(1978)
I Got A Woman	(R)-Sun 524	(1978)
Tweedlee Dee/Lawdy Miss Clawdy	(R)-Sun 525	(1978)
Tweedlee Dee/Louisiana Hayride Interview	(R)-Sun 600	(1978)
Little Sister/Paralyzed	(R)-RCA 13547	(1983)
Heartbreak Hotel/Heartbreak Hotel	(R)-RCA 8760	(1988)

(A Side Elvis/B Side David Keith)
447 Prefix = Gold standards-issued at different times
with different colored labels (black, red, orange, etc..)

Albums

Elvis Presley	-RCA 1254	(1956)
Elvis	-RCA 1382	(1956)
Loving You	-RCA 1515	(1957)
Elvis' Christmas Album	-RCA 1035	(1957)
Elvis' Golden Records	-RCA 1707	(1958)
King Creole	-RCA 1884	(1958)
Elvis' Christmas Album	-RCA 1951	(1958)
For LP Fans Only	-RCA 1990	(1959)
A Date With Elvis	-RCA 2011	(1959)
Elvis' Golden Records, Vol. 2	-RCA 2075	(1959)
Elvis Is Back	-RCA 2231	(1960)
G. I. Blues	-RCA 2256	(1960)

(After 1960 his music changed style)

His Hand In Mine	-RCA 2328	(1961)
Something For Everybody	-RCA 2370	(1961)
Blue Hawaii	-RCA 2426	(1961)
Pot Luck With Elvis	-RCA 2523	(1962)

The Primary Set   63

-Elvis Presley Cont'd-

Girls! Girls! Girls!		-RCA 2621	(1962)
It Happened at the World's Fair		-RCA 2697	(1963)
Fun in Acapulco		-RCA 2756	(1963)
Elvis' Golden Records, Vol. 3		-RCA 2765	(1963)
Kissin' Cousins		-RCA 2894	(1964)
Roustabout		-RCA 2999	(1964)
Girl Happy		-RCA 3338	(1965)
Elvis For Everyone		-RCA 3450	(1965)
Harum Scarum		-RCA 3468	(1965)
Frankie and Johnny		-RCA 3553	(1966)
Paradise Hawaiian Style		-RCA 3643	(1966)
Spinout		-RCA 3702	(1966)
Special Palm Sunday Programing		(DJ)-RCA SP-33-461	(1967)
How Great Thou Art		-RCA 3758	(1967)
Double Trouble		-RCA 3787	(1967)
Clambake		-RCA 3893	(1967)
Special Christmas Programming		(DJ)-RCA 5697	(1967)
Elvis' Golden Records, Vol. 4		-RCA 3921	(1968)
Singer Presents Elvis (Singer Sewing)		-RCA 279	(1968)
Elvis (NBC TV Special)		-RCA 4088	(1968)
Elvis Sings Flaming Star		-Camden 2304	(1969)
From Elvis in Memphis		-RCA 4155	(1969)
From Memphis to Vegas	(2 LP)	-RCA 6020	(1969)
International Hotel Presents Elvis (Giveaway at show)		(DJ)-RCA N/A	(1969)
Let's Be Friends		-Camden 2408	(1970)
On Stage-February, 1970		-RCA 4362	(1970)
Worldwide 50 Gold Hits	(4 LP)	-RCA LP-6401	(1970)
In Person at the International Hotel		-RCA 4428	(1970)
Back in Memphis		-RCA 4429	(1970)
Almost in Love		-Camden 2440	(1970)
That's the Way It Is		-RCA 4445	(1970)
Elvis' Christmas Album		-Camden 2428	(1970)
Elvis Country		-RCA 4460	(1971)
Love Letters From Elvis		-RCA 4530	(1971)
You'll Never Walk Alone		-Camden 2472	(1971)
C'mon Everybody		-Camden 2518	(1971)
The Other Sides	(4 LP)	-RCA 6402	(1971)
I Got Lucky		-Camden 2533	(1971)
The Wonderful World of Christmas		-RCA 4579	(1971)
Elvis Now		-RCA 4671	(1972)
Elvis Sings From His Movies		-Camden 2567	(1972)
Elvis Sings Burning Love		-Camden 2595	(1972)
Madison Square Garden	(2 LP)	(DJ)-RCA 571	(1972)
Madison Square Garden	(2 LP)	-RCA 4776	(1972)

(RCA prefix numbers changed from simple LSP and LSM to others)

Aloha From Hawaii Via Satellite	(2 LP)	-RCA 6089	(1973)
Elvis (Features the song "Fool")		-RCA 0283	(1973)

-Elvis Presley Cont'd-

Raised on Rock/For Ol' Times Sake)		-RCA 0388	(1973)
Elvis (2 LP)	(Mail order item-Brookville Records)	-RCA 2-0056	(1973)
Separate Ways		-Camden 2611	(1973)
A Legendary Performer, Vol. 1		-RCA 0341	(1974)
Good Times		-RCA 0475	(1974)
Live on Stage in Memphis		(DJ)-RCA 0606	(1974)
Live on Stage in Memphis		-RCA 0606*	(1974)
Having Fun With Elvis on Stage		-RCA 0818	(1974)
Elvis Forever (Mail order)		-RCA 7031	(1974)
50,000,000 Fans (reissue of Elvis Gold Records, Vol. 2		(R)-RCA 2075	(1974)
Worldwide 50 Gold Hits (2 LP Record club)		(R)-RCA 213690	(1974)
Having Fun With Elvis on Stage		-RCA CPM1-0818	(1974)
Promised Land		-RCA APL1-0873*	(1975)
Flaming Star	(reissue of Camden 2304)	(R)-Pickwick 2304	(1975)
Let's Be Friends	(reissue of Camden 2408)	(R)-Pickwick 2408	(1975)
Elvis Today		-RCA APL1-1039*	(1975)
Pure Gold		-RCA ANL1-0971	(1975)
The Elvis Presley Story 1975 (13 LP)		(DJ)-Watermark*	(1975)
The Sun Collection		-RCA 1001	(1975)
Elvis' Christmas Album (reissue of Camden 2428)		(R)-Pickwick 2428	(1975)
Almost in Love	(reissue of Camden 2440)	(R)-Pickwick 2440	(1975)
You'll Never Walk Alone (reissue of Camden 2472)		(R)-Pickwick 2472	(1975)
C'mon Everybody	(reissue of Camden 2518)	(R)-Pickwick 2518	(1975)
I Got Lucky	(reissue of Camden 2533)	(R)-Pickwick 2533	(1975)
Elvis Sings Hits From His Movies(reissue of Camden2567)		(R)-Pickwick 2567	(1975)
Burning Love	(reissue of Camden 2595)	(R)-Pickwick 2595	(1975)
Separate Ways	(reissue of Camden 2611)	(R)-Pickwick 2611	(1975)
Double Dynamite		(R)-Pickwick 5001	(1975)
The Sun Sessions		-RCA 1675	(1976)
From Elvis Presley Boulevard		-RCA 1506	(1976)
World Wide 50 Gold Award Hits, Vol. 1 (4 Cassettes)		(R)-RCA 1773-4-R	(1976)
For LP Fans Only	(CD)	(R)-RCA 1990-2-R	(1976)
Elvis in Hollywood		-RCA 2-0168	(1976)
Earth News August 29, 1977		(DJ)-Earth News	(1977)
The Elvis Presley Story (5 LP)		-RCA 0263	(1977)
Songs of Inspiration	(Mail order)	-RCA 0264	(1977)
Elvis: A Three-Hour Special		-Drake-Chenault	(1977)
The Sun Years		(R)-Sun 1001	(1977)
Worldwide 50 Gold Hits (2 LP)		(R)-RCA 6401	(1977)
The Elvis Presley Story, 1977		(DJ)-Watermark 13-LP	(1977)
Reflections of Elvis		-Diamond P	(1977)
A Date With Elvis	(CD)	(R)-RCA 2011-2-R	(1977)
The Million Dollar Quartet	(CD)	-RCA 2023-1-R	(1977)
Elvis' Golden Records, Vol. 2 (digital master)		-RCA 2075E	(1977)
Sound of '77		(DJ)-Billboard	(1977)
Heartbreak Hotel, Hound Dog & Other Top 10	(CD)	-RCA 2079-2-R	(1977)
The Great Performances	(CD)	(R)-RCA 2227-1-R	(1977)

-Elvis Presley Cont'd-

Hits Like Never Before (Essential Elvis, Vol. 3	(CD)		(R)-RCA 2229-2-R	(1977)
Elvis Is Back	(CD)		(R)-RCA 2231-2-R	(1977)
Elvis Sings Flaming Star	(CD)		(R)-Camden 2304	(1977)
Elvis-Greatest Hits, Vol. 1	(CD)		(R)-RCA 2347	(1977)
Pot Luck	(CD)		(R)-RCA 2523-2-R	(1977)
Something for Everybody	(CD)		(R)-2370-2-R	(1977)
Let's Be Friends	(CD)		(R)-Camden 2408	(1977)
Moody Blue	(CD)		(R)-RCA 2428-2-R	(1977)
Almost In Love	(CD)		(R)-Camden 2440	(1977)
You'll Never Walk Alone	(CD)		(R)-Camden 2472	(1977)
C'mon Everybody	(CD)		(R)-Camden 2518	(1977)
Elvis Sings Hits From His Movies	(CD)		(R)-RCA 2567	(1977)
Burning Love and Hits From His Movies, Vol. 2	(CD)		(R)-Camden 2595	(1977)
Separate Ways	(CD)		(R)-Camden 2611	(1977)
Aloha From Hawaii	(CD)		(R)-RCA 3-2645	(1977)
Love Me Tender	(CD)		(R)-Camden 2650	(1977)
Sings For Children	(CD)		-Camden 2704	(1977)
Elvis' Golden Records, Vol. 3	(CD)		(R)-RCA 2765-2-R	(1977)
He Walks Beside Me	(CD)		(R)-RCA 2772	(1977)
Elvis Memories	(3 LP)		(DJ)-ABC Radio 1003	(1978)
Memories of Elvis	(Candelite)	(5 LP)	-RCA 0347	(1978)
Greatest Show on Earth	(Candelite)		-RCA 0348	(1978)
Worldwide 50 Gold Hits	(2 LP Record club)		(R)-RCA 214657	(1978)
Elvis Commemorative Album			(R)-RCA 0056	(1978)
Mahalo from Elvis			-Pickwick 7064	(1978)
From Elvis With Love			-RCA 234340	(1978)
Legendary Command Performances	(Record Club)		-RCA 244047	(1978)
The First Years			-HALW 00001	(1978)
A Legendary Performer, Vol. 3	(Picture Disc)		-RCA 3078	(1979)
A Legendary Performer, Vol. 3			-RCA 3082	(1979)
Elvis' Golden Records	(digital master)		-RCA 1707E	(1979)
1979 Yearbook			(DJ)-Billboard	(1979)
The Legendary Recordings	(Candelite)	(6 LP)	-RCA 0412	(1979)
Elvis! His Greatest Hits		(8 LP)	-RCA 010	(1979)
Our Memories of Elvis			-RCA 3279	(1979)
Girl Happy		(CD)	(R)-RCA 3338	(1979)
Our Memories of Elvis, Vol. 2			-RCA 3448	(1979)
Pure Elvis			-RCA 3455	(1979)
In the Beginning			(DJ)-ATV 1	(1980)
Legend of a King			(DJ)-AOB 1001	(1980)
Greatest Moments in Music	(Candelite)		-RCA-0413	(1980)
Rock 'N' Roll Forever	(Candelite)		-RCA 0437	(1980)
The Legendary Magic	(Candelite)		-RCA 0461	(1980)
Elvis Aaron Presley		(8 LP)	-RCA 8-3699	(1980)
Blue Hawaii		(CD)	(R)-RCA 3683-2-R	(1980)
Elvis Aaron Presley		(8 LP)	-RCA 8-3699	(1980)
Pure Gold			-RCA 3729	(1980)

-Elvis Presley Cont'd-

King Creole	(CD)	(R)-RCA 37332-R	(1980)
G. I. Blues	(CD)	(R)-RCA 3735-2-R	(1980)
How Great Thou Art	(CD)	(R)-RCA 3758-2-R	(1980)
Elvis Aaron Presley		(DJ)-RCA 3781	(1980)
At The International Hotel Las Vegas	(CD)	(R)-RCA 3892	(1980)
The Sun Sessions		(R)-RCA 3893	(1980)
TV Special	(CD)	(R)-RCA 3894	(1980)
Elvis Country		(R)-RCA 3956	(1980)
Elvis Sings "The Wonderful World of Christmas"	(CD)	(R)-RCA 4579-2-R	(1980)
This Is Elvis-	(CD)	(R)-RCA2-2-4031	(1980)
Memories of Christmas---	(CD)	(R)-RCA 4395-2-R	(1980)
Remembering	(CD)	(R)-Pair 2-1037	(1980)
Great Performances	(CD)	(R)-Pair -2-1251	(1980)
Elvis' Golden Records, Vol. 4	(CD)	(R)-RCA 1297-2-R	(1980)
His Hand in Mine	(CD)	(R)-RCA 1319-2-R	(1980)
From Elvis in Memphis		(R)-Mobile Fidelity 059	(1980)
A Legendary Performer, Vol. 2	(CD)	(R)-RCA 1349	(1980)
From Elvis Presley Boulevard	(CD)	(R)-RCA 1506-2-R	(1980)
Loving You	(CD)	(R)-RCA 1515-2-R	(1980)
The Presley Years (Radio Show)		-TM 12 LP	(1980)
Felton Jarvis Talks About Elvis		(DJ)-RCA FJ-1981	(1981)
Elvis Love Songs (Mail order)		-K-Tel 9900	(1981)
Double Dynamite (reissue of Pickwick 5001)		-Pair 1010	(1981)
Rock & Roll Remember, 1982 (48 songs)		-Dick Clark	(1982)
Elvis Sings Inspirational Favorites (Readers Digest) (CD)		-RCA 181	(1983)
The Beginning Years (Louisiana Heyride)		-L Heyride 3061	(1984)
Elvis Sings Country Favorites (Readers Digest)	(CD)	-RCA 242	(1984)
The Elvis Presley Collection (Candlite) (3 LP)		-RCA 0632	(1984)
Memories of Christmas	(CD)	(R)-RCA 4395-2-R	(1984)
Elvis (Special)	(CD)	-SMC S4D-4695	(1984)
Elvis Sings Country Favorites (Readers Digest)		-RCA 242	(1984)
A Legendary Performer, Vol. 4	(CD)	(R)-RCA 4848	(1984)
Elvis' Gold Records, Vol. 5	(CD)	-RCA 4941	(1984)
From Elvis in Memphis	(CD)	(R)-RCA 51456-2	(1984)
A Golden Celebration	(6 CD)	-RCA 5172	(1984)
(previously unissued outtakes, alternate takes, TV, Movies, etc.)			
Elvis (One Night With You)	(CD)	-RCA 0704	(1984)
Rocker	(CD)	-RCA 5182	(1984)
Elvis, The Country Side	(2 LP)	-Creative Radio	(1984)
Savage Young Elvis (tape only)		-RCA 0679	(1984)
He Touched Me	(CD)	(R)-RCA 51923-2	(1984)
Elvis' Golden Records, Vol. 1	(CD)	(R)-RCA 5196	(1984)
Elvis' Golden Records, Vol. 2	(CD)	(R)-RCA 5197	(1984)
Elvis Presley	(CD)	(R)-RCA 5198	(1984)
Elvis	(CD)	(R)-RCA 5199	(1984)
Elvis Country (Mail Order)	(CD)	(R)-K-Tel 393-4	(1984)
An Audio Self Portrait		-RCA 0835	(1985)

-Elvis Presley Cont'd-

Elvis- 50th Anniversary	(6 LP)		(DJ)-Creative Radio	(1985)
Elvis: 50 Years of Hits	(record club)	(3 LP)	-RCA 0710	(1985)
Welcome to My World		(CD)	(R)-RCA 52274-2	(1985)
Pure Gold		(CD)	(R)-RCA 537322-2	(1985)
On Stage		(CD)	(R)-RCA 54362-2	(1985)
Elvis Now		(CD)	(R)-RCA 546781-2	(1985)
A Valentine Gift For You		(CD)	(R)-RCA PCD1-5353	(1985)
Reconsider Baby (Elvis Sings the Blues)			-RCA AYM1-5418	(1985)
Reconsider Baby (Elvis Sings the Blues)		(CD)	-RCA PCD1-5418	(1985)
A Legendary Performer, Vol. 1		(CD)	(R)-RCA CPK1-0341	(1985)
Live on Stage in Memphis--		(CD)	(R)-RCA CPK1-0606	(1985)
Promised Land		(CD)	(R)-RCA 0873-2-R	(1985)
Today		(CD)	(R)-RCA 51039-2	(1985)
Elvis in Concert		(CD)	-RCA 52587-2	(1985)
In Person, at the International Hotel, Las Vegas		(CD)	(R)-RCA 53892-2	(1985)
Always On My Mind (Ballads Collection)		(CD)	(R)-RCA 5430	(1985)
Love Letters From Elvis		(CD)	(R)-RCA 54350-4	(1985)
Live At Madison Square Garden		(CD)	(R)-RCA 54776-2	(1985)
The Elvis Christmas Album		(CD)	(R)-RCA 5486	(1985)
Elvis, The Legend Lives On (Reader's Digest) (7 LP)		(CD)	-RCA 191	(1986)
Double Dynamite		(CD)	-Pair 2-1010	(1986)
NBC TV Special		(CD)	(R)-RCA 61021-4	(1986)
The Lost Album		(CD)	-RCA 61024-2	(1986)
Back In Memphis		(CD)	(R)-RCA 61081-2	(1986)
Elvis Country		(CD)	(R)-RCA 6330-2-R	(1987)
Elvis 10th Anniversary		(6 LP)	-Creative Radio	(1987)
World Wide 50 Gold Award Hits, Vol.1 (Pts 1&2)		(CD)	(R)-RCA 6401-2-R	(1987)
The Memphis Record		(CD)	-RCA 62212-4	(1987)
Christmas With Elvis			(DJ)-Creative Radio	(1987)
The Number One Hits		(CD)	(R)-RCA 6382-2-R	(1987)
The Top Ten Hits		(2 CD)	(R)-RCA 6383-1-R12	(1987)
The Complete Sun Sessions (1954-1955)		(CD)	-RCA 6414-1-R12	(1987)
Essential Elvis-The Movies		(4 CD)	(R)-RCA 6738-1-R	(1988)
Birthday Tribute			(DJ) -Creative Radio	(1988)
The Alternate Aloha (Dress rehearsal 2 days before)		(CD)	(R)-RCA 6985-2R	(1988)
Elvis in Nashville		(CD)	-RCA 8468-2-R	(1989)
Elvis Gospel (1957-1971)		(CD)	-RCA 9586-2-R	(1989)
Between Takes With Elvis		(3 LP)	-Creative Radio	(1989)
Elvis Sings Leiber & Stoller		(CD)	-RCA 3026-2-R	(1991)
Collector's Gold		(CD)	-RCA 3114-2-R	(1991)
(Contains songs from his years in Hollywood, Nashville, and Las Vegas)				
Elvis for Everyone		(CD)	(R)-RCA 3450-2-R	(1991)
The Complete '50's Masters		(CD)	-RCA 66050-2-	(1992)
That's The Way It Is		(CD)	-Mobile Fidelity 560	(1992)
Remembering		(CD)	(R)-Pair 2-1037	(1993)
Roustabout/Viva Las Vegas		(CD)	(R)-RCA 66129-4	(1993)
Stereo '57 (Essential Elvis, Vol. 2)		(CD)	(R)-9589-2-R	(1993)

-Elvis Presley Cont'd-

Roustabout/Viva Las Vegas	(CD)	(R)-RCA 66129-4	(1993)
Elvis Aaron Presley Forever	(CD)	(R)-Pair 2-1185	(1993)
Blue Christmas	(CD)	(R)-RCA 9880-4-R	(1993)
Harum Scarum/ Girl Happy	(CD)	(R)-RCA 66128-2	(1993)
Roustabout/Viva Las Vegas	(CD)	(R)-RCA 66129-4	(1993)
Girls, Girls, Girls/ Kid Galahad	(CD)	(R)-RCA 66130-2	(1993)
It Happened at the World's Fair/Fun in Acapulco	(CD)	(R)-RCA 66131-4	(1993)
I Got Lucky (I'm 10,000 Years Old/Elvis Country	(CD)	(R)-RCA 66279-4-	(1993)

(Candlelite releases were a mail order item)
* These albums were also released in Quad Stereo

Extended Play Mini Albums

EP Complete EP set	(10 Discs)	-RCA SPD-15	(1955)
EP The Sound of Leadership (8 Discs)		-RCA SPD-19	(1956)
EP Elvis Presley (also released as "Blue Suede Shoes"		-RCA EPA-747	(1956)
EP Elvis Presley	(2 records)	-RCA EPB-1254	(1956)
EP Elvis Presley	(2 records)	(DJ)-RCA SPD-22	(1956)
EP Elvis Presley	(3 records)	(DJ)-RCA SPD-23	(1956)
EP Heartbreak Hotel		-RCA EPA-821	(1956)
EP Elvis Presley		-RCA EP-830	(1956)
EP The Real Elvis		-RCA EP-940	(1956)
EP Elvis Presley/Jean Chapel		(DJ)-RCA DJ-7	(1956)
EP TV Guide Presents Elvis		-RCA EPA-8705	(1956)
EP Any Way You Want Me		-RCA EPA-965	(1956)
EP Love Me Tender		-RCA EPA-4006	(1956)
EP Perfect For Parties		(DJ)-RCA SPA 7-37	(1956)
EP Elvis, Vol.1/Jaye P. Morgan (1 record each)		-RCA EPA-992	(1956)
EP Elvis, Vol. 1		-RCA EPA-992	(1956)
EP Elvis, Vol. 2		-RCA EPA-993	(1956)
EP Strickly Elvis	(Elvis, Vol. 3)	-RCA EPA-994	(1956)
EP Elvis Presley/Dinah Shore		(DJ)-RCA DJ-56	(1957)
EP Elvis Country Hits (Part of SPD-26 assorted country hits)		-RCA EP-9113	(1956)
EP Dealers Preview		-RCA SDS-57-39	(1957)
EP Loving You, Vol. 1		-RCA EP1-1515	(1957)
EP Loving You, Vol. 2		-RCA EP2-1515	(1957)
EP Extended Play Sampler (12 EP)		-RCA SDS-61	(1957)
EP Just For You		-RCA EP-4041	(1957)
EP Peace in The Valley		-RCA EP-4054	(1957)
EP Elvis Sings Christmas		-RCA EP-4108	(1957)
EP Jailhouse Rock		-RCA EP-4114	(1957)
EP King Creole, Vol. 1		-RCA EP-4319	(1958)
EP King Creole, Vol. 2		-RCA EP-4321	(1958)
EP Elvis Sails		-RCA EP-4325	(1958)
EP Christmas With Elvis		-RCA EP-4340	(1958)
EP A Touch of Gold, Vol. 1		-RCA EP-5088	(1959)
EP A Touch of Gold, Vol. 2		-RCA EP-5101	(1959)
EP The Real Elvis		-RCA EP-5120	(1959)
EP Peace in the Valley		-RCA EP-5121	(1959)

-Elvis Presley Cont'd-

EP King Creole, Vol. 1		(R)-RCA EP-5122	(1960)
EP A Touch of Gold, Vol. 3		-RCA EP-5141	(1960)
EP Elvis By Request		-RCA SDS-128	(1961)
EP Elvis by Request	(Flaming Star)	-RCA LPC-128	(1961)
EP RCA Family Record Center		(DJ)-RCA SDS-121	(1962)
EP Follow That Dream		-RCA EP-4368	(1962)
EP Kid Galahad		-RCA EP-4371	(1962)
EP Viva Las Vegas		-RCA EP-4382	(1964)
EP Elvis Sails		-RCA EP-5157	(1964)
EP TIckle Me		-RCA EP-4383	(1965)
EP Easy Come, Easy Go		-RCA EP-4387	(1967)
EP Aloha From Hawaii Via Satellite		-RCA O-2006	(1973)

(Most of the EP's were reissued in 1965 and 1969 with same numbers/different color labels)

Odd Ball Releases

Singles

The Hawaiian Wedding Song	-Shaker 1835	
Interview in Memphis	-Memphis Flash 92444	
Interview in San Antonio Texas 1956/That's All Right(Mama)	-Spinout 81677	(1956)
The Truth About Me	-Lynchburg Audio	(1956)
The Truth About Me	(R)-Rainbo	(1956)

Albums

E-Z Pop Programming #5	(Mixed Artists)	(DJ)-RCA F70P-9681	(1955)
E-Z Cntry Programming #2	(Mixed Artists)	(DJ)-RCA G70L-0108	(1955)
E-Z Pop Programming #6	(Mixed Artists)	(DJ)-RCA G70L-0197	(1956)
E-Z Cntry Programming #3 (Mixed Artists)		(DJ)-RCA G70L-0198	(1956)

(Above represents the first releases of Elvis on RCA)

The Presley Years	(12 LP Boxex syndicated radio show)	-TM	(1981)
World of Elvis Presley(one hour weekly radio show 30 discs)		-WOEP	(1983)
Elvis Presley 1954-1961 (Mail order)		-Time-Life 106	(1986)
Elvis the King	(Mail order) (2 LP)	-Time-Life 126	(1989)

Extended Play Mini Albums
Elvis Presley/ Jean Chapel

EP Love Me Tender	-RCA EP-7	(1956)

Elvis Presley/ Marthaa Crson/ Lou Monte/ Herb Jeffries-

EP Dealer's Prevue	(DJ)-RCA EP-2	(1957)

Elvis and other artists-

EP Perfect For Parties	(DJ)-RCA SPA-7-37	(1956)

Elvis /Jaye P. Morgan-

EP Elvis (Volume 1)/Jaye P. Morgan	(2 EP)	(DJ)-RCA EPA-992	(1956)

-Elvis Presley EP's Cont'd-

Elvis Presley/ Vaughn Monroe/ Gogi Grant/ Robert Shaw

EP Pop Transcribed 30 sec. spot   (DJ)-RCA EP-3736   (1958)

Elvis Presley/ Dinah Shore

EP Too Much   (DJ)-RCA EP-56   (1957)

Elvis Presley/ Hank Snow/ Eddy Arnold/ Jim Reeves

EP Old Shep   (DJ)-RCA EP-12   (1956)

CHAPTER 4

Immediate Reactions

After Elvis hit the scene, the craze was on. Every record company searched throughout the back alleys, the bars, the mountains, and the hills of the country, to capture any singer-musician who could perform this type of music.

Decca signed the Rock and Roll Trio (Johnny Burnette, Dorsey Burnette, and Paul Burlison) to its Coral subsidiary. The trio got together while working for the Crown Electric Company; the same company that Elvis drove a truck for.

Johnny Burnette and Dorsey Burnette
The Rock 'n Roll Trio

Johnny Burnette Trio

Dorsey Burnette was born in Memphis, Tennessee, on December 28, 1932, and died in Woodland Hills, California on August 19, 1979. Johnny Burnette was born in Memphis on March 25, 1934, and died in a boating accident in 1963. After his death, Dorsey has been called the Father of Rock and Roll. He contributed greatly to both the rockabilly scene and later to country and western music.

Dorsey and his younger brother, Johnny, learned to play guitar early in life, as did many of the other rockabilly artists, and developed a love for music when they were young. Music was a daily expression in their lives, since their family was totally involved in the music scene.

Dorsey originally considered a career as a professional fighter, but soon realized that there had to be a better life than bloodshed. He worked as an electricians helper to earn money between engagements in his career of singer, entertainer. Johnny had become successful as a fighter, reigning for a time as Golden Gloves champion of Memphis. However, at 22 he decided that show business might be better than boxing In the early 50's, the brothers had their own country music band playing in Arkansas, Louisiana, and Mississippi. They even went to audition for Sam Phillips at Sun Records. Unfortunately, for Sam, he turned them down. So to prove their value, the band went to New York City, to enter the "Ted Mack Amateur Hour" and won four weeks in a row. Afterward they went on tour with the show.

The year 1954 found them working at the Crown Electric Company, where they joined with Paul Burlison to form the Johnny Burnette Trio. Their music was basically country, but they eventually mixed in a blues sound to go with it. Paul Burlison had previously played with Howlin' Wolf, and there was a hard-driving sound to his guitar. It was this driving sound that would eventually become the band's trademark. They appeared on radio broadcasts with Howlin Wolf, and their popularity began to grow. Because of their southern roots and their obvious longing for the black sound, they were referred to as "white niggers" and "white trash." The similarities between the Burnette brothers lives and experiences and those of Elvis are extraordinary.

Recording for Decca's Coral Records division was their big start in the business. They recorded some great driving sounds, including "The Train Kept a-Rollin'," "Rock-Billy Boogie," "Tear It Up," "I Just Found Out," and many more great recordings. These songs represented the full rockabilly sound as we know it. The driving guitars, the screams, and the heavy base sounds all attest to the driving force of the music itself. The band caused riots wherever it went because of its sound, which would influence an enormous amount of artists for years to come.

In 1957 they moved to California, and their luck began to change.

While pushing their writing ability, rather than their musical sound, they got involved with Rick Nelson and wrote many of his hits, including "Waitin' in School," "Just a Little Too Much," "Believe What You Say," and "It's Late."

In 1960, Dorsey hit the charts with "Hey, Little One" and "Tall Oak Tree" on Era Records, and soon Johnny hit on Liberty Records with many strong successful singles and albums, including "You're Sixteen," "Dreamin'," "Big Big City," "The Ballad of the One-Eyed Jacks," and many, many more. Johnny would not be allowed to enjoy his new found success for too long, however. In 1963, he was killed in a boating accident, and his tragic death hurt Dorsey for a long time.

In the mid-60's, Dorsey began to shy away from pop and rock music and returned to the country music roots of his youth. As leader of the house band at the well established Palomino Club, in Hollywood, California, he worked and became close with Johnny Paycheck, Roger Miller, Delaney and Bonnie Bramlett, and Glenn Campbell. Johnny Paycheck, himself, at this time was involved in the rockabilly scene, recording rockabilly on the Decca label, under the name Donnie Young (his real name is Donald Lytle).

Dorsey's interest in country music continued, and during the 70's, he managed a comeback on Capitol Records, with songs such as, "In the Spring" and "Let Another Good One Get Away." One of his most respected songs was a gospel song entitled "Magnificent Sanctuary Band." He moved to Melody Records and had a hit with "Molly (I Ain't Getting Any Younger)."

In 1979, just before he died, Dorsey signed a contract with Elektra/Asylum Records. He died of a heart attack in his California home.

Decca Records tried again to enter the realm of rockabilly (twice actually) with a young man from Lubbock, Texas: Buddy Holly

Charles Harden
"Buddy" Holly

Buddy was born in Lubbock, Texas, on September 7, 1938, the youngest of four children born to Lawrence and

Ella Holley (the spelling of his name was changed accidentally later). He died near Fargo, North Dakota, on February 3, 1959 in an airplane accident that would take the lives of two other extremely popular fellow artists, Richie Valens and J. P. Richardson (the Big Bopper).

In only 21 years, Buddy Holly accomplished more than most artists do in a complete lifetime. At the time of his death, he was approaching the acceptance and popularity of Elvis Presley, and there would have probably been a fight for top honors between them. Like Elvis, he had a tremendous impact not only on up-and-coming artists in the United States but, more importantly, on a number of up-and-comers in the United Kingdom, including the Beatles, the Rolling Stones, and the Who.

Buddy learned to play the violin and piano at age four and took up the guitar when he was seven. He was influenced by Jimmie Rodgers and the Carter Family, among others, in the country and western field.

Buddy started singing in country groups in the early 50's, while he was attending high school. By 1954 he was gaining a reputation as a good, solid, popular artist, playing in small clubs in Texas and around the Southwest. The Buddy, Bob, and Larry trio, comprised of Buddy Holley, Bob Montgomery, and Larry Welborn, would travel upward of 200 miles to a recording studio, as well as to local radio stations, to record their music. The songs would consist of Buddy and Bob harmonizing, with Bob and Buddy on guitar and Larry on bass, sometimes replaced by Don Guess or Sonny Curtis (who was regarded as the best in the area).

In October of 1955, 19-year old Buddy Holley, Larry Wilborn, and Bob Montgomery were the opening act for both Bill Haley and His Comets and Elvis Presley, when each of themplayed Lubbock. The impact of these performances would greatly change the young singer, and would increase his ambition to become a great performer.

Buddy approached Columbia and RCA recording companies, but was turned down by both of them. In 1956, he convinced Sonny Curtis and Don Guess to drive the 100 miles or so with him to Nashville, to find a record company willing to accept him.

In January 1956, he signed a contract with Decca Records to record a few songs, basically as a country artist. At Decca, he was put under the forceful leadership of one of the best producers the company had, Owen Bradley. Unfortunately, the band was not allowed to back up, and Buddy was not allowed any say in what was happening. They recorded "Don't Come Back Knockin'," "Love Me," "That'll Be the Day," and "Blue Days-

Black Nights," as Buddy Holly and the Three Tunes -- none of which went anywhere. To add insult to injury, his name was misspelled on the record label, as Holly, instead of Holley. In early 1957, Decca refused to pick up his option and released him from his contract.

Buddy continued to record various songs as demos during this period, songs such as "You Are My One Desire," "Blue Monday," "Good Rockin' Tonight," "I Ain't Got No Home," "Blue Suede Shoes," "Shake Rattle and Roll," "Brown Eyed Handsome Man," "Bo Diddley," and "Have You Ever Been Lonely?," all of which were later enhanced by Norman Petty and the Fireballs and released as full recordings. His style was developing into an exclusive format of sight and sound, one that he would refuse to deviate from. The Decca mistake would never occur again, as far as he was concerned.

Norman Petty and Buddy became friends at this time. Norman ran a recording studio and was successful in stimulating the careers of many artists, including Roy Orbison ("Ooby Dooby"), the Rhythm Orchids, Buddy Knox and Jimmy Bowen ("Party Doll," and "I'm Stickin' With You"), and a number of others. It was because of the latter two artists' hits that the new Roulette Record Company, in New York, turned down Norman's advances to try and push Buddy on the label. They could only handle the promotion of a few new artists at a time, and Jimmy and Buddy were already there. Norman then sent Buddy to Southern Music, which referred him to Coral Records. Although Coral was a division of Decca, it accepted his sound and his production techniques, which had not been used in the first try at Decca.

Coral Records' attempt was the correct approach, and the heads of Decca Records decided to take advantage of the artist's ability and use him on two of their labels; thus, the solo artist Buddy Holly would sing on Coral Records, and the group, the Crickets, with Buddy as the lead singer, would record for Brunswick Records, which until then was basically for black singers. While the recordings contained the same musicians, these dual recordings allowed Decca to take full advantage of the production capabilities of someone as great as Buddy and still not overload the market with releases by the same, single artist.

The Crickets at the time consisted of Jerry Allison, on drums; Niki Sullivan, on guitar; and Joe Mauldin, who replaced Larry Welborn, on base guitar. In the few years ahead, there would be several different Crickets.

In 1957, on his second release for Coral, he hit the charts with a best-seller of gigantic proportions — "Peggy Sue" — a song named after the girlfriend of one of the Crickets. The original title of which was "Cindy Lou." The second immediate smash was the first release by the Crickets, on Brunswick: "That'll Be the Day" (actually the second version of the song), which broke into the charts and sold over a million copies. The song was co-written by Buddy, Jerry Allison, and Norman Petty. It had previously been recorded under a different style on Decca, and several different versions are still in existence.

Buddy followed up these hits with several songs in 1958, including "Rave On" and "Maybe Baby," along with "Early in the Morning" which was a revenge release by Decca. It seems that after trying for hits on several releases, a young artist named Bobby Darin, on Atco Records, was not doing well. He decided to change his luck by forming a rock group called the Ding Dongs and later the Rinky Dinks and set up to record for Brunswick Records. Just as he recorded two sides, and the company released them, "Early in the Morning," backed with "Now We're One," he hit it big on Atco with his quickly written "Splish Splash." Atlantic Records, the parent of Atco, found out that Darin had taken part in the recordings on Brunswick and threatened to sue the company unless it turned over the masters and pulled the records off the market. Brunswick's reaction was to have Decca's most popular singer, Buddy Holly, do a cover, not only of one, but of both sides of the record. Both versions hit the charts. Atco released the record under the name "Bobby Darin and the Rinky Dinks."

Other hits followed for Buddy: "Oh Boy," by the Crickets, in 1957, and "Think It Over" and "Fools's Paradise" in 1958. In January 1959, Buddy hit with "Heartbeat." He appeared on national TV constantly, on "The Ed Sullivan Show" and "The Arthur Murray Show."

> Although Buddy Holly was a rockabilly artist, he was very different from the rockabilly mainstream. His was a softer music, and his records sounded less neurotic, effervescent instead of turbulent .... In Holly's records, rockabilly deflects from country music toward a more refined, apollonian form, perhaps best exemplified by the music of the Everly Brothers, who thrived from 1957 to 1960. [Tosches, 1985, p. 96-97]

The Crickets continued to argue with Buddy about working as hard as they were, and eventually the band returned to Texas, while Buddy stayed in New York, got married, and started working for the future. He soon began to develop the new sound-on-sound technique of recording one voice over and over until a multiple group of voices is heard. He also started using violins in his songs, which had never been done in rock before.

In January 1956, in New York City, on his own tape recorder, Buddy Holly recorded his last songs: "Peggy Sue Got Married," "Crying, Waiting, Hoping," "That's What They Say," and "Learning the Game."

The hectic schedule he had to follow was partly to blame for his death. He was on tour with Richie Valens, J. P. Richardson, and others, all of whom were tired and sick from the cold. Someone suggested that they charter a plane to fly to their next destination, so Buddy could rest before the next show. Richie and J. P. also thought it a good idea and convinced two members of Buddy's group, one of who was a young bass player by the name of Waylon Jennings, to let them have their seats. The rest is history: on February 3rd, 1959, the plane crashed in a field near Fargo, North Dakota, and they all died.

Buddy did much for Decca and for rockabilly. He created a style of playing guitar that would be copied for decades. He combined country music, blues, Texas swing, and Mexican sounds to form a new style of rockabilly music. His records continued to sell in the '60's and '70's, and well into the '80's with the advent of CD's. Today's teenagers still listen to his songs — songs that are as fresh and timely today as they were then.

> More than any other singer of that era, he brings back a time when music was fun, when rock was fun, was trying to push it as an art form and when sheer animal exuberance was what counted. *[Roxon, 1969, p. 236]*

Ronnie Hawkins

Ronnie Hawkins was born in Huntsville, Arkansas, on January 10, 1935. Early in his life, the family moved to Fayetteville, and Ronnie grew up singing in the church choir and excelling in physical sciences in high school and later at the University of Arkansas.

He formed his first group, the Hawks, in 1952, but unfortunately the band saw little success because all its members, except Ronnie, were black, and the prejudice of the time forced the group to disband.

Ronnie continued to sing, and after the emergence of Elvis, he formed his second version of the Hawks in 1958. He boldly began to spread his sound throughout the Memphis area. Success in recording, however, was not forthcoming, and after many demos and a stint in the U. S. Army, Ronnie and the group decided to head to Canada. In Canada, they recorded a wild version of "Hey Bo Diddley" for Quality Records, which led them to record "Forty Days" for Roulette, in the United States. In June 1959, just four months after the death of Buddy Holly, Ronnie entered the Top-100 with his hit "Forty Days." He Later followed up with another hit, "Mary Lou." Once again, he reorganized the band, and continued to be successful, especially in Canada and in the South.   The group quickly began to drift apart, even with regard to the clothing they wore -- Ronnie, in his $600 black suede suit, and the band in their all white suits, with long lapels. In 1963, he and the band split up, and Ronnie formed his own record label, Hawk. He released a number of successful records on Hawk, among them "Got My Mojo Working," "Bluebirds over the Mountain," and "Little Red Rooster." He was one of the true leaders of rockabilly music, and he constantly spread the word. He was also one of the few innovators who was never struck by tragedy and who is still alive.

The Band

Levon Helm, his drummer, and the Hawks went on to cut a record for Apex entitled "Uh-Uh-Uh," under the name the Canadian Squires. They also recorded two songs for Atco under the name Levon & the Hawks, one of which was not released until 1968. Finally, the group settled on the name the Band and spent some time backing up the new folksinger, Bob Dylan, through his many hits. Later they became very successful themselves on Capitol Records with their releases "The Weight," "Up on Cripple Creek," "Rag Mama Rag," and other songs. They were so popular with the college crowd that they were invited to intertain at Woodstock, in 1969. The band split up forever in 1976, and one of its members, Richard Manuel, committed suicide in 1982. Levon Helm can be found acting in movies, from time to time.

The Band was invited to play at the Woodstock revival program in 1994, and they performed successfully in front of a new and younger audience.

Rick Nelson

Rick Nelson was born in Teaneck, New Jersey, on May 8, 1940. His career in music developed quite by accident, while he was performing in his parents' television show "The Ozzie and Harriet Show." The script had him dressed as Elvis Presley for a costume party. As a joke, he sang two lines from Presley's "Love Me Tender." The result was 10,000 letters in a week, almost all wanting to know when Rick was going to make a recording.

With everyone jumping on the Elvis bandwagon, Ozzie got him a recording with Verve, and Rick sang the songs on the television show for the nation. Both of the songs, "A Teenager's Romance," and "I'm Walkin'," were hits. Rick was beginning to learn how to emanate sex appeal, so the teenage girls would swoon over him. His second release, "You're My One and Only Love," was also a hit, and it, too, was done in the sexy, drooling, teenage craving manner of the first song.

The story goes that Lew Chudd, the head of Imperial Records, heard that Rick had only a verbal contract with Verve and persuaded Ozzie to sign Rick to Imperial Records. The combination of artist and record company was perfect and led to at least a dozen Top-10 records, including "Bee Bop Baby," "Stood Up," "Waitin' in School," and "Poor Little Fool." These songs were more in the rockabilly genre, and he matured in this musical form as the years progressed.

From 1957 to 1963 he remained one of the top pop artists in the country, with sales of around 35 million records. Each song, in turn, showed more and more development, and the background, too, was expanding. All the years were not great, however. There was a slump in the middle, which was broken in 1961.

"Travelin' Man," recorded in 1961, alone sold over 5 million copies worldwide. With the backing of rockabilly guitarist James Burton, Rick's songs began to have a definite country sound, and on several occasions he emulated country stars such as Jim Reeves, and Johnny Cash.

In 1963, Rick signed a 20 year contract with Decca Records, but his hits became fewer and fewer, as he tried turning out pop-sounding records. However, in 1967, he formed his first country band and turned out the country music album *Country Fever* on which he had his first country hit: "You Just Can't Quit." Decca began pushing him toward country music, as that was their strength, at the time.

In 1968, however, he began to form his own style, which would combine the hard sounds of rock with the simple sounds of country, and began to work with the Stone Canyon Band. Now he was getting away from the country sound of James Burton and going more into a smooth rock sound with the likes of Allen Kemp, Rand Meisner, Pat Shanahan, and Tom Bromley on steel guitar (formerly with Buck Owens). Supposedly, he was so impressed with Bob Dylan's *Nashville Skyline* album that he was dedicated to expanding on this new sound.

Rick toured with the band, and began to be invited to entertain at colleges and universities around the country, as well as at rock revival shows and on TV.

In October 1971, in one of the rock revival shows, held at Madison Square Garden, in New York City, he was booed by the audience for playing new material, having an unusual band, long hair and wild jump suit outfits, none of which were associated with his image. Totally frustrated with this response, he wrote the song that would change his life and his sound forever. "Garden Party" zoomed to the top of the pop and country charts and stayed there for a long time. The new sound was clicking.

This song would be the last of the big ones, however, as the takeover of Decca by MCA caused a misunderstanding and a fallout over his 20-year contract. Rick then signed with Epic Records.

Rick worked very hard on a rock concept album, but was frustrated by the results. However, a new album, entitled *Intakes*, was very well received.

In 1979, Rick signed with Capitol Records and began to release some new promising material. He continued to build up his musical following until he died in an airplane accident, in DeKalb, Texas, on December 31, 1985. His two twin boys have since taken to the road with a singing act of their own, carrying out the Nelson tradition.

The following codes and classifications are used in the discography.

R	Reissue of a previous release
Rx	Additional Reissue of previous release
1	The first recording of the song.
2	The second recording... etc.
33	A 33 1/3 speed single release
S	Stereo (noted only on early singles and EP's)
Warner B	Warner Brothers (or Bros)
MF	Mobile Fidelity
ABC/P	ABC/Paramount
EMI/A	EMI/America
Capitol/C	Capitol/CEMA

Recordings are listed chronologically under each artist's heading.
Most CD listings are available on tape with similar numbers
Most LP Records are no longer available
Artists are arranged alphabetically.

Billy Burnette-(and Jawbone)-

(Son Of Dorsey Burnette, Born 5/08/53)
Singles

Frog Prince/One Extreme to the Other	-Warner Bros	(1969)
	-A & M	(1976)
Welcome Home Elvis	-Gusto 167	(1977)
Shoo-Be-Doo	-Polydor 14530	(1978)
I Believe What You Say	-Polydor 14549	(1979)
What's a Little Love Between Friends	-Columbia 12024	(1979)
Don't Say No	-Columbia 12380	(1980)
Let the New Love Begin	-Columbia 12527	(1981)
The Bigger the Love	-Columbia 12699	(1981)
Try Me	-MCA/Curb 5604	(1985)
Soldier of Love	-MCA/Curb 5768	(1986)

Albums

Billy Burnette		-Entrance 31228	(1972)
Welcome Home Elvis		-Gusto SD-994x	
Billy Burnette		-Polydor 6187	(1979)
Between Friends		-Polydor 6242	(1979)
Billy Burnette		-Columbia 3679	(1980)
Gimme You		-Columbia 3746	(1981)
Soldier of Love	(CD)	-MCA/Curb 5768	(1986)
Coming Home	(CD)	-Capricorn 42007-2	(1993)

Dorsey Burnette-
Singles

The Devil's Queen /Let's Fall in Love	-Abbott 188	(1955)
At a Distance	-Abbott 190	(1955)
Bertha Lou/Til the Law Says Stop	-Cee Jam 16	(1957)
It's Late	-Imperial	(1958)
Try/You Came As a Miracle	-Imperial 5561	(1959)
Lonely Train/Misery	-Imperial 5597	(1960)
Way in the Middle of the Night/Your Love	-Imperial 5668	(1960)
Circle Rock/House With a Tin Rooftop	-Imperial 5987	(1960)
Lucy Darlin'/Black Roses	-Merri 206	(1960)
Tall Oak Tree/Hey Little One	-Gusto 2032	(1960)
Tall Oak Tree/Juarez Town	(2) -Era 3012	(1960)
Hey, Little One/Big Rock Candy Mountain	(2) -Era 3019	(1960)
Hey, Little One/Tall Oak Tree	(R)-Era 5003	(1960)
Hey, Little One/Tall Oak Tree	(R)-Era 3	(1960)
The Ghost of Billy Malloo/Red Roses	-Era 3025	(1960)
The River and the Mountain /This Hotel	-Era 3033	(1961)
(It's No) Sin/Hard Rock Mine	-Era 3041	(1961)
Great Shakin' Fever/That's Me Without You	-Era 3045	(1961)
Rainin' in my Heart/A Full House	-Dot 16230	· (1961)
The Feminine Touch/Sad Boy	-Dot 16265	(1961)

-Dorsey Burnette Cont'd-

Dying Ember	-Dot 16305	(1961)
Castle in the Sky/Boys Kept Hanging Around	-Reprise 20093	(1962)
Darling Jane/I'm A Waitin' For Ya Baby	-Reprise 20121	(1962)
Four For Texas/Foolish Pride	-Reprise 20146	(1962)
It Don't Take Much/Hey Sue	-Reprise 20153	(1962)
Invisible Chains/Pebbles	-Reprise 20177	(1963)
One of the Lonely/Where's the Girl	-Reprise 20208	(1963)
Navy Man	-Navy 72896	(196?)
Little Acorn/Cold As Usual	-Mel-o-dy 113	(1964)
Jimmy Brown/Everybody's Angel	-Mel-o-dy 116	(1964)
Ever Since the World Began	-Mel-o-dy 118	(1964)
In the Morning/To Remember	-Smash 2029	(1966)
If You Want To Love Somebody/ Teach Me Little Children	-Smash 2039	(1966)
Tall Oak Tree/I Just Can't Be Tamed	(3) -Smash 2062	(1966)
Ain't That Fine/The House That Jack Built	-Hickory 1458	(1967)
Son You've Got To Make It Alone/I'll Walk Away	-Music Factory 417	(1968)
The Greatest Love/Thin Little, Plain Little, Simple Little Girl	-Liberty 56087	(1969)
Magnificent Sanctuary Band	-Condor 1005	(1970)
One Lump Sum/Call Me Lowdown	-Happy Tiger 563	(1970)
To Be a Man/Fly Away and Hurry Home	-Happy Tiger 546	(1970)
After the Long Drive Home	-Capitol 3073	(1971)
Children of the Universe	-Capitol 3190	(1971)
In the Spring (The Roses Always Turn Red)/ The Same Old You, The Same Old Me	-Capitol 3307	(1972)
I Just Couldn't Let Her Walk Away	-Capitol 3404	(1972)
Cry Mama	-Capitol 3463	(1972)
I Let Another Good One Get Away	-Capitol 3529	(1973)
Keep Out of My Dreams	-Capitol 3588	(1973)
Darlin' (Don't Come Back)	-Capitol 3678	(1973)
Daddy Loves You Honey	-Capitol 3887	(1974)
In the Spring (The Roses Always Turn Red)/The Same Old You, The Same Old Me	-Capitol 6466 (R)	(1974)
Molly (I Ain't Gettin' Any Younger)/I'm Feeling Low	-Melodyland 6007	(1975)
Lyin' In Her Arms Again	-Melodyland 6019	(1975)
Ain't No Heartbreak	-Melodyland 6031	(1976)
	-MC	(1977)
Tennessee Hot Man	-Movie star 102	(1977)
Soon As I Touched Her	-Calliope 8012	(1977)
Here I Go Again/B J Kick-A-Beaux	-Elektra 46586	(1979)
	-Collectables	(1981)

Albums

Tall Oak Tree	-Era EL-102	(1960)
Dorsey Burnette Sings	-Dot DLP-25456	(1963)
Dorsey Burnette's Greatest Hits	-Era ES-800	(1969)
Here and Now	-Capitol 11094	(1972)
Dorsey Burnette	-Capitol 11219	(1973)
Golden Hits of Dorsey Burnette	-Gusto GTS-0050	

-Dorsey Burnette Cont'd-

		-Trip	(1974)
Things I Treasure		-Calliope 7006	(1977)
Rock & Roll	(CD)	-Richmond N5-2134	(198?)

The Texans   **(Dorsey and Johnny Burnette)-**

Singles

Rockin' Johnny Home	-Gothic 001	(1960)
Green Grass of Texas/Bloody River	-Infinity 001	(1960)
Green Grass of Texas/Bloody River	(R)-Vee Jay 698	(1960)
Green Grass of Texas/Bloody River	(R) -Jox	(1964)

Burnette Brothers (Johnny and Dorsey Burnette)-

Singles

Warm Love	-Imperial 5509	(1958)
Blues Stay Away From Me	-Coral 62190	(1960)
Hey Sue/It Don't Take Much	-Reprise 20153	(1963)

Johnny Burnette-

Singles

Go Mule Go	-Von N/A	(1954)
I'm Restless/Kiss Me Baby	-Freedom 44001	(1959)
Me and The Bear/Gumbo	-Freedom 44011	(1959)
Sweet Baby Doll/I'll Never Love Again	-Freedom 44017	(1959)
Settin' the Woods on Fire/Kentucky Waltz	-Liberty 55222	(1960)
Don't Do It/Patrick Henry	-Liberty 55243	(1960)
Dreamin'/Cincinnati Fireball	-Liberty 55258	(1960)
You're Sixteen/I Beg Your Pardon	-Liberty 55285	(1960)
Little Boy Sad/I Go Down to the River	-Liberty 55298	(1960)
Big Big World/Ballad of the One-Eyed Jacks	-Liberty 55318	(1961)
Girls/I've Got a Lot of Things To Do	-Liberty 55345	(1961)
God, Country and My Baby/Honestly I Do	-Liberty 55379	(1961)
Clown Shoes/Way I Am	-Liberty 55416	(1962)
The Fool of the Year /Poorest Boy in Town	-Liberty 55448	(1962)
Damn the Defiant/Lonesome Waters	-Liberty 55489	(1962)
I Wanna Thank You Folks/Giant	-Chancellor 1116	(1962)
Tag-Along/Party Girl	-Chancellor 1123	(1962)
Remember Me/Time Is Not Enough	-Chancellor 1129	(1962)
All Week Long/It Isn't There	-Capitol 5023	(1963)
Opposite/You Taught Me the Way To Love You	-Capitol 5114	(1964)
Sweet Suzie/Walkin' Talkin' Doll	-Capitol 5176	(1964)
Bigger Man/Less Than a Heartache	-Magic Lamp 515	(1964)
Fountain of Love/What a Summer Day	-Sahara 512	(1964)
	(R)-UA	(1984)

-Johnny Burnette Cont'd-
(UA releases are Liberty, renumbered and rereleased)

Dreamin'/Little Boy Sad	(R)-UA 18	(1984)
God, Country And My Baby/Your Sixteen	(R)-UA 19	(1984)

Extended Play Mini Albums

EP Dreamin'	-Liberty LSX-1004	(1961)
EP Johnny Burnette Hits	-LibertyALSX-1011	(1961)

Albums

Dreamin'	-Liberty LST-7179	(1960)
Johnny Burnette	-Liberty LST-7183	(1961)
Johnny Burnette Sings	-Liberty LST-7190	(1961)
Johnny Brunette's Hits and Other Favorites	-Liberty LST-7206	(1962)
Rose Are Red	-Liberty LST-7255	(1963)
Johnny Burnette Story	-Liberty LST-7389	(1964)
Dreamin'	-Sunset SUS-5179	(1967)
Very Best of Johnny Burnette	-UA UA-LA432G	(1975)
Tenth Anniversary Album	-UA 29643	(1975)
Johnny Burnette's Hits and Other Favorites	-Liberty LN-10144	(1981)
You're Sixteen: The Best Of Johnny Burnette (CD)	-Liberty E21Y-9997	(1992)

Johnny Burnette Trio(the Rock 'n Roll Trio)-
(Johnny Burnette, Dorsey Burnette, and Paul Burlison)

Singles

Tear it Up/You're Undecided	-Coral 61651	(1955)
Midnight Train/Oh Baby Babe	-Coral 61675	(1955)
Honey Hush/ The Train Kept a Rollin'	-Coral 61719	(1956)
Lonesome Train/I Just Found Out	-Coral 61758	(1956)
Eager Beaver Baby/If You Want It Enough	-Coral 61829	(1957)
Butterfingers/Drinkin' Wine Spo-Dee-O-Dee	-Coral 61869	(1957)
Rock Billy Boogie/If You Want It Enough	-Coral 61918	(1957)
Blues Stay Away From Me/Midnight Train	-Coral 62190	(1960)

Albums

Johnny Burnette and the Rock 'n' Roll Trip	-Coral CRL-57080	(1956)
Johnny Burnette and the Rock 'n' Roll Trio	-Solid Smoke 8001	(1978)
Johnny and Dorsey Burnette-Together Again	-Solid Smoke 8005	(1980)
Tear It Up (England)	-MCA Coral CP10	
Johnny Burnette's Rock 'n' Roll Trio: A Tribute	-RB 1001	
Johnny Burnette and the Rock 'n' Roll Trio	-MCA 1513	(1982)
Listen to Johnny Burnette	(R)-MCA 1513E	(1982)
The Johnny Burnette Trio 2LP	-MCA 1561	(1982)

Rocky Burnette(and the Rock 'n Roll Trio-son of Johnny Burnette)-

Singles

Tired of Toein' The Line	-EMI/A 8043	(1980)

-Rocky Burnette Cont'd-

Baby Tonight	-EMI/A 8050	(1980)
Fallin' In Love (Being Friends)	-EMI/A 8060	(1980)
Son of Rock & Roll	(R)-Kyd EMC-3323	(1983)

Albums

Son of Rock & Roll	-EMI/A SW-17033	(1980)
Son of Rock & Roll	(R)-EMI/A EMC-323	(1982)
	-Goods	(1982)
Son of Rock & Roll	(R)-Kyd	(1983)

The Crickets-

**(Among others, were Jerry Allison, Sonny Curtis, Jerry Naylor. After
Holly's death, include: Tommy Allsup, Glen Hardin, Joe Mauldin,
Buzz Cason, Jerry Naylor, and Niki Sullivan)**

(With Buddy Holly)

Singles

That'll Be The Day/I'm Lookin' for Someone to Love	-Brunswick 55009	(1957)
Oh Boy!/Not Fade Away	-Brunswick 55035	(1957)
Maybe Baby/Tell Me How	-Brunswick 55053	(1958)
Think It Over/Fool's Paradise	-Brunswick 55072	(1958)
It's So Easy/Lonesome Tears	-Brunswick 55094	(1958)
That'll Be The Day/I'm Lookin' for Someone to Love	(R)-Coral 65618	(1960)

Extended Play Mini Albums

EP Chirping Crickets	-Brunswick 71036	(1957)
EP Sound of The Crickets	-Brunswick 71038**	(1958)
EP The Crickets	-Coral 81192*	(1963)
EP The Crickets Live	-BHMS-100	(1978)

(special by The Buddy Holly Memorial Society)

Albums

The Chirping Crickets	-Brunswick 54038	(1957)

*(buddy holly on one track)

The Chirping Crickets	(R)-MCA 25170	(1988)

(without Buddy Holly)

The Crickets (featuring Jerry Allison)-

Singles

Love's Made a Fool of You/Someone, Someone	-Brunswick 55124	(1959)
When You Ask About Love/Deborah	-Brunswick 55153	(1959)
That'll Be the Day/Looking for Someone to love	-Brunswick 62238	(1960)
More Than I Can Say/Baby My Heart	-Coral 62198	(1960)
Peggy Sue Got Married/Don't Cha Know	-Coral 62238	(1960)
He's Old Enough to Know Better/I'm Feeling Better	-Liberty 55385	(1961)
He's Old Enough to Know Better/I'm Feelng Better	(R)-Liberty 55392	(1962)
Don't Ever Change/I'm Not a Bad Guy	-Liberty 55441	(1962)
Parisian Girl/ I Believe in You	-Liberty 55492	(1962)
Little Hollywood Girl/Parisian Girl	-Liberty 55495	(1962)

-The Crickets (featuring Jerry Allison) Cont'd-

My Little Girl/Teardrops Fall Like Rain	-Liberty 55540	(1963)
April Avenue/Don't Say You Love Me	-Liberty 55603	(1963)
Lonely Avenue/You Can't Be In-Between	-Liberty 55660	(1964)
Please Please Me/From Me to You	-Liberty 55668	(1964)
La Bamba/All Over You	-Liberty 55696	(1964)
I Think I've Caught the Blues/We Gotta Get Together	-Liberty 55742	(1964)
Now Hear This/Everybody's Got a Problem	-Liberty 55767	(1965)
Million Dollar Movie/A Million Miles Apart	-Million 415	(1967)
Million Dollar Movie/A Million Miles Apart	(R)-Music Factory 415	(1968)
True Love Ways/Rockin' '50's Rock And Roll	-Barnaby 2061	(1972)
You're Mine	-MGM 11428	(1973)
For You I Have Eyes	-MGM 11507	(1973)
N/A	-Epic FE-44446	(1989)

Albums

In Style with the Crickets	-Coral 57320	(1960)
Something Old, Something New	-Liberty LST-7272	(1962)
Bobby Vee Meets Crickets	-Liberty LST-7228	(1962)
California Sun	-Liberty LST-7351	(1964)
Rockin' '50's Rock & Roll	-Barnaby Z-30268	(1970)
Remnants	-Vertigo VEL-1020	(1973)
	-Koala	
The Liberty Years	-EMI E21Y-95845	(1991)

Buzz Cason-(Buzz Cason was a member of the Crickets at one time)

Singles

Where Was Love/Endless Circle	-Warner Bros 5663	(1965)
Come to Me/ The Good Side of June	-Monument 938	(1966)
Watermelon/Good Humor Man	-Monument 954	(1967)
Tonight/Debbie and Cherry	-Elf 90026	(1969)
Nashville in the Summer/Adam and Eve	-Elf 90032	(1969)
Funky Street Band/Adam and Eve	(R)-Elf 90036	(1969)
Turning Your Back on Me/Bilpie	-Mega 615-0029	
Texas/Heavy Dudes and Heartaches	-Caprice 1002	
Race Drivin' Man/Come Back	-Caprice 1974	
Rapid Roy (the Stock Car Boy)/Radial Racer	-Caprice 2001	
The Devils Triangle	-Berry Hill 080	
Places/No Place for a Lady	-Janus 258	

Buzz Cason with The Casuals-
Singles

Somebody Help Me/My Love Song for You	-Nu-Sound 101	(1957)
Somebody Help Me/My Love Song for You	(R)-Dot 15557	(1957)
Till You Come Back to Me/Hello Love	-Dot	(1957)
So Though/I Love My Darling	-Back Beat 503	(1958)
Don't Pass Me Bye/Ju Judy	-Back Beat 510	(1958)

-Buzz Cason with The Casuals Cont'd-

So Tough   -ABC 1494

Buzz and Bucky-(Buzz Cason and John Wilkin of Ronnie and The Daytonas)

Singles

Tiger A-Go Go/Bay City   -Amy 924   (1965)

Buzz and Traci-

Singles

My Girl, My Girl/Where's My Baby   -Elf 90005   (1967)

The Campers (the Camps)-
(The Campers were Sonny Curtis and the Crickets)

Singles

Ballad of Batman/Batmobile   -Parkway 974   (1965)

Sonny Curtis-

Singles

Someday You're Gonna Be Sorry/Forever Yours	-Coral 60954	(1954)
The Best Way to Hold a Girl	-Coral 61023	(1955)
Wrong Again/Laughing Stock	-Dot 15754	(1958)
Pretty Girl/Willa Mae Jones	-Dot 15799	(1958)
Talk About My Baby/the Red-Headed Stranger	-Coral 62207	(1960)
So Used to Loving You/Last Song I'm Ever Gonna Sing	-Dimension 1017	(1963)
Unsaintly Judy/You Don't Belong in this Place	-Dimension 1023	(1964)
A Beatle I Want to Be/So Used to Loving You	-Dimension 1024	(1964)
I Pledge My Love to You/Bo Diddley Beach	-Liberty 55710	(1964)
My Way of Life/Last Call	-Viva 602	(1966)
Destiny's Child/The Collector	-Viva 607	(1967)
I Wanna Go Bummin' Around/Gypsy Man	-Viva 617	(1967)
Atlanta Georgia Stray/Day Drinker	-Viva 626	(1968)
The Straight Life/How Little Men Care	-Viva 630	(1969)
Day Gig/ Holiday for Clowns	-Viva 634	(1969)
Girl of the North/Hung Up in Your Eyes	-Viva 636	(1969)
Love Is All Around/Hey There and Everywhere	-Ovation 1006	(1970)
Unsaintly Judy/You Don't Belong in This Place	(R)-Ovation 1023	(1970)
Sunny Mornin'/The Lights of L.A.	-A&M 1359	(1972)
Rock and Roll I Gave You the Best Years/My Momma Sure Left Me Some	-Mercury	(1973)
Lovesick Blues/It's Only a Question of Time	-Capitol 4158	(1975)
Where's Patricia Now?/When It's Just You and Me	-Capitol 4240	(1976)
Cheatin' Clouds/The Cowboy Singer	-Elektra 46526	(1979)
Do You Remember "Roll Over Beethoven?"/Walk Right Back	-Elektra 46568	(1979)
The Real Buddy Holly Story/Ain't Nobody Honest	-Elektra 46616	(1980)
Love Is All Around/The Clone Song	-Elektra 46663	(1980)

-Sonny Curtis Cont'd-

Good Ol' Girls	-Elektra 47129	(1980)
Married Women	-Elektra 47176	(1981)
	-Steem	(1985)

Albums

Beatle Hits Flamenco Guitar Style	-Imperial 12276	(1964)
1st of Sonny Curtis	-Viva 36012	(1968)
The Sonny Curtis Style	-Viva 36021	(1969)
The Sonny Curtis Style	(R)-Elektra 227	(1979)
Love Is All Around	-Elektra 283	(1980)
Sonny Curtis Rollin'	-Elektra 349	(1981)

Ivan (Jerry Ivan Allison)-

Singles

Oh You Beautiful Doll/Real Wild Child	-Coral 62017	(1958)
Frankie Frankenstein/That'll Be Alright	-Coral 62081	(1959)
Everybody's Got A Little Problem/Now Hear	-Liberty 55767	(1965)
Real Wild Child/That'll Be Alright	(R)-Coral 65607	(1967)

Lou Giordano-
(Lou was a friend of the Crickets and Buddy Holly)

Singles

Stay Close to Me/Don't Cha Know	-Brunswick 55115	(1959)

(Buddy Holly plays guitar)

Waylon Jennings-
(Waylon was a Cricket when Buddy Holly Died-As a matter of fact, he gave his seat on the death plane to the Big Bopper)

Singles

Jole Blon/When Sin Stops	-Brunswick 55130	(1959)

(Buddy Holly plays guitar)

Another Blue Day/Never Again	-Trend 102	(1962)
Dream Baby/Crying	-Bat 121639	(1962)
Rave On/Love Denied	-A&M 722	(1963)
Four Strong Winds/Just to Satisfy You	-A&M 739	(1964)

(Most of the recordings on RCA after this are Country or Folk)

Albums

Waylon Jennings at JD's	-Bat 1001	(1964)
Don't Think Twice	-A&M 4238	(1969)
In The Beginning (CD	-Bulldog BDL-1052	(198?)

Jerry Naylor-

Singles

Stop Your Crying/You're Thirteen	-Skyla 1118	(1962)

-Jerry Naylor Cont'd-

Judee Malone/I'm Tired	-Skyla 1123	(1962)
	-Smash	(1965)
	-Tower	(1965-68)
But for Love/Angeline	-Columbia 45106	(1970)
	-MGM	(1971-72)
He'll Have To Go/Once Again	-Melodyland 6012	(1975)

Norman Petty Trio-

Singles

Moondreams/Toy Boy	-Columbia 41039	(1957)

(Buddy Holly on guitar)

Albums

Corsage	-Vik LX-1073	(1957)
Moondreams	-Columbia CL-1092	(1958)

Niki Sullivan-
(One time member of the Crickets)
Singles

It's All Over/Three Steps to Heaven	-Dot 15751	(1958)
Doin' the Dive/My Lost Dream	-Jolie 073	(1958)
It Really Doesn't Matter/You Better Get a Move On	-Jolie 075	(1958)
I Cry All the Time/Then Came the Fall	-Jubilee 5441	(197?)

Statues
(with Buzz Cason as Gary Miles)-

Singles

Blue Velvet/Look For a Star	-Liberty 54564	(1960)
Blue Velvet/Keep the Hall Light Burning	(R)-Liberty 55245	(1960)
Look For a Star/Afraid of Love	(R)-Liberty 55261	(1960)
Look For a Star/Afraid of Love	(R)-Imperial 5674	(1960)
Look For a Star	(Rx)-UA 94	(1960)
Dream Girl/Wishing Well	-Liberty 55279	(1960)
White Christmas/Jeanie with the Light Brown Hair	-Liberty 55292	(1960)
The Commandments of Love/Love At First Sight	-Liberty 55363	(1961)
(Released in Europe on Top Rank Records)		
Candy/Do The Bug	-Liberty 55596	(1963)
Ecstasy/Here Goes a Fool	-Liberty 55714	(1964)

Buddy Holly (and The Three Tunes-and The Crickets)-
(These listings are those of featuring Buddy Holly, and not just the Crickets)

Singles

Blue Days - Black Nights/Love Me	-Decca 29854	(1956)
Modern Don Juan/You Are My One Desire	-Decca 30166	(1956)
That'll Be the Day/Rock Around with Ollie Vee	-Decca 30434	(1957)

-Buddy Holly Cont'd-

Love Me/You Are My One Desire	-Decca 30543	(1958)
Ting-A-Ling/Girl On My Mind	-Decca 30650	(1958)
Words of Love/Mailman, Bring Me No More Blues	-Coral 61852	(1957)
Peggy Sue/Everyday	-Coral 61885	(1957)
I'm Gonna Love You Too/Listen to Me	-Coral 61947	(1958)
Rave On/Take Your Time	-Coral 61985	(1958)
Early in the Morning/Now We're One	-Coral 62006	(1958)
Heartbeat/Well, All Right	-Coral 62051	(1959)
It Doesn't Matter Anymore/Raining in My Heart	-Coral 62074	(1959)
Peggy Sue Got Married/Crying, Waiting, Hoping	-Coral 62134	(1959)
True Love Ways/That Makes It Tough	-Coral 62210	(1960)
You're So Square/Valley of Tears	-Coral 62283	(1961)
Reminiscing/Wait Till the Sun Shines, Nellie	-Coral 62329	(1962)
True Love Ways/Bo Diddley	-Coral 62352	(1963)
Brown Eyed Handsome Man/Wishing	-Coral 62369	(1963)
Rock Around with Ollie Vee/I'm Gonna Love You Too	-Coral 62390	(1964)
Not Fade Away/Maybe Baby	(R)-Coral 62407	(1964)
What To Do/Slippin' and Slidin'	-Coral 62448	(1965)
Rave On/Early in the Morning	(R)-Coral 62554	(1968)
Love Is Strange/You're the One	(R)-Coral 62558	(1969)
I'm Lookin' for Someone To Love/That'll Be the Day	-Coral 62618	(1969)
Peggy Sue/Everyday	(R)-Coral 61885	(1969)
Rave On	(R)-Hep 5	
Peggy Sue/That'll Be the Day	(R)-Memory Lane 771-1	
Peggy Sue/Everyday	(R)-Million Seller 307	
I'm Lookin' for Someone To Love/That'll Be the Day	(R)-MCA 60000	(1973)
Everyday/Peggy Sue	(R)-MCA 60004	(1973)
It Doesn't Matter Anymore/Peggy Sue	(R)-MCA 40905	(1978)

Albums

Buddy Holly	-Coral CRL-57210	(1958)
That'll Be the Day	-Decca DL-86707	(1958)
Buddy Holly Story	-Coral CRL-57279	(1959)
Buddy Holly Story, Vol. 2	-Coral CRL-57326	(1960)
Buddy Holly and the Crickets	-Coral CRL-57405	(1962)
(Repackaging of The Chirping Crickets)		
Reminiscing	-Coral CRL-57426	(1963)
Showcase	-Coral CRL-57450	(1964)
Holly in the Hills	-Coral CRL-57463	(1965)
Best of Buddy Holly (2 LP)	-Coral CXB-8	(1966)
Buddy Holly's Greatest Hits	-Coral CRL-57492	(1967)
Great Buddy Holly	-Vocalion VL-3811	(1967)
(Repackaging of That'll Be The Day)		
Giant	-Coral CRL7-57504	(1969)
Good Rockin'	-Vocalion 73923	(1971)
A Rock and Roll Collection	-Decca DXSE7-207	(1972)
The Great Buddy Holly	-MCA CD-20101	(1975)
Rock and Roll Collection (2 LP)	-MCA 2-4009	(1977)

-Buddy Holly Cont'd-

20 Golden Greats		-MCA 3040	(1978)
Portrait in Music, Vol. 1 (Picture Disc)		-Solid Smoke 8002	(1979)
The Day the Music Died (Picture Disc)	(2 LP)	-Creative Radio	
Portrait in Music, Vol. 2 (Picture Disc)		-Solid Smoke 8003	(1979)
Complete Buddy Holly	(6 CD)	-MCA 6-80000	(1981)
Greatest Hits	(Import)	-MCA CDLM 8007	
Buddy Holly - Legend	(Import)	-MCA CDLM 8024	
Buddy Holly	(Import)	-MCA CDLM 8034	
The "Chirping Crickets"	(Import)	-MCA CDLM 8035	
The Nashville Sessions	(Import)	-MCA CDLM 8038	
Portrait in Music	(Import)	-MCA 2-COPS 4408	
Portrait in Music, Vol. 2	(Import)	-MCA 2-COPS 5616	
Rave On	(Import)	-MCA MFP-50176	
20 Golden Greats	(CD)	(R)-MCA 1484	(1982)
For the First Time Anywhere	(CD)	-MCA 27059	(1983)
Legend	(2 CD)	-MCA 2-4148	(1983)
From the Original Masters	(CD)	-MCAD 5540	(1984)
Buddy Holly and the Picks		-Pick 1111	(1986)
For the First Time Anywhere	(CD)	(R)-MCA 27059	(1987)
The Chirping Crickets	(CD)	(R)-MCA 25170	(1988)
The Great Buddy Holly	(CD)	(R)-MCA 31037	(1989)

Extended Play Mini Albums

EP That'll Be the Day	-Decca EP 2575	(1958)
EP That'll Be the Day	-Coral ECD-2575	(1958)
EP Listen to Me	-Coral EP 81169	(1958)
EP The Buddy Holly Story	-Coral EP 81182	(1959)
EP Peggy Sue Got Married	-Coral EP 81191	(1962)
EP Brown Eyed Handsome Man	-Coral EP 81193	(1963)

Ronnie Hawkins-(the Ronnie Hawkins Quartet)-

Singles

Hey Bo Diddley/Love Me Like You Can	-Quality 6128	(1958)

Ronnie Hawkins (Rockin' Ronald and The Rebels)-

Singles

Kansas City/Cuttin' Out	-Orchid 5005	(1959)
Kansas City/Cuttin' Out	(R)-End 1043	(1959)
Forty Days/One of These Days	-Ric N/A	(1959)
Forty Days/One of These Days	(R)-Roulette 4154	(1959)
Mary Lou/Need Your Lovin'	-Roulette 4177	(1959)
Mary Lou/Forty Days	(R)-Roulette 65	(1959)
Southern Love/Love Me Like You Can	-Roulette 4209	(1960)
Lonely Hours/Clara	-Roulette 4228	(1960)
Ballad of Caryl Chessman/Death of Floyd Collins	-Roulette 4231	(1960)

Ruby Baby/Hay Ride	-Roulette 4249	(1961)

-**Ronnie Hawkin Cont'ds-**

Summertime /Mister and Mississippi	-Roulette 4267	(1961)
Cold Cold Heart/Nobody's Lonesome for Me	-Roulette 4311	(1962)
Come Love/I Feel Good	-Roulette 4400	(1962)
Bo Diddley/Who Do You Love	-Roulette 4483	(1963)
There's a Screw Loose/High Blood Pressure	-Roulette 4503	(1963)
Will the Circle Be Unbroken?/Home From the Forest	-Yorkville 40516	(1967)
Home From the Forest/Bitter Green	-Yorkville 40517	(1967)
Reason to Believe/Mary Jane	-Yorkville 40519	(1968)
I Got My Mojo Workin'/Let the Good Time Roll	-Hawk 102	(1964)
Bluebirds over the Mountain/Diddley Diddley Daddy	-Hawk 106	(1965)
Little Red Rooster/Goin' to the River	-Hawk 107	(1965)
Matchbox/Little Bird	-Hawk 301	(1969)
Down in the Alley/Home from the Forest	(2) -Hawk 302	(1969)
Forty Days/Bitter Green	(3) -Hawk 305	(1970)
Patricia/Black Sheep Boy	-Hawk 1205-01	(1971)
Down in the Alley/Matchbox	(R)-Cotillion 44060	(1970)
Bitter Green/Forty Days	(4) -Cotillion 44067	(1970)
Little Bird/One More Night	-Cotillion 44076	(1970)
Cora Mae/Lawdy Miss Clawdy	-Monument 8548	(1973)
Lonesome Town/Kinky	-Monument 8561	(1973)
Cora Mae/Diddley Diddley Daddy	(2) -Monument 8571	(1972)
Bo Diddley/Lonely Hours	(2) -Monument 8573	(1973)
Lady Came From Baltimore/Will the Circle Be Unbroken?	(R)-Polydor 2065-303	(1976)
	-United Artists	(1979)
	-Accord	(1983)
The Best of Ronnie Hawkins & the Hawks (CD)	-Rhino 70966	(1990)

The Band-
(Robbie Robertson-vocals and lead guitar, Garth Hudson-vocals and organ,
Richard Manuel-vocals and piano, Rick Danko-vocals and bass,
Levon Helm-vocals and drums)

Singles

Jabberwocky/Never Too Much Love	-Capitol 2041	(1968)
The Weight/I Shall Be Released	-Capitol 2269	(1968)
Up on Cripple Creek/The Night They Drove Old Dixie Down	-Capitol 2635	(1969)
Rag Mama Rag/The Unfaithful Servant	-Capitol 2705	(1970)
Time to Kill/The Shape I'm In	-Capitol 2870	(1970)
Life Is a Carnival/The Moon Struck One	-Capitol 3199	(1971)
When I Paint My Masterpiece/Where Do We Go From Here	-Capitol 3249	(1972)
Don't Do It/Rag Mama Rag	-Capitol 3433	(1972)
Hang Up My Rock and Roll Shoes/Caledonia Mission	-Capitol 3500	(1972)
Ain't Got No Home/Get Up Jake	-Capitol 3758	(1973)
Third Man Theme/ W.S. Walcott Medicine Show	-Capitol 3828	(1974)
Stage Freight/(B side by Bob Dylan)	-Asylum 11043	(1974)
Ophellia/Hobo Jungle	-Capitol 4230	(1976)

-The Band Cont'd-

Twilight/Acadian Driftwood	-Capitol 4316	(1976)
Georgia on My Mind/The Night They Drove Old Dixie Down (R)-Capitol 4361		(1976)
The Weight/I Shall Be Released	(R)-Capitol 6158	(1977)
Up on Cripple Creek/The Night They Drove Old Dixie Down (R)-Capitol 6188		(1977)
Ain't Got No Home/Don't Do It	(R)-Capitol 6245	(1977)
Out of the Blue/The Well	-Warner B 6666	(1978)

Albums

Music from Big Pink			-Capitol 2955	(1968)
The Band			-Capitol 132	(1969)
Stage Fright			-Capitol 425	(1970)
In Cahoots			-Capitol 651	(1971)
Rock of Ages (2 LP)			-Capitol 11045	(1972)
Moondog Matinee			-Capitol 11214	(1973)
Northern Lights-Southern Cross			-Capitol 11440	(1975)
The Best of the Band			-Capitol 11553	(1976)
Islands			(R)-Capitol 11602	(1977)
Anthology			-Capitol 11856	(1978)
Last Waltz (3 LP)			-Warner 3WS3146	(1978)
Last Waltz			(DJ)-Warner 737	(1978)
In Cahoots			(R)-Capitol 16003	(1980)
Moondog Matinee			(R)-Capitol 16004	(1980)
Northern Lights-Southern Cross			(R)-Capitol 16005	(1980)
Islands			-Capitol 16007	(1980)
Rock of Ages, Vol. 1			-Capitol 16008	(1980)
Rock of Ages, Vol. 2			-Capitol 16009	(1980)
Music From Big Pink			(R)-MFSL 039	(1980)
Anthology, Vol. 1			(R)-Capitol 16010	(1980)
Music From Big Pink	(CD)	(Ultradisk)	(R)-MF 527	(198?)
The Band	(CD)		(R)-Capitol 16296	(1988)
The Best of the Band	(CD)		(R)-Capitol 16331	(1988)
Music From Big Pink	(CD)		(R)-Capitol/C 46069	(198?)
The Best of the Band	(CD)		(R)-Capitol/C 46070	(198?)
The Band	(CD)		(R)-Capitol/C 46493	(198?)
The Last Waltz	(CD)		(R)-Warner B 3146	(1988)
To Kingdom Come: The Definitive Collection		(CD)	-Capitol/C 92169	(1989)
Islands	(CD)		(R)-Capitol/C 93591	(1990)
Moondog Matinee	(CD)		(R)-Capitol/C 93592	(1990)
Stage Fright	(CD)		(R)-Capitol/C 93593	(1990)
Northern Lights/Southern Cross		(CD)	(R)-Capitol/C 93594	(1990)
Rock of Ages	(2 CD)		(R)-Capitol/C 93595	(1990)

Canadian Squires-
(Levon Helm and other former members of the Band)

Singles

Uh-Uh-Uh/Leave Me Alone	-Apex 76964	(1964)
Uh-Uh-Uh/Leave Me Alone	(R)-Ware 6002	(1964)

Rick Danko-
(Former member of the Band)

Albums

Rick Danko	-Arista 41412	(1977)

Levon Helm-

Singles

Most Likely You'll Go Your Way/Stage Freight	-Asylum 11043	(1974)
Ain't No Way to Forget You	-ABC 12416	(1978)
(One with Johnny Cash)	-A&M	(1980)
	-MCA	(1980)
	-Capitol	(1982)

Album

Levon Helm		-ABC/P AA-1089	(1977)
Levon Helm	(Picture Disc)	-ABC/P SPPD-45	(1978)
		-A&M	(1980)
American Son		-MCA 5120	(1980)
Levon Helm		-Capitol ST-12201	(1982)
Levon Helm	(CD)	(R)-MF 00759	(1992)

Levon Helm & The RCO All-Stars-
(Levon Helm-vocals and drums, Barry Beckett-keyboards,
Steve Cropper-guitar, Scott Edwards-bass)

Singles

Milk Cow Boogie/Blues So Bad		-ABC 12336	(1978)

Albums

Levon Helm & The RCO All-Stars		-ABC/P AA-1017	(1977)
Levon Helm & The RCO All-Stars	(CD)	(R)-MFCD-0761	(1992)

Levon & The Hawks-

Singles

The Stones I Throw/ He Don't Love You	-Atco 6383	(1965)
Go Go Liza Jane/ He Don't Love You	(R)-Atco 6625	(1968)

David Rockinham Trio-(One time member of the Band)

Singles

Dawn/That's All	-Jubilee 913	(1963)
With Midnight/Bee Dee	-Josie 917	(1964)
Jo-De-Vie/Soulful Chant	-Josie 922	(1964)

Rick Nelson-

Singles

A Teenagers Romance/I'm Walkin'	-Verve 10047	(1957)
You're My One and Only Love /(B side is Barney Kessle)	-Verve 10070	(1957)
Be-Bop Baby/Have I Told You Lately That I Love You?	-Imperial 5463	(1957)
Stood Up/Waitin' in School	-Imperial 5483	(1957)
Believe What You Say/My Bucket's Got a Hole in It	-Imperial 5503	(1958)
Poor Little Fool/Don't Leave Me This Way	-Imperial 5528	(1958)
I Got a Feeling/Lonesome Town	-Imperial 5545	(1958)
It's Late/Never Be Anyone Else But You	-Imperial 5565	(1959)
Just A Little Too Much/Sweeter Than You	-Imperial 5595	(1959)
I Wanna Be Loved/Mighty Good	-Imperial 5614	(1959)
Young Emotions/Right By My Side	-Imperial 5663	(1960)
Yes Sir That's My Baby/I'm Not Afraid	-Imperial 5685	(1960)
You Are the Only One/Milk Cow Blues	-Imperial 5707	(1961)
Hello Mary Lou/Travelin' Man	-Imperial 5741	(1961)
Everlovin'/A Wonder Like You	-Imperial 5770	(1961)
Young World/Summertime	-Imperial 5805	(1962)
Teenage Idol	-Imperial 5864	(1962)
It's Up to You/I Need You	-Imperial 5901	(1962)
Teenage Idol/It's Up to You	(R)-Imperial 29	(1962)
That's All/I'm in Love Again	-Imperial 5910	(1963)
Old Enough To Love/If You Can't Rock Me	-Imperial 5935	(1963)
A Long Vacation/Mad Mad World	-Imperial 5958	(1963)
Time After Time/There's Not a Minute	-Imperial 5985	(1963)
Today's Teardrops/Thank You Darling	-Imperial 66004	(1963)
Congratulations/One Minute to Love	-Imperial 66017	(1964)
Everybody But Me/Lucky Star	-Imperial 66039	(1964)
I Got a Woman/You Don't Love Me Anymore	-Decca 31475	(1963)
Gypsy Woman/String Along	-Decca 31495	(1963)
Fools Rush In/Down Home	-Decca 31533	(1963)
For You/That's All She Wrote	-Decca 31574	(1963)
The Very Thought of You	-Decca 31612	(1964)
There's Nothing I Can Say/Lonely Corner	-Decca 31656	(1964)
A Happy Guy/Don't Breath a Word	-Decca 31703	(1964)
Mean Old World/When the Chips Are Down	-Decca 31756	(1965)
Come Out Dancin'/Yesterday's Love	-Decca 31800	(1965)
Love and Kisses/Say You Love Me	-Decca 31845	(1965)
Your Kind of Lovin'/Fire Breathin' Dragon	-Decca 31900	(1966)
Louisiana Man/You Just Can't Quit	-Decca 31956	(1966)
Things You Gave Me/Alone	-Decca 32026	(1966)
Take a Broken Heart/They Don't Give Medals	-Decca 32055	(1966)
Take a City Bride/I'm Called Lonely	-Decca 32120	(1967)
Suzanne on a Sunday Morning/Moonshine	-Decca 32176	(1967)
Dream Weaver/Baby Close Its' Eyes	-Decca 32222	(1967)
I'm Talking About You	-Decca ???	(1968)
Prominade in Green/Don't Blame It on Your Wife	-Decca 32284	(1968)

-Rick Nelson Cont'd-

Don't Make Promises/Barefoot Boy	-Decca 32298	(1968)
She Belongs to Me/Promises	-Decca 32550	(1969)
Come On In/Easy To Be Free	-Decca 32635	(1970)
I Shall Be Released/If You Gotta Go, Go Now	-Decca 32676	(1970)
We Got Such a Long Way To Go/I Look at Mary	-Decca 32711	(1970)
Down Along the Bayou Country/How Long?	-Decca 32739	(1970)
Life/California	-Decca 32779	(1971)
Thank You Lord/Sing Me a Song	-Decca 32860	(1971)
Love Minus Zero/No Limit	-Decca 32906	(1972)
Garden Party/So Long, Mama	-Decca 32980	(1972)
Palace Guard/A Flower Opens Gently By	-MCA 40001	(1973)
She Belongs to Me/Promises	(R)-MCA 60006	(1973)
Garden Party	(R)-MCA 60157	(1973)
Evil Woman Child/Lifestream	-MCA 40130	(1973)
Windfall/Legacy	-MCA 40187	(1974)
One Night Stand/Lifestream	-MCA 40214	(1974)
Louisiana Belle/Try (To Fall in Love)	-MCA 40392	(1974)
Fade Away/Rock and Roll Lady	-MCA 40458	(1975)
Be-Bop Baby/Stood up	(R)-UA 71	(1975)
Lonesome Town/It's Up to You	(R)-UA 72	(1975)
Poor Little Fool/My Buckets' Got a Hole in It	(R)-UA 73	(1975)
Believe What You Say/Travelin' Man	(R)-UA 74	(1976)
Teenage Idol/Young Emotions	(R)-UA 75	(1976)
That's All/Never Be Anyone Else	(R)-UA 76	(1976)
It's Late/Young World	(R)-UA 77	(1976)
Waitin' in School/Just a Little Too Much	(R)-UA 78	(1977)
Hello Mary Lou/Sweeter Than You	(R)-UA 79	(1977)
A Wonder Like You/Everlovin'	(R)-UA 80	(1977)
Gimme a Little Sign/Something You Can't Buy	-Epic 50501	(1978)
Dream Lover/That Ain't The Way Love's Supposed to Be	-Epic 50674	(1979)
It Hasn't Happened Yet/Call It What You Want	-Capitol 4974	(1981)
Believe What You Say/The Loser, Babe, Is You	-Capitol 4988	(1981)
Give 'Em My Number/No Fair Falling in Love	-Capitol 5178	(1982)
(Reissued Imperial Songs)	(R)-Liberty	(1982-83)
You Know What I Mean/Don't Leave Me This Way	(R)-MCA 52781	(1986)
Dream Lover/Rave On	(R)-Epic 06066	(1986)

Extended Play Mini Albums

EP Ricky	-Verve EPV-5048	(1957)
EP Ricky	-Imperial 153-155	(1958)
EP Ricky Nelson	-Imperial 156-158	(1958)
EP Ricky Sings Again	-Imperial 159-161	(1959)
EP Songs by Ricky	-Imperial 162-164	(1959)
EP Ricky Sings Spirituals	-Imperial 165	(1960)
EP For Your Sweet Love	-Decca ED-4419	(1963)
EP Best Always	-Decca ED-4660	(1965)

*Country rock with The Stone Canyon Band

-Rick Nelson Cont'd-
Albums

Teen Time	-Verve 2083	(1957)
Ricky	-Imperial 9048	(1957)
Ricky Nelson	-Imperial 9050	(1958)
Ricky Sings Again	-Imperial 9061	(1959)
Songs by Ricky	-Imperial 9082	(1959)
More Songs by Ricky	-Imperial 9122	(1960)
Rick Is 21	-Imperial 9152	(1961)
Album Seven by Rick	-Imperial 9167	(1962)
Best Sellers by Rick	-Imperial 9218	(1963)
It's Up to You	-Imperial 9223	(1963)
Million Sellers By Rick Nelson	-Imperial 9232	(1963)
A Long Vacation	-Imperial 9244	(1963)
For Your Sweet Love	-Decca 4419	(1963)
The Very Thought of You	-Decca 4459	(1963)
Rick Nelson Sings for You	-Decca 4479	(1963)
Rick Nelson Sings for You	-Imperial 9251	(1964)
Spotlight on Rick	-Decca 4608	(1964)
Best Always	-Decca 4660	(1965)
Love and Kisses	-Decca 4678	(1965)
Rickey Nelson: Teen Time (Verve 2083)	(R)-MGM 4256	(1965)
Bright Lights and Country Music	-Decca 4779	(1966)
Ricky Nelson	-Sunset 5118	(1966)
Country Fever	-Decca 4827	(1967)
On The Flipside (TV Soundtrack)	-Decca 4836	(1967)
Another Side of Rick	-Decca 4944	(1967)

(70000 numbers are in stereo; after this ,all are in stereo)

Perspective	-Decca 75014	(1968)
I Need You	-Sunset 5205	(1968)
Rick Sings Nelson	-Decca 75236	(1970)
Rick Nelson in Concert	-Decca 75162*	(1970)
Rick Nelson Legendary Masters Series (2 LP)	-UA 9960	(1971)
Rudy the Fifth	-Decca 75297*	(1971)
Rick Nelson Legendary Masters Series (2 LP)	-UA 9960	(1971)
Garden Party	-Decca 75391*	(1972)
Windfall	-MCA 3830	(1973)
Rick Nelson Country (2 LP)	-MCA 2-4004	(1973)
Rick Nelson in Concert	(R)-MCA-3*	(1973)
Very Best of Rick Nelson	-United Artists 330	(1975)
Intakes	-Epic KE-34420*	(1977)
The Ricky Nelson Story (3 LP)	-Sessions 1003	(1979)
Ricky	(R)-UA 1004	(1980)
Four You	-Epic N/A	(1981)
Playing to Win	-Capitol	(1981)
Legendary Masters of Rick Nelson	(R)-Liberty L4B-9960	(1981)
The Decca Years	-MCA 1517	(1982)
Rick Nelson Sings Again	(R)-Liberty 10134	(1982)

-Rick Nelson Cont'd-

Rockin' With Ricky		-Ace CH-83	(1982)
Souvenirs		-Liberty 10205	(1983)
Teenage Idol		-Liberty 10253	(1983)
Rick Nelson's Greatest Hits	(CD)	-Rhino R4-70215	(1985)
Rick Nelson's Greatest Hits (Picture Disc)		-Rhino RNDF-259	(1985)
		-MCA/Silver Eagle	(1986)
Rick Nelson In Concert: The Troubadour, 1969 (CD)		(R)-MCA 25983	(1987)
The Best of Rick Nelson	(5 CD)	-EMI/A 21Y-46588	(1987)
All My Best		-Silver Eagle 6163	(1988)
Live, 1983-1985	(2 CD)	-Rhino R2-71114	(1989)
Garden Party	(CD)	(R)-MCA 31364	(1990)
Rick Nelson's Greatest Hits	(CD)	(R)-Curb/CEMA 77372	(1990)
Legendary Masters of Rick Nelson	(CD)	(R)-EMI E21Y-92771	(1990)
The Best of Rick Nelson	(CD)	(R)-Curb/CEMA 77484	(1991)
The Best of Rick Nelson, Vol. 2	(CD)	(R)-EMI E21Y-5219	(1991)

Extended Play Mini Albums

EP Ricky	-Verve EPV-5048	(1957)
EP Ricky	-Imperial 153-155	(1958)
EP Ricky Nelson	-Imperial 156-158	(1958)
EP Ricky Sings Again	-Imperial 159-161	(1959)
EP Songs by Ricky	-Imperial 162-164	(1959)
EP Ricky Sings Spirituals	-Imperial 165	(1960)
EP For Your Sweet Love	-Decca ED-4419	(1963)
EP Best Always	-Decca ED-4660	(1965)

*Country Rock with the Stone Canyon Band

CHAPTER 5

THE SUN INFLUENCE

Without a doubt, the most prominent record label to produce rockabilly records was Sun Records. Sun had more rockabilly artists, including the first, than any other company. Whether Sun signed these artists on purpose, or by accident of location or time, is speculation, but the tastes of its owner, Sam Phillips, tended toward the blues of the south, which led to the sound of white rockabilly music.

Among the not-so-successful or famous singers and musicians on the Sun label were: Billy Lee Riley, the Wildman, part-Native American who had a number of minor hits, but never really scored big; Sonny Burgess, from Newport, Arkansas, who failed to make an impact; Roy Harris, another wild rockabilly singer who literally threw himself into his work; Roy Orbison, who was forced into the genre of rockabilly with "Ooby Dooby," and failed, only to return in the '60's with one of the most successful sounds of the period; Warren Smith, another disappointment for Sun, who remained more of a country music singer than a rockabilly artist, and many more.

Among the greater of the rockabilly musicians to come out of the studios of Sun Records were Johnny Cash, Jerry Lee Lewis, and one of the genuinely pure rockabilly stars who continues to carry on the genre today, Carl Perkins.

Johnny R. Cash

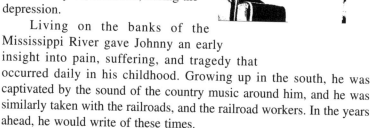

Johnny Cash was born in Kingsland, Arkansas, on February 26, 1932. He was one of five children born to Ray and Carrie Cash. His father was a very hard working poverty-stricken farmer who finally settled in Dyess, Arkansas, during the depression.

Living on the banks of the Mississippi River gave Johnny an early insight into pain, suffering, and tragedy that occurred daily in his childhood. Growing up in the south, he was captivated by the sound of the country music around him, and he was similarly taken with the railroads, and the railroad workers. In the years ahead, he would write of these times.

Johnny never had much as a child and began working in the fields at age 6. By 1940, there were two new children to care for, and times were tough. His only pleasure was listening to the portable radio, and watching his surroundings as he grew to manhood. He spent many a night, as a child, listening to the radio, until his father would demand that he turn it off and go to bed. His mind was filled with the music of Roy Acuff, Jimmie Rodgers, Ernest Tubb, and later, Hank Williams.

Johnny's mother was so impressed with his love of music, that she purchased a $6.98 guitar from Sears, Roebuck. She tried to teach him how to play, but he refused to learn. He preferred sitting and listening, instead. Finally, he sold the guitar to another child in the area.

In the '30's, his brother Roy formed a country band, the Delta Rhythm Ramblers. The band consisted of two guitars, a banjo, a harmonica, and fiddle. They played on radio station KCLN in Blytheville, and rehearsed at home. Johnny listened at every rehearsal, and watched every show with avid enthusiasm. When World War II broke out, the band joined the armed forces, and three of the five were killed.

In the '40's, his brother Jack was killed with a saw, and it took Johnny a long time even to try to get over it. In 1948, at age 16, he got a job on a local work project along the Tyranza River, as a water boy. He would work from 7 A. M., until 6 P. M. with an hour off for lunch. The job didn't last long, because he would listen to the radio in each of the worker's cars, and the batteries would die out.

Johnny's mother decided to buy him singing lessons, and would pay for them by taking in laundry. After one month, the teacher said that his voice was beautiful, and there wasn't any need to improve on it and that his style was his own, and should be left that way.

After graduating from high school, he tried jobs here and there, but nothing seemed to work out for him. He decided to move to Detroit, with a few of his friends, and work in the Fisher Body Plant in Pontiac. However, the job was so tedious and difficult, that he was constantly tired, and he soon quit.

Finally, on July 7, 1950, he joined the U. S. Air Force. On September 21, he started his education as a communications expert. He finished the course four weeks before his fellow students, so he was sent to the Security Service, for more training, after which he was sent to Germany.

While in the Air Force in Germany between 1951 and 1954, he purchased another guitar, and learned a few chords. He formed a country band with a few fellow members from the South, and they began learning and playing country songs. Among his new found friends, were Orvill Rigdon from Louisiana, Ben Pereo from New Mexico, Bill Carnahan from Missouri, Ted Freeman from West Virginia and Reid Cummins from Arkansas. He actually wrote "Folsom Prison Blues" after seeing a movie at the Air Force base theater in Germany, although he wouldn't record it for several years later.

He was discharged on July 3, 1954, and on August 7, 1954, he married his childhood sweetheart, Vivian Liberto, whom he had met in high school. He became an appliance salesman, for the Home Equipment Company, in Memphis, but he hated trying to convince poor blacks that they needed something that they didn't really need, so he decided to go to radio announcers school.

Johnny's brother Roy worked at the Automobile Sales Garage with two good mechanics, Marshall Grant, and Luther Perkins (Carl Perkins's brother), who also played guitar. They soon got together and decided that since they could not all play acoustic guitar, they would have to choose different instruments. Since John would sing, the acoustic guitar was good for him; Luther borrowed an electric guitar from a friend and Marshall took up stand-up bass. The company where Johnny worked as a salesman put up the money to sponsor a 15-minute program on KWEM every Saturday, and thus their career began.

In 1955, after naming the group Johnny Cash and the Tennessee Two, they went to Memphis to audition for Sun Records. At the audition, Johnny sang a song he had been making up lyrics to, for several years, called "Hey Porter." Phillips liked the song, so Johnny wrote "Cry, Cry, Cry!," to use for the flip side. It was good enough for Sun, so they released it. It became a hit in the south, climbing the country charts to number 14 . The group decide to follow up this hit by putting the finishing touches to the song Johnny wrote about Folsom Prison, so Sun released the follow up singles of "So Doggone Lonesome," and "Folsom Prison Blues." "Folsom Prison Blues" did very well, but years later, when he recorded it live at the prison itself, it would become a classic.

Soon after the record was released, Sam Phillips called and asked him if he would like to be booked on the Louisiana Hayride, which, next to WSM, and "The Grand Ole Opry," was the biggest show, on the radio, in country music. The group drove the 350 miles to Shreveport to do the show. (Elvis was also there at the time). When they performed their first two songs, the audience went wild for them, so they were asked to stay as regulars on the show. They received $12 each for performing, and they drove back that night.

Johnny's first royalty check from Sun amounted to $12 also, but now he received his second, for $6,000.00. Bob Neal, a Memphis disc jockey who was booking Elvis agreed to book Johnny as well, so now he began to tour the south in country music packaged shows, from Georgia to Colorado.

In 1956 Sun released "I Walk the Line," which became Johnny's first major hit. It was followed, in rapid succession, by "Train of Love," "There You Go," "Don't Make Me Go," and "Next in Line." "I Walk the Line" would be such a big hit for him that he would use it as his theme song, in the future.

At the tender age of 24, Johnny was a recording star. The record crossed over to the pop charts because of its rhythm and blues influence. The studio pianists, were two newcomers — Charlie Rich, and Jerry Lee Lewis, and both were responsible for the rich sound that emerged.

Johnny had a rich sense of history, and religion, and throughout the years these influences would show up on many of his albums. The unique sound that Luther created on the guitar, by picking cords, one note at a time, with the strings muted by the palm of his hand, was to become Johnny's trademark.

In 1958, Johnny met Don Law, an A & R (Artist & Repertoire) specialist at Columbia Records, who soon convinced him to join the label. Cash agreed, as long as Carl Perkins, his friend, could go, too. He was now on the road for eight months out of the year.

The strain soon began to show on Johnny, the former Arkansas farm boy, and he moved his family to southern California. He left the Grand Ole Opry, moved from Sun Records to Columbia, and decided to try out for the movies.

At Columbia, he had enormous success with "Ballad of a Teenage Queen," "Guess Things Happen That Way," and "Ways of a Woman in Love." Now, however, he began to drift away from the simplicity of his first recordings, at Sun, and to use the echo chamber, choruses, piano, and overdubbing.

In 1959, the 27-year-old man began earning upwards of $250,000 per year. He was becoming moody and depressed and used pills and alcohol as crutches. In the early 60's he moved away from his family and began to frequent New York's Greenwich Village and other centers of folk music throughout the country. He also began performing at night clubs, which he did not like doing. This work led to jobs in the big cities, so he hired a drummer named W. S. Holland, to please his new audience. He didn't really like drums, either.

Despite his mental and physical problems, Johnny managed to continue to sell records to the rock and roll, country, and folk music lovers of the country. He did a remake of Jimmie Rodgers' "I'm in the Jailhouse Now," in 1962, followed by the great "Ring Of Fire" in 1963. This song, co-written by June Carter and Merle Kilgore, more or less symbolized his existence. At this point, June became more and more interested in Johnny and helped him to control his life.

In the mid-'60's June teamed up with him to perform many successful duets, and "Mama" Maybelle and The Carter Family (now Maybelle's sister and her daughters) began to play on his shows and back him on records. June was a steadying influence on Johnny, and they were married in 1967. By now he had moved away from drugs and alcohol and began to rise even more in popularity. He and June recorded "Jackson," "Guitar Pickin' Man," "If I Were a Carpenter," and the fabulous sounding "Daddy Sang Bass" in 1969. The Johnny Cash show, on the road, was one of the most dramatic, polished, professional shows of any recording star in the world. The addition of the Carter Family, and the Statler Brothers, with Carl Perkins, all performing their acts, led to a crescendo of styles and excitement, constantly building, until Cash would step out of the darkness and announce "Hello, I'm Johnny Cash." In 1968, after many national television appearances, ABC offered him his own summer replacement show to be broadcast in 1969. The show was hailed by everyone for its quality of presentation and style. It was during this show, in 1969, that he introduced one of his most popular songs, the novelty "A Boy Named Sue," which sold well over a million copies. While the show continued to do well for several years, eventually the network began squeezing it out.

> Those years [1958 to 1968] were marked by key achievements in repertory expansion, recording activity, and road-show innovations. At the end of that decade came the greatest national recognition any country singer had ever received and a new personal stability, through his breaking the pill habit and his marriage to June Carter — as well as a return to Nashville as a base of operations. *[Malone & McCulloh, 1975, p. 297]*

It was during these years that Johnny became the first country music artist to develop the "concept" album, beginning with *Ride This Train* (1960), and continuing with; *The Lure of the Grand Canyon* (1961), *Blood, Sweat and Tears* (1963), *Bitter Tears* (1964), *Ballads of the True West* (1965), *From Sea to Shining Sea* (1967), *The Holy Land* (1968), *America* (1972), *The Gospel Road* (1973), *Ragged Old Flag* (1974), *The Highwayman* (1985) and *Highwayman 2* (1990), with Waylon Jennings, Willie Nelson, and Kris Kristofferson, and finally, *Heros* (1986), with Waylon Jennings. He also managed to demonstrate his unique sense of humor in a comedy album *Everybody Loves a Nut* (1966), and his children's album, *The Johnny Cash Children's Album* (1975).

The year 1969 was a banner year for Johnny: the Country Music Association named him both Entertainer of the Year, and Male Vocalist of the Year. He also won back-to-back Grammy Awards in 1968 and 1969 as Best Male Country Music Performer, as well as other honors and awards.

During the late '60's and early '70's when Sun Records was taken over by Shelby Singleton, they released most of his old records and smothered a new generation with his sound.

Johnny still remains one of the most respected singers, writers,

and storytellers in country music

Carl Lee Perkins

Carl Perkins was born in Tiptonville, Tennessee, on April 9, 1932, the second of three brothers. He led rather a quiet life, in a large family, as was the typical of the time. The family ran a welfare-supported farm. In the 50's, his family moved near Jackson, Mississippi, where Carl worked in a battery factory. A local black sharecropper sold him a guitar for $3.00, and Carl spent days and nights listening to the radio, and playing his guitar.

When Carl was 15, his family moved east to sharecrop in the hills around Jackson. He worked in the cotton fields for two years and then in a dairy, getting up at 2 A. M. each morning, in order to milk 65 cows. He even tried to become a baker.

In 1947, he relocated in Bemis, as a laborer in a battery plant. When he entered a talent show, he was so impressed with the reaction of the people that he formed the Perkins Brothers Band, with his brothers Jay B. and Clayton, whom he taught to play guitar.

In 1953, he purchased a $150 Les Paul guitar, and began to develop what would be one of the most unique musical styles, which some say crosses the bluegrass sounds of Bill Monroe, with the blues sound of John Lee Hooker. This style would be blended with the Elvis sound, and would be copied by many for years to come.

Carl moved with his wife Valda Crider to Parkview Courts, in Jackson and sent demos out to record companies. In December 1954, Sam Phillips gave him an audition. In February 1955, Carl recorded "Movie Mag" and "Turn Around" on the Flip label, which was an affiliate of Sun Records. The reception around Memphis was very good.

Carl signed with Sun Records in 1955, and began to tour with his brothers, Clayton and Jay B., as well as with W.S. Holland, (Carl's brother Luther was with Johnny Cash) . He released a number of songs that year, but the one that really made it for him was "Blue Suede Shoes," his own composition. It was just this sound that Sam needed to replace

Elvis whom he had just sold to RCA. A few months later, however, RCA released Elvis' version, and the song became Elvis's. Carl's version, however, managed to sell over 2 million copies.

Carl toured with Johnny Cash through out the 50's, and when Cash moved to California, Carl did too. Carl was so close to Johnny that he also began to consume alcohol and pills. Like Cash, he overcame his addiction. He was on his way to stardom; this married man, with three kids would dare to challenge the great Elvis Presley at his own sound. Unfortunately, it was not meant to be, as tragedy would soon hit. On March 22, 1956, on the way to New York City to perform on "The Ed Sullivan Show" and "The Perry Como Hour," his car crashed just outside Delaware. After the accident, he just could not make a comeback; even when he changed to Columbia Records and had some measure of hits on the label, he was never destined for stardom.

> Carl Perkins became the first white southern rock 'n' roller
> to reach the American pop top twenty. "Blue Suede Shoes"
> got there just one week before "Heartbreak Hotel".
> *[Rogers, 1982, p. 36]*

In 1963, Carl moved to Decca Records, and then to Dollie. As a featured artist in "The Johnny Cash Show," both on television, and on the road, from 1969-71, he gained many new fans. This exposure gave him a chance to return to Columbia Records with a new contract, in 1968. Although his career never flew high, several of his records hit the charts, and he gained quite a following.

In 1963, he was asked to join Chuck Berry on a 30 day tour of England, so he set out to make a comeback overseas. In England, he ran into a new group of musicians who called themselves the Beatles. They told him that they were big fans of his, and asked if he would mind if they recorded some of his music. He thought that was great.

His last hitch with Columbia lasted until 1973, when he went to Mercury for one album. He still records and plays with many famous artists, including Johnny Cash, as back up and support vocalist and guitarist.

Carl continues to represent the sounds of rockabilly music on records, more than any other artist in history. He has been a part of "The Johnny Cash Show" for many years, and has remained close with Cash.

Jerry Lee Lewis

Jerry Lee Lewis was born in Ferriday, Louisiana, on September 29, 1935, the second son of Elmo and Mary Ethel Lewis. The first son, Elmo, Jr. was killed in a car accident at the age of 9. He also had two sisters, Frankie Jean and Linda Gail.

For about four decades, Jerry Lee Lewis has outperformed other performers, and outdone many great musicians, first in the genre of rockabilly, then in rock and roll, and finally in country music.

Jerry Lee started playing piano at the age of four. It was at an early age that Jerry Lee and his cousins (Mickey Gilley and Jimmy Swaggart) would sneak into the black areas and go to the local honky tonks to inhale the blues sounds of the times — sounds that were considered sinful to the pure bred country and western and Gospel white people of the south.

Jerry Lee's father would travel around the area and have him perform from the back of his flatbed truck. This was a great training ground for an up-and-coming entertainer, and for his part in the movie *High School Confidential,* which would come much later.

In 1949, he joined in a band plugging a car dealer, where he played for 20 minutes and received $13 in donations, and decided to go pro. By 1950, he was working at the Blue Cat Night Club, in Natchez, and on Saturdays he had a 20-minute radio show on WNAT.

Jerry Lee quit high school and attended Southwestern Bible Institute, in Waxahachie, Texas. The school's rules included clean conduct and conversation, modest appearance in dress, high standards of moral life, and a deep consecration and devotion to spiritual life. Needless to say, Jerry Lee didn't last long, and was expelled.

Next, he became a door-to-door salesman, but he quit in 1952. He was extremely successful as a salesman, but the sheriff was not too enthused with his methods. He began playing drums for a blues pianist. His first marriage was to Dorothy Barton, age 16, who was a preacher's daughter; the marriage lasted one year.

In 1953, he married Jane Mitcham Natchez, who gave birth to Jerry Lee, Jr., who would later turn to drugs. He died in a car accident in 1973. The following year Jerry Lee went to Shreveport, Louisiana to try and join the Louisiana Hayride, but was turned down by Slim Whitman. Although Jerry Lee was raised on gospel music, it would be his love of the blues that kept him going, and later inspired the outbursts of rockabilly music that would overpower the nation in the future.

In 1956, Jerry Lee moved to Memphis, Tennessee, and played backup piano for many artists at Sun Records, with the likes of Carl Perkins, Billy Lee Riley, and even with Elvis. Sun's big break of selling Elvis to RCA was also Jerry Lee's big break because Sun was now hungry for talented artists in the same genre. The label soon signed Jerry Lee to a recording contract after he cornered Jack Clement (Sun's A&R man) one day, and played every kind of music imaginable in a monster test session. His first release was "Crazy Arms," a knockoff of the Ray Price hit. The song was a mild success, but never made the charts.

In his second session, after first recording "It'll Be Me," he was told to play whatever he wanted to. After some time, Jerry finally turned to his band and said, "Hey, let's play that Shakin' thing," and that's how "Whole Lotta' Shakin' Going On" was created. The song went on to sell over one million copies.

This first great hit, "Whole Lotta' Shakin' Going On" was not played by many white radio stations at the time, because of its sexual overtones. The song was taken from the black blues culture, where the overtones were considered normal. Nevertheless, the song managed to stay on the charts for 29 weeks.

Jerry Lee began touring with the various artists at Sun, including Johnny Cash and Carl Perkins. At one of the performances, they both told Jerry Lee that he should move around on stage. He argued that it was easy for them, because they played guitar, but not for him, since he played piano. Carl then asked him if he could play standing up. He said he could play lying down if he had to. During his act, he began to stand up, his boot hit the stool, sending it off the stage. As he bent over his long blond hair came streaming down. He looked like a wild animal, and the audience went crazy. So crazy, that Carl turned to Johnny and said, "Maybe we did the wrong thing." But, as we know, it became the major asset in his performance.

Now, when he did a show, he was reckless. He would generally play the piano with his feet, his elbows, his backside, upside down, or in any style he could imagine that would help the burning style of music and the turbulent pace of his delivery keep going on and on.

It was said that his performances were so unbelievable, that even Elvis was acceptable to the adults, after they saw Jerry Lee perform. He was definitely not Perry Como, or even Pat Boone. In August of 1957 "Whole Lotta" Shakin Going On" would accomplish something that only songs by Elvis would do: it became number one on both the country and the Pop charts at the same time. His music, as well as his piano playing was wild and ridiculous, just what the teenagers wanted to see.

His music led to an appearance on "The Steve Allen Show," on national television, which was the closest competitor to "The Ed Sullivan Show" at the time. Steve soon got into the act, throwing chairs and other objects around the stage area in tune with the wild sounds coming from the piano on the stage. The performance brought an enormous amount of telephone calls from adults, who thought Jerry Lee's performance was "outrageous" and from teenagers, who wanted to know more about the new performer. Rumor had it that he was basically shy, until Carl Perkins and Johnny Cash told him to get wild and carry on.

Sun followed the song with a second smash, "Great Balls of Fire," in November, which proved that Jerry Lee would remain a sensation for some time, or at least that's what everyone thought. In February of 1958, Sun released "Breathless," backed with "Down the Line," but for some reason the record was slow to take off. Sun merged with Dick Clark's sponsor for his new Saturday night show, Beechnut Gum, and they decided to push both the gum and the record with a giant mail order deal. The idea was tremendous; for months, Sam Phillips and everyone else at Sun spent days and nights sending autographed copies of the record to teenagers throughout the country, making both the gum and the record a huge success.

Jerry Lee had always had it written in his contract that he was to be the last person to perform on any road show. On one occasion, on an "Alan Freed Show," in 1958, at the Paramount Theater, in New York, he was told that Chuck Berry was to perform last. When he performed "Whole Lotta' Shakin' Going On" at the end of his performance, he set the piano on fire. As he went off stage, he supposedly turned to Chuck Berry and said "Follow that, Nigger!."

His music would continue to be popular with the teenagers of the time for a number of years, until he married his thirteen year old second cousin, Myra Gail, the daughter of his bass player. this act started a descent from power which he would take years to regain, with a new generation, in a different genre, altogether.

Sun had arranged for a huge tour of Europe, starting in Great Britain. When Jerry Lee landed in London, he dared to make fun of Buckingham Palace and the Queen; he was sarcastic, and egotistical. The British press decided to crucify him. They published the news of his marriage to a child, and wouldn't let up. He was booed wherever he went. In spite of his denial of the problem, he decided to return to the United States. His career would never be the same.

The Sun release of "High School Confidential," backed with "Fools Like Me," a beautiful country song, was a total disappointment to both Jerry Lee and Sun. Even though the record eventually sold over 1 million copies around the world, it was slow getting there. Even the tie in with the movie of the same name couldn't save the record. The sales of his records were sinking. To try and overcome this crisis, in July 1958, Sun released a record in the style of "The Flying Saucers" using Jerry and a popular disc jockey on the record. But no matter what was tried, "The Return of Jerry Lee Lewis" did not work. Also, in 1958, Sam's brother, Judd, left Sun to form Judd Records, in Sheffield, Alabama.

Jerry Lee's next release, "Break Up," though an excellent song, was again somewhat of a disappointment, as would be all the rest of his releases into the '60's including a spectacular version of "What'd I Say," made more popular by Ray Charles.

In 1959, Myra gave birth to their son, Steve Allen Lewis, who would drown in a swimming pool accident in 1962. In 1963, she gave birth to Phoebe Allen Lewis. She and Jerry Lee were divorced in 1970.

Jerry Lee was the longest resident star at Sun records, and continued to record for them up to the end. Starting in 1958, his records were banned from airplay, and his tours were cancelled, all because of his marriage and his attitude. It would not be until later in the mid-'60's when he would be heard from again.

Country music was not exactly a new genre for Lewis, since most of the flip sides of his great rockabilly and rock and roll hits were country songs, even some Hank Williams' tunes. So, in 1964, with Sun Records slowly fading away, one of the last artists to do so left the company to join the Smash Records division of Mercury Records.

For a number of years, Smash tried to continue his efforts in rock, but nothing really hit. It was not until a decision was made to try country music, that success was achieved.

In 1966, Smash released Jerry Lee's first country album entitled *Country Songs*. Jerry Lee followed this with a number of different kinds of sounds on album, but nothing seemed to work for him. He was about to quit the label, when he was convinced to return for one more session, with country music as the genre. The change clicked, and in 1968, Mercury released the next big song, "Another Place, Another Time." Jerry was back on the music charts, this time in country music. He followed this hit with "What's Made Millwaukee Famous Has Made a Loser Out of Me."

During the late 60's and early '70's it was the rock and roll revival shows that kept him going. During the '60's after the takeover of the Sun catalog by Shelby Singleton, a number of his older cuts on Sun became hits, in the Country Music genre: They were "One Minute Past Eternity," "I Can't Seem to Say Goodbye," and "Waiting For a Train."

In 1970, Jerry Lee graduated from the Smash Record subsidiary to the major Mercury label, and continued to have successful releases. In 1971, he married Jaren Pate, and in April of 1972, they had their only child, Lori Leigh Lewis. In 1974, Jaren filed for separation from Jerry Lee. In June of 1982, she was found dead.

In 1979, Jerry Lee made another change, this time to Elektra Records, and cut his first LP in Los Angeles, which was his first session outside Nashville for some time. Again he proved himself with a number of hits, this time with a combination of country, blues, and rock.

In 1981, he suffered physical problems with a tear in his stomach, and the time involved with recuperating drove him crazy; it wasn't until August that he was taken off the critical list. By 1982, he had regained enough strength to continue his trade, which he still does today, in spite of his age, and his physical disabilities.

On June 7, 1983, Jerry Lee married a Shawnee named Michelle Stevens, a 25-year old waitress from Garden City, Michigan. Seventy-eight days later, she was found dead from an overdose of methadone. On April 24, 1984 he married 22 year old Kerrie McCarver.

In the years following, he was arrested for attempted murder on Elvis; he has been arrested for drunkenness, and assault; and he was brought to trial by the Internal Revenue Service, for back taxes. He has suffered near strokes, and heart attacks, but the Killer goes on.

Charlie Rich

He was born in Colt, Arkansas, on December 14, 1932. No other rockabilly artist had to wait as long as Charlie Rich to obtain the star status that he long deserved.

Charlie was schooled in gospel music as a child, and his parents were Missionary Baptists who were very active in the church. His mother played organ, and both parents were members of a gospel quartet, where harmonious singing reigned supreme.

By the time he attended Consolidated High School in Forrest City, his interest and participation in music had expanded. While his environment was that of country music, he began to develop an acute interest in jazz. He also developed a "cute" interest in an attractive young woman by the name of Margaret Ann, whom he married after they graduated from high school.

Margaret Ann was Charlie's biggest supporter as he tried to advance in the music world. He played in many local groups as a teenager, usually normal dance music, but occasionally jazz. He attended the University of Arkansas for a year, as a music major, then he joined the Air Force, in 1951.

While he was stationed in Oklahoma for three years, he formed his own jazz group. He then organized a singing group called the Velvetones, that even had its' own television show for awhile. After the service he tended to lean toward the blues area of music. Now, however, he had a desire to try farming and left music for the weekends.

Margaret Ann urged him to get ahead in music, but not much happened for several years. Finally, she called Bill Justis, A & R man at Sun Records, and asked for a chance to have him hear Charlie's tapes. They liked what they heard and began to use him as a session man for various performers, including Johnny Cash and Roy Orbison, and to use his songs for other artists. Many of these songs became hits for other artists, "The Ways of a Woman in Love" and "I Just Thought That You'd Like to Know" (Johnny Cash), and "Break Up" and "I'll Make It All Up To You" (Jerry Lee Lewis).

At the end of the decade, Sun began releasing a few of Charlie's recordings. On his third release he made the charts with a heavy rockabilly number called "Lonely Weekends." Unfortunately Sun was on the wain by this time, and there was no one to push for him and promote him as was done with the great artists before him.

When Sun faded out of the business in the mid-'60's he turned to Mercury Records under the direction of Shelby Singleton, who would later take over Sun. His first single, on the Smash label, entitled "Mohair Sam," made the charts in 1965. He liked the company, and he liked Jerry Kennedy, who produced most of the country songs for Mercury, but once more, there was no follow-up hit.

About 2 years later, Charlie signed with RCA, and again, he received little promotional push, even though one of the songs, "Big Boss Man" was a fair hit. At this time, Charlie began to hit the pills and the booze. He moved to Hi Records, and still received no noticeable recognition. In 1968, he signed with Epic Records.

Epic teamed him with producer Billy Sherrill, who was pushing out the formatted country music style, and making hits. Billy had great faith in Charlie's style and his ability, and together they worked on finding Charlie's formula for success. But, just as before, they seemed to be going nowhere. Though his songs made the charts, none were at the upper level. Some of the songs that made it were, "Big Boss Man," "Who Will the Next Fool Be," "Nice and Easy," and "Life's Little Ups and Downs," the latter written by Margaret Ann.

When Bill Williams joined Epic, in the promotional department, in Nashville, he fell in love with the latest release by Charlie, entitled "Behind Closed Doors." He began a mountain of promotional material to push the record, and it paid off. The single became a major hit in 1973, and earned a gold record. More important, however, the follow-up record, "The Most Beautiful Girl" earned another gold record. His albums began to reach high levels on the charts, and he was on his way.

At the 1973 Country Music Association Awards celebration, in Nashville, Charlie picked up three awards; Best Song, Best Record and Best Male Artist. When he sang "Behind Closed Doors," his fellow musicians gave him a standing ovation.

His success at Epic would continue, and in 1978 he moved to United Artists, but kept Billy Sherrill at the controls in the studio. He continued to obtain moderate success with his recordings, because he now had a good following.

Roy Orbison

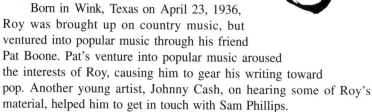

Roy Orbiison's writing and performing from the late '50's through the 60's created a platform for many future artists and earned him the deepest respect of them all.

Born in Wink, Texas on April 23, 1936, Roy was brought up on country music, but ventured into popular music through his friend Pat Boone. Pat's venture into popular music aroused the interests of Roy, causing him to gear his writing toward pop. Another young artist, Johnny Cash, on hearing some of Roy's material, helped him to get in touch with Sam Phillips.

Roy sent Sam Phillips a copy of "Ooby Dooby" because it was the type of music that Sun was using at the time, not the kind of music that Roy wanted to do. Sam loved the song and released it. It was a major hit in 1956, selling 300,000 copies.

Roy soon moved to Nashville, and signed to write songs with Acuff-Rose Music Publishers. One of the first songs he wrote was "Claudette" which became a major hit by the Everly Brothers. After he was in Nashville for awhile, he switched to Monument Records, a relatively new company. Now he was given the chance to write and record ballads, what he wanted to do in the first place.

His second recording for the company, "Only The Lonely," was a beautiful ballad — so beautiful, in fact, that it sold over 2 million copies. It was the song that started the ball rolling, and for Roy the ball continued rolling out of the '50's and into the first half of the 60's. The song "Blue Angel," also released in 1960, sold over a million copies as well.

In 1961, he would sell over one million copies of "Running Scared," "Cryin'" backed with "Candy Man," and "I'm "Hurtin'." In 1962, "Dream Baby," and "Workin' for the Man" would sell over 1 million copies, as would "In Dreams," "Mean Woman Blues" and "I'm Fallin'" in 1963.

Roy continued to knock out hit after hit in his infamous style, with the ya ya's and violins, and large orchestrations. His high pitched voice had an enormous range and seemed to bring the songs to life.

In the summer of 1964, he released his second giant hit "Oh, Pretty Woman" (which sold over one million in the United States alone), and "It's Over." Soon the tall dark-haired man, with the big smile, usually dressed in black and wearing sun glasses, could be seen on TV everywhere. Although his popularity began to fade in the United States after this time, it never faded in England, where he continued to sell.

In 1965, he moved to MGM Records, where he was promised more freedom in the production end of recording, and his first release "Ride Away," was fairly successful. It led him to go over seas to England on a serious concert tour. That year, however, saw his wife, Claudette, killed in a motorcycle accident, a tragedy from which he never really recovered. It would affect his life, and his creative juices for a number of years to come.

Through the late '60's he continued to release one after another for MGM, but none of them seemed to have the impact of his previous hits on Monument. It was a tremendous strain on him, with his memories of his wife, his writing, producing, and performing at a ridiculous pace, and he just couldn't seem to put it all together.

In 1968, just as he seemed to be recovering, 2 of his 3 children died in a fire in his home near Nashville. He never really quite recovered from it all long enough to produce the great sounds of his early years.

In the late '80's he made a major return to recording with his signing to Virgin Records. Once again he was making hits, this time for a new generation of teenagers. He also merged with several greats of music, including Bob Dylan, to form the group The Travelling Wilburys. Roy died of a heart attack, in Madison, Tennessee, on December 8, 1988.

Several television specials and videos have been done for this man, demonstrating his love, his talent and his music. He earned the respect and admiration of almost everyone in the recording business. The reverence in which he was held, by other artists, was evident by these special programs.

His remake of "Crying", as a duet, with K.D. Lang, would make the top ten, after his death, as would his recordings of "Mystery Girl", and "You Got It". So in the end, after many years of failure, he was once again on the top of the charts.

Warren Smith

Warren Smith was born in Louise, Mississippi on February 7, 1932. Sam Phillips had heard him singing at the Cotton Club, in West Memphis, and asked him to cut a few songs. In February of 1956, he recorded "Rock and Roll Ruby" which had moderate success on the charts — not bad for a first shot.

In March 1956, he headed for Sun records with a fiddler, a guitarist, a bass player, and a drummer, and recorded 4 songs: "Who Took My Baby," "Movin' On," " I Couldn't Take a Chance," and "Black Jack David" — none of which were even passable hits. In August, however, he recorded "Ubangi Stomp," which was released in September, and was a smash.

"Ubangi Stomp," was the perfect example of the necessary sound for a hit, in both rock and roll and in the rockabilly genre. It was a wild and crazy nonsense type of song, rather silly, in fact, that implied the "I just don't care" attitude.

Warren left Sun in 1959, and went to Liberty Records where he had seven country hits from 1960-1964. Later, he recorded for Mercury, Skill Records in Texas, and Jubal. His last release was in 1976. On January 30, 1980 he died of a heart attack.

The Others

More than any other record label, Sun was thrust into the midst of the new music; perhaps because its location in the South, or because of the inspiration of Sam Phillips, himself. More rockabilly artists performed on the Sun label than any other: Sonny Burgess, Ray Smith, Onie Wheeler, Malcom Yelvington, Rudy Grayzell, and more. More musicians flocked to Sun's studios to take part in the new creation: Bill Black, James Burton, Scotty Moore, D. J. Fontana, all of whom were blues-inspired musicians that ended up in the rockabilly genre.

Jack Clement would only record a few songs for Sun, and later would record an album for Electra, in 1978, but none of these would be hits, of any kind. Yet, because of his experience at Sun Records, in both the recording and engineering aspects of the business, he would aspire to greater heights behind the scenes,similar to what Jimmy Bowen did.

In 1971, he formed JMI Records, which had several minor hits, but folded in 1974. Jack would become an A & R man, and a producer, with RCA amongst others. He would eventually produce Charlie Pride, and help to establish the sound that would make Charlie a big star in country music.

In the late 70's, he produced many of the duet albums featuring Johnny Cash, and Waylon Jennings.

Ray Smith would have an enormous hit with "Rockin' Little Angel", on Sam's brother's label, Judd, in 1959, and later go on to have several minor hits on many country music labels. The Elvis sound alike curse, however, would get him, and he would never become a star. He eventually committed suicide on November 29, 1979.

The following codes and classifications are used in the discography.

R	Reissue of a previous release
Rx	Additional Reissue of previous release
1	The first recording of the song.
2	The second recording ...etc.
33	A 33 1/3 speed single release
S	Stereo (noted only on early singles and EP's)
CSI	Classical Sound Inc.
Curb/C	Curb/CEMA
KP	Koch Presents
LGP	Live Gold Promotions
Philips Int	Philips International
PSP	Polygram Special Products
	In The '80's and '90's Polygram is used interchangeably with MGM and Polydor is used interchangeably with Mercury.
SMC	Special Music Company
SMSP	Sony Music Special Products
Sun/SSS	Sun/SSS International..Label used for Sun and Philips International product after the takeover of Sun by SSS International.
Warner Bros	Warner Brothers

Recordings are listed chronologically under each artist's heading.
Most CD listings are available on tape with similar numbers
Most LP Records are no longer available
Artists are arranged alphabetically.

Billy Adams(and the Rock-A-Teers)-

Singles

You Heard Me Knocking/True Love Will Come Your Way	-Dot 15689	(1957)
Baby I'm Bugged/Short Hair and a Turtle Neck	-Decca 30724	(1958)
Rock Pretty Mama	-ABC/Paramount	(1958)
You Gotta Have a Duck Tail/Walking Star	-Nau-Voo 802	(1958)
That's My Baby/(Return of)All American Boy	-Nau-Voo 805	(1959)
Blue Eyed Ella/Fun House	-Nau-Voo 808	(1959)
Rock Pretty Mama	-Quincy 932	(1959)
Count Every Star/Peggy's Party	-Capitol 4308	(1960)
Can't Get Enough/The Gods Were Angry With Me	-Capitol m4373	(1960)
Darling, Take My Hand/Tender Years	-Fern 807	(1960)
Tattle Tale/Born to Be a Loser	-Fern 808	(1961)
Betty and Dupree/Got My MoJo Workin'	-Sun 389	(1963)
Trouble in Mind/Lookin' for Mary Ann	-Sun 391	(1964)
Reconsider Baby/Ruby Jane	-Sun 394	(1964)
Big M/My Happiness	-Apt 25072	(1964)
Open The Door Richard/Rock Me Baby	-Sun 401	(1965)

Tommy Blake(and the Rhythm Rebels)-

Singles

Cool It (Baby)	-Buddy 107	
Flat Foot Sam/Lordy Hoody	-Sun 278	(1957)
I Dig You Baby/Sweety Pie	-Sun 300	(1958)
Freedom	-RCA 6925	

Edwin Bruce (Ed Bruce)-

Singles

Rock Boppin' Baby/More Than Yesterday	-Sun 276	(1957)
Sweet Woman/Part of My Life	-Sun 292	(1958)
See The Big Man Cry/You Need a New Love	-Wand 140	(1963)
The Greatest Man	-Wand	(1963)

Sonny Burgess-

Singles

Red Headed Woman/We Wanna Boogie	-Sun 247	(1956)
Restless/Ain't Got a Thing	-Sun 263	(1957)
My Bucket's Got a Hole in It/Sweet Misery	-Sun 285	(1957)
Itchy/Thunderbird	-Sun 304	(1959)
Odessa	-Razorback 136	(1959)
	-International	
Sadie's Back in Town/A Kiss Goodnite	-Philips Int 3551	(1959)

Johnny Cash-

Singles

Hey Porter/Cry! Cry! Cry!	-Sun 221	(1955)
Hey Porter/Cry! Cry! Cry!	(R)-Sun 1	(1955)
Folsom Prison Blues/So Doggone Lonesome	-Sun 232	(1955)
Folsom Prison Blues/So Doggone Lonesone	(R)-Sun 3	(1955)
I Walk the Line/Get Rhythm	-Sun 241	(1956)
I Walk the Line/Get Rhythm	(R)-Sun 7	(1956)
Train of Love/There You Go	-Sun 258	(1956)
Next in Line/Don't Make Me Go	-Sun 266	(1957)
Next in Line/Don't Make Me Go	(R)-Sun 17	(1957)
Home of the Blues/Give My Love to Rose	-Sun 279	(1957)
Home of the Blues/Give My Love to Rose	(R)-Sun 20	(1957)
Ballad of a Teenage Queen/Big River	-Sun 283	(1957)
Ballad of a Tecnage Queen/Big River	(R)-Sun 22	(1957)
Guess Things Happen That Way/Come in Stranger	-Sun 295	(1958)
Guess Things Happen That Way/Come in Stranger	(R)-Sun 27	(1958)
The Ways of a Woman in Love/You're the Nearest		
Thing to Heaven	-Sun 302	(1958)
It's Just About Time/I Just Thought You'd Like to Know	-Sun 309	(1958)
It's Just About Time/I Just Thought You'd Like to Know	(R)-Sun 32	(1958)
Thanks a Lot/Luther Played the Boogie	-Sun 316	(1959)
Thanks a Lot/Luther Played the Boogie	(R)-Sun 35	(1959)
Katy Too/ I Forgot to Remember	-Sun 321	(1959)
Katy Too/ I Forgot to Remember	(R)-Sun 37	(1959)
Goodbye Little Darling/You Tell Me	-Sun 331	(1959)
Goodbye Little Darling/You Tell Me	(R)-Sun 40	(1959)
Straight A's in Love/I Love You Because	-Sun 334	(1960)
Straight A's in Love/I Love You Because	(R)-Sun 41	(1960)
Down the Street to 301/Story of a Broken Heart	-Sun 343	(1960)
Down the Street to 301/Story of a Broken Heart	(R)-Sun 43	(1960)
Mean Eyed Cat/The Port of Lonely Hearts	-Sun 347	(1960)
Oh Lonesome Me/Life Goes On	-Sun 355	(1961)
My Treasure/Sugartime	-Sun 363	(1961)
Blue Train/Born to Lose	-Sun 376	(1962)
Blue Train/Born to Lose	(R)-Sun 54	(1962)
Wide Open Road/Belshazar	-Sun 392	(1964)
Wide Open Road/Belshazar	(R)-Sun 58	(1964)
What Do I Care/ All Over Again	-Columbia 41251	(1958)
Don't Take Your Guns to Town/That's Enough	-Columbia 41313	(1958)
I Still Miss Someone	-Columbia	(1959)
Frankie's Man, Johnny/The Troubadour	-Columbia 41371	(1959)
I Got Stripes/Five Feet High And Rising	-Columbia 41427	(1959)
You Dreamer You	-Columbia	(1959)
Don't Take Your Guns to Town/Five Feet High and Rising	(R)-Columbia 33006	(1959)
I Got Stripes	(R)-Columbia 10279	(1959)
Little Drummer Boy/I'll Remember You	-Columbia 41481	(1960)

-Johnny Cash Cont'd-

Smiling Bill Mccall	-Columbia 41618	(1960)
Second Honeymoon/Honky-Tonk Girl	-Columbia 41707	(1960)
Going to Memphis/Loading Coal	-Columbia 41804	(1960)
Girl in Saskatoon/Locomotive Man	-Columbia 41920	(1961)
(The Rebel) Johnny Yuma	-Columbia 41995	(1961)
Tennessee Flat-Top Box	-Columbia 42147	(1961)
Bonanza/Pick a Bail O'Cotton	-Columbia 42512	(1961)
The Big Battle	-Columbia	(1962)
Busted	-Columbia 42665	(1962)
Ring of Fire/I'd Still Be There	-Columbia 42788	(1962)
The Matador/Still in Town	-Columbia 42880	(1962)
In the Jailhouse Now	-Columbia	(1962)
Understand Your Man/Dark as a Dungeon	-Columbia 42964	(1963)
It Ain't Me Babe/Time and Time Again	-Columbia 43145	(1963)
It Ain't Me Babe/Ring of Fire	(R)-Columbia 33089	(1964)
Understand Your Man/It Ain't Me Babe	(R)-Columbia 33091	(1964)
Orange Blossom Special/All of God's Children Ain't Free	-Columbia 43206	(1964)
Folsom Prison Blues	-Columbia 43313	(1964)
Sons of Katie Elder	-Columbia 43342	(1965)
Mr. Garfield	-Columbia	(1965)
Happy To Be With You	-Columbia	(1965)
I Walk the Line/Orange Blossom Special	(R)-Columbia 33101	(1965)
The One on the Right Is on the Left	-Columbia 43496	(1966)
Put the Sugar to Bed/You Beat All I Ever Saw	-Columbia 43921	(1966)
The One on the Right Is on the Left/Boa Constrictor	(R)-Columbia 33109	(1966)
Folsom Prison Blues/Daddy Sang Bass	(R)-Columbia 33153	(1969)

(Other releases tend to be Country and Folk)

Albums

Johnny Cash with His Hot and Blue Guitar	-Sun SLP-1220	(1956)
Johnny Cash Sings the Songs That Made Him Famous	-Sun SLP-1235	(1958)
The Fabulous Johnny Cash	-Columbia CS-8122	(1958)
Johnny Cash—Greatest!	-Sun SLP-1240	(1959)
Hymns by Johnny Cash	-Columbia CS-8125	(1959)
Songs of Our Soil	-Columbia CS-8148	(1959)
Johnny Cash Sings Hank Williams	-Sun SLP-1245	(1960)
Now, There Was a Song	-Columbia CS-8254	(1960)
Ride This Train	-Columbia CS-8255	(1960)
The Lure of the Grand Canyon	-Columbia CS-8422	(1961)
Now Here's Johnny Cash	-Sun SLP-1255	(1961)
Hymns From the Heart	-Columbia CS-8522	(1962)
The Sound of Johnny Cash	-Columbia CS-8602	(1962)
Blood, Sweat and Tears	-Columbia CS-8730	(1963)
All Aboard the Blue Train	-Sun SLP-1270	(1963)
Ring of Fire:The Best of Johnny Cash	-Columbia CS-8853	(1963)
Christmas Spirit	-Columbia CS-8917	(1963)
The Original Sun Sound of Johnny Cash	-Sun SLP-1275	(1964)
Rock Island Line	-Hilltop JS6101	

-Johnny Cash Cont'd-

Rock Island Line(Longenes Symphonet with Jeannie C. Riley)	-LS-205U	
The Heart of Johnny Cash (radio and TV special 2 LP set)	-Columbia 2000	
I Walk the Line	-Columbia 8990	(1964)
Big River	-Hilltop 6118	
Bitter Tears	-Columbia 9048	(1964)
Orange Blossom Special	-Columbia 9109	(1964)
Mean As Hell	-Columbia 9246	(1965)
The Sons of Katie Elder	-Columbia 2820	(1965)
Johnny Cash Sings Ballads of the True West (2 LP)	-Columbia 2S-838	(1965)
Everybody Loves a Nut	-Columbia 9292	(1966)
I Walk the Line	(R)-Pickwick 6097	(1966)
That's What You Get for Loving Me	-Columbia 9397	(1966)
Happiness Is You	-Columbia 9337	(1966)
From Sea to Shining Sea	-Columbia 9447	(1968)
Golden Sounds of Country Music	-Harmony 11249	(1968)
Legends and Love Songs (Record Club issue)	-Columbia 363	(1968)
Johnny Cash Greatest Hits, Vol.1	-Columbia 9478	(1968)
	-United Artists	(1968)
Johnny Cash at Folsom Prison	-Columbia 9639	(1968)
This is Johnny Cash	-Harmony 11342	(1969)
Original Golden Hits, Vol. 1	-Sun/SSS 100	(1969)
Original Golden Hits, Vol. 2	-Sun/SSS 101	(1969)
Story Songs of the Trains And Rivers	-Sun/SSS 104	(1969)
Get Rhythm	-Sun/SSS 105	(1969)
Show Time	-Sun/SSS 106	(1969)
The Grand Canyon Suite	-Columbia 7425	(1969)
The Holy Land (with 3d picture cover)	-Columbia 9726	(1969)
The Holy Land	-Columbia 9766	(1969)
Johnny Cash at San Quentin	-Columbia 9827	(1969)
The Singing Story Teller	-Sun/SSS 115	(1970)
The Rough-Cut King of Country Music	-Sun/SSS 122	(1970)
Johnny Cash: The Legend	-Sun/SSS 2-118	(1970)
Hello, I'm Johnny Cash	-Columbia 9943	(1970)
The Johnny Cash Show	-Columbia 30100	(1970)
The Walls of a Prison	-Harmony 30138	(1970)
The World of Johnny Cash (2 LP)	-Columbia GP-29	(1970)
Little Fauss & Big Halsy (Movie Soundtrack)	-Columbia 30385	(1970)
I Walk the Line (Movie Soundtrack)	-Columbia 30397	(1970)
The Sound Behind Johnny Cash	-Columbia 30220	(1971)
(played by the Tennessee Three)		
Man in Black	-Columbia 30550	(1971)
The Johnny Cash Collection:His Greatest Hits, Vol. II	-Columbia 30887	(1971)
Understand Your Man	-Harmony 30916	(1971)
Johnny Cash and Jerry Lee Lewis Sing Hank Williams	-Sun/SSS 125	(1971)
Johnny Cash: the Man, the World, His Music (2 LP)	-Sun/SSS 2-126	(1971)
Original Golden Hits, Vol. 3	-Sun/SSS 127	(1971)
A Thing Called Love	-Columbia 31332	(1972)

Johnny Cash Songbook		-Harmony 31602	(1972)
America: A 200 Year Salute in Story and Song		-Columbia 31645	(1972)
Now, There Was a Song		(R)-Columbia 10019	(1973)
The Fabulous Johnny Cash		(R)-Columbia 10063	(1973)
Songs of Our Soil		(R)-Columbia 10064	(1973)
Any Old Wind That Blows		-Columbia 32091	(1973)
I Walk the Line		(R)-Nashville 2108	(1973)
Sunday Morning Coming Down		-Columbia 32240	(1973)
The Gospel Road	(2 LP)	-Columbia 32253	(1973)
Ballads of the American Indian		-Harmony 32388	(1973)
Ragged Old Flag		-Columbia 32917	(1974)
Five Feet High and Rising		-Columbia 32951	(1974)
Junkie and the Juicehead Minus Me		-Columbia 33086	(1974)
Best of Johnny Cash	(2 LP)	-Trip 8500	(1974)
Johnny Cash		-Everest S-278	(1974)
Big River		(R)-Pickwick 6118	
I Walk the Line		(R)-Album Globe 9026	
Folsom Prison Blues		(R)-Share 5001	
The Blue Train		(R)-Share 5002	
Johnny Cash Sings His Greatest Hits		(R)-Share 5003	
Country Gold		-Power Pak 246	
Children's Album		-Columbia 32898	(1975)
Johnny Cash Sings Precious Memories		-Columbia 33087	(1975)
John R. Cash		-Columbia 33370	(1975)
Johnny Cash at Folsom Prison and San Quentin	(2 LP)	-Columbia 33369	(1975)
Look at Them Beans		-Columbia 33814	(1975)
Johnny Cash: Strawberry Cake (Live)		-Columbia 34088	(1976)
One Piece at a Time		-Columbia 34193	(1976)
The Last Gunfighter Ballad		-Columbia 34314	(1977)
The Rambler		-Columbia 34833	(1977)
Johnny Cash: Greatest Hits, Vol.3		-Columbia 35637	(1978)
Superbilly		-Sun/SSS 1002	(1978)
(TV Special)		-Columbia/Suffolk	(1979)
Silver		-Columbia 36086	(1979)
A Believer Sings the Truth	(2 LP)	-Chachet 3-9001	(1979)
(Giveaway Doral cigarettes)		-Doral	(197?)
Rockabilly Blues		-Columbia 36779	(1980)
Classic Christmas		-Columbia 36866	(1980)
Baron		-Columbia 37179	(1981)
Encore		-Columbia 37355	(1981)
The Gospel Road	(2 LP)	(R)-Priority UG-32253	(1982)
Johnny Cash Sings Precious Memories		(R)-Priority PU-33087	(1982)
A Believer Sings the Truth		-Priority PU-38074	(1982)
Everlasting		-Out of Town 8019	(1982)
Original Rockabilly		-Sun/SSS SE-147	(1982)
Biggest Hits: Johnny Cash		-Columbia 38317	(1982)
Years Gone By		-Accord 7208	(1982)

-Johnny Cash Cont'd-

Johnny Cash: Gospel Singer		-Priority 38503	(1983)
Johnny 99		-Columbia 38696	(1983)
First Years	(2 LP)	-Allegiance 5017	(1984)
Johnny Cash Sings Precious Memories	(CD)	(R)-Columbia 33087	(198?)
A Believer Sings the Truth	(CD)	(R)-Columbia 38074	(198?)
Johnny Cash's Greatest Hits, Vol. 1	(CD)	(R)-Columbia 09478	(198?)
Johnny Cash at San Quentin	(CD)	(R)-Columbia 09827	(198?)
Johnny Cash's Greatest Hits, Vol. 2	(CD)	(R)-Columbia 30887	(198?)
First Years	(2 CD)	(R)-Allegiance 5017	(1984)
Johnny Cash's Biggest Hits	(CD)	(R)-Columbia 38317	
This Is Johnny Cash	(CD)	-Camden 3014	
Country Roundup		-Hilltop 6010	
Folsom Prison Blues		(R)-Share 5001	
Folsom Prison Blues		(R)-Hilltop 6114	
Johnny Cash (The Collectores Series)		-SMSP A-8122	
Johnny Cash at Fulsom Prison and San Quentin	(CD)	-Columbia 33639	
Ride This Train	(CD)	(R)-SMSP A-8255	
Classic Cash	(2 CD)	-2 Pair 2-1107	(1986)
The Vintage Years(1955-63)	(2 CD)	-Rhino R2-70229	(1987)
Columbia Records 1958-1986	(CD)	-Columbia 40637	(1987)
Classic Cash(20 Newly Recorded Hits)	(CD)	-Mercury 834526	(1988)
Country Boy (Sun Recodings)	(CD)	-Charly CD-18	
The Sun Years	(2 CD)	-Rhino R2-70950	(1990)
Patriot (ten priviously released songs)	(CD)	-Columbia 45384	(1990)
The Mystery of Life	(2 CD)	-Mercury 848051-2	(1991)
Johnny Cash's Greatest Hits	(CD)	(R)-Classics 40105	(1991)
The Best of Johnny Cash		-Curb/C 77494	(1991)
The Essential Johnny Cash (1955-1983)	(CD)	-Columbia 47991	(1992)
The Gospel Collection	(CD)	-Columbia 48952	(1992)

Extended Play Mini Albums

EP Johnny Cash Sings Hank Williams	-Sun EP-111	(1958)
EP Country Boy	-Sun EP-112	(1958)
EP I Walk the Line	-Sun EP-113	(1958)
EP Johnny Cash-His Top Hits	-Sun EP-114	(1958)
EP Home of the Blues	-Sun EP-116	(1958)
EP Johnny Cash	-Sun EP-117	(1958)
EP The Fabulous Johnny Cash	-Columbia 2531-33	(1958)
EP Hymns by Johnny Cash	-Columbia 2841-43	(1959)
EP Johnny Cash (Sings The Rebel)	-Columbia 2155	(1959)
EP Songs of Our Soil	-Columbia 13391-33	(1959)
EP Now, There Was A Song	-Columbia 14631-33	(1960)
EP Hello, I'm Johnny Cash (Juke Box)	-Columbia 9943	(1969)

Johnny Cash and June (Carter) Cash

Albums

Carryin' On	-Columbia CS-9528	(1966)

Johnny Cash and June (Carter) Cash
Johnny and his Woman   -Columbia 32443   (1973)

Johnny Cash and Jerry Lee Lewis-

Albums

Sunday Down South	-Sun/SSS SE-119	(1970)
Johnny Cash Sings Hank Williams	-Sun/SSS SE-125	(1971)

Johnny Cash, Carl Perkins, Jerry Lee Lewis-

Albums

The Survivors	(CD)	-Columbia 37961	(1985)
Class of 55	(CD)	-Smash 830002	(1986)

Johnny Cash, Waylon Jennings, Willie Nelson, and Kris Kristofferson

Albums

The Highwaymen	-Columbia 40056	(1985)
The Highwaymen 2	-Columbia 45240	(1990)

Johnny Cash and Waylon Jennings-
Albums

Heroes	(CD)	-Columbia 40347	(1986)

Jean Chapel-

Singles

I Won't Be Rockin' Tonight/Welcome to the Club	-Sun 244	(1956)
(She left Sun for RCA at same time as Elvis)		
I Won't Be Rockin' Tonight/Welcome to the Club	-RCA 6681	(1956)
Oo-ba La Baby	-RCA 6892	(1957)
Don't Let Go/Your Tender Love	-Smash 1829	(1962)
Green Paper/Hungry Eyes	-Challenge 59376	(196?)

Jack Clement-

Singles

Ten Years/Your Lover Boy	-Sun 291	(1958)
The Black Haired Man/Wrong	-Sun 311	(1958)
My Voice Is Changing/Time After Time After Time	-Hall-Way 1796	(1962)

Albums

All I Want To Do in Life	-Elektra 6E-122	(1978)

Bill Emerson(Billy "The Kid" Emerson)-

Singles

No Teasing Around/If Lovin' Is Believing	-Sun 195	(1954)
I'm Not Going Home/The Woodchuck	-Sun 203	(1954)
Move Baby Move/When It Rains It Pours	-Sun 214	(1955)
Red Hot/No Greater Love	-Sun 219	(1955)
Little Fine Healthy Thing/Something For Nothing	-Sun 233	(1955)
The Whip	-Mpac 7207	(195?)
You Never Miss the Water	-Vee jay 261	(1957)
Believe Me	-Chess 1728	(1959)

Charlie Feathers-(Claims he sang rockabilly since 1949)

Singles

Tear It Up	-Philwood 223	(195?)
Deep Elm Blues	-Holidy Inn 114	(1952)
I've Been Deceived/Peeping Eyes	-Flip 503	(1955)
Defrost Your Heart/Wedding Gown of White	-Sun 231	(1955)
Tongue-Tied Jill/Get With It	-Meteor 5032	(1956)
Everybody's Lovin' My Baby/Can't Hardly Stand	-King 4971	(1956)
Bottle to the Baby/One Hand Loose	-King 4997	(1956)
Nobody's Woman/When You Decide	-King 5022	(1957)
When You Come Around/Too Much Alike	-King 5043	(1957)
Why Don't You/Jungle Fever	-Kay 1001	(1960)
Jody's Beat/My My	-Kay 1002	(1960)
Dinky John/South Of Chicago	-Wal-May 101	(1960)
Wild Wild Part/Today and Tomorrow	-Memphis 103	(1961)
Nobody's Darlin'/Deep Elm Blues	-Holiday Inn 144	(1963)

Rudy Grayzell-

Singles

Judy/I Think of You	-Sun 290	(1958)
#145, 147, 157	-Abbott	(195?)
The Moon Is Up	-Starday 229	(195?)
Duck Tail	-Starday 241	(195?)
Jig-Ga-Lee-Ga	-Starday 270	(195?)
Let's Get Wild	-Starday 321	(195?)

Hardrock Gunter-

Singles

Gonna Dance All Night/Fallen Angel	-Sun 201	(1954)
Whoo!I Mean Whee!	-Emperor 57	
Whoo!I Mean Whee!	(R)-Emperor 112	
Boogie Woogie On Saturday Night	-Decca 46300	

Hardrock Gunter Cont'd-

I've Done Gone Hog Wild	-Decca 46350
Sixty Minute Man	-Decca 46363
Dixieland Boogie	-Decca 46367
I Won't Tell Who'e To Blame	-King 1416
I'll Give 'Em Rhythm/Put My Britches On	-King 1505

Roscoe Gordon-

Singles

Weeping Blues/Just Love Me Baby		-Flip 227	(1955)
Weeping Blues/Just Love Me Baby	(2)	-Sun 227	(1955)
"The Chicken" (Dance with You)/Love For You, Baby		-Flip 237	(1956)
"The Chicken" (Dance with You)/Love For You, Baby	(2)	-Sun 237	(1956)
Shoobie Dobie/Cheese and Crackers		-Sun 257	(1956)
Sally Jo/Torro		-Sun 305	(1958)
No More Doggin'		-RPM 350	
Two Kinds of Women		-RPM 365	
Too Many Women		-Duke 109	
Ain't No Use		-Duke 114	
Just a Little Bit/Going Home		-Vee Jay 332	

Jimmy Haggett-

Singles

They Call Our Love a Sin/No More	-Sun 236	(1956)
All I Have Is Love	-Caprock 107	(1957)
Gonna Shut You Off Baby	-Meteor 5043	(1958)

Ray Harris-

Singles

Come On Little Mama/Where'd You Stay Last Nite	-Sun 254	(1956)
Greenback Dollar, Watch and Chain/Foolish Heart	-Sun 272	(1957)

Jimmy Isle-

Singles

Baby-O/Hassie	-Bally 1034	(1957)
I've Been Waiting/Diamond Ring	-Sun 306	(1958)
Goin' Wild/You and Johnny Smith	-Roulette 4065	(1958)
Time Will Tell/Without a Love	-Sun 318	(1958)
What a Life	-Sun 332	(1958)
Everybody's Got a Little Girl But Me/Our Town	-Mala 459	(196?)

Sleepy LaBeef-(Still doing rockabilly today)

Singles

Turn Me Loose	-Crescent 102	(1957)
I'm Through/All Alone	-Mercury 71112	(1957)
All The Time/Lonely	-Mercury 71179	(1957)
I'm Through/All Alone	(R)-Starday 292	(1957)
Sure Beats The Heck Outta Settlin' Down/Schneider	-Columbia 44068	(1967)
Completely Destroyed/Go Ahead On, Baby	-Columbia 44261	(1967)
Everyday/If I Go Right, I'm Wrong	-Columbia 44455	(1968)
Too Much Monkey Business/Got You on My Mind	-Plantation 55	(1970)
Blackland Farmer/Got You on My Mind	(R)-Plantation 74	(1970)
Thunder Road	-Sun/SSS 1132	(1971)
Ghost Riders in the Sky	-Sun/SSS 1133	(1971)
There Ain't Much After Texas	-Sun/SSS 1134	(1971)
Good Rockin' Boogie/Good Rockin' Boogie (Part 2)	-Sun/SSS 1137	(1978)
Boogie Woogie Country Girl/Flying Saucers Rock & Roll	-Sun/SSS 1145	(1979)

Albums

The Bull's Night Out		-Sun/SSS 130	(1974)
Western Gold		-Sun/SSS 138	(1976)
1977 Rockabilly		-Sun/SSS 1004	(1978)
Down Home Rockabilly		-Sun/SSS 1014	(1979)
Early, Rare and Rockin' Sides		-Baron 102	(1979)
It Ain't What You Eat(It's the Way You Chew It)	(CD)	-Rounder CD-3052	(1981)
Electricity	(CD)	-Rounder CD-3070	(1986)
Nothin' But The Truth	(CD)	-Rounder CD-3072	(1987)

Rodney Lay(and Wild West)-

Singles

Desert Rock(Gold Rock)	-Sun/SSS 1015	(1979)
Rockabilly Nuggets(Gold Vinyl)	-Sun/SSS 1022	(1980)
Silent Partners(Gold Vinyl)	-Sun/SSS	(198?)

Jerry Lee Lewis-

Singles

Crazy Arms/End of the Road	-Sun 259	(1956)
Crazy Arms/End of the Road	(R)-Sun 14	
Whole Lot of Shakin' Goin On/It'll Be Me	-Sun 267	(1957)
Whole Lot of Shakin' Goin On/It'll Be Me	(R)-Sun 18	(1957)
Great Balls of Fire/You Win Again	-Sun 281	(1957)
Great Balls of Fire/You Win Again	(R)-Sun 21	(1957)
Breathless/Down The Line	-Sun 288	(1958)
Breathless/Down The Line	(R)-Sun 25	(1958)
High School Confidential/Fools Like Me	-Sun 296	(1958)

-Jerry Lee Lewis Cont'd-

High School Confidential/Fools Like Me	(R)-Sun 28	(1958)
Lewis Boogie/The Return of Jerry Lee Lewis	-Sun 301	(1958)
Lewis Boogie/The Return of Jerry Lee Lewis	-Sun 29	(1958)
Break Up/I'll Make It All Up to You	-Sun 303	(1958)
Break Up/I'll Make It All Up to You	(R)-Sun 31	(1958)
I'll Sail My Ship Alone/It Hurts Me So	-Sun 312	(1958)
I'll Sail My Ship Alone/It Hurts Me So	(R)-Sun 34	(1958)
Big Blon' Baby/Lovin' Up a Storm	-Sun 317	(1959)
Big Blon' Baby/Lovin' Up a Storm	(R)-Sun 36	(1959)
The Ballad of Billy Joe/Let's Talk About Us	-Sun 324	(1959)
The Ballad of Billy Joe/Let's Talk About Us	(R)-Sun 38	(1959)
Little Queenie/I Could Never Be Ashamed of You	-Sun 330	(1959)
Little Queenie/I Could Never Be Ashamed of You	(R)-Sun 39	(1959)
In the Mood/I Get the Blues When It Rains	-Philips Int 3559	(1959)
Baby Baby Bye Bye/Old Black Joe	-Sun 337	(1960)
Baby Baby Bye Bye/Old Black Joe	(R)-Sun 42	(1960)
Hang Up My Rock and Roll Shoes/John Henry	-Sun 344	(1960)
Hang Up My Rock and Roll Shoes/John Henry	(R)-Sun 44	(1960)
When I Get Paid/Love Made a Fool of Me	-Sun 352	(1960)
When I Get Paid/Love Made a Fool of Me	(R)-Sun 46	(1960)
What'd I Say/Livin' Lovin' Wreck	-Sun 356	(1961)
What'd I Say/Livin' Lovin' Wreck	(R)-Sun 48	(1961)
It Won't Happen to Me/Cold Cold Heart	-Sun 364	(1961)
It Won't Happen to Me/Cold Cold Heart	(R)-Sun 50	(1961)
Save the Last Dance for Me/As Long As I Live	-Sun 367	(1961)
Save the Last Dance for Me/As Long As I Live	(R)-Sun 51	(1961)
Bonnie B/Money	-Sun 371	(1961)
Bonnie B/Money	(R)-Sun 52	(1961)
I've Been Twistin'/Ramblin' Rose	-Sun 374	(1962)
I've Been Twistin'/Ramblin' Rose	(R)-Sun 53	(1962)
Sweet Little Sixteen/How's My Ex Treating You?	-Sun 379	(1962)
Sweet Little Sixteen/How's My Ex Treating You?	(R)-Sun 55	(1962)
Good Golly Miss Molly/I Can't Trust You	-Sun 382	(1962)
Good Golly Miss Molly/I Can't Trust You	(R)-Sun 56	(1962)
Teenage Letter/Seasons Of My Heart	-Sun 384	(1963)
Teenage Letter/Seasons Of My Heart	(R)-Sun 57	(1963)
Breathless/Whole Lotta' Shakin Going On	(2)-Smash 1412	(1963)
Great Balls of Fire/High School Confidential	(2)-Smash 1413	(1963)
Pen and Paper/Hit the Road Jack	-Smash 1857	(1963)
I'm on Fire/Bread and Butter Man	-Smash 1886	(1964)
She Was My Baby/He Said He'd Die for Me	-Smash 1906	(1964)
High Heel Sneakers/You Went Back on Your Word	-Smash 1930	(1964)
Carry Me Back to Old Virginia/I Know What It Means	-Sun 396	(1965)
Carry Me Back to Old Virginia/I Know What It Means	(R)-Sun 59	(1965)
I Believe in You/Baby, Hold Me Close	-Smash 1969	(1965)
Rockin' Pneumonia and the Boogie Woogie Flu/ This Must Be the Place	-Smash 1992	(1965)

Baby(You've Got What It Takes)/Green, Green Grass of Home	-Smash 2006*	(1965)
What a Heck of a Mess!/Sticks 'N' Stones	-Smash 2027	(1966)
Memphis Beat/If I Had To Do It All Over	-Smash 2053	(1966)
Holdin' On/It's a Hang Up Baby	-Smash 2103	(1967)
Turn on Your Love Light/Shotgun Man	-Smash 2122	(1967)
Another Place, Another Time/I'm Walking the Floor Over You	-Smash 2146	(1968)
What's Made Milwaukee Famous/All the Good Is Gone	-Smash 2164	(1968)
She Still Comes Around/Slipping Around	-Smash 2186	(1968)
Let's Talk About Us/To Make Love Sweeter For You	-Smash 2202	(1969)
Don't Let Me Cross Over/We Live In Two Different Worlds	-Smash 2220*	(1969)
One Has My Name/I Can't Stop Loving You	-Smash 2224	(1969)
Invitation to Your Party/I Could Never Be Ashamed of You	(R)-Sun/SSS 1101	(1969)
She Even Woke Me Up to Say Goodbye/Echoes	-Smash 2244	(1969)
One Minute Past Eternity/Frankie and Johnny	(R)-Sun/SSS 1107	(1969)
Roll Over, Beethoven/Secret Places	-Smash 2254	(1969)
One Minute Past Eternity/Invitation to Your Party	(Rx)-Sun/SSS 68	(1969)
Once More With Feeling/You Went Out of Your Way	-Smash 2257	(1970)
Can't Seem to Say Goodbye/Goodnight Irene	(R)-Sun/SSS 1115	(1970)
What's Made Milwaukee Famous/ Another Place, Another Time	(R)-Mercury 35020	(1970)
Who's Sorry Now/Come on In	-Mercury 35021	(1970)
Roll Over Beethoven/Don't Let Me Cross Over	(R)-Mercury 35022	(1970)
She Even Woke Me Up To Say Goodbye/One Has My Name	(R)-Mercury 35023	(1970)
There Must Be More To Love Than This/ Home Away from Home	-Mercury 73099	(1970)
Waiting For a Train/Big Legged Woman	(R)-Sun/SSS 1119	(1970)
Waiting For a Train/Can't Seem To Say Goodbye	(Rx) -Sun/SSS 69	(1970)
	-Buddah	(1971)
I Can't Have a Merry Christmas Without You/ In Loving Memories	-Mercury 73155	(1971)
I Can't Have a Merry Christmas Without You/ In Loving Memories	(R)-Mercury 73192	(1971)
Would You Take Another Chance/Touchng Home	(R)-Mercury 35028	(1971)
There Must Be More To Love Than This/ When He Walks on You	(R)-Mercury 35028	(1971)
Love on Broadway/Matchbox	(R)-Sun/SSS 1125	(1971)
When He Walks on You (Like You Have Walked On Me)/ Foolish Kind of Man	(Rx)-Mercury 73227	(1971)
Me and Bobbie Mcgee/Would You Take Another Chance On Me	-Mercury 73248	(1971)
I Can't Trust Me in Your Arms Anymore/Your Loving Ways	-Sun 1128 (R)	(1972)
Chantilly Lace/Think About It Darlin'	-Mercury 73273	(1972)
Chantilly Lace/Who's Gonna Play This Old Piano	(R)-Mercury 35034	(1972)
Turn on Your Love Light/Lonely Weekends	-Mercury 73296	(1972)
Handwriting on the Wall/Me and Jesus	-Mercury 73303	(1972)
Who's Gonna Play This Old Piano/ No Honky Tonks in Heaven	(R)-Mercury 73328	(1972)

-Jerry Lee Lewis Cont'd-

No More Hanging On/Mercy of a Letter	-Mercury 73361	(1973)
Drinking Wine Spo-Dee O'dee/Rock and Roll Melody	-Mercury 73374	(1973)
No Headstone on My Grave/Jack Daniels # 7	-Mercury 73402	(1973)
No Headstone on My Grave/Jack Daniels # 7	(R)-Mercury 73405	(1973)
Sometimes a Memory Ain't Enough/Think I Need to Pray	-Mercury 73423	(1973)
I'm Left, You're Right, She's Gone/I've Fallin' to the Bottom	-Mercury 73452	(1974)
I Can't Trust Me in Your Arms Anymore/ Good Rockin' Tonight	(R)-Sun/SSS 1130	(1974)
Just A Little Bit/Meat Man	-Mercury 73462	(1974)
Tell Tale Signs/Cold,Cold Morning Light	-Mercury 73491	(1974)
He Can't Fill My Shoes/Tomorrow's Taking My Baby Away	-Mercury 73618	(1974)
I Can Still Hear the Music in the Restroom/Remember Me	-Mercury 73661	(1975)
Boogie Woogie Country Man/I'm Still Jealous of You	-Mercury 73685	(1975)
A Damn Good Country Song/When I Take My Vacation in Heaven	-Mercury 73729	(1975)
Don't Boogie Woogie/That Kind of Fool	-Mercury 73763	(1976)
Jerry Lee's Rock and Roll Revival Show/ Let's Put It Back Together Again	-Mercury 73822	(1976)
The Closest Thing to You/You Belong to Me	-Mercury 73872	(1976)
Middle Age Crazy/Georgia on My Mind	-Mercury 55011	(1976)
Come On In/Who's Sorry Now	-Mercury 55021	(1978)
I'll Find It Where I Can/Don't Let The Stars Get in Your Eyes	-Mercury 55028	(1978)
I'll Find It Where I Can/Touching Home	-Mercury 55028	(1978)
Save the Last Dance for Me/Am I To Be the One?	(R)-Sun/SSS 1138**	(1978)
Save the Last Dance for Me/Am I To Be the One?	(R)-Sun/SSS 1139**	(1978)
Middle Age Crazy/I'll Find It Where I Can	(R)-Mercury 35044	(1978)
Cold, Cold Heart/Hello Josephine	(R)-Sun/SSS 1141	(1979)
Who Will the Next Fool Be?	-Electra 44067	(1979)
Rockin' My Life Away/I Wish I Was Eighteen Again	-Electra 46030	(1979)
Who Will the Next Fool Be?	(R)-Electra 46067	(1979)
Be-Bop-A-Lulu	(R)-Sun/SSS 1151	(1979)
When Two Worlds Collide/Rita May	-Electra 46591	(1980)
Honky Tonk Stuff	-Electra 46642	(1980)
Over the Rainbow	-Electra 47026	(1980)
Thirty Nine and Holding	-Electra 47095	(1981)
Forever and Forgiving	-MCA 52151	(1982)
	-MCA	(1982-83)
	(R)-Sun/SSS	(to 1984)
	-Scr	(1985)
	(R)-America Smash	(1986)

* Sung with sister Linda Gail Lewis
** A side with Elvis Presley
B side with Charlie Rich
(Both artists were with Sun at the time.)

Albums

Jerry Lee Lewis	-Sun 1230	(1958)
Jerry Lee's Greatest	-Sun 1265	(1961)

-Jerry Lee Lewis Cont'd-

Golden Rock Hits of Jerry Lee Lewis	-Smash 67040	(1964)
Greatest Live Show on Earth	-Smash 67056	(1964)
The Return of Rock	-Smash 67063	(1965)
Country Songs for City Folks	-Smash 67071	(1965)
Memphis Beat	-Smash 67079	(1966)
By Request	-Smash 67086	(1966)
The Return of Rock	-Wing 12340	(1967)
Jerry Lee Lewis: Soul My Way	-Smash 67097	(1967)
Another Place, Another Time	-Smash 67104	(1968)
In Demand	-Wing 16340	(1968)
She Still Comes Around	-Smash 67112	(1968)
Jerry Lee Lewis Sings the Country Music Hall of Fame Hits, Vol. 1	-Smash 67117	(1969)
Jerry Lee Lewis Sings the Country Music Hall of Fame Hits, Vol. 2	-Smash 67118	(1969)
Legend of Jerry Lee Lewis (2 LP)	-Wing 16406	(1969)
Together(W/Linda Gail)	-Smash 67126	(1969)
All Country	-Smash 67171	(1969)
Original Golden Hits, Vol. 1	-Sun/SSS 102	(1969)
Original Golden Hits, Vol. 2	-Sun/SSS 103	(1969)
Rockin' Rhythm and Blues -	-Sun/SSS 107	(1969)
Golden Cream of the Country	-Sun/SSS 108	(1969)
She Even Woke Me Up To Say Goodbye	-Smash 67128	(1970)
Best of Jerry Lee Lewis	-Smash 67131	(1970)
A Taste of Country	-Sun/SSS 114	(1970)
Sunday Down South	-Sun/SSS 119	(1970)
Memphis Country	-Sun/SSS 120	(1970)
Ole Tyme Country Music	-Sun/SSS 121	(1971)
High Heal Sneakers	-Pickwick 3224	(1970)
Jerry Lee Lewis Live at the InterNational Las Vegas	-Mercury 61278	(1970)
Monsters	-Sun/SSS 124	(1971)
Original Golden Hits, Vol. 3	-Sun/SSS 128	(1971)
In Loving Memories	-Mercury 61318	(1971)
There Must Be More To Love Than This	-Mercury 61323	(1971)
Touching Home	-Mercury 61343	(1971)
Would You Take Another Chance on Me?	-Mercury 61346	(1971)
Breathless (2 LP)	-Pickwick 2055	(1972)
Roll Over Beethoven	-Pickwick 6110	(1972)
Rural Route #1	-Pickwick 6120	(1972)
Who's Gonna Play This Old Piano?	-Mercury 61366	(1972)
The Killer Rocks On	-Mercury 1-637	(1972)
Drinkin' Wine Spo-Dee-O-Dee	-Pickwick 3344	(1973)
Sometimes a Memory Ain't Enough	-Mercury 1-677	(1973)
Southern Roots- A Jerry Lee Lewis Radio Special	-Mercury MK-3	(1973)
Southern Roots- Back Home to Memphis	-Mercury 1-690	(1973)
The Session (2 LP)	-Mercury 2-803	(1973)
Breathless (2 LP)	(R)-Pickwick 1002	(1974)

-Jerry Lee Lewis Cont'd-

Title		Label	Year
Jerry Lee Lewis: From the Vaults of Sun		-Power Pak PO-247	(1974)
The Best of Jerry Lee Lewis (2 LP)		-Trip TLX-8501	(1974)
I-40 Country		-Mercury 1-710	(1974)
Boogie Woogie Country Man		-Mercury 1-1030	(1975)
The Killer Rocks On		-Buckboard 1025	(1975)
Jerry Lee Lewis		(R)-Everest FS-298	(1975)
Odd Man In		-Mercury 1-1064	(1975)
Country Class		-Mercury 1-1109	(1976)
Country Memories		-Mercury 1-5004	(1977)
Golden Rock & Roll		-Sun/SSS 1000	(1977)
The Sun Story, Vol. 5		-Sunnyvale9330-905	(1977)
The Best of Jerry Lee Lewis, Vol. 2		-Mercury 1-5006	(1978)
Original Jerry Lee Lewis		-Sun/SSS 1005	(1978)
Jerry Lee Lewis Keeps Rockin'		-Mercury 1-5010	(1978)
Jerry Lee Lewis		-Elektra 6E-184	(1979)
Great Balls of Fire		-Koala AW-14109	(1979)
When Two Worlds Collide		-Elektra 6E-254	(1980)
Killer Country		-Elektra 6E-291	(1980)
Great Balls of Fire		(R)-Accord SN-7133	(1981)
Golden Rock Hits of Jerry Lee Lewis		-Smash SL-7001	(1982)
The Best of Jerry Lee Lewis		-Elektra E1-60191	(1982)
The Lousiana Fireball		-Aura A-1021	(1982)
My Fingers Do the Talkin'	(CD)	-MCA 5387	(1982)
Roots		-Sun/SSS 145	(1982)
Great Balls of Fire(The Killer)	(3 LP)	-Grudge 4513	(1989)
Jerry Lee Lewis	(CD)	(R)-Rhino 70656	(1989)
Country Gold		-Out of Town 8018	(1982)
Doin' Just Fine		-Accord SJA-7903	(1982)
Jerry Lee Lewis' Original Sun Greatest	(CD)	-Rhino R2-70255	(1983)
I Am What I Am	(CD)	-MCA 5478	(1984)
		-SCR	(1985)
I'm on Fire(Early 60's)	(CD)	-Polydor 826139	(1985)
Jerry Lee Lewis	(CD)	(R)-Everest 298	
Jerry Lee Lewis/Unlimited		(R)-Wing SRW-16406	
Rockin' With Jerry Lee Lewis	(CD)	(R)-Design DLP-165	
(Repackaging of The Legend of Jerry Lee Lewis)			
The Ferriday Fireball(Sun Song)	(CD)	-Charly CD-1	(1986)
Solid Gold	(2 Tapes)	-2 Pair PDK2-1132	(1986)
The Session	(CD)	(R)-Mercury 822751	(1987)
Best of Jerry Lee Lewis, Vol.2	(CD)	-Mercury 822789	(1987)
The Golden Rock Hits of Jerry Lee Lewis	(CD)	-Smash 826251	(1987)
Would You Take Another Chance on Me?	(CD)	(R)-Mercury 830399	(1987)
The Greatest Live Show on Earth	(CD)	(R)-Smash 830528	(1987)
Jerry Lee's Greatest	(CD)	(R)-Rhino 70657	(1989)
Killer: The Mercury Years	(CD)	-Mercury 836935	(1989)
Killer: Vol. 2 (1969 - 72)	(CD)	-Mercury 836938	(1989)
Killer: Vol.3 (1973 - 77)	(CD)	-Mercury 836941	(1989)

-Jerry Lee Lewis Cont'd-

Original Sun Greatest Hits	(4 CD)	-Rhino 70255	(1989)
Jerry Lee Lewis (1st Album)	(CD)	(R)-Rhino 70656	(1989)
Jerry Lee Lewis At His Best	(CD)	-Camden CPK-5009	
Live at the Vapors Club	(CD)	-Ace CDCH-326	
Honky Tonk Rock'N'Roll Piano Man	(CD)	-Ace CDCH-332	
Pretty Much Country	(CD)	-Ace CDCH-348	
A Private Party	(CD)	-LGP 70007/8	
Jerry Lee Lewis (2nd Album)	(CD)	(R)-Rhino 70657	(1989)
Wild One: Rare Tracks From Jerry Lee Lewis	(CD)	-Rhino 70899	(1989)
Milestone(Sun & Smash 1956-77)	(CD)	(R)-Rhino 71499	(1989)
Greatest Hits Live	(CD)	-SMC SCD-4811	
The Best of Jerry Lee Lewis	(CD)	-Curb/C 77446	(1991)
Jerry Lee Lewis: Greatest Hits	(CD)	-K P399-538	(1991)
The Complete Palamino Club Recordings	(CD)	-Tomato 70385	(1991)
Rockin' My Life Away	(CD)	-Warner B 26689-2	(1991)
Live at the Star Club, Hamburg 1964	(CD)	-Rhino 70268	(1992)
Rockin' My Life Away	(CD)	-Tomato 70392	(1992)
Heartbreak	(CD)	-Tomato R2-70697	(1992)
Rocket 88	(CD)	-Tomato R2-70698	(1992)
Great Balls of Fire	(CD)	-CSI 75312	(1992)
All Killer, No Filler:The Anthology of Jerry Lee Lewis(2CD)		-Rhino 2--71216	(1993)

Extended Play Mini Albums

EP Jerry Lee Lewis: The Great Ball of Fire	-Sun EPA-107	(1957)
EP Jerry Lee Lewis	-Sun EPA 108-110	(1958)
EP Golden Cream of Country	-Sun EP-108	(1969)
EP D.J. Open End Interview With Jerry Lee Lewis	-Smash DJS-28	(1969)
EP Jerry Lee Lewis (Jukebox)	-Smash SEP-2	(1969)
EP A Taste of Country	-Sun EP-114	(1969)
EP Special Radio Cuts from the Killer Rocks On	-Mercury MEPL-6	(1971)
EP Special Radio Cuts From the Great Ball of Fire	-Mercury MEPL-14	(1972)

Jerry Lee, And Friends(Jimmy Ellis & Charlie Rich)

Singles

Save The Last Dance For Me		-Sun/SSS 1139	(1980)

Albums

Duets	(CD)	-Sun/SSS 1011	(1978)

Jerry Lee Lewis/ Curly Bridges/ Frank Motley

Albums

Jerry Lee Lewis/ Curly Bridges/ Frank Motley	-Design	(1963)

Jerry Lee Lewis/ Roger Miller/ Roy Orbison

Albums

Jerry Lee Lewis/ Roger Miller/ Roy Orbison	-Pickwick

Jerry Lee Lewis and Johnny Cash -

Albums
Sunday Down South	-Sun/SSS SE-119	(1970)
Johnny Cash Sings Hank Williams	-Sun/SSS SE-125	(1971)

-Johnny Cash, Carl Perkins, Jerry Lee Lewis-

Albums
The Survivors	(CD)	-Columbia 37961	(1985)
Class of 55	(CD)	-Smash 830002	(1986)

Jerry Lee Lewis/ Charlie Rich/ Johnny Cash

Albums
Jerry Lee Lewis/ Charlie Rich/ Johnny Cash	-Power Pak

Jerry Lee Lewis, Carl Perkins, and Charlie Rich

Albums
Trio(with Jimmy Ellis)	-Sun/SSS 1018	(1978)

Carl Mann(born 8/24/42 in Huntingdon, Tn)-

Singles
Gonna Rock & Roll Tonight/Rockin' Love	-Jaxon 502	(1957)
Mona Lisa/Foolish One	-Philips Int 3539	(1959)
Pretend/Rockin' Love	-Philips Int 3546	(1959)
Some Enchanted Evenings/I Can't Forget	-Philips Int 3550	(1959)
South of the Border/I'm Coming Home	-Philips Int 3555	(1960)
Wayward Wind/Born To Be Bad	-Philips Int 3564	(1960)
I Ain't Got No Home/If I Could Change You	-Philips Int 3569	(1960)
Mountain Dew/When I Grow Too Old To Dream	-Philips Int 3579	(1961)
The Serenade of the Bells	-Monument 974	(196?)
Mona Lisa	(R)-Sun/SSS 64	(1969)
Pretend	(R)-Sun/SSS 65	(1969)
Some Enchanted Evening	(R)-Sun/SSS 66	(1969)

Albums
Like Mann(Featuring Carl Mann)	-Phillips Int 1960	(1960)
Carl Mann(The Sun Story,Vol.6)	-GRT/Sunnyvale 906	(1977)

Miller Sisters-

Singles
I Knew You Would/Someday You Will Pay	-Flip 504	(1955)
There's No Right Way To Do Me Wrong/You Can Tell Me	-Sun 230	(1955)

-Miller Sisters Cont'd-

Ten Cats Down/Finders Keepers	-Sun 255	(1956)
I Miss You So	-Rayna 5001	
Walk On	-Rayna 5004	
You Got To Reap What You Sow	-Glodis 1003	

Roy Orbison(and The Teen Kings-and The Roses)-

(Rockabilly Only)

Singles

Ooby Dooby/Trying to Get to You	-JeWel 101	(1956)
(Different than the one on Sun)		
Ooby Dooby/Go, Go, Go	-Sun 242	(1956)
Ooby Dooby/Go, Go, Go	(R)-Sun 8	(1956)
Rock House/You're My Baby	-Sun 251	(1956)
Rock House/You're My Baby	(R)-Sun 12	(1956)
Devil Doll/Sweet and Easy	-Sun 265	(1956)
Devil Doll/Sweet and Easy	(R)-Sun 16	(1956)
Chicken Hearted/I Like Love	-Sun 284	(1957)
Devil Doll/Sweet and Easy	(R)-Sun 353	(1956)
	(R)-Sun/SSS	(1969)
	(R)-Collectables	(1985)

Albums

At the Rockhouse	-Sun LP-1260	(1961)
Orbiting With Orbison	-Spectrum DLP-164	
The Original Sound of Roy Orbison	-Sun/SSS 113	(1969)
Golden Hits	-Buckboard 1015	
Best of Roy Orbison	-Trip 8505	(1974)
	-Sunnyvale	(1977)
The Sun Years	-Rhino 70916	(1989)

Extended Play Mini Albums

EP Roy Orbison and the Teen Kings	-Stars, Inc	(1959)

Tracy Pendarvis(and The Swampers)-

Singles

A Thousand Guitars/Is It Too Late?	-Sun 335	(1959)
Is It Me?/Southbound Line	-Sun 345	(1960)
Bell of the Swanee/Eternally	-Sun 359	(1961)
First Love	-Des Cant 1234	
It Don't Pay	-Scott 1202	
All You Gotta Do	-Scott 1203	

Dick Penner-

Singles

Cindy Lou/Your Honey Love   -Sun 282   (1957)

Carl Perkins-

Singles

Movie Magg/Turn Around	-Flip 501	(1955)
Let the Juke Box Keep on Playing/Gone Gone Gone	-Sun 224	(1955)
Let the Juke Box Keep on Playing/Gone Gone Gone	(R)-Sun 2	
Blue Suede Shoes/Honey Don't	-Sun 234	(1956)
Blue Suede Shoes/Honey Don't	(R)-Sun 4	
Tennessee/Sure To Fall	-Sun 238	(1956)
Tennessee/Sure To Fall	(R)-Sun 5	
Boppin the Blues/All Mama's Children	-Sun 243	(1956)
Boppin the Blues/All Mama's Children	(R)-Sun 10	
Dixie Fried/I'm Sorry I'm Not Sorry	-Sun 249	(1956)
Dixie Fried/I'm Sorry I'm Not Sorry	(R)-Sun 12	
Your True Love/Matchbox	-Sun 261	(1957)
Your True Love/Matchbox	(R)-Sun 15	
Forever Yours/That's Right	-Sun 274	(1957)
Forever Yours/That's Right	(R)-Sun 19	
Glad All Over/Lend Me Your Comb	-Sun 287	(1957)
Glad All Over/Lend Me Your Comb	(R)-Sun 24	
Pink Pedal Pushers/Jive After Five	-Columbia 41131	(1958)
Levi Jacket/Pop, Let Me Have the Car	-Columbia 41207	(1958)
Y-O-U/This Life I Lead	-Columia 41296	(1958)
Pointed Toe Shoes/Highway to Love	-Columbia 41379	(1959)
One Ticket to Loneliness/I Don't See Me in Your Arms Anymore	-Columbia 41449	(1959)
L-O-V-E-V-I-L-L-E/Too Much for a Man To Understand	-Columbia 41651	(1960)
Just for You/Honey, 'Cause I Love You	-Columbia 41825	(1960)
Any Way The Wind Blows/The Unhappy Girls	-Columbia 42061	(1961)
Hollywood City/ The Fool I Used To Know	-Columbia 42405	(1961)
Twister Sister/Hambone	-Columbia 42514	(1961)
Forget Me Next Time Around/I Just Got Back From There	-Columbia 42753	(1962)
Help Me Find My Baby/For a Little While	-Decca 31548	(1963)
After Sundown/I Wouldn't Have You	-Decca 31591	(1963)
Let My Baby Be/The Monkeyshine	-Decca 31709	(1964)
One of These Days/Mama of My Song	-Decca 31786	(1964)
Helpless/Woman in the Darkness	-Columbia 44343	(1964)
Restless/11-43	-Columbia 44723	(1965)
For Your Love/Four Letter Word	-Columbia 44883	(1966)
Country Boy's Dream/If I Could Come Back	-Dollie 505	(1967)
Shine, Shine, Shine/Almost Love	-Dollie 508	(1967)
Without You/You Can Take the Boy Out of the Country	-Dollie 512	(1967)

-Carl Perkins Cont'd-

Back to Tennessee/My Old Home Town	-Dollie 514	(1967)
	(R)-SSS/Sun	(1968-72)
All Mama's Children/Step Aside	-Columbia 45107	(1968)
My Son, My Son/State of Confusion	-Columbia 45132	(1968)
What Every Little Boy Ought To Know/Just As Long	-Columbia 45253	(1969)
Me Without You/Red Headed Woman	-Columbia 45347	(1970)
Cotton Top/About All I Can Give You Is Love	-Columbia 45466	(1971)
Take Me Back to Memphis/High On Love	-Columbia 45582	(1971)
Someday/ The Trip	-Columbia 45694	(1972)
Help Me Dream/You Tore My Heaven All to Hell	-Mercury 73393	(1973)
(Let's Get)Dixie Fried/One More Loser Goin' Home	-Mercury 73425	(1973)
Sing My Song	-Mercury 73495	(1973)
You'll Always Be a Lady to Me/Low Class	-Mercury 73653	(1974)
The E.P. Express/big bad blues	-Mercury 73690	(1975)
The E.P. Express/big bad blues	(R)-Mercury 55009	(1977)
Blue Suede Shoes	-Mercury 55054	(1977)
Ballad of Little Fauss and Big Halsy	-Jet AE-32	(1979)
Rock-A-Billy Fever/Till You Get Thru With Me	-Suede 102	(1981)
	(R)-American Smash	(1986-87)

Albums

Carl Perkins Dance Album	-Sun LP-1225	(1957)
Whole Lotta Shakin'	-Columbia CL-1234	(1958)
Tennessee	-Design SDLP-611	(1961)
Teen Beat: Best of Carl Perkins	(R)-Sun LP-1225	(1961)
(Repackage of Dance Album)		
Country Boys Dream	-Dollie LP-4001	(1967)
Carl Perkins' Greatest Hits	-Columbia CS-9633	(1969)
Carl Perkins on Top	-Columbia CS-9931	(1969)
Original Golden Hits	-Sun/SSS 111	(1969)
Blue Suede Shoes	-Sun/SSS 112	(1969)
Boppin' the Blues	-Columbia CS-9981	(1970)
(With NRBQ-Rock Blues Group)		
Brown-Eyed Handsome Man	-Harmony 31179	(1972)
Carl Perkins	-Harmony 31185	(1972)
The Greatest Hits of Carl Perkins	(R)-Harmony 31792	(1972)
My Kind Of Country	-Mercury 1-691	(1973)
Carl Perkin's Greatest Hits	(R)-Columbia 10117	(1974)
The Best of Carl Perkins (2 LP)	-Trip 8503	(1974)
Rocking Guitar Man	-Charly	(1975)
Original Carl Perkins	-Charly	(1976)
Long Tall Sally	-CBS	(1977)
The Sun Story, Vol. 3	-GRT/Sunnyvale	(1977)
Sun Sounds Special	-Charly	(1978)
Ol' Blue Suede's Back	-Jet KZ-35604	(1978)
Ol' Blue Suede's Back	(R)-Jet JT-LA856-H	(1978)
Country Soul	-Album Globe 8118	(1979)
That Rockin' Chair Man	-Album Globe 9016	(1979)

-Carl Perkins Cont'd-

Goin' Back to Memphis		-Album Globe 9037	(1980)
Country Soul		-Koala AW-14164	(1980)
Carl Perkins and The C.P. Express		-Suede 002	(1981)
Presenting Carl Perkins		-Accord SN-7169	(1982)
Boppin' the Blues		-Accord SJA-7915	(1982)
Boppin' the Blues	(CD)	(R)-Columbia 9981	(1982)

(With NRBQ-Rock Blues Group)

Dixie Fried (Sun Records product)	(CD)	-Charly CD-2	(1983)
That Rockin' Guitar Man-Today		-WAA 9016	(1983)
The Heart and Soul Of Carl Perkins (With Johnny Cash)		-Allegiance 5001	(1984)
Introducing Carl Perkins	(CD)	-Boplicity BOP-8	(1985)
Up Through the Years(1954- 57)	(CD)	-Bear Family 15246	(1986)
Original Sun Greatest Hits	(CD)	-Rhino 75890	(1986)
Twemtu Golden Pieces	(CD)	-Bulldog 2034	
Whole Lotta Shakin' (Collector's Series)	(CD)	-SMSP A-1234	
Born to Rock	(CD)	-Liberty C21K-90079	
Honky Tonk Gal: Rare and Unissued Sun Masters)	(CD)	-Rounder SS-27	(1989)
Born to Rock		-Universal 76001	(1989)
Jive After Five: The Best of Carl Perkins	(CD)	-Rhino R2-70958	(1990)
The Best of Carl Perkins	(CD)	-Sound CD-929	(1991)
Restless: The Columbia Years w/NRBQ	(CD)	-Legacy CK-48896	(1992)
The Best of Carl Perkins	(CD)	-Curb/C 77598	(1993)
Carl Perkins & Sons	(CD)	(R)-RCA 66216-2	(1993)
Take Me Back	(CD)	(R)-RCA 66217-2	(1993)
Disciple in Blue Suede Shoes	(CD)	(R)-RCA 66218-2	(1993)

Extended Play Mini Albums

EP Carl Perkins-Dance Album	-Sun EP 115	(1958)
EP Whole Lotta Shakin'	-Columbia EP12341	(1958)

Carl Perkins, Johnny Cash, Jerry Lee Lewis-

Albums

The Survivors	(CD)	(R)-Columbia 37961	(1985)
Class of '55	(CD)	(R)-Smash 830002	(1986)

Carl Perkins, Johnny Cash, Jerry Lee Lewis & Roy Orbison

Albums

(Mail order)		-America	(1986)
	(CD)	-America/Smash	(1986)

Carl Perkins/Sonny Burgess-

Albums

	-Sun/SSS	(1970)

Earl Peterson(Michigan's Singing Cowboy-

Singles

Boogie Blues/In the Dark   -Sun 197   (1954)

Doug Poindexter(and The Starlite Wranglers)-

Singles

My Kind of Carryin' On/More For Me   -Sun 202   (1954)

Johnny Powers(with Stan Getz and The Tom Cats-and His Rockets)-

Singles

Honey, Let's Go(To a Rock and Roll Show)/Your Love	-Fortune 199	(1955)
Honey, Let's Go(To a Rock and Roll Show	(R)-Hi-Q 5044	(1956)
Rock Rock/Long Blonde Hair, Red Rose Lips	-Fox 916/917	(1957)
Be Mine All Mine/With Your Love, With Your Kiss	-Sun 327	(1959)
A Teenager's Prayer/A Young Boy's Heart	-Tridex 103	(1960)

Elvis Presley-

Singles

That's All Right (Mama)/Blue Moon of Kentucky	-Sun 209	(1954)
Good Rockin' Tonight/I Don't Care If the Sun Don't Shine	-Sun 210	(1954)
Milkcow Blues Boogie/You're a Heartbreaker	-Sun 215	(1955)
I'm Left, You're Right, She's Gone/Baby Let's Play House	-Sun 217	(1955)
Mystery Train/I Forgot To Remember To Forget	-Sun 223	(1955)
The Lady Loves Me	(R)-Sun 101*	(1978)
Jailhouse Rock	(R)-Sun 102*	(1978)
Let's Have a Party	(R)-Sun 103*	(1978)
Mean Woman Blues	(R)-Sun 104*	(1978)
Heartbreak Hotel/Shake, Rattle and Roll	(R)-Sun 227*	(1978)
Tiger Man/Harbor Lights	-Sun 520*	(1978)
Blue Suede Shoes/My Baby's Gone	(R)-Sun 521*	(1978)
Money Honey/Blue Moon	(R)-Sun 522*	(1978)
Tutti Frutti	(R)-Sun 523*	(1978)
I Got A Woman	(R)-Sun 524*	(1978)
Tweedlee Dee/Lawdy Miss Clawdy	(R)-Sun 525*	(1978)
Tweedlee Dee/Louisiana Hayride Interview	(R)-Sun 600*	(1978)

*Special release from RCA using the Sun label

Albums

The Sun Sessions	(R)-RCA AYMI-3893	(1980)
The Sun Years (CD)	(R)-Sun 1001	(1977)

-Elvis Presley Cont'd-

The Beginning Years	(Louisiana Heyride)	-L Heyride 3061	(1984)
Elvis- 50th Anniversary	(6 LP)	(DJ)-Creative Radio	(1985)
The Million Dollar Quartet	(CD)	-RCA 2023-2R	(1990)

(Elvis, Johnny Cash, Jerry Lee, Carl Perkins)

Slim Rhodes-

Singles

Uncertain Love/Don't Believe	-Sun 216	(1955)
The House of Sin/Are You Ashamed of Me?	-Sun 225	(1955)
Gonna Romp and Stomp/Bad Girl	-Sun 238	(1956)

(With Sandy Brooks)

Take and Give/Do What I Do	-Sun 256	(1956)

The Rhythm Rockers-

Singles

Thinkin' About You	-Oasis 104	
Fiddle Bop/Juke Box, Help Me Find My Baby	-Cross Country 524	(1956)
Fiddle Bop/Juke Box, Help Me Find My Baby	(R)-Sun 248	(1956)
We Belong Together/Oh, Boy	-Satin 921	(1960)

Charlie Rich-

Singles

Whirlwind /Philadelphia Baby	-Phillips Int 3532	(1958)
Big Man/Rebound	-Phillips Int 3542	(1958)
Lonely Weekends/Everything I Do Is Wrong	-Phillips Int 3552	(1959)
Gonna Be Waiting/School Days	-Phillips Int 3560	(1959)
Stay/On My Knees	-Phillips Int 3562	(1960)
Who Will the Next Fool Be?/Caught in the Middle	-Phillips Int 3566	(1960)
Just a Little Sweet/It's Too Late	-Phillips Int 3572	(1961)
Easy Money/Midnight Blues	-Phillips Int 3576	(1961)
Sittin' and Thinkin'/Finally Found Out	-Phillips Int 3582	(1962)
There's Another Place I Can't Go/I Need Your Love	-Phillips Int 3584	(1962)
She Loved Everybody But Me/ The Grass Is Always Greener	-Groove 580020	(1963)
Big Boss Man	-Groove 580025	(1963)
The Ways of a Woman in Love/My Mountain Dew	-Groove 580035	(1964)
Nice And Easy	-Groove 580041	(1965)
There Won't Be Anymore	-RCA 47-8536	(1965)
Mohair Sam	-Smash 1430	(1965)
Mohair Sam/I Washed My Hands in Muddy Water	(R)-Smash 1993	(1965)
The Dance of Love/I Can't Go On	-Smash 2012	(1965)
Something Just Came Over Me/Hawg Jaw	-Smash 2022	(1966)
Tears Ago/No Home	-Smash 2038	(1966)

-Charlie Rich Cont'd-

That's My Way	-Smash 2060	(1966)
Only Me	-Hi 2134	(1967)
Set Me Free	-Epic 5-10287	(1968)
Ragedy Ann	-Epic 5-10358	(1968)
Life's Little Ups and Downs	-Epic 5-10492	(1969)
Who Will the Next Fool Be/Stay	(R)-Sun/SSS 1110	(1969)
Lonely Weekends/Everything I Do Is Wrong	(R)-Sun/SSS 67	(1969)
July 12, 1939	-Epic 5-10585	(1970)
July 12, 1939/Life's Little Ups and Downs	(R)-Epic 15-2291	(1970)
Sittin' and Thinkin'/Who Will the Next Fool Be	-Sun/SSS 70	(1970)
Nice and Easy/I Can't Even Drink It Away	(2) -Epic 5-10662	(1971)
Nice and Easy/Life's Little Ups and Downs	(DJ) -Epic AE7-1065	(1971)
A Part of Your Life	-Epic 5-10809	(1971)
I Take It on Home	-Epic 5-10867	(1972)
The Most Beautiful Girl	-Epic 5-11040	(1973)
Tomorrow Night	-RCA 74-0983	(1973)
A Very Special Love Song/I Can't Even Drink It Away	-Epic 11091	(1973)
There Won't Be Anymore	(R)-RCA apbo-0195	(1973)
I Take It on Home/Behind Closed Doors	(R)-Epic 15-2336	(197?)
I Love My Friend	-Epic 20066	(1974)
I Don't See Me in Your Eyes Anymore	(R)-RCA APBO-0260	(1974)
She Called Me Baby	(R)-RCA PB-10062	(1974)
There Won't Be Anymore/Tomorrow Night	(R)-RCA PB-10159	(1975)
It's All Over Now	(R)-RCA PB-10256	(1975)
I Love My Friend/The Most Beautiful Girl	(R)-Epic 15-2343	(1975)
My Elusive Dreams	-Epic 8-50064	(1975)
Every Time I Touch You	-Epic 8-50103	(1975)
Every Time I Touch You/Nice and Easy	(R)-Epic 15-2345	(1975)
Since I Fell for You	-Epic 8-50182	(1975)
Down by the Riverside	-Epic 8-50222	(1976)
My Mountain Dew/Nice and Easy	(R)-RCA PB-10859	(1976)
Road Song	-Epic 8-50268	(1976)
Road Song	(R)-Epic 15-2359	(1976)
	(R)-RCA	(1974-77)
Easy Look	-Epic 8-50328	(1977)
Rollin' with the Flow	-Epic 8-50392	(1977)
Rollin' with the Flow/A Very Special Love Song	(R)-Epic 15-2379	(1977)
Spanish Eyes	-Epic 8-50701	(1979)
Even a Fool Would Let Go	-Epic 8-50869	(1980)
A Field of Daisies	-Mercury 73498	(1973-74)
	-Electra	(1978-81)
Puttin' In Overtime Overtime At Home	-UA 1193	(1978)
I Still Believe In Love	-UA 1223	(1978)
I Lost My Head	-UA 1280	(1979)
Life Goes On	-UA 1307	(1979)
You're Gonna Love Yourself in the Morning	-UA 1325	(1979)
	-Arista	(1980)

-Charlie Rich Cont'd-
Albums

Lonely Weekends with Charlie Rich	-Phillips Int 1970	(1960)
Charlie Rich	-Groove GS-1000	(1964)
That's Rich	-RCA LSP-3352	(1965)
Big Boss Man	-RCA LSP-3537	(1966)
Many New Sides of Charlie Rich	-Smash 67070	(1965)
Charlie Rich(Best Years)	-Smash 67078	(1966)
Charlie Rich Sings Country and Western	-Hi SHL-32037	(1967)
Set Me Free	-Epic BN-26376	(1968)
The Fabulous Charlie Rich	-Epic JE-26516	(1969)
Lonely Weekends	(R)-Sun/SSS 110	(1969)
A Lonely Weekend	(R)-Wing 16375	(1969)
A Time For Tears	-Sun/SSS 123	(1970)
The Fabulous Charlie Rich	(R)-Epic BN-26516	(1970)
She Loved Everybody But Me	-Camden 2417	(1970)
Boss Man	-Epic E-30214	(1970)
The Best of Charlie Rich	-Epic KE-31993	(1972)
Entertainer of the Year	-Hilltop 6160	
Tomorrow Night	-RCA APL1-0258	(1973)
I Do My Swingin' at Home	-Harmony 32166	(1973)
Behind Closed Doors	-Epic PE-32247	(1973)
There Won't Be Anymore	(R)-RCA APL1-0433	(1974)
She Called Me Baby	-RCA APL1-0686	(1974)
Very Special Love Songs	-Epic KE-32531	(1974)
The Silver Fox	-Epic PE-33250	(1974)
There Won't Be Anymore	(R)-Power Pak 241	(1974)
Arkansas Traveller	-Power Pak 245	(1974)
Greatest Hits, Vol. 1	-Power Pak 248	(1974)
Greatest Hits, Vol. 2	-Power Pak 249	(1974)
Fully Realized (2 LP)	-Mercury 2-7505	(1974)
Charlie Rich Sings the Songs of Hank Williams and Others	-Hi SHL-32084	(1974)
Charley Rich- The Early Years	-Sun/SSS 132	(1974)
Golden Treasures	-Sun/SSS 134	(1974)
The Memphis Sound	-Sun/SSS 133	(1974)
The Best of Charlie Rich (2 LP)	-Trip 8502	(1974)
Greatest Hits- Charlie Rich	-RCA APL1-0857	(1975)
Sun's Best of Charlie Rich	-Sun/SSS 135	(1975)
Too Many Teardrops	-Camden	(1975)
	(R)-Buckboard	
The Silver Fox	-Epic PE-33250	(1975)
Every Time You Touch Me I Get High	-Epic PE-33455	(1975)
Greatest Hits of Charlie Rich	-Epic PE-34240	(1976)
The World of Charlie Rich	-RCA APL1-1242	(1976)
Silver Lining	-Epic KE-33545	(1976)
Tomorrow Night	(R)-RCA ANL1-1542	(1976)
Everything You Always Wanted to Hear by Charlie Rich	(DJ)-Epic AS-139	(1976)
Take Me	-Epic KE-34440	(1977)

-Charlie Rich Cont'd-

So Lonesome I Could Cry		(R)-Hi 8006	(1977)
Big Boss Man/My Mountain Dew		-RCA APLI-2260	(1977)
She Called Me Baby		(R)-RCA ANL1-2424	(1977)
Rollin' with the Flow		-Epic PE-34891	(1977)
		-Phonorama	
		-51 West	
Greatest Hits/Best of Charlie Rich	(2 LPS)	-CBS EGT-38568	(1976)
Classic Rich		-Epic JE-35394	(1978)
Classic Rich, Vol. 2		-Epic JE-35624	(1978)
I Still Believe in Love		-UA UALA876H	(1979)
20 Golden Hits		-Sun/SSS 1003	(1979)
Fool Strikes Again		-UA UALA925H	(1979)
Nobody But You		-UA LT-998	(1979)
The Original Charlie Rich		-Sun/SSS 1007	(1979)
Once a Drifter		-Elektra 6E-301	(1980)
I Do My Swingin' at Home		-Epic	(1981)
Greatest Hits/Best of Charlie Rich	(2CDS)	(R)-CBS EGT-38568	(1982)
Behind Closed Doors	(CD)	(R)-Epic PE-32247	(1983)
Greatest Hits of Charlie Rich	(CD)	(R)-Epic PE-34240	(1983)
Midnight Blue		-Quicksilver 1005	(198?)
American Originals	(CD)	-Columbia 45073	(1989)
The Complete Smash Sessions	(CD)	-Mercury 512643-2	(1992)
Pictures and Paintings	(CD)	-Blue Horizon26730	(1992)
Unchained Melody	(CD)	-Intersound 5003	(1992)

(As Bobby Sheridan)-

Red Man/Sad News	-Sun 354	(1960)

Jimmy Richards-

Singles

Strollin' and Boppin'/Cool As a Moose	-Columbia 4-41083

Rudi Richardson-

Singles

Fool's Hall of Fame/Why Should I Cry	-Sun 271	(1957)

Billy Lee Riley(and The Little Green Men-born 10/05/33 in Pocahontas, Arkansas)-

Singles

Trouble Bound/Rock with Me Baby	-Sun 245	(1955)
Flyin' Saucers Rock and Roll/I Want You Baby	-Sun 260	(1956)
Flyin' Saucers Rock and Roll/I Want You Baby	(R)-Sun 72	(1956)
Red Hot/Pearly Lee	-Sun 277	(1957)

-Billy Lee Riley Cont'd-

Wouldn't You Know/Baby Please Don't Go	-Sun 289	(1958)
(As Bill Riley)		
Down by the Riverside/No Name Girl	-Sun 313	(1958)
Is That All to the Ball(Mr.Hall?)	-Brunswick 55085	(1958)
Got the Water Boiling/One More Time	-Sun 322	(1959)
Flip, Flop and Fly	-Home Of Blues 233	(1961)
You've Lost That Lovin' Feeling	-Verve 10637	(1964)
Bo Didley/Memphis	-Mercury 72314	(1964)
Mojo Workout	-Mercury 72385	(1965)
	-GNP/Crescndo	(1966)
Mississippi Delta	-MoJo 8001	(1967)
Family Portrait	-Hi 8006	(1968)
Show Me Your Soul	-Hi 8011	(1969)
	-Hip	(1968)
	-Atlantic	(1968)
I Got a Thing About You Baby	-Entrance 7508	(1969)
Kay (Reissue From SSS)	-Sun/SSS 1100	(1970)
Albums		
	-Crown	(1963)
	-Mercury	(1964-65)
	-GNP/Crescendo	(1966)
Billy Lee Riley in Action	-Crescent	(1966)
	-Mojo	(1979)
Blue Collar Blues	-Hightone 8040	(1992)

Gene Simmons(Jumpin' Gene Simmons-(Morris Gene Simmons)-

Singles

Drinkin' Wine/I Done Told You	-Sun 299	(1958)
Waiting Game/Shenandoah Waltz	-Sandy 1027	(1960)
Bad Boy Willie	-Checker 2086	(1960)
Teddy Bear/Your True Love	-Hi 2034	(1961)
No Other Guys	-Hi 2039	(1961)
Caldonia/Be Her Number One	-Hi 2050	(1962)
Haunted House/Hey, Hey Little Girl	-Hi 2076	(1963)
The Dodo/The Jump	-Hi 2080	(1964)
Skinny Minnie/I'm a Ramblin' Man	-Hi 2086	(1964)
Folsom Prison Blues	-Hi 2092	(1965)
Batman/Bossy Boss	-Hi 2102	(1965)
Keep That Meat in the Pan	-Hi 2113	(1966)
I'm Just A Loser/Lila (Don't Worry)	-Mala 12012	(1968)
Don't Worry 'Bout Me/Back Home Again	-Agp 119	(1968)
Hop Scotch/Little Rag Doll	-Tupelo	(1969)
Magnolia Street/She's There When I Come Home	-Epic 10601	(1970)
	-Hurshey	(1973)
	-Deltune	(1978)

Ray Smith-

Singles

Gone Baby Gone	-Heart 250	(1956)
So Young/Right Behind You Baby	-Sun 298	(1958)
Why, Why, Why/You Made a Hit	-Sun 308	(1958)
Rockin' Bandit/Sail Away	-Sun 319	(1959)
Rockin' Little Angel/That's All Right	-Judd 1016	(1959)
Put Your Arms Around Me Honey/Marie Elena	-Judd 1017	(1959)
Makes Me Feel Good/One Wonderful Love	-Judd 1019	(1960)
Blonde Hair, Blue Eyes/You Don't Want Me	-Judd 1021	(1961)
Traveling Salesman/Won't Miss You	-Sun 372	(1961)
Turn on the Moonlight/After This Night Is Through	-Infinity 003	(1961)
Let Yourself Go/Johnny the Hummer	-Infinity 007	(1961)
Candy Doll/Big Boss Man	-Sun 376	(1962)
Those Four Precious Years/Room 503	-Smash 1787	(1962)
Almost Alone/A Place with Me in My Heart	-Toppa 1071	(1962)
Did We Have a Party/Here Comes My Baby Back Again	-Tollie 9029	(1962)
Turn On The Moonlight/After This Night Is Through	-Zirkon 1055	(1962)
Turn Over a New Leaf/I'm Snowed	-Warner Bros 5371	(1963)
Deep in My Heart/She's Mine	-Nu-tone 1182	(1964)
I Walk the Line/Fool Number One	-Celebrty Crcl 6901	(1964)
Robbin' The Cradle/Rockin' Robin	-Vee Jay 579	(1964)
Everybody's Goin' Somewhere/Au Go Go Go	-Diamond 193	(1965)
	-SSS Int	(1968)
	-Sun/SSS	(1969)
Tilted Cup of Love	-Cinnamon 755	(1972)
It Wasn't Easy/It's Just Not The Same	-Cinnamon 760	(1972)
I Guess I Better Move Along/Four Seasons of My Life	-ABC 351	(1973)
Walk on By/Did He Hurt You All That Bad?	-ABC 4100	(1973)
Let The Four Winds Blow/I'm in Love Again	-ABC 7130	(1973)
	(R)-Cinnamon	(1974)
Fool Number 1/I Walk the Line	(R)-Collectables 6901	(1974)
	-Corona	(1975-77)
Piss Factory/Hey Joe ??	N/A	
Break Up/Room Full of Roses	-Wix 101	(1978)
Me & Bobby McGee/Whole Lotta' Shakin' Goin On	-Wix 102	(1978)
Rockin' Little Angel	(R)-Oldies 45's 26	
Rockin' Little Angel	(R)-Sire 3109	

Albums

Travelin' with Ray	-Judd JLPA-701	(1960)
The Best of Ray Smith	-T 56062	(196?)
Ray Smith's Greatist Hts	-Columbia CL-1937	(1963)
Ray Smith and Patt Cupp	-Crown CLP-5364	(1963)
I'm Gonna Rock Some More	-Wix 1000	(1978)
	-Boot	(1978)

Warren Smith-

Singles		
Rock and Roll Ruby/I'd Rather Be Safe Than Sorry	-Sun 239	(1956)
Ubangi Stomp/Black Jack David	-Sun 250	(1956)
So Long I'm Gone/Miss Frogie	-Sun 268	(1957)
I've Got Love If You Want It/ I Fell in Love	-Sun 286	(1958)
Sweet Sweet Girl/Goodbye Mr. Love	-Sun 314	(1958)
	-Warner Brothers	(1959)
Cave In/I Don't Believe I'll Fall In Love Today	-Liberty 55248	(1959)
A Whole Lot of Nuthin'/Odds and Ends	-Liberty 55302	(1960)
Old Lonesome Feeling/Call of the Wild	-Liberty 55336	(1960)
Why Baby Why/Why I'm Walking(with Shirlie Collie)	-Liberty 55361	(1961)
Bad News Gets Around/Five Minutes of the Latest Blues	-Liberty 55409	(1961)
Book of Broken Hearts/160 Pounds of Hurt	-Liberty 55475	(1962)
Big City Ways	-Liberty 55615	(1962)
Blue Smoke	-Liberty 55699	(1964)
Future x	-Skill 45-007	
	-Mercury	(1968)
'Till You Can Make It on Your Own/Between the		
Devil and the Deep Blue Sea	-Jubal 172	(1971)
I Don't Believe I'll Fall in Love Today/Did You Tell Him	(2) -Jubal 272	(1972)
	-Sun/SSS	(1980)
Albums		
The First Country Collection of Warren Smith	-Liberty LSP-3199	(1961)

Vernon Taylor-

Singles		
The Black Haired Man/Wrong	-Sun 311	(1958)
Breeze/Today Is Blue Day	-Sun 310	(1958)
I've Got the Blues/	-Dot 15632	(1957)
You're the Beat in My Heart	-Dot 15697	(1957)

Onie Wheeler-

Singles		
No, I Don't Guess I Will	-Columbia 21500	
21371-21523-40917	-Columbia	(1954-57)
Sandyland Farmer	-Epic 09540	
Run 'Em Off/	-Okeh 18022	(1958)
Little Mama	-Okeh 18049	(1958)
Would You Like To Wear an Onie Wheeler	-Okeh 18058	(1958)
Jump Right Out of this Juke Box/Tell 'Em Off	-Sun 315	(1959)
The Dirt Behind My Ears	-Jab 9013	
John's Been Shuckin' My Corn	-Royal American 76	(1972)

-Onie Wheeler Cont'd-
Albums

John's Been Shuckin' My Corn	-Onie 100	
Something New and Something Old	-Brylen 4448	

Bobby Wood-

Singles

Everybody's Searchin'/Human Emotions	-Sun 369	(1961)
Everybody's Searchin'/Human Emotions	(R)-Pen 113	(1961)
	-Challange	(1962)
That's All I Need	-Joy 279	(1963)
If I'm a Fool For Loving You/Boing Boing Boing	-Joy 285	(1963)
That's All I Need You To Know	-Joy 288	(1963)

Malcom Yelvington(and The Star Rhythm Boys)-

Singles

Drinkin' Wine Spodee-O-Dee/Just Rolling Along	-Sun 211	(1955)
Rockin' with My Baby/It's Me Baby	-Sun 246	(1956)
	-Mala	(1968)
	-MGM	(1967-69)
	-Luckey Eleven	(1973)
	-Cinnamon	(1974)

The Complete 45 Sun Discography

Because of the enormous contribution of Sun Records, and
Sam Philips, to the Rockabilly genre, we feel that we should
include the complete list of single releases from Sun.

The Sun Sessions

174 Jackie Boy And Little Walter	Sellin' My Whiskey/Blues In My Condition	
175 Johnny London	Drivin' Slow/Flat Tire	
176 Walter Bradrod		
& Big City 4	Dreary Night/Nuthin' But Blues	
177 Handy Jackson	Got My Application Baby/	
	Trouble (will Bring You Down)	
178 Joe Hill Louis	We All Gotta Go Sometime/She May Be Yours	
179 Willie Nix		
-Memphis Blues Boys	Seems Like A Million Years/Barber Shop Boogie	
180 Jimmy And Walter	Easy/Before Long	
181 Rufus "Hound Dog" Thomas, Jr.	Bearcat/Walkin' In The Rain	
182 Dusty Brooks And His Tones	Tears And Wine/Heaven Or Fire	
183 D. A. Hunt	Lonesome Ol' Jail/Greyhound Blues	
184 Big Memphis Marainey-		
Onzie Horn Combo	Call Me Anything But Call Me/No Means No	
185 Jimmy Deberry	Take A Little Chance/Time Has Made A Change	
186 Prisonaires	Just Walkin' In The Rain/Baby Please	
187 Little Junior's Blue Flames	Feelin' Good/Fussin' And Fightin' Blues	(1954)
188 Rufus Thomas, Jr.	Tiger Man/Save That Money	(1954)
189 Prisionaires	My God Is Real/Softly & Tenderly	(1954)
190 Ripley Cotton Choppers	Silver Bells/Blues Waltz	(1954)
191 Prisonaires	A Prisoner's Prayer/I Know	(1954)
192 Little Junior's Blue Flames	Mystery Train/Love My Baby	(1954)
193 Doctor Ross	Come Back Baby/Chicago Breakdown	(1954)
194 Little Milton	Beggin' My Baby/Somebody Told Me	(1954)
195 Billy "The Kid" Emerson	No Teasing Around/If Lovin' Is Believing	(1954)
196 Hot Shot Love	Wolf Call Boogie/Harmonica Jam	(1954)
197 Earl Peterson-Michigan's		
Singing Cowboy	Boogie Blues/In The Dark	(1954)
198 Howard Seratt	Troublesome Waters/I Must Be Saved	(1954)
199 James Cotton	My Baby/Straighten Up Baby	(1954)
200 Little Milton	If You Love Me/Alone And Blue	(1954)
201 Hardrock Gunter	Gonna Dance All Night/Fallen Angel	(1954)
202 Doug Poindexter And The		
Starlite Wranglers	My Kind Of Carryin' On/Now She Cares	
	No More For Me	(1954)
203 Bill (The Kid) Emerson	I'm Not Going Home/The Woodchuck	(1954)
204 Raymond Hill	Bourbon Street Jump/The Snuggle	(1954)
205 Harmonica Frank	Rockin' Chair Daddy/The Great Medical	
	Menagerist	(1954)
206 James Cotton	Hold Me In Your Arms/Cotton Crop Blues	(1954)
207 Prisonaires	There Is Love In You/What'll You Do Next	(1954)
208 Buddy Cunningham	Right Or Wrong/Who Do I Cry	(1954)
209 Elvis Presley-Scotty & Bill	That's All Right/Blue Moon Of Kentucky	(1954)
210 Elvis Presley-Scotty & Bill	Good Rockin' Tonight/	
	I Don't Care If The Sun Don't Shine (1954)	

211 Malcom Yelvington And Star Rhythm Boys	Drinkin' Wine Spodee-O-Dee/ Just Rolling Along	(1955)
212 Doctor Ross	The Boogie Disease/Juke Box Boogie	(1955)
213 The Jones Brothers	Every Night/Look To Jesus	(1955)
214 Bill (The Kid) Emerson	Move Baby Move/When It Rains It Pours	(1955)
215 Elvis Presley-Scotty & Bill	Milkcow Blues Boogie/You're A Heartbreakr	(1955)
216 Slim Rhodes	Don't Believe/Uncertain Love	(1955)
217 Elvis Presley-Scotty & Bill	Baby Let's Play House/ I'm Left,You're Right, She's Gone	(1955)
218 Sammy Lewis-Willie Johnson	So Long Baby/I Feel So Worried	(1955)
219 Billy "The Kid" Emerson	Red Hot/No Greater Love	(1955)
220 Little Milton	Lookin' For My Baby/Homesick For My Baby	(1955)
221 Johnny Cash & Tennessee Two	Hey Porter/Cry! Cry! Cry!	(1955)
01 Johnny Cash & Tennessee Two	Hey Porter/Cry! Cry! Cry! (R)	(1955)
222 The Five Tinos	Sitting By My Window/Don't Do That	(1955)
223 Elvis Presley-Scotty & Bill	Mystery Train/ I Forgot To Remember To Forget	(1955)
224 Carl Perkins	Let The Juke Box Keep On Playing/ Gone Gone Gone	(1955)
02 Carl Perkins	Let The Juke Box Keep On Playing/ Gone Gone Gone (R)	(1955)
225 Slim Rhodes	The House Of Sin/Are You Ashamed Of Me?	(1955)
226 Eddie Snow	Ain't That Right/Bring Your Love Back Home	(1955)
227 Roscoe Gordon	Just Love Me Baby/Weeping Blues	(1955)
228 Smokey Joe	The Signifying Monkey/Listen To Me Baby	(1955)
229 Maggie Sue Wimberly	How Long/Daydreams Come True	(1955)
230 The Miller Sisters	There's No Right Way To Do Me Wrong/ You Can Tell Me	(1955)
231 Charlie Feathers	Defrost Your Heart/Wedding Gown Of White	(1955)
232 Johnny Cash	Folsom Prison Blues/ So Doggone Lonesme	(1955)
03 Johnny Cash (R)	Folsom Prison Blues/ So Doggone Lonesme	(1955)
233 Billy "The Kid" Emerson	Little Fine Healthy Thing/ Something For Nothing	(1955)
234 Carl Perkins	Blue Suede Shoes/Honey Don't	(1956)
04 Carl Perkins	Blue Suede Shoes/Honey Don't (R)	(1956)
235 Carl Perkins	Sure To Fall/Tennessee	(1956)
05 Carl Perkins	Sure To Fall/Tennessee (R)	(1956)
236 Jimmy Haggett	No More/They Call Our Love A Sin	(1956)
237 Rosco Gordon	"The Chicken"/Love For You Baby	(1956)
238 Slim Rhodes	Gonna Romp And Stomp/Bad Girl	(1956)
239 Warren Smith	Rock 'N' Roll Ruby/I'd Rather Be Safe Than Sorry	(1956)
06 Warren Smith	Rock 'N' Roll Ruby/I'd Rather Be Safe Than Sorry (R)	(1956)
240 Jack Earls & The Jimbos	Slow Down/A Fool For Lovin' You	(1956)

241 Johnny Cash & Tennessee Two	I Walk The Line/Get Rhythm		(1956)
07 Johnny Cash & Tennessee Two	I Walk The Line/Get Rhythm	(R)	(1956)
242 Roy Orbison & The Teen Kings	Ooby Dooby/Go, Go, Go		(1956)
08 Roy Orbison & The Teen Kings	Ooby Dooby/Go, Go, Go (R)		(1956)
243 Carl Perkins	Boppin' The Blues/All Mama's Children		(1956)
10 Carl Perkins	Boppin' The Blues/All Mama's Children	(R)	(1956)
244 Jean Chapel	I Won't Be Rockin' Tonight/		
	Welcome To The Club		(1956)
245 Billy Riley	Trouble Bound/Rock With Me Baby		(1956)
246 Malcom Yelvington	Rockin' Wth My Baby/Its Me Baby		(1956)
247 Sonny Burgess	Red Headed Woman/We Wanna Boogie		(1956)
248 Rhythm Rockers	Fiddle Bop/		
	Juke Box, Help Me Find My Bby		(1956)
249 Carl Perkins	Dixie Fried/I'm Sorry, I'm Not Sorry		(1956)
11 Carl Perkins	Dixie Fried/I'm Sorry, I'm Not Sorry	(R)	(1956)
250 Warren Smith	Ubangi Stomp/Black Jack David		(1956)
251 Roy Orbison-Teen Kings	Rockhouse/You're My Baby		(1956)
12 Roy Orbison-Teen Kings	Rockhouse/You're My Baby	(R)	(1956)
252	(Never released)		
253 Barbara Pitman	I Need A Man/No Matter		
	Who's To Blame		(1956)
254 Ray Harris	Come On Little Mama/		
	Where'd You Stay Last Night		(1956)
255 Miller Sisters	Ten Cats Down/Finders Keepers		(1956)
256 Slim Rhodes Featuring			
Sandy Brooks	Take And Give/Do What I Do		(1956)
257 Rosco Gordon	Shoobie Oobie/Cheese And Crackers		(1956)
258 Johnny Cash & Tennessee Two	Train Of Love/There You Go		(1956)
13 Johnny Cash & Tennessee Two	Train Of Love/There You Go (R)		(1957)
259 Jerry Lee Lewis	Crazy Arms/End Of The Road		(1956)
14 Jerry Lee Lewis	Crazy Arms/End Of The Road	(R)	(1957)
260 Billy Riley And His Little			
Green Men	Flyin' Saucers Rock & Roll/I Want You Bby		(1956)
261 Carl Perkins	Your True Love/Matchbox		(1957)
15 Carl Perkins	Your True Love/Matchbox	(R)	(1957)
262 Ernie Chaffin	Lonesome For My Baby/Flyin' Low		(1956)
263 Sonny Burgess	Restless/Ain't Got A Thing		(1956)
264 Glenn Honeycutt	I'll Be Around/I'll Wait Forever		(1956)
265 Roy Orbison And The Roses	Devil Doll/Sweet And Easy		(1957)
16 Roy Orbison And The Roses	Devil Doll/Sweet And Easy	(R)	(1957)
266 Johnny Cash & Tennessee Two	Next In Line/Don't Make Me Go		(1957)
17 Johnny Cash & Tennessee Two	Next In Line/Don't Make Me Go	(R)	(1957)
267 Jerry Lee Lewis	Whole Lot Of Shakin' Going On/It'll Be Me		(1957)
18 Jerry Lee Lewis	Whole Lot Of Shakin' Going On/It'll Be Me	(R)	(1957)
268 Warren Smith	So Long I'm Gone/Miss Froggie		(1957)
269 Wake & Dick The College Kids	Bop Bop Baby/Don't Need Your Lovin'		(1957)
270 Jim Williams	Please Don't Cry Over 'Em/		
	That Depends On You		(1957)

271 Rudi Richardson	Fools Hall Of Fame/Why Should I Cry		(1957)
272 Ray Harris	Greenback Dollar, Watch And Chain/		
	Foolish Heart		(1957)
273 Mack Self	Easy To Love/Every Day		(1957)
274 Carl Perkins	Forever Yours/That's Right		(1957)
19 Carl Perkins	Forever Yours/That's Right	(R)	(1957)
275 Ernie Chaffin	I'm Lonesome/Laughin' And Jokin		(1957)
276 Edwin Bruce	Rock Boppin' Baby/ More Than Yesterday		(1957)
277 Billy Riley-Little Green Men	Red Hot/Pearly Lee		(1957)
278 Tommy Blake-Rhythm Rebels	Flat Foot Sam/Lordy Hoody		(1957)
279 Johnny Cash & Tennessee Two	Home Of The Blues/		
	Give My Love To Rose		(1957)
20 Johnny Cash & Tennessee Two	Home Of The Blues/		
	Give My Love To Rose (R)		(1957)
280 Dickey Lee & The Collegiates	Memories New Grow Old/Good Lovin'		(1957)
281 Jerry Lee Lewis	Great Balls Of Fire/You Win Again		(1957)
21 Jerry Lee Lewis	Great Balls Of Fire/You Win Again	(R)	(1957)
282 Dick Penner	Your Honey Love/Cindy Lou		(1957)
283 Johnny Cash & Tennessee Two	Ballad Of A Teenage Queen/Big River		(1957)
22 Johnny Cash & Tennessee Two	Ballad Of A Teenage Queen/Big River	(R)	(1958)
284 Roy Orbison	Chicken-Hearted/I Like Love		(1957)
23 Roy Orbison	Chicken-Hearted/I Like Love	(R)	(1957)
285 Sonny Burgess	My Bucket's Got A Hole In It/Sweet Misery		(1957)
286 Warren Smith	I've Got Love If You Want It/I Feel In Love		(1957)
287 Carl Perkins	Glad All Over/Lend Me Your Comb		(1957)
24 Carl Perkins	Glad All Over/Lend Me Your Comb	(R)	(1958)
288 Jerry Lee Lewis	Breathless/Down The Line		(1958)
25 Jerry Lee Lewis	Breathless/Down The Line	(R)	(1958)
289 Billy Riley-Little Green Men	Wouldn't You Know/Baby Please Don't Go		(1958)
290 Rudy Grayzell	Judy /I Think Of You		(1958)
291 Jack Clement	Ten Years/Your Lover Boy		(1958)
292 Edwin Bruce	Sweet Woman/Part Of My Life		(1958)
293 The Sun-Rays	The Lonely Hours/Love Is A Stranger		(1958)
294 Magel Friesman	I Feel So Blue/Memories Of You		(1958)
295 Johnny Cash & Tennessee Two	Guess Things Happen That Way/		
	Come In Stranger		(1958)
27 Johnny Cash & Tennessee Two	Guess Things Happen That Way/		
	Come In Stranger	(R)	(1958)
296 Jerry Lee Lewis	High School Confidential/Fools Like Me		(1958)
28 Jerry Lee Lewis	High School Confidential/Fools Like Me	(R)	(1958)
297 Dickey Lee	Fool, Fool, Fool/Dreamy Nights		(1958)
298 Ray Smith	Right Behind You Baby/So Young		(1958)
299 Gene Simmons	Drinkin' Wine/I Done Told You		(1958)
300 Tommy Blake	Sweetie Pie/I Dig You Baby		(1958)
301 George And Louis	The Return Of Jerry Lee/ Lewis Boogie		(1958)
29 George And Louis	The Return Of Jerry Lee/Lewis Boogie	(R)	(1958)
302 Johnny Cash & Tennessee Two	The Ways Of A Woman In Love/You're		
	The Nearest Thing To Heaven		(1958)

30 Johnny Cash & Tennessee Two	The Ways Of A Woman In Love/You're		
	The Nearest Thing To Heaven(R)		(1958)
303 Jerry Lee Lewis	Break-Up/I'll Make It All Up To You		(1958)
31 Jerry Lee Lewis	Break-Up/I'll Make It All Up To You	(R)	(1958)
304 Sonny Burgess	Itchy/Thunderbird		(1958)
305 Rosco Gordon	Sally Jo/Torro		(1958)
306 Jimmy Isle	I've Been Waiting/Diamond Ring		(1950)
307 Ernie Chaffin	My Love For You/Born To Lose		(1950)
308 Ray Smith	Why, Why, Why/You Made A Hit		(1958)
309 Johnny Cash & Tennessee Two	It's Just About Time/I Just Thought		
	That Y'oud Like To Know		(1958)
32 Johnny Cash & Tennessee Two	It's Just About Time/I Just Thought		
	That Y'oud Like To Know	(R)	(1958)
310 Vernon Taylor	Breeze/Today Is Blue Day		(1958)
311 Jack Clement	The Black Haired Man/Wrong		(1958)
312 Jerry Lee Lewis	I'll Sail My Ship Alone/It Hurt Me So		(1958)
34 Jerry Lee Lewis	I'll Sail My Ship Alone/It Hurt Me So	(R)	(1958)
313 Bill Riley	Down By The Riverside/No Name Girl		(1958)
314 Warren Smith	Sweet, Sweet Girl/Goodbye Mr. Love		(1958)
315 Onie Wheeler	Jump Right Out Of This Juke Box/		
	Tell 'Em Off		(1959)
316 Johnny Cash & Tennessee Two	Thanks A Lot/Luther Played The Boogie		(1959)
35 Johnny Cash & Tennessee Two	Thanks A Lot/Luther Played The Boogie(R)		(1959)
317 Jerry Lee Lewis	Lovin' Up Storm/Big Blon' Baby		(1959)
36 Jerry Lee Lewis	Lovin' Up Storm/Big Blon' Baby	(R)	(1959)
318 Jimmy Isle	Time Will Tell/Without A Love		(1959)
319 Ray Smith	Rockin' Bandit/Sail Away		(1959)
320 Ernie Chaffin	Don't Ever Leave Me/Miracle Of You		(1959)
321 Johnny Cash & Tennessee Two	Katy Too/I Forgot To Remember To Forget		(1959)
37 Johnny Cash & Tennessee Two	Katy Too/I Forgot To Remember To Forget (R)		(1959)
322 Bill Riley	Got The Water Boiling/One More Time		(1959)
323 Alton And Jimmy	Have Faith In My Love/		
	No More Crying The Blues		(1959)
324 Jerry Lee Lewis	Let's Talk About Us/Ballad Of Billy Joe		(1959)
38 Jerry Lee Lewis	Let's Talk About Us/Ballad Of Billy Joe	(R)	(1959)
325 Vernon Taylor	Mystery Train/Sweet And Easy To Forget		(1959)
326 Jerry McGill & The Top Coats	I Wanna Make Sweet Love/ Love Struck		(1959)
327 Johnny Powers	With Your Love, With Your Kiss/		
	Be Mine, All Mine		(1959)
328 Sherry Crane	Willie, Willie/Winnie The Parakeet		(1959)
329 Will Mercer	You're Just My Kind/Ballad Of St. Marks		(1959)
330 Jerry Lee Lewis	Little Queenie/I Could Never		
	Be Ashamed Of You		(1959)
39 Jerry Lee Lewis	Little Queenie/I Could Never		
	Be Ashamed Of You	(R)	(1959)
331 Johnny Cash & Tennessee Two	Goodbye, Little Darling/ You Tell Me		(1959)
40 Johnny Cash & Tennessee Two	Goodbye, Little Darling/ You Tell Me	(R)	(1959)
332 Jimmy Isle	What A Life/Together		(1959)

333 Ray B. Anthony	Alice Blue Gown/St. Louis Blues		(1959)
334 Johnny Cash & Tennessee Two	Straight A's In Love/I Love You Because		(1959)
41 Johnny Cash & Tennessee Two	Straight A's In Love/I Love You Because	(R)	(1960)
335 Tracy Pendarvis & Swampers	A Thousand Guitars/Is It Too Late		(1960)
336 Mack Owen	Walkin' And Talkin'/		
	Somebody Just Like You		(1960)
337 Jerry Lee Lewis	Old Black Joe/Baby, Baby Bye Bye		(1960)
42 Jerry Lee Lewis	Old Black Joe/Baby, Baby Bye Bye	(R)	(1960)
338 Paul Ricky	Legend Of Big Steeple/Brokn Hearted Willie		(1960)
339 Rayburn Anthony	There's No Tomorrow/Whose Gonna Shine		
	Your Pretty Little Feet		(1960)
340 Bill Johnson	Bobaloo/Bad Times Ahead		(1960)
341 Sonny Wilson	The Great Pretedr/I'm Gonna Take A Walk		(1960)
342 Bobbie Jean	You Burned The Bridges/Cheatrs Never Win		(1960)
343 Johnny Cash & Tennessee Two	Down The Street To 301/		
	Story Of A Broken Heart		(1960)
43 Johnny Cash & Tennessee Two	Down The Street To 301/		
	Story Of A Broken Heart	(R)	(1960)
344 Jerry Lee Lewis	John Henry/Hang Up My		
	Rock And Roll Shoes		(1960)
44 Jerry Lee Lewis	John Henry/Hang Up My		
	Rock And Roll Shoes	(R)	(1960)
345 Tracy Pendarvis	Is It Me/Southbound Line		(1960)
346 Bill Strength	I Guess I'd Better Go/Senorita		(1960)
347 Johnny Cash & Tennessee Two	Mean Eyed Cat/Port Of Lonely Hearts		(1960)
45 Johnny Cash & Tennessee Two	Mean Eyed Cat/Port Of Lonely Hearts	(R)	(1960)
348 Lance Roberts	The Good Guy Always Wins/		
	The Time Is Right		(1960)
349 Tony Rossini	I Gotta Know Where I Stand/Is It Too Late		(1960)
350 The Rockin' Stockings	Yulesville U.S.A./Rockin' Old Lang Syne		(1960)
351 Ira Jay II	You Don't Love Me/More Than Anything		(1960)
352 Jerry Lee Lewis	When I Get Paid/Love Made A Fool Of Me		(1960)
46 Jerry Lee Lewis	When I Get Paid/Love Made A Fool Of Me	(R)	(1960)
353 Roy Orbison	Devil Doll/Sweet & Easy To Love		(1960)
354 Bobby Sheridan	Red Man/Sad News (This is Charlie Rich)		(1960)
355 Johnny Cash & Tennessee Two	Oh, Lonesome Me/Life Goes On		(1960)
47 Johnny Cash & Tennessee Two	Oh, Lonesome Me/Life Goes On	(R)	(1961)
356 Jerry Lee Lewis	What'd I Say/Livin' Lovin' Wreck		(1961)
48 Jerry Lee Lewis	What'd I Say/Livin' Lovin' Wreck	(R)	(1961)
357	(not released)		
358 George Klein	U.T. Party (Part 1)/U.T. Party (Part 2)		(1961)
359 Tracy Pendarvis	Bell Of The Suwanee/Eternally		(1961)
360 Wade Cagle And The Escorts	Groovey Train/Highland Rock		(1961)
361 Anita Wood	I'll Wait Forever/ I Can't Show		
	Here How I Feel		(1961)
362 Harold Dorman	There They Go/I'll Stick By You		(1961)
363 Johnny Cash & Tennessee Two	My Treasure/Sugartime		(1961)
49 Johnny Cash & Tennessee Two	My Treasure/Sugartime	(R)	(1961)

364 Jerry Lee Lewis	It Won't Happen With Me/		
	Cold, Cold Heart		(1961)
50 Jerry Lee Lewis	It Won't Happen With Me/		
	Cold, Cold Heart	(R)	(1961)
365 Shirley Sisk	I Forget To Remember To Forget/Other Side		(1961)
366 Tony Rossini	Well I Ask Ya/Darlena		(1961)
367 Jerry Lee Lewis	Save The Last Dance For Me/		
	As Long As I Live		(1961)
51 Jerry Lee Lewis	Save The Last Dance For Me/		
	As Long As I Live	(R)	(1961)
368 Don Hosea	Since I Met You /U Huh Unh		(1961)
369 Bobby Wood	Everybody's Searchin'/Human Emotions		(1961)
370 Harold Dorman	Uncle Johah's Place/Just One Step		(1961)
371 Jerry Lee Lewis	Money/Bonnie Bee		(1961)
52 Jerry Lee Lewis	Money/Bonnie Bee	(R)	(1961)
372 Ray Smith	Travelin' Salesman/I Won't Miss You		(1961)
373 Rayburn Anthony	How Well I Know/Big Dream		(1961)
374 Jerry Lee Lewis	I've Been Twistin'/Rambln Rose		(1962)
53 Jerry Lee Lewis	I've Been Twistin'/Rambln Rose	(R)	(1962)
375 Ray Smith	Candy Doll/Hey, Boss Man		
376 Johnny Cash & Tennessee Two	Blue Train/Born To Lose		(1962)
54 Johnny Cash & Tennessee Two	Blue Train/Born To Lose	(R)	(1962)
377 Harold Dorman	Wait 'Til Saturday Night/In The Beginning		(1962)
378 Tony Rossini	After School/Just Around The Corner		(1962)
379 Jerry Lee Lewis	Sweet Little Sixteen/		
	How's My Ex Treating You		(1962)
55 Jerry Lee Lewis	Sweet Little Sixteen/		
	How's My Ex Treating You	(R)	(1962)
380 Tony Rossini & The Chippers	You Make It Sound So Easy/		
	New Girl In Town		(1962)
381 The Four Upsetters	Crazy Arms/Midnight Soiree		(1962)
382 Jerry Lee Lewis	Good Golly, Miss Molly/		
	I Can't Trust Me (In Your Arms)		(1962)
56 Jerry Lee Lewis	Good Golly, Miss Molly/		
	I Can't Trust Me (In Your Arms)	(R)	(1962)
383	(never released)		
384 Jerry Lee Lewis	Teenage Letter/Seasons Of My Heart		(1963)
57 Jerry Lee Lewis	Teenage Letter/Seasons Of My Heart	(R)	(1963)
385	(never released)		
386 The Four Upsetters	Wabash Cannonball/ Surfin' Calliope		(1963)
387 Tony Rossini	Moved To Kansas City/Nobody		(1963)
388 The Teenangels	Ain't Gonna Let You/ Tell Me My Love		(1963)
389 Billy Adams	Betty And Dupree/Got My Mojo Working		(1963)
390 Bill Yates And His T-Birds	Don't Step On My Dog/Stop, Wait, Listen		(1964)
391 Billy Adams	Trouble In Mind/Lookin For Mary Ann		(1964)
392 Johnny Cash	Wide Open Road/Belshazar		(1964)
58 Johnny Cash	Wide Open Road/Belshazar	(R)	(1964)
393 Smokey Joe	Signifying Monkey/Listen To Me Baby		(1964)

394 Billy Adams	Reconsider Baby/Ruby Jane		(1964)
395 Randy And The Radiants	Peek-A-Boo/Mountain High		(1964)
396 Jerry Lee Lewis	Carry Me Back To Old Virginia/		
	I Know What It Means		(1965)
59 Jerry Lee Lewis	Carry Me Back To Old Virginia/		
	I Know What It Means	(R)	(1965)
397 Gorgeous Bill	Carleen/Too Late To Right My Wrong		(1965)
398 Randy And The Radiants	My Ways Of Thinking/Truth From My Eyes		(1965)
399 Bill Yates	Big, Big World/I Dropped My M & M's		(1965)
400 The Jesters	My Babe/Cadillac Man		(1965)
401 Billy Adams	Open The Door Richard/Rock Me baby		(1965)
402 Dane Stinit	Don't Knock What You Don't Under Stand/		
	Always On The Go		(1965)
403 David Houston	Sherry's Lips/Miss Brown		(1965)
404 The Climates	No You For Me/Breaking Up Again		(1965)
405 Dane Stinit	Sweet Country Girl/That Muddy Ole' River		(1965)
406 Gospel Series:Brother	I'm Gonna Move In The Room With		
James Anderson	The Lord/My Soul Needs Resting		(1965)
407 "Load Of Mischief"	Back In My Arms Again/I'm A Lover		(1965)
72 Billy Riley And His Little			
Green Men (R)	Flyin' Saucers Rock & Roll/I Want You Baby		(1965)

CHAPTER 6

THE BLACK INFLUENCE

Charles Edward Anderson Berry

Chuck Berry was born in San Jose, California on January 15, 1926. His father moved the family to St. Louis when Chuck was very young, and he grew up in the Elleardsville section, which contained pleasant, quiet, clean streets.

Chuck began to learn the guitar in his teens, mainly as a hobby. He was into jazz, swing, and blues. In 1944, he entered reform school after being arrested for a failed robbery attempt. In 1947, when he was released, he ended up working as an assembler at the GM Fisher Body Plant, after working at several types of odd jobs. In his search for an occupation, he learned to be a hairdresser and cosmetologist by taking night courses.

In the early '50's he was married with two children, so he supplemented his hairdressing income by playing in small clubs. He soon formed a trio with Johnny Johnson on piano and Ebby Harding on drums. The trio performed regularly at the Cosmopolitan Club in East St. Louis, and soon gained a large following of steady fans.

By now, Chuck had been accustomed to adding his own verses to many of the popular songs, as well as to songs that he created himself, so he decided to try his luck at playing and writing. Loaded up with his songs. He headed for Chicago to seek a career and take in some of the blues artists, such as Muddy Waters, who constantly played in the area. While he was at one of Muddy Waters's shows, he sat in with Muddy, who was so impressed with him that he recommended that Chuck audition for Leonard Chess of Chess Records.

Chess had been receiving many records from southern companies that recorded them and licensed them to Chess. One of these companies was Sun Records of Memphis, Tennessee. This was primarily how Sun survived before it produced some hits.

One of Chuck's songs, "Ida Red", which Chess heard stood out among the rest. Unfortunately, there was another song by the same name, so Chess renamed it "Maybellene" and released it. The song was a monstrous hit, with the help of Alan Freed, who played it frequently on his New York disc jockey show. The official list of co-writers on the song are Chuck Berry, Alan Freed, and Russ Frato. Putting Freed's name on the song was the cost of doing business with him. With this record, Chuck went to the top of the world.

He followed "Maybellene" with "Roll Over Beethoven", which immediately rose to tremendous heights on the national charts. Crowds began to follow him and show up at his performances, and he soon developed a better stage presence than most performers accumulate in a lifetime of work.

Chuck travelled with a midyear tour that covered 101 stages in 101 days and followed that up by appearing on stage at the Paramount Theater, in Brooklyn, New York, where he walked like a duck while he played. This bit of style tore the house down, and became his trademark.

By the end of the '50's Chuck had become rich and famous. He lived in a beautiful mansion in the better section of St. Louis, and his Club Bandstand was one of the most popular clubs in the area. But just as he was riding high, tragedy occurred: He was indicted on a morals charge. The hatcheck girl at his club accused him of taking her from New Mexico to St. Louis for immoral purposes. She also claimed to be only 14 years old.

After several years of questioning, and fighting in the courts, testimony came to light that she had been a prostitute, and had gone with him of her own free will. Chuck claimed that he used her only to learn Spanish. Unfortunately, possibly because he was black, but at least because of his outgoing, sometimes arrogant, manner, he was sent to jail for the crime.

He spent the next few years at the Federal Penitentiary in Terre Haute, Indiana.

By the time he got out of prison, the world had changed, and everything was different: His club was closed, his family had left him, and rock and roll music had changed. Though his records continued to sell, he was no longer the star that he used to be.

Chuck worked on creating an amusement park and country club complex in, of all places, Wentzville, Missouri. He spent several years on this project, which never really amounted to much, although he had a dream of establishing a type of Disneyland there.

In the late '60's Mercury Records offered him a favorable contract. He would record his songs, in his own studio, and forward them to Mercury. Nothing in the way of hits really came from this deal, and he returned to Chess.

In 1972, he had the distinction of playing in Las Vegas and was warmly received. It looked like a comeback was in order. In 1972, he hit the charts again, this time with a cute performance of a song that he had used in his act for years, recorded live during one of his concerts, "My Ding-a-Ling". Today, he is still doing shows, performing, and recording, and has appeared in many movies and TV specials concerning his own life and performances, and those of others.

Bo Diddley (Ellas Bates)

Bo Diddley definitely ranked among the founding fathers of rock and was a precursor of the sounds of rockabilly. By combining blues and jazz sounds, and constantly stressing loud music and heavy use of lead guitars, he provided inspiration to many aspiring guitar players and other musicians of the '60's and early '70's. Even with all this going for him, somehow, he slowly disappeared from the charts in the mid '60's However, you must remember that at that time he had already been performing for over thirty years.

Born in McComb, Mississippi, on December 30, 1928, Bo Diddley was adopted by his mother's cousin, Gussie McDaniel, as a baby, and she and Bo moved to Chicago.

He took up the guitar at the age of 10 and began playing on street corners for nickels and dimes, with two other boys, one playing guitar and one a washboard.

Throughout his teens, and early '20s, he played for parties and dances, but earned most of his living working at unskilled jobs. Hanging around clubs, taking in the atmosphere of professional blues people, and continuing to practice and teach himself the guitar was his way of life for several years. However, it seemed to him that he was going nowhere.

In 1951, using his original name, Ellas McDaniel, he gained his first regular night club gig at the 708 Club in Chicago. Here, he came to the attention of Chess Records. It was after an audition that Leonard Chess gave him the stage name of Bo Diddley, supposedly because it meant "funny storyteller" in the colloquialism the streets.

Bo used his new name as the lyric for his first record, on Chess's new Checker label, and it became one of the biggest hits of 1955. After this, he recorded another top single "I'm A Man," and he was well on his way. Plugged by the Chess connection with Alan Freed, who constantly pushed his records, he soon had a national following.

He became the proverbial record-producing machine, continuously producing fast selling records for the younger generation of blues lovers during the '60's His effect on the new generation of rock artist was phenomenal, especially in England, with the likes of Eric Burdon and the Animals, the Rolling Stones, the Yardbirds, and countless others.

The story goes that he and his band were invited to play on "The Ed Sullivan Show". When they arrived for rehearsals, however, Ed sent word that they were not to be allowed to do "Bo Diddley," and were to do "Sixteen Tons," a popular song, instead. After a full week of practicing this song, the time for the show finally came. When the cameras moved to him, he led out with the familiar refrains of "Bo Diddley" and the band followed him.

After the show, he was asked why he did not do the song that he was told to do, and he answered, "Well, we practiced "Sixteen Tons," and the cuecards read "Sixteen Tons," but my heart yelled "Bo Diddley"". He was never again invited to perform on the show.

Bo Diddley had the outgoing personality necessary to overcome the suppression of the period, as did Chuck Berry, and he continued to ad-lib and make up lyrics and licks for years to come. He made jokes of everything from sex to politics, so you had to be strong to avoid his bite.

The hard guitar sounds prevalent in his recordings were the types of licks that rockabilly artists would grab and change to fit their own personalities.

Still releasing records occasionally, and now on TV commercials, he plays well today, as does his son. He is very successful on rock and roll revival shows throughout the world.

The following codes and classifications are used in the discography.

R	Reissue of a previous release
Rx	Additional Reissue of previous release
1	The first recording of the song.
2	The second recording ...etc.
33	A 33 1/3 speed single release
S	Stereo (noted only on early singles and EP's)

Recordings are listed chronologically under each artist's heading.
Most CD listings are available on tape with similar numbers
Most LP Records are no longer available
Artists are arranged alphabetically.

Chuck Berry-

Singles		
Maybellene/Wee Wee Hours	-Chess 1604	(1955)
Thirty Days/Together	-Chess 1610	(1955)
No Money Down/Downbound Train	-Chess 1615	(1956)
Roll Over Beethoven/Drifting Heart	-Chess 1626	(1956)
Too Much Monkey Business/Brown Eyed Handsome Man	-Chess 1636	(1956)
You Can't Catch Me/Havana Moon	-Chess 1645	(1956)
School Day/Deep Feeling	-Chess 1653	(1957)
Oh Baby Doll/La Juanda	-Chess 1664	(1957)
Rock And Roll Music/Blue Feeling	-Chess 1671	(1857)
Sweet Little Sixteen/Reelin' and Rockin'	-Chess 1683	(1957)
Johnny B. Goode/Around and Around	-Chess 1691	(1958)
Beautiful Delilah/Vacation Time	-Chess 1697	(1958)
Carol/Hey Pedro	-Chess 1700	(1958)
Sweet Little Rock and Roller/Joe Joe Gun	-Chess 1709	(1958)
Run Rudolph Run/Merry Christmas Baby	-Chess 1714	(1959)
Almost Grown/Little Queenie	-Chess 1716	(1959)
Anthony Boy/That's My Desire	-Chess 1722	(1959)
Dear Dad/Lonely School Days	-Chess 1726	(1959)
Back in the U.S.A./Memphis, Tennessee	-Chess 1729	(1959)
Childhood Sweetheart/Broken Arrow	-Chess 1737	(1959)
Too Pooped to Pop/Let It Rock	-Chess 1747	(1960)
Bye Bye Johnnie/Worried Life Blues	-Chess 1754	(1960)
Mad Lad/I Got To Find My Baby	-Chess 1763	(1961)
Jaguar and the Thunderbird/Our Little Rendezvous	-Chess 1767	(1961)
Little Star/I'm Talking About You	-Chess 1779	(1962)
Go Go Go/Come On	-Chess 1799	(1962)
I Say You're Driving Me Crazy	-Little Star	(1962)
Don't Give Me Love	-Big Three 401	
I'm Talking About You/Diploma For Two	-Chess 1853	(1964)
Sweet Little Sixteen/Memphis	(R)-Chess 1866	(1964)
Nadine/Orangatang	-Chess 1883	(1965)
No Particular Place To Go/You Two	-Chess 1898	(1965)
You Never Can Tell/Brenda Lee	-Chess 1906	(1966)
Little Marie/Go Bobby Soxer	-Chess 1912	(1966)
	-Philo	(1966)
Maybellene/Sweet Little Sixteen	-Mercury 30143	(1966)
Memphis Tennessee/School Days	-Mercury 30144	(1966)
Roll Over, Beethoven/Johnny B. Goode	-Mercury 30145	(1966)
Johnny B. Goode/Rock & Roll Music	-Mercury 30146	(1966)
Laugh and Cry/Club Nitty Gritty	-Mercury 72643	(1967)
Back to Memphis/I Do Really Love You	-Mercury 72680	(1967)
Promised Land/Things I Used To Do	(R)-Chess 1916	(1967)
Chuck's Beat/(B Side Is Bo Diddley)	-Checker 1069	(1967)
Dear Dad/Lonely School Days	(R)-Chess 1926	(1967)
Feelin' It/It Hurts Me Too	-Mercury 72748	(1967)

-Chuck Berry Cont'd-

It Wasn't Me/Welcome Back Pretty Baby	-Chess 1943	(1968)
ST. Louie To Frisco/Ma Dear	-Mercury 72840	(1968)
Lonely School Days/Ramona, Say Yes	(R)-Chess 1963	(1969)
Good Looking Woman/It's Too Dark in There	-Mercury 72963	(1969)
Maybellene/Roll Over, Beethoven (Flex Disc)	-Hip Pocket 34 *	(1969)
Tulane/Have Mercy Judge	(R)-Chess 2090	(1970)
My Ding-A-Ling/Johnny B. Goode	(R)-Chess 2131	(1971)
Reelin' and Rockin'/Let's Boogie	(R)-Chess 2136	(1971)
Bio/Roll 'Em Pete	-Chess 2140	(1972)
Shake, Rattle and Roll/Baby What You Do To Me	-Chess 2169	(1972)
	(R)-Eric	(1973)
Johnny B. Goode/Little Queenie	(R)-Chess 101	
Back in the USA/Rock & Roll Music	(R)-Chess 102	
Carol/Sweet Little Rock & Roller	(R)-Chess 103	
Roll Over Beethoven/Nadine	(R)-Chess 9010	(1973)
Maybellene/Rock & Roll Music	(R)-Chess 9020	(1973)
Memphis Tennessee/School Days	(R)-Chess 9030	(1973)
Sing Sang A Song	-Ode 66120	(1976)
	-Atco	(1979)
Oh, What a Thrill/California	-Atco 7203	(1979)

Albums

After School Session	-Chess LP-1426	(1957)
One Dozen Berry's	-Chess LP-1432	(1958)
Chuck Berry's on Top	-Chess LP-1435	(1959)
Rockin' at the Hops	-Chess LP-1448	(1959)
Chuck Berry's New Juke Box Hits	-Chess LP-1458	(1961)
Chuck Berry Twist	-Chess LP-1466	(1962)
Chuck Berry on Stage	-Chess 1480E	(1963)
St. Louis to Liverpool	-Chess LPS-1488	(1964)
Two Great Guitars	-Checker LP-2992	(1964)
Fresh Berry's	-Chess LPS-1498	(1965)
More Chuck Berry	-Chess 1465E	(1963)
Chuck Berry's Greatest Hits	-Chess 1485E	(1964)
Chuck Berry in London	-Chess LPS-1495	(1965)
Chuck Berry's Golden Decade, Vol. 1 (2 LP)	-Chess 1514	(1967)
Chuck Berry's Golden Hits	-Mercury 61103	(1967)
Chuck Berry in Memphis	-Mercury 61123	(1967)
Live at the Filmore Auditorium	-Mercury 61138	(1967)
From St. Louis to Frisco	-Mercury 61176	(1968)
Concerto in B. Goode	-Mercury 61223	(1969)
Chuck Berry Live in Concert	-Magnum MR-703	(1969)
Pop Origins	-Chess LP-1544	(1969)
Back Home	-Chess LPS-1550	(1970)
San Francisco Dues	-Chess CH-50008	(1971)
Johnny B. Goode	-Pickwick SPC-3327	(1971)
Sweet Little Rock and Roller	-Pickwick SPC-3345	(1971)
Wild Berry's	(R)-Pickwick SPC-3392	(1972)

-Chuck Berry Cont'd-

Flashback	-Pickwick 2061	(1972)
St. Louie to Frisco to Memphis (2 LP)	-Mercury 2-6501	(1972)
Chuck Berry Bio	-Chess CH-50043	(1973)
London Sessions	-Chess 60020	(1973)
Chuck Berry's Golden Decade, Vol. 2 (2 LP)	-Chess 60023	(1973)
Chuck Berry and His Friends	-Brookville 1274	(1973)
Chuck Berry's Golden Decade, Vol. 3 (2 LP)	-Chess 60028	(1974)
Chuck Berry	-Chess 60032	(1975)
Chuck Berry (2 LP)	-Chess 706	(1976)
Chuck Berry's Greatest Hits	-AOFJ 321	
Chuck Berry's Greatest Hits	-Everest 321	(1976)
Best of Chuck Berry	-Gusto GT-0004	(1978)
Rock It	-Atco SD-38-118	(1979)
All-Time Hits	-Upfront 199	(1979)
	-Accord	(1982)
Two Great Guitars Chuck Berry & Bo Didley(CD)	-Chess CHD-9170	
New Juke Box Hits (CD)	-Chess CHD-9171	
The Best of Chuck Berry + Percy Sledge (CD)	-DeLuxe 7858	
The Incredible Chuck Berry (CD)	-Camden CPK-5010	
School Days (CD)	-Blues 490	
Sweet Little Sixteen (CD)	-Blues 491	
St. Louie to Liverpool (CD)	(R)-Chess CHD-9186	(1986)
	(R)-MCA	(1986)
Rock 'N' Roll Rarities (2 CD)	-Chess CHD-92521	(1986)
More Rock 'N' Roll Rarities From the Golden Era Chess	-Chess CHD-9190	(1986)
Chuck Berry on Top (CD)	(R)-Chess CHD-9256	(1987)
Rockin' at the Hops (CD)	(R)-Chess CHD-9259	(1987)
Chuck Berry's Golden Hits (CD)	(R)-Mercury 826256	(1987)
Roll Over Beethoven (CD)	-Allegaince CD	(1988)
Hail! Hail! Rock'n'Roll (CD)	(R)-MCA 6217	(1988)
After School Session (CD)	(R)-Chess CH-9284	(1989)
London Sessions (CD)	-Chess CH-9295	(1989)
The Best of Chuck Berry (CD)	-Vogue CD-600033	(1989)
The Chess Box (71 Hits) (6 CD)	-Chess CH6-80001	(1989)
To Kingdom Come (2 CD)	-Chess C22V-92169	(1989)
Chuck Berry Great Twenty-Eight (2 CD)	-Chess CH2-92500	(1989)
Chuck Berry Is On to (CD)	-MCA 31260	
Chuck Berry Live Hits (CD)	-Quicksilver 1017	
Missing Berries:Rareties, Vol. 3 (CD)	-Chess CHD-9318	(1990)
21 Greatest Hits of Chuck Berry	-Zeta 520	

Extended Play Mini Albums

EP After School Sessions	-Chess 5118	(1957)
EP Rock & Roll Music	-Chess 5119	(1958)
EP Sweet Little Sixteen	-Chess 5121	(1958)
EP Pickin' Berries	-Chess 5124	(1958)
EP Sweet Little Rock & Roller	-Chess 5126	(1958)

Bo Diddley-

Singles

Bo Diddley/I'm a Man	-Checker 814	(1955)
Diddley Daddy/She's Fine, She's Mine	-Checker 819	(1955)
Pretty Thing/Bring It to Jerome	-Checker 827	(1955)
Diddy Wah Diddy/(I'm) Looking For a Woman	-Checker 832	(1956)
Who Do You Love/I'm Bad	-Checker 842	(1956)
Cops and Robbers/Down Home Special	-Checker 850	(1957)
Hey Bo Diddley/Mona(I Need You Baby)	-Checker 860	(1957)
Say Boss Man/Before You Accuse Me	-Checker 878	(1958)
Hush Your Mouth/Dearest Darling	-Checker 896	(1958)
Willie and Lillie/Bo Meets the Monster	-Checker 907	(1958)
I'm Sorry/Oh Yea	-Checker 914	(1959)
Crackin' Up/The Great Grandfather	-Checker 924	(1959)
Say Man/The Clock Strikes 12	-Checker 931	(1959)
Road Runner/My Story	-Checker 942	(1960)
She's Allright/Say Man, Back Again	-Checker 936	(1959)
Walkin' and Talkin'/Crawdad	-Checker 951	(1960)
(Bo Diddley's A)Gun Slinger/Signifying Blues	-Checker 965	(1960)
Not Guilty/Aztec	-Checker 976	(1961)
Pills(Or Love's Labor Lost)/Call Me	-Checker 985	(1961)
Bo Diddley/I'm a Man	-Checker 997	(1962)
You Can't Judge a Book by the Covr/I Can Tell	-Checker 1019	(1962)
Greatest Lover in the World/Surfr's Love Call	-Checker 1045	(1963)
Mama Keep Your Big Mouth Shut/Jo-ann	-Checker 1083	(1964)
Chuck's Beat/Bo's Beat	-Checker 1089*	(1964)
Hey Good Lookin'/You Ain't Bad(As You Claim)	-Checker 1098	(1964)
500 Percent More Man/Let the Kids Dance	-Checker 1123	(1965)
We're Gonna Get Married/Do the Frog	-Checker 1142	(1966)
Ooh Baby/Back to School	-Checker 1158	(1967)
Ooh Baby/Back to School	-Chess 15167	(1967)
Wreckin' My Love Life/Boo-Ga-Loo Before You Go	-Checker 1168	(1967)
Wreckin' My Love Life/Boo-Ga-Loo Before You Go	-Checker 15545	(1967)
Another Sugar Daddy/I'm High Again	-Checker 1200	(1968)
Bo Diddley 1969/Soul Train	-Checker 1213	(1969)
The Shape I'm In/Polluted	-Checker 1238	(1969)
I Said Shut Up Woman/I Love You More Than You'll Ever Know	-Chess 2117	(1971)
Bo Diddley- It Is/Inflation	-Chess 2129	(1972)
Husband In Law/Bo Jam	-Chess 2134	(1972)
I'm A Man/Bo Diddly	(R)-Chess 9031	
Diddly Daddy/I'm Sorry	(R)-Chess 9053	
Not Fade Away/Drag On	-RCA 10618	(1976)
The Clock Strikes Twelve/Say Man	(R)-Goldies 2638	

*Sung with Chuck Berry

Albums

Bo Diddley	-Chess 704	(1956)

-Bo Diddley Cont'd-

Bo Diddley		(R)-Chess 1431	(1957)
Go Bo Diddley		-Checker 1436	(1957)
Have Guitar Will Travel		-Checker 2974	(1959)
Bo Diddley in the Spotlight		-Checker 2976	(1960)
Bo Diddley is a Gunslinger		-Checker 2977	(1961)
Bo Diddley is a Lover		-Checker 2980	(1961)
Bo Diddley's a Twister		-Checker 2982	(1962)
Bo Diddley		(R)-Checker 2984	(1962)
Bo Diddley & Company		-Checker 2985	(1963)
Surfin' With Bo Diddley		-Checker 2987	(1963)
Bo Diddley's Beach Party		-Checker 2988	(1963)
Bo Diddley's 16 All Time Greatest Hits		-Checker 2989	(1963)
Two Great Guitars(with Chuck Berry)		-Checker 2991	(1964)
Hey Good Lookin'		-Checker 2992	(1965)
500% More Man		-Checker 2996	(1964)
The Originator		-Checker 3001	(1966)
Road Runner		-Checker 2982	(1967)
Go Bo Diddley		(R)-Checker 3006	(1967)
Boss Man		(R)-Checker 3007	(1967)
Super Blues(with Muddy Waters and Little Walter)	(CD)	-Checker 3008	(1968)
The Super Blues Band (Muddy Waters and Howlin Wolf)(CD)		-Checker 3010	(1968)
Black Gladiator		-Checker 3013	(1969)
Another Demension		-Chess 50001	(1971)
Where It All Began		-Chess 50016	(1972)
Got My Own Bag of Tricks	(2CD)	-Chess 60005	(1972)
The London Bo Diddley Sessions	(CD)	-Chess 50029	(1973)
Big Bad Bo	(CD)	-Chess 50047	(1974)
20th Aniversary of Rock & Roll	(CD)	-RCA 1229	(1976)
I'm a Man	(2 CD)	(R)-MF 2002	(1977)
Toronto Rock And Roll Revival, Vol. 5		-Accord SN-7812	(1982)
Bo Diddley/Go Bo Diddley	(2CD)	-Chess 5094	(1984)
His Greatest Sides	(CD)	-Chess 9106	
This Should Not Be	(CD)	-XXX 51017	
Say Man	(CD)	-Blues 872	
Two Great Guitars: Chuck Berry & Bo Didley	(CD)	-MCA 9170	
Super Blues(with Muddy Waters and Little Walter)	(CD)	(R)-MCA 9168	
The Super Blues Band(with Muddy Waters and Howlin' Wolf)	(CD)	-MCA 9169 (R)	
Bod Diddley (1955-58)	(CD)	(R)-Chess 9194	(1987)
In the Spotlight	(CD)	(R)-Chess 9264	(1988)
Give Me a Break	(CD)	(R)-Check Mate 1960	(1988)
Bo Diddley Is a Gunslinger	(2CD)	(R)-Chess 9285	(1989)
The Chess Box (45 Songs)	(2 CD)	-Chess CHD2-19502	(1990)
Rare and Well Done	(CD)	-MCA 9331	

Extended Play Mini Albums

EP Bo Diddley	-Chess 5125	(1958)

CHAPTER 7

THE SOUND TAKES HOLD

With the resounding success of rockabilly, every record company now scrambled for rockabilly artists. The problem was that most record companies did not really know what a rockabilly artist was, or how rockabilly should sound. For the most part, they took anyone who looked wild, young, and sexy, put a guitar in his hand; added a lot of echo and guitar work to the recording; and voila, the thought they had rockabilly.

Even the large record companies, which had up to this time never allowed rock and roll artists on their labels, were scrambling to find record stars. Eventually, every label found one. Capitol had Gene Vincent; MGM found Conway Twitty; Columbia tried with Guy Mitchell, who was just country, and not really rockabilly, and with Marty Robbins; Liberty had Eddie Cochran, with Ricky Nelson on their Imperial label; Mercury tried with the Big Bopper and Johnny Preston; Roulette had Ronnie Hawkins, Jimmy Bowen, and Buddy Knox; Coral, Brunswick, and Decca had Buddy Holly, the Crickets, and Bill Haley. The small labels were also in the act with Clyde Stacey, Marvin Rainwater, Charlie Gracie, Ray Smith, Ral Donner, Jack Scott, Terry Stafford, Lonnie Donnegan, to name a few. Although these came later, they were still definitely rockabilly.

Phil Everly and Don Everly
The Everly Brothers

The Everly Brothers were born in Brownie, Kentucky. Don was born on February 1, 1937, and Phil on January 19, 1939. Both had a tremendous influence on many of the rock and roll artists from the '60's through the '80's

The Everly family was deeply into the country and gospel genre of music, long before Don and Phil began performing. Ike and Margaret Everly travelled the southern and Midwestern states from the '30's to the '50's.

As soon as they were old enough, the boys were trained musically. At ages six and eight, they made their first appearance on radio station KMA in Shenandoah, Iowa. They also toured with their parents during the summer.

After they graduated from high school, they decided to continue with their music, and moved to Nashville, Tennessee, where they began playing the club scene. They received their first recording contract from Columbia Records, in 1956. However, they were dropped within a year.

At Acuff-Rose Publishing, they met Felice and Boudreaux Bryant, prominent country and western music writers of the day, as well as producers. They played their version of "Bye Bye Love," and the Bryants loved it, recorded it, and helped to release it on the Cadence label, which coincidentally was begun by the former music director of Columbia Records, Mitch Miller. The song rose to number one on the charts, both popular music and country and western. They soon followed with "Wake Up Little Susie," which was quite controversial at the time, "All I Have to Do Is Dream," "Bird Dog," and "Devoted to You."

In late 1958 they switched to Warner Brothers Records and recorded their own composition "Cathy's Clown," followed in 1959 with their own "Till I Kissed You". Between their releases on Cadence, and those on Warner Brothers, they were constantly in the top-ten on the music charts. Try these for hits: "Problems," "Take a Message to Mary," "Let It Be Me," "When will I Be Loved," "So Sad," "Ebony Eyes," "Don't Blame Me," "Crying in the Rain," and, in 1962, "That's Old Fashioned." Their albums were constantly best sellers.

In the early '60's Don enlisted in the Marine Corps, and while it meant breaking up the act on the road, records were still released. It was during these years that the boys matured and developed a solid act for TV shows.

In the late '60's they were a regular act on "The Smother's Brothers Comedy Hour," which helped to broaden their style and finesse. While not gaining anything like the mass following they had in the '50's they did continue to draw good crowds at shows and appearances. But it was on TV where they demonstrated their ability and their professionalism. In 1970 they had their own summer replacement show on TV.

When their contract ran out at Warner Brothers, they joined RCA records, but nothing seemed to catch on with the public, and the younger audience seemed to be heading toward heavy rock. While they still maintained a strong following on the road, the brothers began to drift apart. Just like married couples, they seemed to develop their own individual styles, and started to record separately.

In mid 1973 they formally announced their breakup, and gave their final performance at Knott's Berry Farm, in California. They were both sick of doing the same thing over and over and decided to pursue new areas, on their own. They continued to record and play by themselves until they again reunited in 1987.

Liberty records would soon jump on the bandwagon of rockabilly music with the acquisition of Eddie Cochran.

Eddie Cochran

Born in Albert Lea, Minnesota, on October 3, 1938, Eddie grew up in the mid west, the son of two Oklahoma country and western music fans. He later moved with the family to Bell Gardens, California. He was the youngest of five children, and he had a pretty normal, happy upbringing.

Eddie became attracted to country and western music early. Having grown up in the mid west, he certainly came in contact with it enough. When he was 12, he asked his parents to buy him an instrument so that he could join the school orchestra. He wanted to be a drummer, but when he was told that he would have to study some piano first, he decided on the trombone. His teacher thought that his mouth was not shaped properly for the trombone, and suggested the clarinet. While Eddie and his mother were at the music store shopping for the clarinet, he fell in love with the guitar. The orchestra, however, had no openings for a guitarist, but that didn't bother him. He picked up a few chords here and there and rapidly taught himself how to play.

He organized a local band and started playing gigs at various local parties and such. By 1955, however, the band had broken up, and Eddie joined in a duo with his namesake, Hank Cochran, who was no relation.

Eddie met his future partner, Jerry Capehart, in a music store, in Bell Gardens, in the fall of 1955, while looking through records. Jerry needed someone to sing and play demos of his songs, and the first disc was "Tired and Sleepy," by the Cochran Brothers. Hank eventually moved to Nashville, to be closer to the country music scene.

In 1955, he signed with American Music, and recorded his first solo, "Skinny Jim," which flopped, on their Crest label. Capehart flew to Los Angeles, and convinced Liberty Records to invest in the future of Eddie Cochran. In 1956, he was asked to do a cameo in the movie *The Girl Can't Help It*, because his style would fit in as part of the representation of rock music, in the film. Liberty wanted him to record "Twenty Flight Rock," as his first release. Before they released the record, however, Liberty came upon a John D. Laudermilk song called "Sittin' In the Balcony," which they became very excited about. After talking it over with Jerry, they decided to go with the song as his first release.

The record was simultaneously released by the author, under the name of Johnny Dee. Both versions became hits. This early rockabilly song used all the powerful tools that the genre could come up with, including: the sexy sounds, the cute lyrics, the echo, and the guitar as the main musical instrument. Eddie's follow-up song, "Mean When I'm Mad," was a bomb, however. The song was co-written by Jerry and Eddie.

In the fall of 1957, he made the charts with "Drive-in Show," and again with "Jeannie, Jeannie, Jeannie" in early 1958. Now he began appearing in several cameo rolls in movies, such as *Flaming Youth*, with Mamie Van Doren, and in *The Girl Can't Help It*, with Jane Mansfield, singing "Twenty Flight Rock." He also appeared in several rock and roll shows, including Alan Freed's.

In 1958, his "Summertime Blues" was the rage, hitting the teenagers where they live and soaring up the charts. It started in May, and stayed on the charts throughout the summer. It was the perfect time of year to release the song, as every teenage boy would be out "cattin'" and "lookin'" for girls then. Once again, it was heavy on guitars, with lyrics whose main themes were love, sex, and girls.

In the summer of 1958, Eddie and Jerry wrote another excellent song that would become a classic "C'mon Everybody." The record was received with open arms by the teenagers who were just waiting for that next release from Eddie. If it was "Summertime Blues" that made him a star, it was "C'mon Everybody" that kept him there.

Eddie also assembled a backup band for one night stands called the Kelly Four, with Connie "Guybo" Smith on bass, later replaced by Dave Shreiber, Gene Ridgio on drums, and several different musicians on piano, sax, and other instruments.

He was close to Buddy Holly, and Richie Valens, and was originally scheduled to be on the show with them when they were killed. A screwup in scheduling, however, prevented him from being on the plane. After their death, he always had the feeling that he was living on borrowed time.

In 1959 he toured the country and appeared in several television shows on the networks. This year was great: He continued to turn out hits — "Three Steps to Heaven" and "Something Else." The latter tried to revive the popular hard sound of "Summertime Blues."

In the 60's, he began recording hits right from the start, with "Cut Across Shorty," the bluesy "Hallelujah, I Love Her So," and "Weekend." He was just beginning to become a household word, and on the minds of every teenager growing up in America. He was the good-looking boy with the charming smile and the sexy voice who every female desired.

As popular as Eddie was in the United States, he was even more popular in Europe, and was as influential as any other star ever was. In 1960 he was booked for a giant European tour with other artists, including Gene Vincent and English star Billy Fury. The show would appear in several countries, and several English cities. Supposedly George Harrison, of the soon to be Beatles, attended most of the performances.

The tour ended in April, and he was scheduled to return to California. On April 17, Eddie, Gene Vincent, and Sharon Sheely, a friend and songwriter, headed for the airport in a chauffeured limousine. There was an accident on the way to the airport; the car blew a tire, the driver lost control, and the car rammed into a lamp post. Eddie Cochran died within a few hours from multiple head wounds.

Sharon has stated many times that the night before the accident, she found him in his room playing Buddy Holly records, which he had not done since Buddy's death. He mumbled something about seeing Buddy real soon. On the way to the airport, Eddie mentioned to Gene that he felt he was going to die shortly.

While other artists were singing of love and hate, Eddie made his mark by singing of the pain, sorrow, heartache, and happiness of what it was like to be a teenager. Eddie, more than any other artist, was the symbolic representation of the teenager of the 50's. He went to the congressman for help, and the congressman said, "I'd like to help you, son, but you're too young to vote."

Capitol Records would vie for a piece of the action with the sensational Gene Vincent.

Gene Vincent (Vincent Gene Craddock)

Gene Vincent was born in Norfolk, Virginia, on February 11, 1935. His real name was Vincent Gene Craddock. His destiny was to become a flaming star. Overnight, he would rise to lofty heights, and then disappear into obscurity.

He spent most of his youth in Norfolk, and learned to play guitar in his teens. Naturally, his taste in music was geared toward country music. When the Korean War broke out, he joined the navy. He continually entertained his shipmates with his country songs and his own accompaniment on the guitar. His military career, however, came to an abrupt end when his leg was severely injured in one of the battles at sea.

The truth of how he was injured was never really known: Sometimes he said he stepped on a land mine, sometimes he was shot, and sometimes he was in a motorcycle accident. In any case, the injury was bad enough to warrant amptation, but he did not allow it. He returned to Norfolk to recuperate, and build a new career. His mother suggested that he should go into entertaining.

He began working on his original material and playing locally in the mid 50's. Supposedly, he and a friend were looking one night at Little LuLu, a comic book and he explained to his friend that it was a Be-bop-a-lulu, and that's how the they picked the title of the song. But soon after, Bill Davis, Gene's future manager, would offer the friend $25.00 for his share. He would sell it to Bill, against Gene's wishes.

Soon after his release from the navy, Gene started dating Ruth Ann Hand, a 15 year old high school girl, from his hometown. After only a few months of going out together, they became engaged. Gene's mother, Louise Craddock, thought that he and Ruth were too young for marriage. Nevertheless, on Gene's 21st birthday, February 11, 1956, he and Ruth Ann were married in a large church ceremony. Gene wore his naval uniform.

Roy Lamear, station manager of WCMS, and deejay "Sheriff Tex" Davis met with Gene to Book him as an act. They got Gene together with some of the finer local talent at the radio studios: The group consisted of: Willie Williams, on acoustic guitar; Jack Neal, on standup bass; Cliff Gallup, on electric lead guitar; and Dickie Harrell, on drums.

The group recorded and practiced two of Gene's songs, "Be-Bop-A-Lula" and "Race with the Devil." Roy was so impressed that he made them cut a one sided acetate demo of "Be-Bop-A-Lula," and he sent it along to Capitol Records. The wait seemed like an eternity to Gene, but Capitol was impressed, and wanted to record Gene in Nashville.

In 1956, Gene recorded a song called "Woman Love." The record was released on June 2, 1956 , with "Be-Bop-A-Lula" on the flip side. With Gene sounding a lot like Elvis, the song was too suggestive for most radio stations, and disk jockeys began playing the flip side. It wasn't long before "Be-Bop-A-Lula" shot to the top of the charts, and earned Gene his first gold record with Capitol.

The music was pure undiluted rockabilly; with heavy echo, loud guitars, and heavy mumbling of somehow unknown or unheard sexy lyrics. At the recording session, Gene's voice was so soft that the engineer could barely mix it correctly, with the background. Since the toilet was tile, the engineer made him stand in the toilet, with his earphones on, to get the correct echo effect.

In 1956, Gene recorded a song called "Woman Love." The record was released on June 2, 1956 , with "Be-Bop-A-Lula" on the flip side. With Gene sounding a lot like Elvis, the song was too suggestive for most radio stations, and disk jockeys began playing the flip side. It wasn't long before "Be-Bop-A-Lula" shot to the top of the charts, and earned Gene his first gold record with Capitol.

The music was pure undiluted rockabilly; with heavy echo, loud guitars, and heavy mumbling of somehow unknown or unheard sexy lyrics. At the recording session, Gene's voice was so soft that the engineer could barely mix it correctly, with the background, so he made him stand in the toilet, with his earphones on, to get the correct echo effect

The group began touring with the likes of the Johnny Burnette

Trio, Chuck Berry, Carl Perkins, Frankie Lymon and the Teenagers, and others. In September 1956, Capitol released an album titled *Blue Jean Bop*, plus a single with the title tune backed by "Who Slapped John." Both were wild rockabilly sounds. After the tour, Gene got into a contract dispute with Lamear, so Gene decided that Bill Davis should represent him. Willie Williams and Cliff Gallup decided to leave the group — Willie to spend more time with his wife, and Cliff, because he was tired of travelling. Gene replaced Willie with Teddy Crutchfield, a guitarist from Norfolk, but Cliff would be hard to replace. Just before Cliff left, Gene had taken on Paul Peek, for rhythm guitar; Paul would later become NRC Records' first artist.

From 1956 through 1958 Gene Vincent and his four-piece group, the Blue Caps were very hot on the performance circuit. He consistently produced high-selling songs, such as "Little Lover," "Race with the Devil," "She She Little Sheila," "Blue Jean Bop," "Lotta' Lovin'," backed with "Wear My Ring" and "Yes I Love You Baby." Above all, the songs were totally Gene Vincent, and it would be hard to imagine anyone else singing them. The albums produced were wild and crazy, fast paced and incapable of being duplicated by many others, at the time. They toured extensively throughout the country and were featured on "The Ed Sullivan Show," and other national television shows. With each tour. The stress and strain of the tour began showing, and Gene began drinking. He soon became a quick-tempered, hard nosed leader. Calm and relaxed offstage, on stage he was the wild and crazy showman. Gene soon broke up with Ruth Ann.

The girls always flocked around Gene, and were taken in and fascinated by his style of singing. It wasn't too long before he met a young attractive divorcee, Darlene Hicks, who worked as a ticket seller at the auditorium in Vancouver, Washington. Gene was completely captivated by her, and before long they were married.

In the late 50's Gene's popularity began to fade, and his record sales actually went down in The United States, but he was still a star in Europe. It was during this period that the whole category of rock and roll in general went down in sales. Instead, it was the good-looking, clean-cut teenagers who made the hits, supported, of course, by good-looking, clean-cut Dick Clark.

In 1960, Gene toured Europe with Eddie Cochran and he and Eddie became close friends. They went everywhere together. They drank together, yelled together, pulled off tricks together, and argued together.

Although Gene survived the now-famous car crash, on April 17th, 1960, in which Eddie was killed, the accident succeeded in irritating his already bad leg, and left him morally, spiritually, and physically beat. Eddie had been his best friend. He decided, after this, to settle in London for awhile, but actually spent his time between California and London. He now had a new band, overseas, called "The Echoes."

Gene earned a living playing around Europe throughout the 60's In the mid-60's EMI, Capitol Records' parent company in England, released two albums of his greatest hits, which sold fairly well in Europe, but were never released in the United States. For the most part, however, Gene was a popular artist without a hit record to his name. Darlene soon became disenchanted with him, and left.

In December of 1963, his new record company, Columbia Records, released "Where Have You Been All My Life" backed with "Love 'Em Leave 'Em Kind of Guy," but neither song made the charts. In 1963, Capitol Records of France released the album, *The Crazy Beat Of Gene Vincent*, a strange compilation of older and newer songs. Now, with the Beatles beginning to go full swing, he hired a band called the Shouts, and went back on the road.

In early 1964, he entered the recording studio, with his new band, and recorded an album called *Shakin' Up A Storm*, but was criticized because it was made in only a few days, and it showed. The highlight of the album was the song "Baby Blue."

Columbia soon released "Private Detective" and "You Are My Sunshine," but the only Americans making the charts were Chuck Berry , Elvis, or Roy Orbison. Gene's recording career was at a complete standstill. He futzed around with tours for the next few years.

In 1969, Gene joined Dandelion Records in England, whose records were released in the United States through Electra/Asylum Records, and in mid-1969, he recorded an album in Los Angeles. After the sessions, he started playing in all sorts of rock and roll revival shows throughout Canada and the United States, with other great stars of the past. The tours were representative of the past achievements of the artists. This is exactly what his new record companies — Challenge, Playground, Forever, Kama Sutra, Dandelion — were trying to achieve. They wanted to make money on his past achievements, and were not interested in any current attempts at popularity. None of them were successful in instigating a comeback for either Gene Vincent or his style.

In late 1969, Capitol released an album of his early hits entitled

Gene Vincent's Greatest, and in January of 1970, Dandelion/Reprise released the album *I'm Back and I'm Proud*. Although neither album became a smash, they sold well. His comeback tries were failing.

In the fall of 1971, he was in Newhall, California visiting his father when he fell ill. He suffered internal hemorrhaging and died, on October 12 at the young age of 36.

Conway Twitty
(Harold Lloyd Jenkins)

Conway Twitty was born in 1933, in Helena, Arkansas. His professional name was derived from the names of two cities in Texas, which he spotted while travelling there.

He began singing and playing the guitar at age 5, usually in the pilot house of a Mississippi River ferryboat, which his father sailed back and forth between Arkansas and Mississippi. By age 10, he had organized his first musical group, the Phillips County Ramblers.

In the 50's he had to make a difficult choice between music and sports. He had been offered a contract to play baseball with the Philadelphia Phillies when he was discharged from the army. Eight years later, he had to face another choice: between rock and roll, at which he had become successful, and his love for country music.

In 1958, he began his recording career with Mercury Records, with three releases. Nothing, however, really hit for him. He began to get down in the mouth, just as his career was beginning. He switched labels to MGM Records.

Later that year, the flip side of a song he recorded took the country by storm; the song was "I'll Try," and the flip side was "It's Only Make Believe." It didn't take long for him to become a stable entity in rock, with one release after another on MGM, throughout the 1950's.

In 1965, however, he decided to cross over to country music and switched labels to Decca Records. His repertoire was growing.

It was a slow start at Decca, in a completely different field, but it was an area where Decca had enormous strength, and they stuck with him. There were no big hits, for awhile, but he started to make good sales with "Next in Line," in 1968. In 1970, he recorded two songs that would make him a star forever; "Hello Darlin'," and "Fifteen Years Ago." From then on, it was as if he was magnetically attached to every hit song that came along.

In 1970, he teamed up with Loretta Lynn, to form the magical duo that existed for many years. The Country Music Association awarded them their Vocal Duo of the Year for four consecutive years, from 1972-1975. Their records together strengthened both of their careers, and they fast became the most popular duet in country music.

He became so strong, in fact, that MGM began to release his older songs in all sorts of compilations, including a group of album cuts, and never-before released songs, in a country style, which they titled Conway Twitty Sings the Blues. The album, released in 1972, included a unique version of Elvis's "Hound Dog" which was never released before. He had finally established himself as the star he always was, instead of a sound-alike of Elvis.

In the mid-80's, he grew tired of the way Decca (now MCA) was pushing his material, so he chanced on over to Warner Brothers, who was trying to establish a country music division. He continued to have hits for several years, but toward the end of the 80's, he went back to MCA.

In May of 1993, he went into the hospital for a thorough examination, which he passed completely. On June 5, 1993, during an appearance in Branson, Missouri, he was rushed to Cox Medical Center., in Springfield. Immediate surgery was performed in order to repair an abdominal aortic aneurysm. He died on the operating table. His contribution to rockabilly, and country and western music was enormous. He will be remembered for many years to come.

Jack Scott
(Jack Scafone, Jr)

Jack Scott was born on January 24, 1936 in Windsor Ontario, Canada. His first recordings were on the ABC-Paramount label; "TwoTimin' Woman," was the first, in October of 1957. In 1958, he signed with Carlton Records, and "Leroy," which he wrote, was released in April to a moderate reception by the teenage audience. However when some of the disk jockeys turned the record over, they

they discovered "My True Love," which became a solid hit. Where "Leroy" was a rollicking mover, "My True Love" was a slow, impressive ballad; it was the ballads that made him strong from then on. The uniqueness of Jack's voice was probably the most important part of the acceptance by the teenagers. The deep resonance was what every male desired, to show the world that he was now a man. While he was basically a shy person, the strength of his voice was more than enough to carry forth even a very weak song, and make it strong.

The next single was also a two sided hit: "With Your Love," backed with "Geraldine," the latter a pure rockabilly sound, with echo, and cute lyrics. This slow, fast formula would continue to work throughout the Carlton Records phase of his career. His appearances on national television, mainly with Dick Clark, would increase his popularity immeasurably. By the time Jack signed with the Guaranteed label, the influence of Hank Williams, and country music in general, was obvious. His first release, "What Am I Living For," backed with "Indiana Waltz," would set the pace for future songs of the slow, sexy style that would become popular with the teenagers. Here, the faster songs tended to be on the A side, where as the slower songs would remain on the B side.

When Jack moved to Top Rank, the influence of Hank Williams reigned supreme, and he recorded one of the best albums of Hank Williams' songs ever recorded, entitled *I Remember Hank Williams*. His song "What in the World's Come Over You," was excellently received by his audience, and "Burning Bridges," later released on Capitol Records in an album, sold for many years as a strong standard in the field.

By this time, however, the fire was out. The movement to Capitol Records really didn't accomplish much by way of advancing his career. Neither did the moves to RCA, Groove, Jubilee, and finally, in the '60's to Dot Records, although some of these recordings are considered to be his best. Even today, he is constantly asked for copies of his records, and has rerecorded several of them on his own. He currently makes a living selling cars, somewhere in Indiana.

It is difficult to understand why the public reacts the way it does to many singers, and artists, but Jack Scott deserved more than he received. His album of Hank Williams' songs, alone, was one of the best albums I have ever heard. He had an emotional understanding of the songs, and it was evident in his presentation. Through his disappearance from the American music scene, the world has lost a great artist.

The following codes and classifications are used in the discography.

R	Reissue of a previous release
Rx	Additional Reissue of previous release
1	The first recording of the song.
2	The second recording ...etc.
33	A 33 1/3 speed single release
S	Stereo (noted only on early singles and EP's)
Warner	Warner Brothers
MF	Mobile Fidelity
ABC/P	ABC/Paramount
EMI/A	EMI/America
Curb/C	Curb/CEMA
PSP	Polygram Special Products
	In The '80's and '90's Polygram is used interchangeably with MGM and Polydor is used interchangeably with Mercury.

Recordings are listed chronologically under each artist's heading.
Most CD listings are available on tape with similar numbers
Most LP Records are no longer available
Artists are arranged alphabetically.

Jimmy Bowen-

Singles		
I'm Stickin' With You/Party Doll(B.Knox)	-Triple D 797	(1957)
I'm Stickin' With You/Ever Lovin' Fingers	-Roulette 4001	(1957)
Warm Up to Me Baby/I Trusted You	-Roulette 4010	(1957)
I'm Stickin' With You/Warm Up to Me Baby	(R)-Roulette	(1957)
Don't Tell Me Your Troubles/Ever Since That Night	-Roulette 4017	(1958)
Cross Over/It's Shameful	-Roulette 4023	(1958)
By the Light of the Silvery Moon/The Two Step	-Roulette 4083	(1958)
My Kind of Woman/Blue Moon	-Roulette 4102	(1958)
Wish I Were Tied To You/Always Faithful	-Roulette 4122	(1959)
You're Just Wasting Your Time/Walkin on Air	-Roulette 4175	(1959)
(I Need)Your Loving Arms/Oh Yeah! Mm Mm	-Roulette 4224	(1960)
Don't Drop It/Someone To Love	-Crest 1085	(1961)
Teenage Dreamworld/It's Against the Law	-Capehart 5005	(1961)
It's Such a Pretty World Today/Raunchy	-Reprise 392	(1964-66)
Albums		
Jimmy Bowen	-Roulette R-25004	(1957)
Buddy Knox and Jimmy Bowen	-Roulette R-25048	(1958)
Sunday Morning With the Comics	-Reprise RS-6210	(1966)
Extended Play Mini Albums		
EP Jimmy Bowen	-Roulette 302	(1957)

Eddie Cochran-

Singles		
Skinny Jim/Half Loved	-Crest 1026	(1956)
Sittin' in the Balcony/Dark Lonely Street	-Liberty 55056	(1957)
Mean When I'm Mad/One Kiss	-Liberty 55070	(1957)
Drive-In Show/Am I Blue	-Liberty 55087	(1957)
Twenty Flight Rock/Cradle Baby	-Liberty 55112	(1958)
Jeannie, Jeannie, Jeannie/Pocketful of Hearts	-Liberty 55123	(1958)
Pretty Girl/Teresa	-Liberty 55138	(1958)
Summertime Blues/Love Again	-Liberty 55144	(1958)
C'mon Everybody/Don't Ever Leave Me	-Liberty 55166	(1958)
Summertime Blues/Teenage Heaven	-Liberty 54503	(1959)
Teenage Heaven/I Remember	(R)-Liberty 55177	(1959)
Somethin' Else/Boll Weevil Song	-Liberty 55203	(1959)
Hallelujah, I Love Her So/Little Angel	-Liberty 55217	(1959)
Three Steps to Heaven/Cut Across Shorty	-Liberty 55242	(1960)
Sweetie Pie/Lonely	-Liberty 55278	(1960)
Rough Stuff	-Capehart	(1960)
Weekend/Lonely	-Liberty 55389	(1961)
(Items Below rereleased On United Artists)		
Teenage Cutie/Twenty Flight Rock	(R)-UA 618	(1972)
C'mon Everybody/Three Stars	(R)-UA 5367	(1984)

-Eddie Cochran Cont'd-

Cut Across Shorty/Summertime Blues	(R)-UA 014	(1984)
C'mon Everybody/Three Steps to Heaven	(R)-UA 015	(1984)
Sittin' in the Balcony/Somethin' Else	(R)-UA 016	(1984)

Albums

Singin' to My Baby	-LRP-3061	(1958)
Eddie Cochran (Memorial Album)	-LRP-3172	(1959)
Never To Be Forgotten	-LRP-3220	(1962)
Summertime Blues	-Sunset SUN-1123	(1966)
The Legendary Masters of Eddie Cochran(2 LP)	-UA UAS-9959	(1971)
Very Best of Eddie Cochran	-UA UA-la428e	(1975)
Memorial Album	-Liberty LRP-3172	(1980)
Twelve of His Biggest Hits	-Liberty LRP-3172	(1980)
Great Hits	-Liberty LRP-10204	(1982)
Legendary Masters No. 4	(R)-UA 9959	(1971)
Eddie Cochran Singles Album	-UA 30244 Imp	
20th Anniversary Box Set	-UA EC SP20 Imp	
On the Air	-EMI Amrca 17245	(1987)
The Best of Eddie Cochran (CD)	-EMI Amrca 46580	(1987)
Eddie Cochran: The Early Years (CD)	-Ace CHA-237	(1988)
The Legendary Masters of Eddie Cochran (2 CD)	-EMI E21Y-92809	(198?)
Eddie Cochran and Gene Vincent Greatest Hits (CD)	(R)-Curb/CD21K-7371	(1990)
Singin' to My Baby/Never To Be Forgotten (CD)	-EMI E21Y-80240	(1993)

Extended Play Mini Albums

EP Singin' to My Baby	-Liberty-3061	(1958)

The Cochran Brothers(Eddie Cochran and Hank Cochran)-

Singles

Two Blue Singing Stars/Mr. Fiddle	-Ekko 1003	(1954)
Guilty Conscience/Your Tomorrows Never Come	-Ekko 1005	(1955)
Tired and Sleepy/Fool's Paradise	-Ekko 3001	(1955)

(Cochran Brothers With Jerry Capehart)

Singles

Walkin' Stick Boogie/Rollin'	-Cash 1021	(1955)

Jerry Capehart(Partner and Friend of Eddie Cochran)-

Singles

Song of New Orleans/The Young and Blue	-Crest 1101	(1962)
(With Eddie Cochran)		

Jerry Capehart-(as Jerry Neal)

Singles

Scratchin'/I Hate Rabbits	-Dot 15810	(1958)
(Eddie Cochran on Guitar)		

Lee Denson-

Singles

Strollin' Guitar/Guybo	-Silver 1001	(1955)
Annie Had a Party/So Fine, Be Mine	-Silver 1006	(1955)
(Eddie Cochran plays guitar on record)		
New Shoes/Climb Love Mountain	-Vik 0281	(1956)
(Eddie Cochran plays guitar on record)		

The Galaxies-

Singles

My Tattle Tale/Love Has Its Way	-Guaranteed 216	(1960)
(Eddie Cochran plays guitar on record)		

Jewel And Eddie(Jewel Akens And Eddie Cochran)-

Singles

Opportunity/Doin' the Hully Gully	-Silver 1004	(1960)
Opportunity/Strollin' Guitar	-Silver 1004	(1960)
Sixteen Tons/My Eyes Are Crying for You	-Silver 1008	(1960)

Don Everly-

Singles

Tumbling Tumbleweeds/Only Me	-Ode 66009	(1970)
Warmin' Out the Band	-Ode 66046	(1974)
Yesterday Just Passed My Way Again	-Hickory 368	(1975)
Love at First Sight	-ABC/Hickry 54002	(1976)
Since You Broke My Heart	-ABC/Hickry 54005	(1976)
Brother Jukebox/Oh What a Feeling	-ABC/Hickry 54012	(1977)

Albums

Don Everly	-Ode '70 77005	(1970)
Sunset Towers	-Ode '70 77023	(1974)
Brother Jukebox	-ABC/Hickry 44003	(1976)

Phil Everly-

Singles

Sweet Grass Country/God Bless Older Ladies	-RCA ABPO 0064	(1973)
Old Kentucky River/Summershine	-Pye 71014	(1974)
New Old Song/Better Than Now	-Pye 71036	(1975)
Better Than Now/Friends	-Pye 71050	(1975)
Words in Your Eyes/Back When the BandsPlayed to Ragtime	-Pye 71055	(1976)
Living Alone/I Just Don't Feel Like Dancing	-Elektra 46519	(1979)
You Broke It/Buy Me a Beer	-Elektra 46556	(1979)

-Phil Everly Cont'd-

Dare to Dream Again/Lonely Days, Lonely Days	-Curb 5401	(1980)
Sweet Southern Love/In Your Eyes	-Curb 02116	(1981)
Who's Gonna Keep Me Warm?/One Way Love	-Capitol 5197	(1983)

Albums

Star Spangled Springer	-RCA APL1-0092	(1973)
Phil's Diner	-Pye 12104	(1975)
Mystic Line	-Pye 12121	(1976)
	-Elektra	(1979)

Everly Brothers-

Singles

Keep A-Loving Me/The Sun Keeps Shining	-Columbia 21496	(1956)
Bye Bye Love/I Wonder If I Care As Much	-Cadence 1315	(1957)
Wake Up Little Suzie/Maybe Tomorrow	-Cadence 1337	(1957)
This Little Girl of Mine/Should We Tell Him?	-Cadence 1342	(1957)
All I Have to Do Is Dream/Claudette	-Cadence 1348	(1958)
Bird Dog/Devoted to You	-Cadence 1350	(1958)
Problems/Love of My Life	-Cadence 1355	(1958)
Take a Message to Mary/Poor Jenny	-Cadence 1364	(1958)
('Til) I Kissed You/Oh, What a Feeling	-Cadence 1369	(1959)
Let It Be Me/Since You Broke My Heart	-Cadence 1376	(1959)
When Will I Be Loved?/Be Bop a Lula	-Cadence 1380	(1959)
Like Strangers/A Brand New Heartache	-Cadence 1388	(1959)
I'm Here to Get My Baby Out of Jail/Lightning Express	-Cadence 1429	(1960)
Cathy's Clown/Always It's You	-Warner 5151	(1960)
So Sad/Lucille	-Warner 5163	(1960)
Ebony Eyes/Walk Right Back	-Warner 5199	(1961)
Temptation/Stick With Me Baby	-Warner 5220	(1961)
Crying in the Rain/I'm Not Angry	-Warner5250	(1961)
That's Old Fashioned/How Can I Meet Her?	-Warner 5273	(1962)
Don't Ask Me to Be Friends/No One Can Make My Sunshine Smile	-Warner 5297	(1962)
Nancy's Minuet/So It Always Will Be	-Warner 5346	(1962)
It's Been Nice/I'm Afraid	-Warner 5362	(1963)
The Girl Sang The Blues/Love Her	-Warner 5389	(1963)
Hello Amy/Ain't That Loving You Baby	-Warner 5422	(1963)
The Ferris Wheel/Don't Forget To Cry	-Warner 5441	(1964)
You're the One I Love/Ring Around My Rosie	-Warner 5466	(1964)
Gone, Gone, Gone/Torture	-Warner 5478	(1964)
Don't Blame Me/Muscrat	-Warner 5501	(1965)
You're My Girl/Don't Let the Whole World Know	-Warner 5600	(1965)
That'll Be the Day/Give Me a Sweetheart	-Warner 5611	(1965)
The Price of Love/It Only Costs a Dime	-Warner 5628	(1965)
Follow Me/I'll Never Get Over You	-Warner 5635	(1965)
Love Is Strange/A Man with Money	-Warner 5649	(1965)
It's All Over/I Used to Love You	-Warner 5682	(1966)
The Doll House Is Empty/Lovely Kravezit	-Warner 5698	(1966)

-Everly Brothers Cont'd-

Leave My Girl Alone/(You Got) The Power of Love	-Warner 5808	(1966)
Somebody Help Me/Hard, Hard Year	-Warner 5833	(1966)
Like Everytime Before/Fifi the Flea	-Warner 5857	(1967)
The Devil's Child/She Never Smiles Anymore	-Warner 5901	(1967)
Bowling Green/I Don't Want to Love You	-Warner 7020	(1967)
Mary Jane/Talking to the Flowers	-Warner 7062	(1967)
Voice Within/Love of the Common People	-Warner 7088	(1967)
Cathy's Clown/So Sad	(R)-Warner 7110	(1968)
Crying in the Rain/Lucille	(R)-Warner 7111	(1968)
Bird Dog/Wake Up Little Susie	(R)-Warner 7120	(1968)
All I Have To Do Is Dream/Bye Bye Love	(R)-Warner 7121	(1968)
Bowling Green/That's Old Fashioned	(R)-Warner 0311	(1968)
Empty Boxes/It's My Time	-Warner 7192	(1968)
Milk Train/Lord of the Manor	-Warner 7226	(1968)
The Price of Love/It Only Cost a Dime	-Warner 5628	(1968)
I Wonder If I Care As Much/T For Texas	-Warner 7262	(1969)
I'm On My Way Home Again/Cuckoo Bird	-Warner 7290	(1969)
Carolina on My Mind/My Little Yellow Bird	-Warner 7326	(1969)
Yves/The Human Race	-Warner 7425	(1970)
('Til) I Kissed You/Oh, What a Feeling	(R)-Barnaby 500	(1970)
Maybe Tomorrow/Wake Up Little Susie	(R)-Barnaby 501	(1970)
Bye Bye Love/I Wonder If I Care As Much	(R)-Barnaby 502	(1970)
Should We Tell Him/This Little Girl of Mine	(R)-Barnaby 503	(1971)
Love of My Life/Problems	(R)-Barnaby 504	(1971)
Poor Jenny/Take a Message to Mary	(R)-Barnaby 505	(1971)
Let It Be Me/Since You Broke My Heart	(R)-Barnaby 506	(1972)
When Will I Be Loved/Be-Bop-a-Lula	(R)-Barnaby 507	(1972)
Ridin' High/Stories We Should Tell	-RCA 74-0717	(1972)
Lay It Down/Paradise	-RCA 74-0849	(1972)
Ladies Love Outlaws/Not Fade Away	-RCA 74-0901	(1973)
Brand New Heartache/Like Strangers	(R)-Barnaby 508	(1973)
All I Have To Do Is Dream/Claudette	(R)-Barnaby 509	(1973)
Bird Dog/Devoted To You	(R)-Barnaby 510	(1973)
I'm Here To Get My Baby Out of Jail/Lightning Express	(R)-Barnaby 511	(1973)
When Will I Be Loved?/Be Bop a Lula	(R)-Barnaby 606	(1974)
All I Have To Do Is Dream/Claudette	(R)-Barnaby 609	(1974)
Maybe Tomorrow/Wake Up Little Susie	(R)-Eric	

Albums

The Everly Brothers	-Cadence 3003	(1958)
Songs Our Daddy Taught Us	-Cadence 3016	(1958)
The Everly Brothers Best	-Cadence 3025	(1959)
Fabulous Style of the Everly Brothers	-Cadence 25040	(1960)
Folk Songs of the Everly Bros	-Cadence 25029	(1962)
15 Everly Hits 15	-Cadence 25062	(1963)
It's Everly Time	-Warner 1381	(1960)
A Date With the Everly Brothers	-Warner 1395	(1961)
The Everly Brothers(Both Sides of an Evening)	-Warner 1418	(1961)

-Everly Brothers Cont'd-

Title		Label	Year
Souvenir Sampler		(DJ)-Warner 135	(1961)
Instant Party		-Warner 1430	(1962)
Golden Hits of the Everly Brothers		-Warner 1471	(1962)
Christmas with the Everly Brothers		-Warner 1483	(1962)
The Everly Brothers Sing Great Country Hits		-Warner 1513	(1963)
Very Best of the Everly Bros		-Warner 1554	(1964)
Rock N' Soul		-Warner 1578	(1965)
Gone, Gone, Gone		-Warner 1585	(1965)
Beat N' Soul		-Warner 1605	(1965)
In Our Image		-Warner 1620	(1966)
Two Yanks in London		-Warner 1646	(1966)
Hit Sound of the Everly Bros		-Warner 1676	(1967)
The Everly Brothers Sing		-Warner 1708	(1967)
Roots		-Warner 1752	(1968)
The Everly Brothers		(R)-Harmony 11304	(1968)
Christmas With the Everly Brother		(R)-Harmony 11350	(1969)
The Everly Brothers Show	(2 LP)	-Warner 1858	(1970)
Chained to a Memory		-Harmony 11388	(1970)
Original Greatest Hits		-Barnaby BGP-350	(1970)
The End of an Era		-Barnaby 30260	(1971)
Stories We Could Tell		-RCA Victor 4620	(1972)
Pass the Chicken and Listen		-RCA Victor 4781	(1972)
History of the Everly Brothers		-Barnaby 2-15008	(1973)
The Everly Brothers Greatest Hits		-Barnaby 2-6006	(1974)
(Special TV offer)		-Ronco	
Magical Golden Hits of the Everly Brothers		-Candelite OP-2505	(1976)
The Fabulous Everly Brothers		-Ace CH-006	(1980)
Rip It Up	(CD)	-Ace CHM-64	(1981)
Songs Our Daddy Taught Us	(CD)	(R)-Ace CHM-75	(1983)
	(CD)	-Arista	(1984)
	(CD)	(R)-Pair	(1984)
Reunion Concert	(CD)	-Passport 4006	(1984-86)
The Everly Brothers: The Mercury Years	(CD)	-Mercury 514905	(1984)
Rockin' in Harmony	(CD)	-Crown GEM-002	(1984)
24 Original Classics 9	(2LP)	-Arista AL9-8207	(1984)
EB '84	(CD)	-Mercury 822431	(1984)
Pure Harmony	(CD)	-Ace CH-118	(1984)
The Best of The Everly Brothers	(CD)	-Rhino R2-70173	(1984)
Home Again	(CD)	-RCA AFL1-5401	(1985)
The Everly Brothers: The Early Recordings, Vol.1	(CD)	-Rhino R2-70211	(1985)
The Everly Brothers: Songs Our Daddy Taught Us Vol.4		(R)-Rhino R2-70212	(1985)
The Everly Brothers:The Fabulous Style Of, Vol. 2	(CD)	-Rhino R2-70213	(1985)
All They Had To Do Was Dream	(3 CD)	-Rhino R2-70214	(1985)
Reunion Concert(Live at Albert Hall, 9/23/83)	(2 CD)	-Mercury 824479	(1985)
In the Studio	(CD)	-Ace CH-159	(1985)
The Everly Bros: Heartaches and Harmonies, Vol. 3	(CD)	-Rhino R2-70258	(1985)
Cadence Classics: Their 20 Greatest Hits	(CD)	-Rhino R2-75258	(1985)

-Everly Brothers Cont'd-

Golden Hits of the Everly Brothers	(CD)	(R)-Warner WS-1471-2	(1985)
Rip It Up/Pure Harmony	(2 CD)	-Ace CHC-804	(1986)
Born Yesterday	(CD)	-Mercury 826142	(1986)
The Everly Brothers: Living Legends	(2 LP)	-2 Pair PDK2-1063	(1986)
Very Best of the Everly Bros	(CD)	(R)-Warner WS-1554	(1986)
The Best of the Everly Brothers (1957-60)	(CD)	-Rhino R4-70173	(1987)
The Everly Bros: The Greatest Recordings		-Ace CHA-194	(1987)
The Everly Bros: The Greatest Recordings	(CD)	-Ace CDCH-903	(1987)
Some Hearts(W/Brian and Dennis Wilson)	(CD)	-Mercury 832520	(1989)
All Time Greatest Hits	(CD)	-Curb/C D21K-77311	
The Everly Brothers Golden Hits	(CD)	-Hollywood/IMG 439	
The Fabulous Style of The Everly Brothers	(CD)	-Ace CDCH-932	
The Everly Brothers Pure Solo Classics	(CD)	-Curb/CD21S-77472	(1991)
In The Studio: The Mercury Years	(CD)	(R)-Mercury 51490502	(1993)

Extended Play Mini Albums

EP The Everly Brothers	-Cadence 104-107	(1958)
EP Songs Our Daddy Taught Us	-Cadence 108-110	(1958)
EP The Everly Brothers	-Cadence 111	(1959)
EP The Everly Brothers	-Cadence 118	(1960)
EP The Very Best of the Everly Brothers	-Cadence 121	(1960)
EP Rockin' With the Everly Bros	-Cadence 333	(1961)
EP Dream With the Everly Bros	-Cadence 334	(1961)
EP Foreverly Yours	-Warner Bros 1381	(1961)
EP Especially For You	-Warner Bros 1382	(1960)
EP Everly Brothers Plus Two Oldies	-Warner Bros 5501	

Buddy Knox-

Singles

Party Doll/I'm Stickin' with You	-Triple D 797	(1957)
(Flip side is Jimmy Bowen)		
Party Doll/My Baby's Gone	-Roulette 4002	(1957)
Rock Your Little Baby to Sleep/Don't Make Me Cry	-Roulette 4009	(1957)
Party Doll/Rock You Little Baby to Sleep	(R)-Roulette 42	(1957)
Hula Love/Devil Woman	-Roulette 4018	(1957)
Swingin' Daddy/Whenever I'm Lonely	-Roulette 4042	(1958)
Somebody Touched Me/C'mon Baby	-Roulette 4082	(1958)
Hula Love/Swinging Daddy	(R)-Roulette 43	(1958)
Teasable, Pleasable You/That's Why I Cry	-Roulette 4120	(1959)
I Think I'm Gonna Kill Myself/To Be With You	-Roulette 4140	(1959)
I Ain't Sharin' Sharon/Taste of the Blues	-Roulette 4179	(1959)
Long Lonely Nights/Storm Clouds	-Roulette 4262	(1960)
Lovey Dovey/I Got You	-Liberty 55290	(1960)
Ling-Ting-Tong/The Kisses	-Liberty 55305	(1960)
All By Myself/Three-Eyed Man	-Liberty 55366	(1961)
Chi-Hua-Hua/Open	-Liberty 55411	(1961)
She's Gone/Now There's Only Me	-Liberty 55473	(1961)

-Buddy Knox Cont'd-

Three Way Love Affair/Dear Abby		-Liberty 55503	(1962)
Tomorrow Is a Comin'/Shadaroom		-Liberty 55592	(1962)
Hitch-Hike Back to Georgia/Thanks a Lot		-Liberty 55650	(1962)
All Time Loser/Good Lovin'		-Liberty 55694	(1963)
Ling-Ting-Tong/Lovey Dovey	(RX)	-Liberty 54525	(1963)
Good Time Girl/Livin' In a House Full of Love		-Reprise 0395	(1965)
A Lover's Question/You Said Goodbye		-Reprise 0431	(1865)
A White Sport Coat/That Don't Do Me No Good		-Reprise 0463	(1966)
Love Has Many Ways/16 Feet of Patio		-Reprise 0501	(1966)
Jo-ann/Don't Make a Ripple		-Ruff 101	(1966)
Gypsy Man/This Time Tomorrow		-UA 50301	(1968)
Tonight My Sleepless Night's Gone to Town/			
A Million Years or So		-UA 50463	(1968)
God Knows I Love You/Night Runners		-UA 50526	(1969)
Salt Lake City		-UA 50596	(1969)
Back to New Orleans		-UA 50644	(1970)
Glory Train/White Dove		-UA 50722	(1970)
Travelin' Light/Come Softly to Me		-UA 50789	(1971)
Party Doll/My Babys Gone		(RX)-ABC 2516	(1970)
Ling-Ting-Tong/Lovey Dovey		(RX)-UA 040	(1975)
Party Doll/My Baby's Gone		(RX)-Goldies 2516	

Albums

Buddy Knox	-Roulette R-25003	(1957)
Buddy Knox's Golden Hits	-Liberty LRP-3251	(1962)
Gypsy Man	-UA UAS-6689	(1969)
	-Accord	(1982-83)

Buddy Knox & Jimmy Bowen-(Originally of the same group)

Albums

Buddy Knox & Jimmy Bowen	-Roulette R-25048	(1958)

Extended Play Mini Albums

EP Buddy Knox	-Roulette 301	(1958)

Jack Scott(Jack Scafone)-

Singles

Baby She's Gone/You Can Bet Your Bottom Dollar	-ABC/P 9818	(1957)
Two Timin' Woman/I Need Your Love	-ABC/P 9860	(1957)
Before the Bird Flies/Insane	-ABC/P 10843	(1957)
My True Love/Leroy	-Carlton 462	(1958)
With Your Love/Geraldine	-Carlton 483	(1958)
Goodbye Baby/Save My Soul	-Carlton 493	(1958)
I Never Felt Like This/Bella	-Carlton 504	(1959)
The Way I Walk/Midgie	-Carlton 514	(1959)
There Comes a Time/Baby Marie	-Carlton 519	(1959)
What Am I Living For?/Indiana Waltz	-Guaranteed 209	(1960)

-Jack Scott Cont'd-

Go Wild, Little Sadie/No One Will Ever Know	-Guaranteed 211	(1960)
What in the World's Come Over You/Baby, Baby	-Top Rank 2028	(1960)
Burning Bridges/Oh Little One	-Top Rand 2041	(1960)
It Only Happened Yesterday/Cool Water	-Top Rank 2055	(1960)
Patsy/Old Time Religion	-Top Rank 2075	(1961)
Is There Something On Your Mind?/ Found a Woman	-Top Rank 2093	(1961)
A Little Feeling Called Love/Now That	-Capitol 4554	(1961)
My Dream Come True/Strange Desire	-Capitol 4597	(1961)
Steps 1 and 2/One of These Days	-Capitol 4637	(1961)
Cry, Cry, Cry/Grizzly Bear	-Capitol 4689	(1962)
The Part Where I Cry/You Only See What You Want To See	-Capitol 4738	(1962)
Sad Story/I Can't Hold Your Letters	-Capitol 4796	(1962)
If Only/Green, Green Valley	-Capitol 4855	(1963)
Strangers/Laugh and the World Laughs With You	-Capitol 4903	(1963)
All I See Is Blue/Me-O My-O	-Capitol 4955	(1963)
There's Trouble Brewing/Jingle Bell Slide	-Groove 0027	(1963)
I Knew You First/Blue Skies	-Groove 0031	(1964)
Wiggle on Out/What a Wonderful Night Out	-Groove 0037	(1964)
Thou Shalt Not Steal/I Prayed for an Angel	-Groove 0042	(1964)
Tall Tales/Flakey John	-Groove 0049	(1964)
I Don't Believe in Tea Leaves/Separation's Now Granted	-RCA 8505	(1965)
Looking For Linda/I Hope, I Think, I Wish	-RCA 8685	(1965)
Don't Hush the Laughter/Let's Learn To Live and Love Again	-RCA 8724	(1965)
Burning Bridges/Goodbye Baby	(2)-Gusto 2088	
Before the Bird Flies/Insane	(R)-ABC/Paramount	(1966)
My Special Angel/I Keep Changing My Mind	-Jubilee 5606	(1967)
Burning Bridges/What I Would	(R)-Capitol 6077	
Billy Jack/Mary Marry Me	-GRT 35	(1970)
May You Never Be Alone/Face To The Wall	-Dot 17475	(1973)
You're Just Getting Better/Walk Throu My Mind	-Dot 17504	(1974)
Spirit of '76	-Ponie 4104-30	
	-Eric	
My True Love	(R)-Oldies 89	
My True Love	(R)-Collectables 3021	

Albums

Jack Scott	-Carlton ST-LP 107	(1958)
What Am I Living For?	-Carlton ST-LP 122	(1960)
I Remember Hank Williams	-Top Rank RS-319	(1960)
What in the Worlds Come Over You	-Top Rank RS-326	(1961)
The Spirit Moves Me	-Top Rank RS-348	(1961)
Burning Bridges	-Capitol ST-2035	(1964)
Great Scott	-Jade 33-202	
Soul Stirring	-Sesac 4201	(196?)
	-Ponie	(1974-77)
Burning Bridges	(R)-Cesp 9775	

-Jack Scott Cont'd-

The Greatest Hits of Jack Scott	(CD)	-Curb/C K-77255	(1990)
Jack Scott (Capitol Collectors Series)	(CD)	-Capitol Y-93192	(1990)

Extended Play Mini Albums

EP Presenting Jack Scott	-Carlton EP1070-71	(1958)
EP Jack Scott Sings	-Carlton EP1072	(1959)
EP Starring Jack Scott	-Carlton EP1073	(1959)
EP Jack Scott (What in the World's Come Over You)	-Top Rank 1001	(1960)

Conway Twitty(Harold Jenkins)-

Singles

I Need Your Lovin'/Born To Sing the Blues	-Mercury 71086	(1957)
Shake It up/Maybe Baybe	-Mercury 71148	(1957)
Double Talk Baby/Why Can't I Get Through to You?	-Mercury 71384	(1958)
It's Only Make Believe/I'll Try	-MGM 12677	(1959)
It's Only Make Believe/I'll Try	(S) -MGM 50107	(1959)
The Story of My Love/Make Me Know Your Mine	-MGM 12748	(1959)
Hey Little Lucy/When I'm Not with You	-MGM 12785	(1959)
Mona Lisa/Heavenly	-MGM 12804	(1960)
Danny Boy/Halfway to Heaven	-MGM 12826	(1960)
Danny Boy/Halfway to Heaven	(S) -MGM 50130	(1960)
Lonely Blue Boy/Star Spangled Heaven	-MGM 12857	(1960)
Lonely Blue Boy/It's Only Make Believe	(R)-MGM 144	(1960)
What Am I Living For/The Hurt in My Heart	-MGM 12886	(1960)
Is a Blue Bird Blue?/She's Mine	-MGM 12911	(1960)
Tell Me One More Time/What a Dream	-MGM 12918	(1961)
I Need You So/Teasin'	-MGM 12943	(1961)
Whole Lot of Shakin' Going On/The Flame	-MGM 12962	(1961)
C'est Si Bon/Don't You Dare Let Me Down	-MGM 12969	(1961)
The Next Kiss (Is the Last Goodbye)/Man Alone	-MGM 12998	(1961)
A Million Teardrops/I'm In a Blue, Blue Mood	-MGM 13011	(1961)
Sweet Sorrow/It's Drivin' Me Wild	-MGM 13034	(1962)
Portrait of a Fool/Tower of Tears	-MGM 13050	(1962)
Comfy 'N Cozy/A Little Piece of My Heart	-MGM 13072	(1962)
Unchained Melody/There's Something on Your Mind	-MGM 13089	(1962)
The Pickup/I Hope, I Think, I Wish	-MGM 13112	(1963)
Got My Mojo Working/She Ain't No Angel	-MGM 13149	(1963)
Lonely Blue Boy/It's Only Make Believe	(R)-MGM 509	
Go On And Cry/She Loves Me	-ABC/P 10507	(1963)
My Baby Left Me/Such a Night	-ABC/P 10550	(1964)
(Country Music)	-Decca	(1965-72)
(Country Music)	-MCA	(1973-90)
Lonely Blue Boy/It's Only Make Believe	(R)-MGM 14172	(1971)
What Am I Living For/I'll Try	(R)-MGM 14205	(1971)
What a Dream/Long Black Train	(R)-MGM 14274	(1971)
It's Too Late/I Hope, I Think, I Wish	(R) -MGM 14355	(1972)
Walk on By/Hey, Miss Ruby	(R)-MGM 14088	(1972)

-Conway Twitty Cont'd-

Boss Man/Fever		(R) -MGM 14447	(1973)
Danny Boy/The Pickup		(R) -MGM 14582	(1974)
(Country Music)		-Warner Bros	(1985-87)

Albums

Conway Twitty Sings		-MGM 3744	(1959)
Saturday Night With Contway Twitty		-MGM 3786	(1959)
Lonely Blue Boy		-MGM 3818	(1960)
Conway Twitty's Greatest Hits		-MGM 3849	(1960)
(Reissued again in 1968)			
The Rock & Roll Story		-MGM 3907	(1961)
The Conway Twitty Touch		-MGM 3943	(1961)
Conway Twitty Sings Portrait of a Fool		(R)-MGM 4019	(1962)
R&B '63		-MGM 4089	(1963)
Hit the Road!		-MGM 4217	(1964)
It's Only Make Believe		(R)-Metro 512	(1965)
You Can't Take the Country Out of Conway		-MGM 4650	(1969)
Conway Twitty		-MGM GA-110	(1970)
Conway Twitty Hits		-MGM 4799	(1971)
Conway Twitty Sings the Blues		-MGM 4837	(1972)
Conway Twitty		(R)-Demand 0020	(1972)
Shake It Up		(R)-Picwick SPC-3360	(1972)
20 Great Hits(2 LP)		-MGM 4884	(1973)
Early Favorites (Repackage of Demand 0020)		(R)-Accord 7167	(1982)
Conway Twitty		(R)-Trolly Car 5002	(1982)
You Made Me What I Am		-Allegiance 5012	(1984)
Conway Twitty Greatest Hits	(CD)	-Curb/C K-77365	(1991)
#1's Volume 1	(CD)	-Liberty Y-96293	(1991)
#1's Volume 2	(CD)	-Liberty Y-96679	(1991)
The Best of Conway Twitty, Volume 1, The Rockin' Years	(CD)	-Mercury 849574	(1991)
It's Only Make Believe	(4 CD)	-PSP 837-668-2	(1992)

Extended Play Mini Albums

EP It's Only Make Believe	-MGM X-1623	(1958)
EP Saturday Night With Conway Twitty	-MGM X1678-1680	(1959)
EP Conway Twitty Sings	-MGM X1640-1642	(1959)
EP Lonely Blue Boy	-MGM X1701	(1960)

Gene Vincent(Gene Vincent Craddock)

Singles

Be-Pop-A-Lulu/Woman Love	-Capitol 3450	(1956)
Race with the Devil/Gonna Back Up Baby	-Capitol 3530	(1956)
Bluejean Bop/Who Slapped John	-Capitol 3558	(1956)
Crazy Legs/Important Words	-Capitol 3617	(1956)
Bi-Bickey-Bi-Bo-Bo-Go/Five Days, Five Days	-Capitol 3678	(1957)
Lotta Lovin'/Wear My Ring	-Capitol 3763	(1957)

-Gene Vincent Cont'd-

Title		Label	Year
Dance to the Bop/I Got It		-Capitol 3839	(1957)
Walkin' Home from School/I Got a Baby		-Capitol 3874	(1957)
Baby Blue/True to You		-Capitol 3959	(1958)
Rocky Road Blues/Yes, I Love You Baby		-Capitol 4010	(1958)
Git It/Little Lover		-Capitol 4051	(1958)
Say Mama/Be Bop Boogie Baby		-Capitol 4105	(1959)
Who's Pushin' Your Swing/Over the Rainbow		-Capitol 4153	(1959)
Summertime/Frankie and Johnnie	(Imp)	-Capitol 15035	(1959)
Right Now/ The Night Is So Lonely		-Capitol 4237	(1959)
Wild Cat/Right Here on Earth		-Capitol 4313	(1960)
My Heart/I Gotta Get To You Yet	(Imp)	-Capitol 15115	(1960)
Pistol Packin' Mama/Anna-Annabelle		-Capitol 4442	(1960)
Pistol Packin' Mama/Weeping Willow	(Imp)	-Capitol 15136	(1960)
Anna-Annabelle/Accentuate the Positive	(Imp)	-Capitol 15169	(1961)
Jezebel/Maybe	(Imp)	-Capitol 15179	(1961)
If You Want My lovin'/Mister Loneliness		-Capitol 4525	(1961)
She She Little Sheila/Love of a Man	(Imp)	-Capitol 15202	(1961)
I'm Goin' Home/Love of a Man	(Imp)	-Capitol 15215	(1961)
Brand New Beat/Unchained Melody	(Imp)	-Capitol 15231	(1961)
Lucky Star/Baby Don't Believe Him		-Capitol 4665	(1961)
King of Fools/Be Bop-A-Lula '62	(Imp)	-Capitol 15264	(1962)
Held For Questioning/You're Stll in My Heart	(Imp)	-Capitol 15290	(1962)
Crazy Beat/High Blood Pressure	(Imp)	-Capitol 15309	(1962)
Where Have You Been?/Temptation Baby	(Imp)	-Columbia 7174	(1962)
Humpity Dumpity/Love 'Em Leave 'Em Kinda Guy	(Imp)	-Columbia 7218	(1963)
La Den Da Den Da Da/Beginning of the End	(Imp)	-Columbia 7293	(1963)
Private Detective/You Are My Sunshine	(Imp)	-Columbia 7343	(1964)
Be-Bop-A-Lula/Lotta Lovin'		(R)-Capitol 6042	(1965)
Bird Doggin'/Ain't That Too Much		-Challange 59337	(1967)
Bird Doggin'/Ain't That Too Much	(Imp)	-London 10079	(1967)
Lonely Street/I've Got My Eyes on You		-Challange 59347	(1967)
Lonely Street/I've Got My Eyes on You	(Imp)	(R) -London 10099	(1967)
Born to Be a Rolling Stone/Hurtin' for You, Baby		-Challange 59365	(1967)
Be-Bop-A-Lula/Say Mama	(Imp)	(R)-Capitol 15546	(1967)
Be-Bop-A-Lula '69/Ruby Baby	(Imp)	-Dandelion 4596	(1968)
Story of the Rockers/Pickin' Poppies		-Playground 100	(1968)
Story of the Rockers/Pickin' Poppies	(Imp)	-Spark 1091	(1968)
Story of the Rockers/Pickin Poppies		(R)-Forever 6001	(1969)
Sunshine/Geese		-Kama Sutra 514	(1970)
White Lightning/Scarlet Ribbons	(Imp)	-Dandelion 4974	(1971)
The Day the World Turned Blue/How I Love Them Old Sngs		-Kama Sutra 518	(1971)
The Day The World Turned Blue/High on Livin'		(R)-Kama Sutra2013018	
Say Mama/Lotta Lovin'/Race with the Devil	(Imp)	-Capitol 15906	
Be-Bop-A-Lulu/Lotta Lovin'		(R)-Capitol 6042	

Albums

Bluejean Bop		-Capitol T-764	(1957)
Gene Vincent and The Blue Caps		-Capitol T-811	(1957)

-Gene Vincent Cont'd-

Gene Vincent Rocks and The Blue Caps Roll		-Capitol T-970	(1958)
Hot Rod Gang (Soundtrack)		-Capitol T-985	(1958)
A Gene Vincent Record Date		-Capitol T-1059	(1958)
Sounds Like Gene Vincent		-Capitol T-1207	(1959)
Twist Crazy Times		-Capitol ST-1342	(1960)
The Crazy Beat of Gene Vincent		-Capitol T-20453	(1966)
Shakin' Up a Storm	(Imp)	-Columbia 33-1646	(1967)
Gene Vincent	(Imp)	-London HLH 8333	(1968)
Rock on With Gene	(Imp)	-Capitol 50463	
Gene Sings Vincent	(Imp)	-Capitol 068-86309	
Rock 'N' Roll Heroes	(Imp)	-Rockstar 1004	
Eddie Cochran and Gene VincentTheir Finest Years	(Imp)	-Music For Pleasure 50535	
Gene Vincent with Interview By Red Robinson	(Imp)	-Great Northwest	
Gene Vincent's Greatest		-Capitol DKAO-380	(1969)
I'm Back and I'm Proud		-Dandelion D9-102	(1970)
Gene Vincent(If Only You Could See Me Today)		-Kama Sutra 2019	(1970)
Gene Vincent(Sampler)		-Kama Sutra SP-19	(1970)
The Day the World Turned Blue		-Kama Sutra 2027	(1971)
The Crazy Beat of Gene Vinvent	(Imp)	(R)-Capitol T-20453	(1972)
Gene Vincent Memorial Album	(Imp)	-Capitol	
The Best of Gene Vincent, Vol. 1	(Imp)	-Capitol T-20957	(1973)
The Best of Gene Vincent, Vol. 2	(Imp)	-Capitol T-21144	(1973)
Shakin' Up a Storm	(Imp)	(R)-Columbia 33-1646	(1973)
Gene Vincent	(Imp)	(R)-London HLH 8333	(1973)
The Bop That Just Won't Stop		-Capitol SM-11826	(1974)
Gene Vincent and The Blue Caps		(R)-Capitol ST-11287	(1974)
Rock 'N' Roll Legend	(Imp)	-Capitol	(1977)
Gene Vincent's Greatest		(R)-Capitol SM-380	(1978)
Forever		-Rollin' Rock 022	(1980)
The Bop That Just Won't Stop	(CD)	(R)-Capitol N-16209	(1981)
Gene Vincent's Greatest	(CD)	-Capitol N-16208	(1981)
Rockabilly Fever	(CD)	-Intermedia QS-5074	
Eddie Cochran and Gene Vincent Greatest Hits	(CD)	(R)-Curb/C K-77371	(1990)
Gene Vincent (Capitol Collector's Series)	(CD)	-Capitol Y-94074	(1990)
Gene Vincent and his Blue Caps	(CD)	(R)-Curb/C K-77623	(1993)

Extended Play Mini Albums

EP Bluejean Bop		(3 EP's)	-Capitol EPA 764	(1957)
EP Dance to the Bop		(DJ)	-Capitol PRO 438	(1957)
EP Geme Vomcemt and His Blue Caps		(3 EP's)	-Capitol EPA 811	(1957)
EP Gene Vincent Rocks and the Blue Caps Roll		(3 EP's)	-Capitol EPA 970	(1958)
EP Hot Rod Gang(Soundtrack)			-Capitol EPA 985	(1958)
EP A Gene Vincent Record Date		(3 EP's)	-Capitol EPA 1059	(1958)
EP If You Want My Lovin'		(Imp)	-Capitol EAP 20173	(1961)
EP Race With the Devil		(Imp)	-Capitol EAP 20354	(1963)
EP Crazy Beat of Gene Vincent	(3 EP's)	(Imp)	-Capitol EAP 20453	(1964)
EP True To You		(Imp)	-Capitol EAP 20461	(1964)
EP The Last Word in Lonesome		(Imp)	-Sat Club Radio	
EP Rainy Day Sunshine		(Imp)	-Magnum Force 003	

CHAPTER 8

The After Effects

During the late '50's, the most common interest for any new singer from the South seemed to be rockabilly. It was for this reason, that the country music genre was fast becoming void of talent as everyone recorded at least one rockabilly song.

Some of the country singers who tried rockabilly were Marty Robbins; Johnny Horton; Guy Mitchell; Bobby Bare; Wanda Jackson; Sonny James; George Hamilton, IV; Bob Luman; Little Jimmy Dickens; and Stonewall Jackson. These artists were never really known for this style of music, but it was worth a try as far as the record companies were concerned.

Terry Stafford, Ral Donner, and Ray Smith

These artists were doomed from the beginning: They sounded just like Elvis. They each had a chance, with one or more hits, but never really made it because of their disability.

Terry Stafford, from Amarillo, Texas, had an excellent singing style, as noted by his one hit "Suspicion," which even Elvis covered, but that was all. His album of the same name was actually very good, but the similarity to Elvis was his downfall. He tried to make it with several different labels, but failed to do so.

Ral Donner, whose real name was Ralph, was born on February 10,

1943, in Chicago. Ral was performing at the age of 14, and was the band vocalist at the Club Hollywood, in Chicago, for many years. He was discovered by Sammy Davis, Jr., while they were both booked into the Chez Paree, in Chicago. Sammy brought him to the Apollo Theater in New York to perform in a show hosted by Steve Allen. Ral won over the audience without any trouble.

It was from there, that he was brought to the attention of George Goldner, of Gone Records, who signed him to a recording contract. He hit the charts with "The Girl of My Best Friend," on which he sounded more like Elvis than Elvis did. Ral made several very good attempts, including using Scotty Moore and the Jordanaires, but to no avail. Even an attempted comeback, in 1970, was futile. He managed to sound impressive as the voice of Elvis in the movie, This is Elvis., just as he did on his records. He died of cancer, at age 41, on April 6, 1984.

Ray Smith, who was born in Paducah, Kentucky, on October 31, 1938, had a slightly different story. His career began before Elvis, at Sun Records, yet he never really made a hit until Sam's brother, Judd, put him on his Judd Records label, in 1960, singing "Rockin' Little Angel." The song was a big hit, but Ray disappeared from the rock scene when Elvis came out of the army. In the early '70's however, he did make a comeback attempt in the country music genre. While he recorded some excellent sounding songs, he made no impact on the industry. No one, even today, has been able to make it on his own as long as he sang like Elvis. Many of them also died early in life, as Elvis did. Ray committed suicide on November 29, 1979.

Buddy Knox and Jimmy Bowen

Buddy   Wayne Knox was born on April 14, 1933, in Happy, Texas. He earned a degree in psychology and business administration from West Texas State University, but hit it big with "Party Doll" in 1957, as the lead singer of the Rhythm Orchids. Jimmy Bowen was the base player and second singer of the group.

Their careers both began when Norman Petty pushed the record with Roulette Records, in New York. Buddy was given credit for the A side, and Jimmy the B side.

After Buddy's instant success on Roulette began to wain, he moved to Liberty Records and continued to make decent hits into the mid-'60's, when he faded. An attempted comeback, in 1968, on the United Artists label produced no sparks, and he faded away to obscurity.

Jimmy Bowen was not as good a singer as Buddy, so his career on Roulette fizzled out much quicker than Buddy's did. Jimmy was born on November 30, 1937, in Santa Rita, New Mexico. He managed to make the charts to the number 14 position in 1957, with Roulette's release of "I'm Stickin' With You." After that, it was a matter of going down hill as a singer, and up hill as an administrator, and producer.

After his sad attempt at a comeback on several labels, he managed to fill a void in the production departments of several companies, including United Artists/Liberty, and Reprise. He remained in this area for several years, and after EMI took over the United Artists/Liberty labels, he stayed on as a producer, and vice president of the company. Today, he not only produces many popular country artists, including Garth Brooks, but he has resurrected the Liberty Records label, among others, as strong country music divisions of EMI.

Some Minor Performers

Some of the minor, yet interesting, rockabilly acts to come along after Knox and Bowen are still important in the development of the music.

Ersel Hickey came from New York City, which is not a very good place for either a rockabilly or country and western singer to come from. He had a very unusual hit in 1958 with the shortest song ever heard, "Bluebirds over the Mountain." After this, he cut several more records for Epic, and other labels, and then disappeared.

Guy Mitchell (Al Cernik), from Detroit, had a hit in 1957 with "Rock-A-Billy," and though a few of his songs, both before and after this, reflect some of the style, he was never a rockabilly artist.

Mickey Gilley, Jerry Lee Lewis' cousin, was born on March 9, 1937 in Natchez, Louisiana. He had a terrible time getting started, as evidenced by the many record companies he recorded for: Minor, Dot, Rex, Khoury's, Potomac, Lynn, Sabra, Princess, Supreme, San, Daryl, Astro, Goldband, Epic, Tcg-hall, Act-1, Paula, GRT, Resco, Playboy, Asylum, Liberty. He finally made hits on Epic, when Playboy went out of business. No-one in the history of music has ever recorded for as many labels, and he even recorded on his own Gilley label. His basic problem was that he played and sang too similar to his cousin, Jerry Lee. He does, however, hold the distinction of owning the largest nightclub in the world, Gilley's Club, located in Pasadena, Texas.

Charlie Gracie (Charles Graci) born on January 13, 1936, in Philadelphia, came on the scene in the late '50's with a number of beautiful rockabilly songs, "Butterfly," which was covered in pop by Andy Williams, and "I Love You So Much It Hurts Me." Both songs were excellent sounding, and so was his voice. In spite of the fact that he was on at least 11 labels, nothing more was heard from him.

The Big Bopper (Jules Perry Richardson) born in Sabine Pass, Texas, on October 24, 1930 was a former disc jockey on KTRM, in Beaumont, Texas, and hit it big with the rockabilly sound in a song called "Chantilly Lace," as did his friend Johnny Preston, with "Running Bear." Preston was born on August 18, 1930, in Port Arthur, Texas. The Big Bopper had a few strong hits before he was killed with Buddy Holly and Richie Valens in an airplane crash, and Johnny Preston had a number of good hits before completely disappearing from the record scene. The Big Bopper, who wrote "Running Bear" for Johnny, was joined by George Jones, in vocal harmony as Indians in the background on the record.

All of the following had a quick shot at stardom and then disappeared from the scene: Jody Reynolds who hailed from Los Angeles, played with a group called the Storms, and released an audition record called "Endless Sleep" on Demon Records in 1958. Sanford Clark, who was born in Tulsa, Oklahoma, in 1935, worked with Duane Eddy and Lee Hazelwood, developing a number of good songs on Dot with "The Fool," and a second version of "Swanee River Rock," in competition with Ray Charles's version. Thomas Wayne (Thomas Wayne Perkins, brother of

Carl and Luther), was born in Baltsville, Mississippi, on July 22, 1940, and attended the same high school as Elvis did. He hit the charts with "Tragedy" on Fernwood Records. This was the result of an appointment set up by Scotty Moore, in 1959. He suffered his own tragedy when he was killed in an auto crash on August 15, 1971. Buzz Clifford from Berwyn, Illinois, had a good chance for stardom in 1960 with "Baby Sittin' Boogie." Clyde Stacy. born in Eufala, Oklahoma, on August 11, 1936, recorded a number of great songs for Fernwood and other labels, including "So Young" which he had a hit with on Candlelight in 1957, and then again on Argyle in 1959. Marvin Rainwater, born in Wichita, Kansas, on July 2, 1925, a Native American Indian, had one hit with "Gonna Find Me A Bluebird." The Fendermen, Jim Sundquist and Phil Humphrey, from Wisconson, had a tremendous hit with "Mule Skinner Blues" only to have faded out to nothing. Carl Mann, a prodigy of Sam Phillips, on the Phillips label, was born on August 24, 1942, in Huntington, Texas; he had a few hits with "Mona Lisa" and "Pretend" — both done by Nat King Cole, incidently — and disappeared. Bobby Helms, born on August 15, 1935, in Bloomington, Indiana, disappeared from the scene in the early '60's, after some great hits like "My Special Angel," and "Fraulein," and reappeared on Little Darlin' and then Certron as a producer and writer. To this day, he still has the one of the great repeating hits every year with "Jingle Bell Rock."

BOBBY BARE

Far from a traditionalist in music, Bobby Bare, born in Ironton, Ohio, on April 7, 1935, has a totally laid-back style, both as a singer and a writer. He came from a relatively poor family. His mother died when he was five years old, and his sister gave him up for adoption. Bobby left school at 15, built a guitar out of an old tin can, a stick, and a string; and began to perform with a country band in the Ohio area.

Bobby received a contract on Capitol Records, in 1957, but the songs recorded never really amounted to much, so he decided to join the armed forces.

The day before he was to enter the service, he recorded the song "All American Boy" for Fraternity Records. The song was written by Bobby, but sold to Bill Parsons, and was inadvertently released as being sung by Bill, which it wasn't. The song told a story basically paralleling the life of Elvis, done in a laid back, comedy style. The song was an immediate hit, staying on the top-40 charts for thirteen weeks, and making it to number two.

Since Bobby was in the service, Bill went around the country lip-synching the record. Bobby continued to record his songs for Fraternity, but most of them were unsuccessful; it looked like his attempts at rock and roll were going nowhere.

After Bobby was discharged from the service, he continued to entertain. He was grabbed up by Chet Atkins, in 1962, for RCA Victor Records. In the able hands of Chet Atkins, his laid back style would be used to his advantage. He had some fairly large records for RCA, including "Shame on Me," "Detroit City," and "500 Miles Away From Home," all were crossover records that made the pop charts, as well as the country ones.

In 1970, several artists left RCA to go elsewhere, Bobby was one of them. Bobby went to Mercury, under the direction of Jerry Kennedy. Many fine albums were released by Mercury, including: *This Is Bare Country* (1970), *Where Have All the Seasons Gone?* (1971), and *What Am I Gonna Do Now?* (1972), but very few hits caught on.

After a short stint at Rice Records, in the 1973-74 season, he moved to Columbia Records, where he would spend his final days. Unfortunately, while his albums continued to sell fairly well, mostly because he continued touring, there were no hits.

Bobby found Waylon Jennings playing in a night club in Arizona, and practically forced Chet Atkins to hire him for the label. Bobby later pushed Billy Joe Shaver, and helped Mickey Newbury, and Kris Kristofferson, and went crazy over his good friend Shel Silverstein, later recording his songs, "Daddy What If?," "Marie LaVeaux," "Alimony," "The Winner," and "Red Neck Hippie Romance."

Dale Hawkins
(Delmar Allen Hawkins)

Dale was born in Bossier, Louisiana, on August 22, 1938. He entered the late '50's as one of the most promising stars on the horizon. He was loved and pushed by great promoters such as Dick Clark and his "American Bandstand Show," and other deejays across the country, but for some reason all he had was a short little sprint at greatness.

He was exposed at an early age to gospel and country music influences throughout the South. By his teens, he was already singing with various groups, locally , and he was soon won over by the unique sounds of Elvis and Jerry Lee, and the other new stars of his day.

In the mid-50's, he signed with Chess Records in Chicago. Chess released a number of his songs, which were regional, but not national favorites. A member of his band, at the time, was James Burton, a super guitarist who later went on to back up Ricky Nelson, and had the licks of rockabilly down just fine.

In 1957, he gained national recognition with "Oh Susie Q.." As a result of this single he would begin to travel across the country and appear on TV shows both locally and nationally.

He made the charts again with "La-Do-Dada," and "A House, a Car, and a Wedding Ring" in 1958 and with "Yeah Yeah" in 1959. Although he continued to record on several different labels for years afterward, including: Atlantic, ABC-Paramount, Tilt, Zonk, and Lincoln, and a comeback try in 1970 on Bell Records; he never amount to anything.

George Hamilton, IV

Born in Winston-Salem, North Carolina, on July 19, 1937, George, although not a great contributor to rockabilly, did make some definite contributions. His early sweet, echo-enhanced sounds made light of love and sex. After 1959, however, he turned directly to country music, and away from the sound of his roots.

Having been raised in North Carolina certainly contributed to his appeal for country music, and both his parents were strong fans of the Grand Ole Opry Show. In high school, he turned his ability to play guitar, which he learned in his early teens, to the rock and roll scene that was rushing through the country at the time. He played with local bands, at meetings and dances, and soon his work came to the attention of ABC-Paramount Records. In spite of a recording contract, however, he continued his education, and entered the University Of North Carolina in 1955.

He happened to hear John D. Laudermilk play one of his own compositions on a local radio station, and got to be friends with him. He managed to record "A Rose And a Baby Ruth." The song was an instant hit, in 1956, and later sold one million copies. His smooth, creamy sound was totally different from the rough, loud sounds of the other rock artists, and allowed him to hit it big. The song featured heavy echo, and it was melodic, with sweet sounds.

In the late '50's, George became very popular, placing many songs on the charts, both of his own composition, and those of others. These songs included "Why Don't They Understand," "Now And For Always," "Only One Love," and "I Know Where I'm Goin'." While working for his college degree, he opened his own TV show in Washington, D.C., and went on to perform on many national TV shows throughout the late '50's. He also became popular with the college crowd , and played colleges throughout the country, turning to folk music, when the movement came.

At the start of the '60's, with his maturity, he found his interest in rock fading, and began to shift towards his old country music, and more importantly the new folk music that was beginning to take over the country.

In 1961, he left ABC-Paramount to sign with RCA, under Chet Atkins, as a country music artist. He provided RCA with a number of hit records for several years, including "Abilene;" "Ft. Worth, Dallas and Houston;" and "The Urge For Going."

He joined the Grand Ole Opry in the late '50's, and still remains a loyal member to this day. He now has taken his son into the fold, and they perform together.

Bob Glynn Luman

Bob was born on April 15, 1937 in Nacadoches, Texas, and he died in Nashville, Tennessee on December 27, 1978. In his short forty years, he managed to leave a musical mark on the rockabilly world, that will be hard to replace.

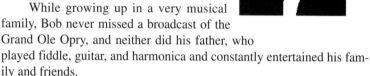

While growing up in a very musical family, Bob never missed a broadcast of the Grand Ole Opry, and neither did his father, who played fiddle, guitar, and harmonica and constantly entertained his family and friends.

Bob developed excellent athletic abilities through high school and was generally very skillful in sports. When the family moved to Kilgore, he became a star on the Kilgore High School baseball team.

His musical abilities and attributes were developing, as well, and he leaned toward making music his career, although he was given many offers to try out for professional baseball. After winning a talent show, he was given a chance to go to the Louisiana Hayride in the mid-50's.

At the height of rock and roll, in 1957, Imperial Records released his, "Red Cadillac and a Black Mustache," and "Red Hot," both heavy rockabilly sounds. But there were no big hits.

As his career grew, he received a contract with Warner Brothers Records, but his recordings were poorly accepted. At this time, he was given a chance to sign a baseball contract with The Pittsburgh Pirates, but he held off. A chance meeting with the Everly Brothers turned his head, because they suggested that he record one of Boudleaux Bryant's songs, "Let's Think About Living." The result was a total smash on both the country and pop charts. His follow-up hit "The Great Snowman" assured his success.

In 1960, he was drafted, and when he returned, he found it hard to start up again. His fans, however, continued to follow him, and in 1965 he became a member of the Grand Ole Opry.

During the mid-'60's he recorded for Hickory Records, but with little success; although his songs were melodic, they did not sound like Bob Luman. In the late 60's he decided to change to Epic Records, and his luck began to change. In 1968, he hit the charts with "Ain't Got Time To Be Unhappy." For the next 10 years, he would be a popular country music artist.

He toured, with his own show, first in this country, and then overseas on a 28 day tour of Great Britain, Scottland, and Ireland. He was constantly featured on many TV shows, both in The United States and Canada.

In December of 1978, just after he signed with Polydor Records, he came down with pneumonia, and entered Nashville Hospital. On December 19, just eight days later, he died of complications.

In his early, and later music, he established a style which was definitely his own, and would be tough to replace.

Narvel Felts

Born near Bernie, Missouri, on November 11, 1938, Narvel grew up on a farm, and was totally swept away by the rock revolution in the mid-'50's, after which he slowly returned to his country music roots.

As a child, he was fascinated by the Grand Ole Opry, and by Ernest Tubb. He picked cotton enough to earn $15 to send away for a Sears guitar, as did many others in the country field. The Sears catalog, in those days, was probably the only place a country boy could get his hands on a new guitar.

In 1956, Narvel entered a talent contest, and won, which led to a position in the radio station's band. After the band leader left, he took over the band.

He drifted around doing various gigs, and recorded some songs for Sun Records, along with Charlie Rich and worked around the south and the Midwest.

Although he recorded some songs for Sun and then for Mercury, nothing seemed to he happening. In the '60's, however, he went with a small company, Pink Records, and had moderate success on the national charts, with "Honey Love," and "3000 Miles." Most of his work appeared to be aimed at the pop and rockabilly genre. In 1960, he left

Pink and didn't do much until he signed with Groove, in 1963.

In 1967, he went to Hi Records, in Nashville, and soon worked with a new independent company, Cinnamon Records. His first breakthrough into the top 5 was "Drift Away," in 1973. Later in the same year, he hit with "All in the Name of Love." In 1974, "When Your Good Love Was Mine," and several other releases hit the charts. While he was well on his way, he was now into the country music genre.

After a short stint at ABC Records, from 1975-77, he came to the attention of MCA, which absorbed the label in the late-'70's. Not including the labels mentioned, Narvel recorded for nine labels, right up to the mid-'80's.

A Few Other Performers

Sonny James (James Loden), born on May 1, 1929, in Hackleburg, Alabama, did not have much success as a young artist on Capitol Records until he hit it big with "Young Love." This record actually sold over a million twice; once on his version, and once on a version by Tab Hunter, a young movie star, and another by the author Ric Carty, on RCA. All were released at the same time. Although Sonny was around for many years, for the most part he disappeared into the country music scene, rather than the pop, even though his music was still rockabilly. While he had only two songs in the top-40, he had 16 consecutive number one songs, on the country and western charts, from 1967-1971.

Wanda Jackson, born on October 20, 1937, in Maud, Oklahoma, who was also on Capitol Records, was one of the few women to pursue rockabilly, and it turned her records into successful sellers. Her young loving touch added sentimentality to the genre.

Her cover of Elvis' "Let's Have a Party," and her "Right or Wrong" are a definite part of the rockabilly chapter in modern music. She managed to have three songs reach the top-40 in 1960 and

1961, before she turned to country and western music.

In England, the reaction to rockabilly developed Skiffle Music, which was similar to it, but used instruments other than the guitar.

Lonnie Donegan (Anthony James Donegan) born in Glasgow, Scottland, on April 29, 1931, was probably the most important factor in its rise to power. He released "Rock Island Line" on London Records in 1956 and "Does Your Chewing Gum Lose Its Flavor on the Bedpost Overnight" on Dot in 1958. The latter was a stiff until Boston area disc jockey Arnie "WooWoo" Ginsburg began pushing it, and it became a hit.
While only two of his songs made the top-40 in the United States, he was a constant chartbuster in Europe.

The more modern sounds of rock, during the late '60's, '70's and '80's brought in more unusual artists with a taste for rockabilly.

Allman Brothers Band

The Allman Brothers Band had several good albums, mostly double sets, in their attempt to write blues, rock and country. Duane Allman's use of the slide guitar brought the blues into the sound, and several of the songs could have survived if only the band had.

The band was formed in Macon, Georgia, in 1968. It consisted of Duane Allman on lead guitar, Gregg Allman on keyboard, Dickey Betts on guitar, Berry Oakley on bass, and two drummers, Jai Johnny Johanson and Butch Trucks. They were first known as the Allman Joys, and later the Hour Glass. They managed to reach the number two position on the top-40, in 1973, with "Ramblin Man."

Duane was killed in a motorcycle crash on October 28, 1971, and Oakley was killed in a motorcycle crash on November 11, 1972. Oakley was replaced by Lamar Williams, and later, Chuck Leavitt was added for keyboards. The band regrouped in 1978, and managed to have 2 songs in the top-40, in the next few years. They were an extremely popular representation of southern rock.

Amazing Rhythm Aces

The group basically consisted of Russell Smith, Butch McDade, Jeff Davis, Billy Earhart III, Barry Burton, and, later James Hooker. In 1977, Burton was replaced by Duncan Cameron. It was a Memphis based group that combined country music, rhythm and blues, rock, gospel, and swing music. It was formed in 1972 because its members were disillusioned with what was happening in rock and in country music at the time and wanted to expand to something else.

Area Code 615

Area Code 615 was a pure backup artists' attempt to bring rockabilly back, using the down-home sound of bluegrass, with steel guitar mixed with harmonica. It was done in a truly professional way. The group consisted of Charlie McCoy, Welden Myric, David Briggs, Norbert Putman, Elliot Mazer, Bobby Thompson, and Wayne Moss. All of these artists were, and still are, excellent musicians.

Asleep at the Wheel

As far back as 1972, the group consisted of Roy Benson, Lucky Oceans (Reuben Gosfield), Chris O'Connell, Danny Levin, Pat "Taco" Ryan, and Link Davis, Jr. (Paul Arthur). Others in the group were Floyd Domino, LeRoy Preston, Tony Garnier, Chris York, Bill Mabry. As of 1982, the group consisted of Benson, Oceans, O'connell, Levin, Ryan, Preston, Domino, Garnier, York, and Mabry.

The group is a total mixture of music from the Midwest, Texas, and country and swing music, with the major influence of Bob Wills thrown in for spice. The strangest part is that most of the members of the band are from the Northeast.

Hoyt Axton

Born on March 25, 1938, in Duncan, Oklahoma. Hoyt is known for his huge size and his tender heart. His mother had gone from teacher to songwriter, when she wrote "Heartbreak Hotel" for Elvis. Hoyt felt from the beginning that it was a lot easier to write and entertain than to labor for a living.

Hoyt wrote a tremendous amount of songs, for many people, including Three Dog Night and Kenny Rodgers, and such songs as "Greenback Dollar," "The Pusher," and "Joy to the World."

He was another artist who attempted to expand the rockabilly sound. This giant weirdo of the music business has no record contract, no manager, no producer, yet continues to create like crazy due to his highly commercial songs. His discography shows a large number of labels, but none for any length of time. He has a tremendous, impressive voice, and is a giant of a man.

The Beatles

The story of the Beatles is certainly well known, from their meager beginnings as the Quarrymen, with John Lennon, Eric Griffiths, Pete Shotton, and Colin Hanson, in 1955. Paul McCartney joined them in 1956, and George Harrison joined them in 1958. Then, they changed their name from the Rainbows to the Silver Beatles, and finally, to the Beatles, when Richard Starkey joined them on drums, in 1960. But rather than duplicate what's already been written about them , this section will discuss only certain aspects of their development that are related to rockabilly.

In the early years of their career, the influence of rockabilly was heavy with the sounds of Buddy Holly, Gene Vincent, Eddie Cochran, and even more noticeably with the sounds of Chuck Berry. The early live club albums certainly demonstrate this influence with their various versions of "Roll Over Beethoven," "Hippy Hippy Shake," and "Long Tall Sally."

The influence is more than evident in their versions of "Matchbox," and "Slow Down," released in 1964, as well as the Gene Vincent style of "Ain't She Sweet," and "Sweet Georgia Brown." "I Saw Her Standing There," released in January 1964, was a fun song, as was most of the rockabilly songs. Rockabilly is also heard in the guitar work of "And I Love Her," "Ticket to Ride" and 1965's "Act Naturally," which was country and western, with shades of Chuck Berry, as well.

Thus, the Beatles, who began as an ordinary rock group, because they were in the right place at the right time, developed their own styles of music, both collectively, and individually, and even showed us the basis of genius in the development of their works.

The latest artists to push for the revival of rockabilly, in its pure form, are the Stray Cats. This young group of musicians tends to sound like a cross between Gene Vincent and Eddie Cochran, and has done its best to revive the sound in todays market.

The beginning form of rock, known as rockabilly, brought with it a tremendous amount of bad luck, and few of the artists have survived.

> Beginning with Elvis (inducted into he army in 1958), Jerry
> Lee Lewis (whose marriage to his 14 year old cousin ended
> his career in 1958), Carl Perkins whose 1956 car crash put
> him out of the market place just when his "Blue Suede
> Shoes" began to take off, Eddie Cochran who was killed in
> a 1960 taxi crash in London, in which Gene Vincent suffered
> and made worse a crippling leg injury suffered earlier in life,
> Buddy Holly, Richie Valens, all dead. *[Miller, 1976, p. 51-52]*

In later tragedies that occurred. all the artists died young or at least suffered: Elvis; Bob Luman; and the two Burnette brothers, Dorsey and Johnny, all died young, and Johnny Cash had problems with drugs and booze. All of these tragedies are a part of the flavor of the music, and all of them will help to see that the music will survive.

The sounds of rockabilly tended to overshadow the other sounds of rock, during its' infancy, even to the extent of trying to cover up its rhythm and blues base, but it never really had a great deal of control over the genre. Although most of the artists mentioned in this book were the dominant factors in the early development of rock, there were others, who helped to broaden the boundaries of its' existence.

Rockabilly managed to survive the '60's -- '70's because of the support and love given to the music throughout the world by record collectors, and small clubs, especially in Europe. England was also the stomping grounds for these artists and musicians, where they not only survived, but thrived, as evident by the life of Gene Vincent.

The Philips division of Phonogram originally held the rights to the Sun label and put out three volumes of rockabilly budget-priced albums in 1974. In 1975, the French label Charly bought the rights and set up in England with massive reissues of this material. MERCURY, MCA, Capitol, and other record companies soon followed suit. Thus, the music lived through several more generations of teenagers than it should have.

The future of rockabilly music lies in the hands of the followers of the artists mention here; the younger performers who have idolized the likes of Eddie Cochran, Gene Vincent, and others enough to continue their style of playing and singing.

Although it is doubtful that rockabilly will ever be as successful as it once was, there can be no doubt that it will survive in the hearts of the old, and will be rejuvenated by the young.

The following codes and classifications are used in the discography.

R	Reissue of a previous release
Rx	Additional Reissue of previous release
1	The first recording of the song.
2	The second recording ...etc.
33	A 33 1/3 speed single release
S	Stereo (noted only on early singles and EP's)
ABC/P	ABC/Paramount
Captl/CEMA	Capitol/CEMA
Caprcn	Capricorn
CESP	CEMA Special Products (Capitol)
Celebrity Circ	Celebrity Circle
CSP	Columbia Special Products
Curb/C	Curb/CEMA
EMI/A	EMI/America
House Sound	House of Sound
MF	Mobile Fidelity
PSP	Polygram Special Products
Warner	Warner Brothers
WSP	Warner Brothers Special Products

In The '80's and '90's Polygram is used
interchangeably with MGM and Polydor is used
interchangeably with Mercury.

Recordings are listed chronologically under each artist's heading.
Most CD listings are available on tape with similar numbers
Most LP Records are no longer available
Artists are arranged alphabetically.

Allman Brothers-

Singles

Black Hearted Woman/Every Hungry Woman	-Capricorn 8003	(1970)
Revival(Love Is Everywhere)/Leave My Blues at Home	-Capricorn 8011	(1971)
Midnight Rider/Whipping Post	-Capricorn 8014	(1971)
Melissa/Blue Sky	-Capricorn 0007	(1972)
One Way Out/Stand Out	-Capricorn 0014	(1972)
Ramblin' Man/Penny Boy	-Capricorn 0027	(1973)
Jessica/Come and Go Blues	-Capricorn 0036	(1973)
Melissa/Ramblin Man	(R)-Capricorn 0051	(1972)
Midnight Rider/Don't Mess Up a Good Thing	-Capricorn 0053	(1975)
Louisiana Lou & Three Card Monty/Nevertheless	-Capricorn 0246	(1975)
Crazy Love	-Capricorn 0320	(1979)
Can't Take It With You	-Capricorn 0326	(1979)
Angeline	-Arista 0555	(1980)
Straight from the Heart	-Capricorn 0618	(1981)

Albums

The Allman Brothers		-Atco SD-33-308	(1969)
Idlewild South		-Capricorn 0197	(1969)
Idlewild South		(R)-Atco SD-33-342	(1970)
Allman Brothers Band		-Capricorn 0196	(1970)
Allman Brothers: At Fillmore East		-Capricorn SD2-802	(1971)
Eat a Peach		-Capricorn C20-102	(1972)
Beginnings		-Atco SD-2-805	(1973)
Brothers and Sisters		-Capricorn 0111	(1973)
Early Allman (Allman Joys)		-Dial DL-6005	(1973)
Beginnings		(R)-Caprcrn 2CX-0132	(1974)
Allman Brothers: At Fillmore East		(R)-Caprcrn2CX4-0131	(1974)
Eat a Peach		(R)-Caprcrn 2S4-0102	(1975)
Win, Lose or Draw		-Caprcrn CP-0156	(1975)
The Road Goes on Forever		-Caprcrn 2CP-0164	(1975)
Wipe the Window, Check the Oil Dollar Worth of Gas		-Caprcrn 0177	(1976)
Enlightened Rogues		-Caprcrn CPN-0218	(1979)
Super Groups in Concert	(Promo)	-ABC Radio*	(1979)
Fantastic Allman Brothers Originals		-K-Tel NI-471	
At Fillmore East	(CD)	(R)-Nautilus NR-30	(1980)
Reach for the Sky	(CD)	(R)-Arista AL9535	(1980)
Best of the Allman Brothers	(2 CD)	(R)-Polydor PD1-6339	(1981)
Brothers of the Road	(CD)	-Arista AL-9564	(1981)
Eat a Peach	(2 CD)	(R)-MFSL 157	(1984)
Back to Back /Atlanta Rhythm Section	(CD)	-K-Tel 219-4	(198?)
The Allman Brothers Live at Fillmore East	(2 CD)	(R)-Polydor 823273	(1987)
The Allman Brothers' Band	(2 CD)	(R)-Polydor 823653	(1987)
Eat a Peach	(2 CD)	(R)-Polydor 823654	(1987)
Best of the Allman Brothers	(2 CD)	(R)-Polydor 825092	(1987)
Allman Brothers: Brothers and Sisters	(2 CD)	-Polydor 825092	(1987)
Win, Lose or Draw	(2 CD)	(R)-Polydor 827586	(1987)

-Allman Brothers Cont'd-

Beginnings	(2 CD) (R)-Polydor 827588	(1987)
Best of the Allman Brothers	(2 CD) (R)-Polydor 827563	(1987)
Enlightened Rogues	(2 CD) (R)-Polydor 831589	(1987)
Wipe the Window, Check the Oil Dollar Worth of Gas	(2 CD) -Polydor 831595(R)	(1987)
Seven Turns	(CD) -Epic 46144	(1987)
Eat a Peach	(2 CD) (R)-MF 10513	(1988)
Idlewild South	(2 CD) (R)-Polydor 833334	(1988)
Allman Brothers: Dreams	(6 CD) -Polydor 839417	(1989)
Live at Ludlow Garage: 1970	(CD) -Polydor 843260	(1990)
Ramblin' Man	(2 CD) (R)-PSP 843771-4	(1990)
Shades of Two Worlds	(CD) -Epic 47877	(1991)
A Decade of Hits	(2 CD) -Polydor 511156-2	(1991)
Live at the Fillmore East (Ultradisk)	(CD) (R)-M F 20588	(1992)
An Evening With The Allman Brothers Band: First Set	(CD) -Epic 48998	(1992)
The Fillmore Concerts (Cronicles series)	(2 CD) (R)-Polydor 517294-2	(1992)

Extended Play Mini Albums

EP Brothers And Sisters	(33)-Capricorn 0111	(1973)
EP Beginnings	(33)-Atlantic 805	(1973)

(Most albums are two-record sets)

Allman Joys (Duane & Gregg Allman)-

Singles

Spoonful/You Deserve Each Other	-Dial 4046	(1973)
The Allman Joys (Dial with live performances added)(CD)	-Mercury518040	(1993)

Duane And Greg Allman-

Singles

Morning Dew/Morning Dew	-Bold 200	(1973)

Albums

Duane and Gregg Allman	-Bold 33-301	(1972)
Duane and Gregg Allman	(R)-Bold 33-302	(1973)

Duane Allman-

Albums

An Anthology	-Caprcrn 2CP-0108	(1972)
Dialogs	(DJ)-Caprcrn PRO-45	(1972)
Anthology, Vol. 2	-Caprcrn 2cp-0139	(1974)
Best of Duane Allman (CD)	-Polydor 827563	(1987)
Anthology (2LP) (CD)	(R)-Polydor 831444	(1987)
Anthology, Vol. 2 (CD)	(R)-Polydor 831445	(1987)

Greg Allman-

Singles

Midnight Rider	-Capricorn 35	(1973)
Please Call Home	-Capricorn 42	(1974)
Crying Shame	-Capricorn 279	(1977)

Albums

Laid Back		-Capricorn CP-0116	(1973)
Gregg Allman Tour		-Capricorn 2C-0141	(1974)
Playin' Up a Storm		-Capricorn CP-0181	(1977)
Gregg Allman Tour	(CD)	(R)-Polydor 831490	(1987)
Laid Back	(CD)	(R)-Polydor 831941	(1987)
Playin' Up a Storm	(CD)	(R)-Polydor 831942	(1987)
I'm No Angel	(CD)	-Epic FE-40531	(1987)
Just Before the Bullets Fly	(CD)	-Epic OE-44033	(1988)

Amazing Rhythm Aces-
(Russell Smith, James Brown, Jr, Byrd Burton, Stick Davis,
Billy Earhart III,James Hooker,Butch McDade)

Singles

Third Rate Romance	-ABC 12078	(1975)
Third Rate Romance	(R)-ABC 2762	(1975)
The End Is Not in Sight	-ABC 12202	(1976)
Dancing the Night Away	-ABC 12242	(1976)
Third Rate Romance	(R)-MCA 2762	(1976)
The End Is Not in Sight	(R)-MCA 2818	(1976)
Two Can Do It, Too	-ABC 12272	(1977)
Burning the Ballroom Down	-ABC 12359	(1978)
Love and Happiness	-Columbia 10983	(1979)
What Kind of Love Is This	-Warner Bros 49543	(1980)

Albums

Stacked Deck	-ABC D-913	(1975)
Too Stuffed To Jump	-ABC D-940	(1976)
Two can Do It, Too	-ABC 1005	(1976)
Burning the Ballroom Down	-ABC 1063	(1978)
Amazing Rhythm Aces	-ABC AA-1123	(1979)
Amazing Rhythm Aces	-Columbia JC-36083	(1979)
How the Hell Do You Spell Rhythm (CD)	-Wrnr Brs BSK3476	(1980)

Area Code 315-

Singles

Ruby/Why Ask Why	-Polydor 14012	(1970)
Stone Fox Chase	-Polydor 14215	(1973)

Albums

| Area Code 615 | | -Polydor 24-4002 | (1969) |
| Trip in the Country | | -Polydor 24-4025 | (1970) |

John Ashley-

Singles

| Born to Rock | | -Dot 15775 | (1958) |

Asleep at the Wheel-

Singles

Take Me Back to Tulsa		-UA 245	(1973)
Choo Choo Ch'boogie		-Epic 8-50045	(1974)
The Letter That Johnny Walker Read		-Capitol 4115	(1975)
Bump Bounce Boogie		-Capitol 4187	(1976)
Nothing Takes the Place of You		-Capitol 4238	(1976)
Blues for Dixie		-Capitol 4357	(1976)
The Trouble With Lovin' Today		-Capitol 4393	(1976)
Somebody Stole His Body		-Capitol 4438	(1977)

Albums

Comin' Right at Ya		-UA LA038-F	(1973)
Asleep at the Wheel		-Epic KE-33097	(1974)
Fathers and Sons	(2LP)	-Epic BG-33782	(1975)
Texas Gold		-Capitol ST-11441	(1975)
Wheelin' and Dealin'		-Capitol ST-11546	(1976)
The Wheel		-Capitol ST-11620	(1977)
Collision Course		-Capitol SW-11726	(1978)
Served Life		-Capitol ST-11945	(1979)
Framed		-MCA 742	(1980)
Framed	(R)	-MCA 5131	(1981)
		-MCA	(1980-84)
		-Epic	(1981)
Asleep at the Wheel	(CD)	(R)-Epic Pet 3097	
Asleep at the Wheel Ten	(CD)	(R)-Epic 40681	(1987)
Asleep at the Wheel	(CD)	-MCA 31281	(1988)
Western Standard Time	(CD)	-Epic 44213	(1988)
Keepin' Me Up Nights	(CD)	-Arista 8550	(1990)
Greatest Hits : Live & Kicking	(CD)	-Arista 18698	(1992)
The Swingin' Best of Asleep at the Wheel (CD)		-Epic 53049	(1992)
Route 66	(CD)	-Lbrty/CEMA98925	(1992)

Hoyt Axton-

Singles

San Fernando	-Colgems 1005	(1967)
Ease Your Pain	-Capitol 3167	(1971)
Greenback Dollar	-Horizon 351	(1972)
Less Than the Song	-A&M 1437	(1973)
When the Morning Comes	-A&M 1497	(1974)
Boney Fingers	-A&M 1607	(1974)
Flash of Fire	-A&M 1811	(1976)
Nashville	-A&M 1657	(1975)
Lion in the Winter	-A&M 1683	(1975)
Southbound	-A&M 1713	(1975)
Della and the Dealer	-Jeremiah 1000	(1979)
A Rusty Old Halo	-Jeremiah 1001	(1979)
Wild Bull Rider	-Jeremiah 1003	(1980)
Evangelina	-Jeremiah 1005	(1980)
Boozers Are Loosers	-Jeremiah 1006	(1980)
She's Too Lazy to Be Crazy	-Jeremiah 1014	(1982)
There Stands the Grass	-Jeremiah 1015	(1982)
Wild Storm and Wild Flowers	-Jeremiah 1017	(1982)

Albums

The Balladeere	-Horizon 1601	(1962)
Thunder'N Lightnin'	-Horizon 1613	(1963)
Saturday's Child	-Horizon 1621	(1963)
Hoyt Axton Explodes	-Vee-Jay 1098	(1964)
Best of Hoyt Axton	-Vee-Jay 1118	(1964)
Greenback Dollar	-Vee-Jay 1126	(1964)
Saturday's Child	(R)-Vee Jay 1127	(1964)
Thunder'N Lightnin'	(R)-Vee-Jay 1128	(1964)
Mr. Greenback Dollar	-Surrey 1005	(1965)
Hoyt Axton Sings Bessie Smith	-Exodus EXS-301	(1966)
My Griffin Is Gone	-Columbia CS-9766	(1969)
Joy to the World	-Capitol SMAS-788	(1971)
Country Anthem	-Capitol SMAS-850	(1971)
Less Than the Song	-A&M SP-4376	(1973)
My Griffin Is Gone	(R)-Columbia C-33103	(1974)
Life Machine	-A&M SP-4422	(1974)
Hoyt Axton Gold	-V J INT 2-1005	(1974)
Bessie Smith My way	(R)-V J INT 7306	(1974)
Southbound	-A&M SP-4510	(1975)
Fearless	-A&M SP-4571	(1976)
Road Songs	-A&M SP-4669	(1977)
Long Old Road	-V J INT VJS-6001	(1977)
Snowblind Friend	-MCA 2263	(1977)
Free Sailin'	-MCA 2319	(1978)
A Rusty Old Halo	-Jeremiah JH-5000	(1979)
Where Did the Money Go?	-Jeremiah JH-5001	(1980)

-Hoyt Axton Cont'd-

Hoyt Axton Live	(2LP)	-Jeremiah JH-5002	(1981)
Best of Hoyt Axton		-Lake Shore 831	(1981)
Pistol Packin' Mama		-Jeremiah JH-5003	(1982)
Double Dare		-Brylen BN-4400	(1982)
Heartbreak Hotel		-Accord SN-7197	(1982)
Down and Out	(CD)	-Allegiance 5023	(1984)
Down and Out	(CD)	(R)-Allegiance5023	(1987)
Life Machine	(CD)	(R)-A&M SP-4422	(1987)
Fearless	(CD)	(R)-A&M SP-4571	(1987)
Road Songs	(CD)	(R)-A&M SP-4669	(1987)
Free Sailin'/Snowblind Friends	(CD)	-MCA 38036	(1987)
Hoyt Axton (American Originals)	(CD)	-Captl/CEMA 99920	(1993)

Bobby Bare-

Singles

Another Love Has Ended	-Capitol 3557	(1956)
Life of a Fool	-Capitol 3686	(1956)
The Livin' End	-Capitol 3771	(1957)
The All American Boy/ Rubber Dolly	-Fraternity 835*	(1958)
Educated Rock and Roll/ Carefree Wanderer	-Fraternity 838*	(1958)
I'm Hanging Up My Rifle/That's Where I Want	-Fraternity 861	(1959)
More Than a Poor Boy Could Give/Sweet Singing Sam	-Fraternity 867	(1959)
No Letter from My Baby/Lynchin' Party	-Fraternity 871	(1960)
Book of Love/Lorena	-Fraternity 878	(1961)
Island of Love/Sailor Man	-Fraternity 885	(1961)
Brooklyn Bridge/Zig Zag(Twist)	-Fraternity 890	(1961)
That Mean Old Clock/The Day My Rainbow Fell	-Fraternity 892	(1961)
All American Boy/Rubber Dolly	(R)-Era 033	(1961)
Shame On Me/Above And Beyond	-RCA 8032	(1962)
To Whom It May Concern	-RCA 8083	(1962)
I'd Fight the World	-RCA 8146	(1963)
Detroit City/Heart of Ice	-RCA 8183	(1963)
500 Miles Away from Home/It All Depends on Linda	-RCA 8238	(1963)
Miller's Cave/Jeannie's Last Kiss	-RCA 8294	(1963)
Have I Stayed Too Long/More Than a Poor Man	-RCA 8358	(1964)
He Was a Friend Of Mine	-RCA 8395	(1964)
Four Strong Winds/Take Me Home	-RCA 8443	(1964)
Miller's Cave/Jeannie's Last Kiss	(R)-RCA 447-0746	(1964)
Times Are Gettin' Hard	-RCA 8509	(1965)
It's Alright	-RCA 8571	(1965)
Just to Satisfy You	-RCA 8654	(1965)
Talk Me Some Sense/Delia's Gone	-RCA 8699	(1965)
In the Same Old Way	-RCA 8758	(1966)
Streets of Baltimore	-RCA 8851	(1966)
Homesick	-RCA 8988	(1966)

-Bobby Bare Cont'd-

Charlestown RR Tavern	-RCA 9098	(1966)
The Piney Wood Hills	-RCA 9314	(1967)
The All American Boy/Rubber dolly	(R)-Goldies 2542	

(Songs after this were mostly country)
*Released under the name Bill Parsons in error

Albums

	-Columbia	(1978-85)
Detroit City	-RCA LSP-2776	(1963)
500 Miles Away from Home	-RCA LSP-2835	(1963)
500 Miles Away from Home	(R)-Camden ACL-7003	(1963)
The Travelin' Bare	-RCA LSP-2955	(1964)
Tunes For Two	-RCA LSP-3336	(1965)
Constant Sorrow	-RCA LSP-3395	(1965)
Tender Years	-Pickwick 6026	(1965)
The Best of Bobby Bare	-RCA LSP-3479	(1966)
Talk Me Some Sense	-RCA LSP-3515	(1966)
Streets of Baltimore	-RCA LSP-3618	(1966)
This I Believe	-RCA LSP-3688	(1966)
The Game of Triangles	-RCA LSP-3764	(1967)
A Bird Named Yesterday	-RCA LSP-3831	(1967)
English Country Side	-RCA LSP-3896	(1967)
Best of Bobby Bare, Vol. 2	-RCA LSP-	(1968)
Folsom Prison Blues	-Camden CAS-2290	(1968)
Lincoln Park Inn	-RCA LSP-4177	(1969)
This Is Bare Country	-Mercury SR-61290	(1970)
The Real Thing	-RCA LSP-4422	(1971)
Where Have All the Seasons Gone	-Mercury SR-61316	(1971)
I Need Some Good News Bad	-Mercury SR-61342	(1971)
I'm a Long Way From Home	-Camden CAS-2465	(1971)
What Am I Gonna Do	-Mercury SR-61363	(1972)
Sings "Lullabys, Legends, And Lies"	-RCA CPl2-0290	(1973)
This Is Bobby Bare	(2LP) -RCA VPS-6090	(1973)
Bobby Bare-I Hate Goodbyes	-RCA APL1-0040	(1973)
Memphis, Tennessee	-Camdn ACL1-0150	(1973)
Singin' in the Kitchen	-RCA APL1-0700	(1974)
Singin' in the Kitchen	(R)-RCA DJL1-0079	(1974)
Bobby Bare's Greatest Hits	-Sun 136	(1974)

(Production ceased as soon as released by SSS)

The Very Best of Bobby Bare	-UA UA-LA427	(1975)
Cowboys and Daddys	-RCA AHL1-1222	(1975)
Memphis Tennessee	-Camdn ACL1-0150	(1975)
Paper Roses	-Camdn ACL1-0533	(1975)
Sunday Morning Coming Down	-RCA ANL1-0560	(1975)
I'm a Long Way from Home	-Camden S-2465	(1975)
500 Miles Away From Home	(R)-Pickwick ACL7003	(1975)
Hard Time Hungrys	-RCA APL1-0906	(1975)
This Is Bare Country	-UA UA-LA621	(1976)

-Bobby Bare Cont'd-

Country Boy And Country Girl	-RCA AHL1-1244	(1976)
Winner And Other Losers	-RCA AHL1-1786	(1976)
Me and McDill	-RCA APL1-2179	(1977)
Folsom Prison Blues	(R)-Pickwick ACL7045	(1977)
Bare	-Columbia KC35314	(1978)
Sleeper Wherever I Fall	-Columbia KC35645	(1978)
Sunday Mornin' Comin' Down	(R)-RCA ANL1-0560	(1979)
Singin' in the Kitchen	(R)-Pickwick ACL7082	(1980)
Down and Dirty	-Columbia JC-36323	(1980)
Drunk and Crazy	-Columbia JC-36785	(1980)
My Country America	-RCA	(1980)
The Bobby Bare Radio Show	(DJ)-Columbia AS-747	(1980)
Greatest Hits of Bobby Bare	-RCA AYL1-4118	(1981)
As Is	-Columbia FC37157	(1981)
Encore	-Columbia FC37351	(1981)
Biggest Hits-Bobby Bare	-Columbia FC38311	(1982)
Bobby Bare-Country Classc	-Columbia P-16917	(1983)
Drinkin' from the Bottle, Singin' from the Heart	-Columbia FC38670	(1983)
	-EMI America	(1985-86)
Down and Dirty	(R)-Columbia JC36323	(198?)
Folsom Prison Blues	(CD) (R)-Camden 2290	(198?)

Barefoot Jerry-

Singles

If There Were Only Time for Love	-Monument 8623	(1974)
Watchin' TV(With the Radio On)	-Monument 8607	(1974)
(T D's Boogie Woogie) Boogie Woogie	-Monument 8611	(1974)
(Recorded with Charlie McCoy)		
The West Side of Mississippi	-Monument 8664	(1975)
The Battle of New Orleans	-Monument 204	(1976)
Barefootin'	-Monument 220	(1977)

Albums

Southern Delights	-Capitol ST-786	(1971)
Barefoot Jerry	-Warnr Brs BS-2641	(1973)
Watchin' TV	-Monument 32926	(1974)
You Can't Get Off with Your Shoes On	-Monument 33381	(1975)
Barefoot Jerry's Grocery (2LP)	-Monument 3909	(1975)
Keys to the Country	-Monument 34252	(1976)
You Can't Get Off with Your Shoes On	(R)-Monument 6631	(1977)
Watchin' TV	(R)-Monument 7601	(1977)
Keys to the Country	(R)-Monument 7605	(1977)
Barefootin'	-Monument 7610	(1977)
Barefoot Jerry's Grocery (2LP)	(R)-Monument 8603	(1977)

Benny Barnes(and the Echoes)-

Singles

Gold Records in the Snow	-D 1052	
Bar With No Beer	-Hallway 1203	
No Fault of Mine	-Starday 236	(1956)
A Poor Man's Riches/Those Who Know	(1) -Starday 262	(1957)
Mine All Mine	-Mercury 71119	(1957)
Lonely Street/Moon Over My Shoulder	-Mercury 71284	(1958)
Yearning/Go On, Go On	-Mercury 71806	(1961)
Heartache's Comin'	-Musicor 1127	(1965)
Headed for a Heartbreak	-Kapp 859	(1967)
It's My Mind That's Broken	-Kapp 912	(1968)
You're Everywhere	-RCA 47-9830	(1970)
A Poor Man's Riches/Those Who Know	(2) -Starday 978	(1974)
I'm So Afraid of Losing You	-Guyden 6005	(1975)
Forget You Sits on My Table	-Guyden 6008	(1975)
I've Got Some Gettin' Over You To Do	-Playboy 5808	(1976)
Little Brown Paper Bag Blues	-Playboy 6084	(1977)

Chuck Barr(and the Rockabillies)-

Singles

Susie or Mary Lou	-Elsan 100

Dean Beard-

Singles

Rakin' and Scrapin'/On My Mind Again	-Edmoral 1011	(1957)
Rakin' and Scrapin'/On My Mind Again	(R)-Atlantic 1137	(1957)
Egad, Charlie Brown	-Challange 59033	(1957)
Party Party	-Atlantic 1162	(1958)
Little Lover	-Challange 59048	(1958)

The Beatles-
(Rockabilly was only involved in their early period)

Singles

Please, Please Me/Ask Me Why	-Vee Jay 498	(1963)
From Me to You/Thank You Girl	-Vee Jay 522	(1963)
Please, Please Me/From Me to You	(R)-Vee Jay 581	(1964)
Do You Want to Know a Secret/Thank You Girl	-Vee Jay 587	(1964)
Ask Me Why/Anna	(R)-Vee Jay DJ8	(1964)
Twist And Shout/There's a Place	-Tollie 9001	(1964)

-The Beatles Cont'd-

Love Me Do/P.S. I Love You	-Tollie 9008	(1964)
Do You Want to Know a Secret/Thank You Girl	(R)-Oldies OL-149	(1964)
Please, Please Me/From Me to You	(R)-Oldies OL-150	(1964)
Love Me Do/P.S. I Love You	(R)-Oldies OL-151	(1964)
Twist And Shout/There's a Place	(R)-Oldies OL-152	(1964)
(Souvenir of Their Visit To America)	-Vee Jay 903	(1964)
She Loves You/I'll Get You	-Swan 4152	(1964)
Sie Liebt Dich/I'll Get You	-Swan 4182	(1964)
My Bonnie/The Saints	-MGM 13213	(1964)
Why/Cry for a Shadow	-MGM 13227	(1964)
Sweet Georgia Brown/Take Out Some Insurance	-Atco 6302	(1964)
Ain't She Sweet/Nobody's Child	-Atco 6308	(1964)
I Want To Hold Your Hand/I Saw Her Standing	-Capitol 5112	(1964)
(A Gift from Your Holiday Inn Keeper)	-Capitol/Holday Inn	(1964)
Music City KFW Beatles/You Can't Do That	-Capitol RB2637/38	(1964)
Can't Buy Me Love/You Can't Do That	-Capitol 5150	(1964)
A Hard Day's Night/I Should Have Known Better	-Capitol 5222	(1964)
I'll Cry Instead/I'm Happy Just to Dance	-Capitol 5234	(1964)
And I Love Her/If I Fell	-Capitol 5235	(1964)
Matchbox/Slow Down	-Capitol 5255	(1964)
I Feel Fine/She's a Woman	-Capitol 5327	(1964)
Eight Days a Week/I Don't Want to Spoil the Party	-Capitol 5371	(1965)
Ticket To Ride/Yes It Is	-Capitol 5407	(1965)
Help!/I'm Down	-Capitol 5476	(1965)
Yesterday/Act Naturally	-Capitol 5498	(1965)
Twist And Shout/There's a Place	-Capitol 6061	*(1965)
Love Me Do/P.S. I Love You	-Capitol 6062	*(1965)
Please, Please Me/From Me To You	(R)-Capitol 6063	*(1965)
Do You Want to Know a Secret/Thank You Girl	(R)-Capitol 6064	*(1965)
Roll Over Beethoven/Misery	-Capitol 6065	*(1965)
Kansas City/Boys	-Capitol 6066	*(1965)
We Can Work It Out/Day Tripper	-Capitol 5555	(1965)
Nowhere Man/What Goes On	-Capitol 5587	(1966)
Paperback Writer/Rain	-Capitol 5651	(1966)
Yellow Submarine/Eleanor Rigby	-Capitol 5715	(1966)
Penny Lane/Strawberry Fields Forever	-Capitol 5810	(1967)
All You Need Is Love/Baby, You're a Rich Man	-Capitol 5964	(1967)
Hello, Goodbye/I Am The Walrus	-Capitol 2056	(1967)
Lady Madonna/The Inner Light	-Capitol 2138	(1968)
Hey Jude/Revolution	-Apple 2276	(1968)
Hey Jude/Revolution	(R)-Americom 2276	(1968)
Get Back/Don't Let Me Down	-Apple 2490	(1969)
Get Back/Don't Let Me Down	(R)-Americom 335	(1969)
Ballad of John and Yoko/Old Brown Shoes	-Apple 2531	(1969)
Something/Come Together	-Apple 2654	(1969)
Let It Be/You Know My Name	-Apple 2764	(1970)
(Dialogue from the Motion Picture Let It Be)	(DJ)-Beatles 1970	(1970)

-The Beatles Cont'd-

Let It Be/(One Side Only)	(R)-UA 42370	(1970)
The Long and Winding Road/For You Blue	-Apple 8232	(1970)

*Special Starline series

Albums

Introducing the Beatles	-Vee-jay 1062	(1963-64)
American Tour With Ed Rudy	-Radio Plsbt News	(1964)
Ain't She Sweet (4 Tracks)	-Atco SD-33-169	(1964)
Beatles With Tony Sheridan and Guests	-MGM SE-4215	(1964)
Chartbusters, Vol IV	-Capitol ST-2094	(1964)
Big Hits from England and the USA	-Capitol ST-2125	(1964)
The Savage Young Beatles	-Savage BM-69	(1964)
Discoteque in Astrosound	-Clarion MS-609	(1964)
Jolly What! The Beatles and Frank Ifield on Stage	-Vee-Jay S1085	(1964)
Amazing Beatles and Other Groups	-Clarion MS-601	(1964)
Beatles and Frank Ifield	-Vee-Jay m1085	(1964)
Beatles Vs. Four Seasons	-Vee-Jay DXS-30	(1964)
Meet the Beatles!	-Capitol ST-2047	(1964)
The Beatles Second Album	-Capitol ST-2080	(1964)
Something New	-Capitol ST-2108	(1964)
The Beatles Story	-Capitol STBO2222	(1964)
A Hard Day's Night	-UA 6366	(1964)
Songs, Pictures and Stories	(R)-Vee Jay 1092	(1964)

(Repackaging of 1062)

Hear the Beatles Tell All	(DJ)-Vee Jay PRO-202	(1964)

(rereleased 1979 and 1987)

Beatlemania Tour (Open End Interview)	-NS Radio News 1	(1964)
American Tour with Ed Rudy	-Radio Pulsebeat	(1964)
This Is Where It Started	-Metro MS-563	(1964)
Great New Releases	(DJ)-Capitol PRO-2538	(1964)
A Hard Day's Night (Open End Interview)	(DJ)-UA SP-2359	(1964)
A Hard Day's Night (Radio Spots)	(DJ)-UA SP-2362	(1964)
A Hard Day's Night	(R)-UA ST-90828	(1964)
Beatles '65	-Capitol ST-2228	(1965)
The Early Beatles	-Capitol ST-2309	(1965)
Beatles VI	-Capitol ST-2358	(1965)
Help! (Radio Spots)	(DJ)-UA Help A/B	(1965)
Help! (Open End Interview)	(DJ)-UA Help INT	(1965)
Help! (One Sided-Open End Interview)	(DJ)-UA Help Show	(1965)
Help!	-Capitol SMAS-2386	(1965)
Rubber Soul	-Capitol ST-2442	(1965)
The Great American Tour	-Lloyds ER-MCLTD	(1965)
1965 Talk Album with Ed Rudy	(DJ)-Radio Pulsebeat	(1965)
Yesterday and Today	-Capitol ST-2553	(1966)
Revolver	-Capitol ST-2576	(1966)
Sgt. Pepper's Lonely Hearts Club Band	-Capitol SMAS-2653	(1966)
Magical Mystery Tour	-Capitol SMAL-2835	(1966)
The Amazing Beatles and Others	-Clarion 601	(1966)

-The Beatles Cont'd-

I Apologize	-Sterling Prodctins	(1966)
The Savage Young Beatles	(R)-Savage BM-69	(1968)
The Beatles (The White Album)	-Apple 101	(1968)
The Beatles Second Album	-Captl/Appl ST-080	(1969)
Yellow Submarine	(R)-Apple KAL-1004	(1969)
Yellow Submarine	-Apple SW-153	(1969)
Abbey Road	-Apple SW-383	(1969)
Hey Jude	-Apple SW-385	(1970)
Beatles VI	(R)-Captl/Appl ST-2358	(1970)
In The Beginning/Circa 1960	-Polydor 24-4504	(1970)
Meet The Beatles!	(R)-Apple ST-2047	(1970)
The Beatles Second Album	(R)-Apple ST-2080	(1970)
Something New	(R)-Apple ST-2108	(1970)
Let It Be	(R)-Apple AR-34001	(1970)
The Beatles Christmas Album	(DJ)-Apple SBC-100	(1970)
The Beatles Story	(R)-Apple STBO-2222	(1970)
Beatles '65	(R)-Apple ST-2228	(1970)
The Early Beatles	(R)-Apple ST-2309	(1970)
Beatles VI	(R)-Apple ST-2358	(1971)
Help	(R)-Apple ST-2386	(1971)
Rubber Soul	(R)-Apple ST-2442	(1971)
Revolver	(R)-Apple ST-2576	(1971)
Sgt Peppers Lonely Hearts	(R)-Apple SMAS-2653	(1971)
Magical Mystery Tour	(R)-Apple SMAL-2835	(1971)
The Beetles/1962-1966	-Apple ST-3403	(1973)
The Beetles/1967-1970	-Apple ST-3404	(1973)
Beatles 1962-1966	-Apple SKBO-3403	(1973)
Beatles 1962-1966(Red)	-Apple SKBO-3403	(1973)
Beatles 1967-1970	-Apple SKBO-3404	(1973)
The Beatles Special Limited Edition	(DJ)-Apple	(1974)
The Beatles 10th Anniversary Box Set	(DJ)-Capitol	(1974)

(Apple numbers were duplicated on Capitol through 1980's)

Meet the Beatles!	(R)-Capitol ST-2047	(1976)
Something New	(R)-Capitol ST-2108	(1976)
The Beatles Story	(R)-Capitol STBO-2222	(1976)
The Early Beatles	(R)-Capitol ST-2309	(1976)
Beatles and Tony Sheridan	(R)-Pickwick CN-2007	(1977)
Rock 'N' Roll Music	(2 LP) (R)-Capitol 11537	(1977)
Live at the Hollywood Bowl	(R)-Capitol11638	(1977)
Live at the Star Club in Hamburg, Germany	(R)-Lingasong 7001	(1977)
Live at the Star Club in Hamburg, Germany	(2 LP) (R)-Atlantic SD2-7001	(1977)
Love Songs	(2 LP) -Capitol 11711	(1977)
	-Grt Northwst Music	(1978)
Beatles 1967-1970(Blue vinyl)	(R)-Apple SKBO-3404	(1978)
Tne Beatles: The White Album	(2 LP) -Apple SWBO-101	(1978)
The Beatles Collection	(13 LP) -Capitol BC-13	(1978)
Sgt. Pepper's Lonely Hearts Club Band	(R)-Capitol 11840	(1978)

-The Beatles Cont'd-

The Beatles	(2LP)	(R)-Capitol SEBX11841	(1978)
The Beatles 1962-1966 (2LP)		(R)-Capitol SEBX11842	(1978)
The Beatles 1967-1970 (2LP)		(R)-Capitol SEBX11843	(1978)
Abbey Road		(R)-Capitol SEAX11900	(1978)
		-PBR International	(1978)
Recorded Live in Hamburg 1962(3 Vols)		(R)-Pickwk BAN90051	(1978)
First Live Recordings, Vol. 1		-Pickwick SPC-3661	(1979)
First Live Recordings, Vol. 2		-Pickwick SPC-3662	(1979)
The Beatles Collectors Items*		-Capitol SPRO-9463	(1979)
A Hard Day's Night		(R)-Capitol 11921	(1979)
The Beatles Rarities		(R)-Capitol SN-12009	(1979)
Rarities		(DJ)-Capitol SPRO8969	(1980)
* Rarities		(R)-Capitol SHAL12080	(1980)
Reel Music		-Capitol SV-12199	(1982)
The Platinum Collection (18 LP Boxed)		(DJ)-Capitol	
Beatles Collection	(13 LP)	-Capitol BC-13	(1978)
Beatles Collectors Items		-Capitol SPRO-9463	(1979)
Abbey Road (1/2 speed)		(R)-MFSL 023**	(1979)
American Tour W/Ed Rudy#2		-I-N-S Radio News	(1980)
The Beatles' Rarities		(R)-Capitol 12060	(1980)
* Rock 'N' Roll Music, Vol. 1		(R)-Capitol 16020	(1980)
* Rock 'N' Roll Music, Vol. 2		(R)-Capitol 16021	(1980)
Magical Mystery Tour (1/2 speed)		(R)-MFSL 047**	(1981)
Dawn of the Silver Beatle		(R)-PAC/UDL 2333	(1981)
Tne Beatles Star Club		(R)-Hall of Music2200	(1981)
		-Raven	(1981)
* Reel Music		-Capitol SV-12199	(1982)
The Beatles (1/2 speed)		(R)-MFSL 072**	(1982)
		-Silhouette	(1981-84)
Sgt. Pepper's Lonely Hearts Club Band**		(R)-MFSL/UHQR 100	(1982)
		-Heritage Sound	(1982)
First Movement		-Audio Fdelty 339	(1982)
The Complete Silver Beatles		-Audio Rarities2452	(1982)
Like Dreamers Do*	(3LP)	-Backstage 1111	(1982)
		-Backstage*	(1983)
*(4 different issues...most 3 LP sets)			
The Beatles 20 Greatest Hits		(R)-Capitol 12245	(1982)
The Beatles Starclub		(R)-Hall of Music 2200	(1982)
The Beatles, the Collection**(13 LP)		-MFSL 1	(1982)
		-Phoenix 10	(1982)
		-Phoenix 20	(1982)
In The Beginning		(R)-Polydr 24-4504	(1984)
Sgt. Pepper's Lonely Hearts Club Band		(R)-MFSL 100**	(1984)
Please Please Me		(R)-MFSL 101**	(1984)
With the Beatles		(R)-MFSL 102**	(1984)
A Hard Day's Night		(R)-MFSL 103**	(1984)
Beatles for Sale		(R)-MFSL 104**	(1984)

-The Beatles Cont'd-

Yesterday and Today	(CD)		(R)-Capitol/C 90447	(1987)
The Early Beatles	(CD)		(R)-Capitol/C 90451	(1987)
Revolver	(CD)		(R)-Capitol/C 90452	(1987)
Rubber Soul	(CD)		(R)-Capitol/C 90453	(1987)
Help	(CD)		(R)-Capitol/C 90454	(1987)
* Please Please Me	(CD)	(Imp)	(R)-Capitol 46435	(1987)
* With the Beetles	(CD)	(Imp)	(R)-Capitol 46436	(1987)
* A Hard Day's Night	(CD)	(Imp)	(R)-Capitol 46437	(1987)
* The Beatles For Sale	(CD)	(Imp)	-Capitol 46438	(1987)
* Help	(CD)	(Imp)	(R)-Capitol 46439	(1987)
* Rubber Soul	(CD)	(Imp)	(R)-Capitol 46440	(1987)
* Revolver	(CD)	(Imp)	(R)-Capitol 46441	(1987)
* Sgt. Pepper's Lonely Hearts Club Band	(CD)	(Imp)	(R)-Capitol 46442	(1987)
* The Beatles	(CD)	(Imp)	(R)-Capitol 46443	(1987)
* Yellow Submarine	(CD)	(Imp)	(R)-Capitol 46445	(1987)
* Abbey Road	(CD)	(Imp)	(R)-Capitol 46446	(1987)
* Let It Be	(CD)	(Imp)	(R)-Capitol 46447	(1987)
* Magical Mystery Tour	(CD)	(Imp)	(R)-Capitol 48062	(1987)
In The Beginning: The Early Tapes	(CD)		(R)-Polydor 823701	(1987)
In The Beginning	(CD)		(R)-Polydor 825073	(1988)
Past Masters Vol.1 & 2	(2 CD)		-Capitol/C 91135	(1988)
The Ultimate Box Set	(16 CD)		-Capitol/C 91302	(1989)
The Beatles' Compact Disc Singles Collection	(CD)		-Capitol/C 15901	(1992)

* The Original versions as released in the United Kingdom

Extended Play Mini Albums

EP Souvenir of Their Visit to America		-Vee-jay 1-903	(1964)
EP Four By the Beatles		-Capitol EAP1-2121	(1964)
EP Four By the Beatles		-Capitol EPR-5365	(1964)
EP (Open End Interview with the Beatles)		-Capitol PRO2348-49	(1964)
EP (The Beatles Second Open End Interview)	(33)	-Capitol PRO2598	(1964)
EP Meet the Beatles	(33)	-Capitol SXA-2047	(1967)
EP The Beatles' Second Album (Jukebox Only)	(33)	-Capitol SXA-2080	(1967)
EP Something New	(33)	-Capitol SXA-2108	(1967)

** MFSL Disks are cut from original masters, at half speed.

Boyd Bennett(and His Rockets-and the Southlanders)-

Singles

I'm Wasting My Time	-King 1201	(1953)
Waterlou/I've Had Enough	-King 1413	(1954)
Poison Ivy/You Upset Me Baby	-King 1432	(1954)
Boogie at Midnight/Everlovin'	-King 1443	(1954)
Seventeen/Little Old You-all	-King 1470	(1955)
Tennessee Rock and Roll /Oo-Oo-Oo	-King 1475	(1955)
My Boy Flat Top/Banjo Rock and Roll	-King 1494	(1955)

-The Beatles Cont'd-

Help	(CD)	(R)-MFSL 105**	(1984)
Rubber Soul	(CD)	(R)-MFSL 106**	(1984)
Revolver	(CD)	(R)-MFSL 107**	(1984)
Yellow Submarine	(CD)	(R)-MFSL 108**	(1984)
Let It Be Me	(CD)	(R)-MFSL 109**	(1984)
The Beatles	(CD)	(R)-Capitol 101	(1984)
Yellow Submarine	(CD)	(R)-Capitol 153	(1984)
Abbey Road	(CD)	(R)-Capitol 383	(1984)
Hey Jude	(CD)	(R)-Capitol 385	(1984)
Meet the Beatles	(CD)	(R)-Capitol ST-2047	(1984)
The Beatles Second Album	(CD)	(R)-Capitol ST-2080	(1984)
Something New	(CD)	(R)-Capitol ST-2108	(1984)
The Beatles Story	(CD)	(R)-Capitol 2222	(1984)
Beatles '65	(CD)	(R)-Capitol ST-2228	(1984)
The Early Years	(CD)	(R)-Capitol ST-2309	(1984)
Beatles VI	(CD)	(R)-Capitol ST-2358	(1984)
Help	(CD)	(R)-Capitol2386	(1984)
Rubber Soul	(CD)	(R)-Capitol ST-2442	(1984)
Yesterday and Today	(CD)	(R)-Capitol ST-2553	(1984)
Revolver	(CD)	(R)-Capitol ST-2576	(1984)
Sgt. Pepper's Lonely Hearts Club Band	(CD)	(R)-Capitol 2653	(1984)
Magical Mystery Tour	(CD)	(R)-Capitol 2835	(1984)
A Hard Day's Night	(CD)	(R)-Capitol/C 11921	(1984)
Let It Be	(CD)	(R)-Capitol/C 11922	(1984)
The Beatles 20 Greatest Hits		(R)-Capitol/C 12245	(1984)
		-Music Interntional	(1985)
		-Cicadelic	(1985-87)
Live at the Hollywood Bowl	(CD)	(R)-Capitol/C 11638	(1986)
Love Songs	(CD)	(R)-Capitol/C 11711	(1986)
A Hard Day's Night	(CD)	(R)-Capitol/C 11921	(1986)
Rarities	(CD)	(R)-Capitol/C 12060	(1986)
Reel Music	(CD)	(R)-Capitol/C 12199	(1986)
The Beatles 20 Greatest Hits	(CD)	(R)-Capitol/C 12245	(1986)
The Compact Disk EP Collection	(CD)	-Capitol/C 15852	(1986)
Rock 'N' Roll Music, Vol 1	(CD)	(R)-Capitol/C 16020	(1986)
Rock 'N' Roll Music, Vol. 2	(CD)	(R)-Capitol/C 16021	(1986)
Past Masters Vol. 1	(CD)	-Capitol/C 90043	(1987)
Past Masters Vol. 2	(CD)	-Capitol/C 90044	(1987)
1962-66	(CD)	(R)-Capitol/C 90435	(1987)
1967-70	(CD)	(R)-Capitol/C 90438	(1987)
Meet the Beatles	(CD)	(R)-Capitol/C 90441	(1987)
Hey Jude	(CD)	(R)-Capitol/C 90442	(1987)
Something New	(CD)	(R)-Capitol/C 90443	(1987)
Second Album	(CD)	(R)-Capitol/C 90444	(1987)
Beatles VI	(CD)	(R)-Capitol/C 90445	(1987)
Beatles '65	(CD)	(R)-Capitol/C 90446	(1987)
The Beatles Past Masters	(CD)	-CapitolC 91135	(1988)

Boyd Bennett (and His Rockets-and the Southlanders)-

Singles

I'm Wasting My Time	-King 1201	(1953)
Waterlou/I've Had Enough	-King 1413	(1954)
Poison Ivy/You Upset Me Baby	-King 1432	(1954)
Boogie at Midnight/Everlovin'	-King 1443	(1954)
Seventeen/Little Old You-all	-King 1470	(1955)
Tennessee Rock and Roll/Oo-Oo-Oo	-King 1475	(1955)
My Boy Flat Top/Banjo Rock and Roll	-King 1494	(1955)
The Most/Desperately	-King 4853	(1956)
Right Around the Corner/Partners for Life	-King 4874	(1956)
Blue Suede Shoes/Mumbles Blues	-King 4903	(1956)
The Groovy Age/Let Me Love You	-King 4925	(1956)
Hit That Five Jack/Rabbit Eye Pink & Charcoal Black	-King 4953	(1956)
Rockin' Up a Storm/A Lock of Your hair	-King 4985	(1957)
Put the Chain on the Door/Big Boy	-King 5049	(1957)
Move	-King 5115	(1957)
Cool Disc Jockey(DJ)/High School Hop	-King 5282	(1959)
My Boy Flat Top/Seventeen	(2)-King 5374	(1959)
Teenage Years	-King 5738	(1963)
Tear It Up/Tight Tights	-Mercury 71409	(1959)
Boogie Bear/A Boy Can Tell	-Mercury 71479	(1959)
Naughty Rock & Roll/Lover's Night	-Mercury 71537	(1960)
It's Wonderful/Amos, Amas, Amat	-Mercury 71605	(1960)
Seventeen/Sarasota	(2)-Mercury 71648	(1960)
Big Junior/Hershey Bar	-Mercury 71724	(1961)
The Brain/Coffee Break	-Mercury 71813	(1961)
Everything's Getting Bigger But Our Love/Kiss And Run	-Mercury 72912	(1961)
Who"s Knocking On My Door/Paralyzed	-Psycho Suave 1033	(196?)
Seventeen/My Boy Flat Top	(R)-Gusto 2080	(196?)

Albums

Boyd Bennett	-King 594	(1957)

Extended Play Mini Albums

EP Rock & Roll	-King 377	(1957)
EP Rock & Roll	(R)-King 383	(1957)

Joe Bennett & The Sparkletones-

Singles

	-Columbia	(1950-56)
The Little Rock and Roll	-Columbia 2521	(1956)
Black Slacks/Bopin Rock Boogie	-ABC /P 9837	(1957)
Black Slacks/Boppin Rock Boogie	(R)-ABC /P 1228	(1957)
Penny Loafers & Bobby Sox/Rocket	-ABC /P 9867	(1957)
Cotton Pickin' Rocker/I Dig You Baby	-ABC/ P 9885	(1957)
We've Had It/Little Turtle	-ABC/ P 9929	(1958)

-Joe Bennett & The Sparkletones Cont'd-

Do The Stop/Late Again	-ABC/ P 9959	(1958)
Run Rabbit Run/Well-Dressed Man	-ABC/ P10659	(1958)
Bayou Rock/Beautiful One	-Paris 530	(1959)
Boys Do Cry/What the Heck	-Paris 537	(1959)
Boys Do Cry	(R)-Paris 3	(1959)
Are You From Dixie/Beautiful One	-Paris 542	(1960)
Boys Do Cry	(R)-Roulette 3	(1960)
Black Slacks	(R)-Roulette 126	(1960)
Black Slacks	(R)-ABC 1228	(1973)
Black Slacks	(R)-MCA 2402	(1973)

The Big Bopper(J.P. Richardson, Jape Richardson)-

Singles

* Beggar to a King/Before They Make Me Run	-Mercury 71219	(1957)
* Teenage Moon/Monkey Song	-Mercury 71312	(1958)
Chantilly Lace/Purple People Eater Meets the Witch Doctor	-D 1008	(1958)
Chantilly Lace/Purple People Eater Meets the Witch Doctor	-Mercury 71343	(1958)
Big Bopper's Wedding/Little Red Riding Hood	-Mercury 71375	(1958)
Walking Through My Dreams/Someone Watching Over You	-Mercury 71416	(1959)
It's the Truth, Ruth/That's What I'm Talking About	-Mercury 71451	(1959)
Pink Petticoats/The Clock	-Mercury 71482	(1959)

*(Recorded as Jape Richardson)

Albums

Chantilly Lace	-Mercury 20402	(1959)
(Released with same number 1964, 1971, 1981, 1987)		
The Big Bopper	-Pickwick	(1973)
Hello Baby!: The Best of the Big Bopper, 1954-1959(CD)	-Rhino 70164	(1989)

Billy the Kid-

Singles

Apron Strings	-Kapp 261	(1959)

Bob and the Rockabillies-

Singles

Your Kind of Love	-Blue Chip 011	(195?)

Eddie Bond(and his Stompers)-

Singles

Talkin' Off the Wall	-Ekko 1015	(1955)
Love Makes a Fool	-Ekko 1016	(1955)

-Eddie Bond Cont'd-

Rockin' Daddy/I've Got a Woman	-Mercury 70826	(1956)
Slip Slip Slippin' In/Flip Flop Mama	-Mercury 70882	(1956)
Boppin' Bonnie/Baby, Baby, Baby	-Mercury 70941	(1956)
You're Part of Me	-Mercury 71067	(1957)
Hershey Bar	-Mercury 71153	(1957)
Here Comes The Train	-Erwin 2001	(1957)
Here Comes The Train	-Memphis 115	(1957)
Backslidin'	-Mercury 71237	(1958)
Frump/Blacksmith Blues	-Mercury 72111	(1958)
Quarter to Four Stomp/Foolish One	-Landa 684	(195?)
You'll Never Be a Stranger	-Stomper Time 1156	(195?)
The Monkey and the Baboon	-Diplomat 8566	(195?)
Caution	-Enterprise 9057	(1972)

Albums

Eddie Bond Sings the Greatest Country Gospel Hits	-Phillips Int 1980	(1961)
Favorite Country Hits From Down Home	-Millionaire 1618	(1967)
My Choice Is Eddie Bond	-M.C.C.R. 660	(1969)
My Choice Is Eddie Bond	(R)-Country Crcl 8352	(1969)
Eddie Bond Sings the Legend of Buford Pusser	-Enterprise 1038	(1973)

Johnny Bond-

Singles

Honky Tonk Fever	-Columbia 40842	(1956)
Wild Cat Boogie	-Columbia 21160	(1957)
Stealin'	-Columbia 21294	(1957)
Louisiana Swing	-Columbia 21383	(1957)
Somebody's Pushin'	-Columbia 21448	(1957)
Loaded for Bear	-Columbia 21494	(1957)
The Little Rock and Roll	-Columbia 21521	(1957)
Lonesome Train	-Columbia 21565	(1957)
Hot Rod Lincoln/Five Minute Love Affair	-Republic 2005	(1959)
X-15/The Way a Star Is Born	-Republic 2008	(1959)
Side Car Cycle/Like Nothin' Man	-Republic 2010	(1959)
Hot Rod Lincoln/Ten Little Bottles	(R)-Starday 8026	(1960)
Mister Sun/I'll Step Aside	-Smash 1761	(1962)
How To Succeed with Girls/Don't Mention Name	-Starday 618	(1962)
Cimarron	-Starday 636	(1963)
Three Sheets To The Wind/Let the Tears Begin	-Starday 649	(1963)
Hot Rod Surfin' Beatle Hootananny/ Don't Mama Count Anymore?	-Starday 678	(1963)
Bachelor Bill	-Starday 690	(1963)
Divorce Me COD/Three Sheets in the Wind	(R)-Starday 7027	(1964)
10 Little Bottles/Let It Be Me	-Starday 704	(1964)
The Man Who Comes Around/Sick, Sober and Sorry	-Starday 721	(1965)

-Johnny Bond Cont'd-

The Great Figure Eight Race	-Starday 731	(1965)
Hot Rod Lincoln/Ten Little Bottles	(R)-Gusto 2939	(1965)
Silent Walls/They Got Me	-Starday 749	(1966)
Fireball	-Starday 758	(1966)
Your Old Love Letters/Si Si	-Starday 803	(1966)
Don't Bite the Hand That's Feeding You	-Starday 813	(1967)
Invitation to the Blues	-Starday 847	(1967)
It Only Hurts When I Cry/ The Girl Who Carries the Torch for Me	-Starday 893	(1970)
Here Come The Elephants	-Starday 916	(1971)
The Bottles Empty/The Late and Great Myself	-Starday 931	(1971)
Put the Country Back in Country Music	-Starday 951	(1972)
Rose of Reynosa	-MGM 14596	(1973)
Hot Rod Lincoln	(R)-Trip 135	(197?)
	-Lamb & lion	(1974)
	-Orchid	(1989)

Albums

That Wild, Wicked But Wonderful West	-Starday SLP-147	(1961)
Live It Up and Laugh It Up	-Starday SLP-187	(1962)
Songs That Made Him Famous	-Starday SLP-227	(1963)
Johnny Bond's Best	-Harmony HL-7308	(1964)
Hot Rod Lincoln-Three Sheets in the Wind	-Starday SLP-298	(1964)
Bottled In Bond	-Harmony HL-7353	(1965)
Ten Little Bottles	-Starday SLP-333	(1965)
Famous Hot Rodders I Have Known	-Starday SLP-354	(1965)
The Man Who Comes Around	-Starday SLP-368	(1966)
Bottles Up	-Starday SLP-378	(1966)
Branded Stock of Johnny Bond	-Starday SLP-388	(1966)
Ten Nights in a Barroom	-Starday SLP-402	(1967)
Little Ole Wine Drinker	-Starday SLP-416	(1967)
Drink Up and Go Home	-Starday SLP-426	(1968)
Best of Johnny Bond	-Starday SLP-444	(1969)
Something Old, New Patriotic and Blue	-Starday SLP-456	(1970)
Johnny Bond Rides Again	-Shasta SH-516	(1971)
Sick, Sober and Sorry	-Nashville NLP-2039	(1971)
Three Sheets in the Wind	-Nashville NLP-2054	(1971)
Here Come the Elephants	-Starday SLP-472	(1971)
How I Love Them Old Songs	-Lamb&Lion 4002	(1974)
Best of Johnny Bond	-Starday SLP-954	(1974)
	-CMH	(1977)
The Best of Country	(CD)	-Rounder 2155	(198?)
The Best of Comedy	(CD)	-Rounder 2195	(198?)
That Wild But Wonderful West	(CD)	(R)-Starday 147	(198?)

Extended Play Mini Albums

EP Johnny Bond and His Red River Valley Boys	-Columbia B-2820	(1958)
EP Hot Rod Lincoln	-Republic EP-100	(1960)

Billy Briggs-

Singles

Chew Tobacco Rag	-Imperial	(1950)

Donnie Brooks-

Singles

Lil' Sweetheart/If You're Lookin'	-Era 3004	(1959)
White Orchid/Stay and Move with the Beat	-Era 3007	(1960)
Mission Bell/Do It For Me	(1)-Era 3018	(1960)
Doll House/Round Robin	(1)-Era 3028	(1960)
Memphis/That's Why	-Era 3042	(1961)
All I Can Give/Wishbone	-Era 3049	(1961)
Boomerang/How Long?	-Era 3052	(1961)
Sweet Lorraine/Up To My Ears in Tears	-Era 3059	(1961)
Up To My Ears in Tears/Goodnight, Judy	(R)-Era 3063	(1961)
Your Little Boy's Come Home/Goodnight, Judy	(R)-Era 3071	(1962)
Oh, You Beautiful Doll/Just a Bystander	-Era 3077	(1962)
It's Not That Easy/Cries My Heart	-Era 3095	(1962)
Love Is Funny That Way	-Era 3194	(1962)
Doll House/Mission Bell	(R)-Era 1	(196?)
Doll House/Cries from My Heart	(R)-Era 5038	(196?)

Albums

The Happiest	-Era 105	(1961)

James Burton(Guitarist)-

Albums

Corn Pickin' and Slick Slidin'	-Capitol ST-2822	(1968)
James Burton	-A&M SP-4293	(1971)

(Backup for Dale Hawkins, Rick Nelson, Elvis Presley, Emmie Lou
Harris, John Denver, and many more)

Dick Bush-

Singles

Hollywood Party	-Era 1067	(1958)

Aubrey Cagle-

Singles

Real Cool/Want to Be Wanted Blues	-House Sound 504	(1957)
Be Bop Blues/Just For You	-Glee 1000	(1960)

-Aubrey Cagle Cont'd-

Come Along Little Girl/Blue Lonely World	-Glee 1001	(1960)
Bop 'n' Stroll	-Glee 1003	(1960)

Ray Campi(and His Rockabilly Rebels)-

Singles

Play It Cool	-TNT 145	(1957)
It Ain't Me/Give That Love to Me	-Dot 15617	(1957)

Albums

Ray Campi Rockabilly		-Rollin' Rock 001	(1976)
Rockabilly Rebel		-Rollin' Rock 006	(1976)
Ray Campi-The Eager Beaver Boy		-Rollin' Rock 008	(1976)
Born to Rock		-Rollin' Rock 011	(1977)
Rockabilly Rocket		-Rollin' Rock 013	(1977)
Rockabilly Music		-Rollin' Rock 023	(1977)
Rockabilly Lives		-Rollin' Rock 104	(197?)
Rockabilly Rebellion		-Rollin' Rock 6901	(197?)
Ray Campi		-Rollin' Rock 6902	(197?)
Rockin' at the Ritz	(CD)	-Rounder 3046	(198?)
Gone, Gone, Gone	(CD)	-Rounder 3047	(198?)
Ray Campi with Friends in Texas	(CD)	-Flying Fish 70518	(1991)

Extended Play Mini Albums

EP Ray Campi and Merl Travis	-Rollin' Rock 031	(197?)

Johnny Carrol(and His Hot Rocks)-

Singles

Rock and Roll Ruby/Trying to Get to You	-Decca 29940	(1956)
Wild Wild Women/Corrine, Corrina	-Decca 29941	(1956)
Hot Rock/Crazy, Crazy Lovin'	-Decca 30013	(1956)

Ric Carty-

Singles

Young Love/Oooh-eee	-Stars 539	(1956)
Young Love/Oooh-eee	-RCA 6751	(1956)
Heart Throb	-RCA 6828	(1956)
Let Me Tell You About Love	-RCA 6920	(1957)
My Babe	-RCA 7011	(1957)
Something in My Eye	-ABC/P 10415	(1958)
Scratchin' on My Screen	-NRC 503	(1959)

Sanford Clark-

Singles

The Fool/Lonesome for a Letter	-MCI 1003	(1955)
The Fool/Lonesome for a Letter	(R)-ABC 2707	(1955)
The Fool/Lonesome for a Letter	(R)-Dot 15481	(1956)
A Cheat/Usta Be My Baby	-Dot 15516	(1956)
9 Lb Hammer/Ooo Baby	-Dot 15534	(1957)
The Glory of Love/Darling Dear	-Dot 15556	(1957)
Love Charms/Lou Be Doo	-Dot 15585	(1957)
Swannee River Rock/Man Who Made an Angel Cry	-Dot 15646	(1957)
Modern Romance/Travelin' Man	-Dot 15738	(1958)
Sing 'Em Some Blues / Still as the Night	-Jamie 1107	(1958)
(A-side ith Duane Eddy-Flip side is with Al Casey)		
Bad Luck/My Jealousy	-Jamie 1120	(1959)
Run Boy Run/A New Kind of Fool	-Jamie 1129	(1959)
Son of a Gun	-Jamie 1139	(1959)
Pledging My Love/Go On Home	-Jamie 1153	(1960)
It Hurts Me Too/Guess It's Love	-Trey 3016	(1961)
Tennessee Walk/Give The Boy Love	-Project 5004	(196?)
She Tought Me	-Warner 5473	(1964-65)
The Fool/Lonesome for a Letter	(R)-Ramco 1872	(1966)
Shades	-Ramco 1976	(1966)
Footprints In Her Yard	-LHI 9	(1967)
Hickory Hollars Tramp	-LHI 1203	(1968)
Farm Labor Camp #2	-LHI 1213	(1968)
The Fool/Lonesome For A Letter	(R)-ABC	(1974)
The Fool/Lonesome For A Letter	(R)-Goldies 2707	(197?)

Albums

The Fool	-ACE CH-83	(1986)

Buzz Clifford-

Singles

Hello Mr. Moonlight/Blue Lagoon	-Columbia 41774	(1960)
Baby Sitter Boogie/Driftwood (Original Title)	-Columbia 41876	(1960)
Baby Sittin' Boogie/Driftwood	(R)-Columbia 41876	(1960)
Baby Sittin' Boogie/Driftwood	(R)-Columbia13-33217	(1961)
Three Little Fishes/Simply Because	-Columbia 41979	(1961)
I'll Never Forget/The Awakening	-Columbia 42019	(1961)
Moving Day/Loneliness	-Columbia 42177	(1961)
Baby Sittin' Boogie/Driftwood	(R)-Columbia 41876	(1961)
I'll Never Forget/The Awakening	-Columbia 42019	(1961)
I'll Never Forget	(2)-Jason 45021	(1961)
Forever/Magic Circle	-Columbia 42290	(1962)
More Dead Than Alive/No One Loves Me Like You	-Roulette 4451	(1962)
My Girl/Pretend	-Roulette 4500	(1963)

-Buzz Clifford Cont'd-

-RCA	(1966)
-Capitol	(1967)
-Dot	(1969-70)

Albums

Baby Sittin' Boogie	-Columbia 1616	(1961)
Baby Sittin' With Buzz	(R)-Columbia 8416	(1961)
See Your Way Clear	-Dot 25965	(1969)
	-Eric	(1983)

Jackie Lee Cochran-

Singles

Ruby Pearl/Mama Don't You Think I Know	-Decca 30206	(1957)
Buy a Car	-ABC/P 9930	(1958)
Georgia Lee Brown/I Want You	-Jaguar 3031	(195?)
Pity Me/Endless Love	-Spry 120	(195?)
Hip Shakin' Mama	-Sims 107	(195?)
Buy a Car/I Want You	(R)-Viv 102	(195?)
Buy a Car/I Want You	(R)-Viv 988	(195?)

Albums

Swamp Fox	-Rollin' Rock 005	(1976)
Rockabilly Legend	-Rollin' Rock 010	(1976)

Commander Cody-

Singles

Midnight Man	-Arista 4125	(1978)
Flying Dreams	-Arista 4183	(1978)

Commander Cody and His Lost Planet Airmen-

Singles

Hot Rod Lincoln	-Paramount 146	(1972)
Beat Me Daddy Eight to the Bar	-Paramount 169	(1972)
Mama Hated Diesels/Truck Stop Rock	-Paramount 178	(1973)
Watch My 38	-Paramount 193	(1973)
Smoke Smoke Smoke(That Cigarette)	-Paramount 216	(1973)
Oh Mama Mama/Riot in Cell Block Number Nine	-Paramount 278	(1974)
Hot Rod Lincoln/Beat Me Daddy Eight to the Bar	(Rx)-ABC 2741	(1974)
Hot Rod Lincoln/Beat Me Daddy Eight to the Bar	(Rx)-MCA 2741	(1974)
Don't Let Go	-Warner Bros 8073	(1975)
Roll Your Own	-Warner Bros 8164	(1975)

Albums

Lost in the Ozone	-Paramount 6017	(1972)
Hot Licks, Cold Steel and Trucker's Favorites	-Paramount 6031	(1972)

-Commander Cody and His Lost Planet Airmen Cont'd-

Hot Licks, Cold Steel and Trucker's Favorites		(R)-MCA 660	(1972)
Country Casanova		-Paramount 6054	(1973)
Country Casanova		(R)-MCA	(1973)
Live From Deep in the Heart of Texas		-Paramount 1017	(1974)
Live From Deep in the Heart of Texas		(R)-MCA 659	(1974)
Commander Cody and His Lost Planet Airmen		-Warner Bros 2847	(1975)
Tales From the Ozone		-Warner Bros 2883	(1975)
We've Got a Live One Here (2 LP)		-Warner Bros 2939	(1976)
Midnight Man		-Arista 4125	(1977)
Flying Dreams		-Arista 4183	(1978)
Lost in the Ozone		-MCA 31185	(198?)
Sleazy Roadside Stories	(CD)	-Relix 2028	(198?)
Hot Licks, Cold Steel and Trucker's Favorites	(CD)	(R)-MCA 660	(1989)
Country Casanova	(CD)	(R)-MCA 661	(1989)
Aces High	(CD)	-Relix 2041	(1989)
Lost in Space	(CD)	-Relix 2061	(1990)
Live From Deep in the Heart of Texas	(CD)	(R)-MCA 659	(1990)
Let's Rock	(CD)	-Relix 2086	(1991)
Too Much Fun: The Best of Commander Cody	(CD)	-MCA 10092	(1992)

Creedence Clearwater Revival-

Singles

Brown Eyed Girl	-Scorpio 404	(1965)
Don't Tell Me No Lies	-Fantasy 590	(1965)
You Came Walking	-Fantasy 597	(1965)
You Got Nothin' on Me	-Fantasy 599	(1965)
Fragile Child	-Scorpio 405	(1966)
Walking on the Water	-Scorpio 406	(1966)
Porterville/Call It Pretending	-Scorpio 412	(1968)
Susie Q/Susie Q Part 2	-Fantasy 616	(1967)
I Put A Spell on You/Walk On Water	-Fantasy 617	(1967)
Proud Mary/Born on the Bayou	-Fantasy 619	(1967)
Bad Moon Rising/Lodi	-Fantasy 622	(1968)
Green River/Commotion	-Fantasy 625	(1968)
Down on the Corner/Fortunate Son	-Fantasy 634	(1969)
Travelin' Band/Who'll Stop the rain?	-Fantasy 637	(1969)
45 Revolutions Per Minute	-Fantasy 2838	(1969)
Up Around the Bend/Run Through the Jungle	-Fantasy 641	(1970)
Lookin' Out My Back Door/Long As I Can See the Light	-Fantasy 645	(1971)
Have You Ever Seen the Rain?/Hey Tonight	-Fantasy 655	(1972)
Sweet Hitch-Hiker/Door to Door	-Fantasy 665	(1973)
Someday Never Comes/Tearin' Up the Country	-Fantasy 676	(1974)
Heard It Through the Grapevine/Good Golly	-Fantasy 759	(1976)
Tombstone Shadow/Commotion	-Fantasy 908	(1981)
Medley U.S.A./Bad Moon Rising	-Fantasy 917	(1981)

-Creedence Clearwater Revival Cont'd-

Cottonfields/Lodi	-Fantasy 920	(1981)
Susie Q	(R)-America 17005	(198?)
Creedence Medley (12-inch single)	(R)-Fantasy 238	(1985)

Albums

Creedence Clearwater Revival	-Fantasy 8382	(1968)
Bayou Country	-Fantasy 8387	(1969)
Green River	-Fantasy 8393	(1969)
Willy and the Poor Boys	-Fantasy 8397	(1969)
Cosmo's Factory	-Fantasy 8402	(1970)
Pendulum	-Fantasy 8410	(1970)
Mardi Gras	-Fantasy 9404	(1972)
Creedence Gold	-Fantasy 9418	(1972)
Green River	(R)-Liberty	(197?)
Live In Europe (2 LP)	-Fantasy CCR-1	(1973)
More Creedence Gold	-Fantasy 9430	(1973)
The Golliwogs: pre Creedence	-Fantasy 9474	(1974)
Green River	(R)-Sweet Thunder	(1975)
Chronicle	-fantasy CCR-2	(1976)
Cosmo's Factory(1/2 speed)	-MFSL 037	(1979)
Royal Albert Hall Concert	-Fantasy MPF-4501	(1980)
The Concert	(CD)	-Fantasy MPF-4501	(1981)
Creedence Country	-Fantasy F-4509	(1981)
Tne Concert	(R)-Fantasy MPF-4501	(1984)
Creedence Country	(CD)	(R)-Fantasy MPF-4509	(1984)
Greatest Hits	-Warner Spec 3514	(1985)
The Movie Album	(CD)	-Fantasy MPF-4522	(1985)
Creedence Gold	(CD)	(R)-Fantasy 9418	(1986)
Chooglin'	(CD)	-Fantasy 9621	(1986)
More Creedence Gold	(CD)	(R)-Fantasy 9430	(1986)
The Golliwogs: Pre Creedence	-Fantasy 9474	(1986)
Creedence Clearwater Revival	(CD)	(R)-Fantasy ORC 4512	(1987)
Bayou Country	(Tape)	(R)-Fantasy ORC 4513	(1987)
Bayou Country	(CD)	(R)-Fantasy 8387	(1987)
Green River	(CD)	(R)-Fantasy ORC 4514	(1987)
Willy and the Poor Boys	(CD)	(R)-Fantasy ORC 4515	(1987)
Cosmo's Factory	(CD)	(R)-Fantasy ORC 4516	(1987)
Chronicle	(CD)	-fantasy CCR-2	(1987)
Chronicle Vol. 2	(CD)	-fantasy CCR-3	(1987)
Pendulum	(CD)	(R)-Fantisy ORC 4517	(1987)
Mardi Gras	(CD)	(R)-Fantasy ORC-4518	(1987)
live In Europe	(2 CD)	(R)-Fantasy CCR-1	(1987)
Chronicle, Vol. 1	(CD)	(R)-Fantasy CCR-2 2	(1987)
Chronicle, Vol. 2	(CD)	(R)-Fantasy CCR-3 2	(1987)
Live in Europe	(CD)	-Fantasy 4526	(1987)
1968/69	(CD)	-Fantasy CCR-68	(1989)
1969	(CD)	-Fantasy CCR-69	(1989)
1970	(CD)	-Fantasy CCR-70	(1989)

Golliwogs(John Fogerty's First Band)-

Singles

Don't Tell Me No lies/Little Girl, Does Your Mama Know?	-Fantasy 590	(1964)
You Came Walking/Where Have You Been?	-Fantasy 597	(1965)
You Got Nothin' on Me/You Can't Be True	-Fantasy 599	(1965)
Brown Eyed Girl/You Better Be Careful	-Scorpio 404	(1965)
Fight Fire/Fragile Girl	-Scorpio 405	(1966)
Walking on the Water/You Better Get It	-Scorpio 408	(1967)
Porterville/Call It Pretending	-Scorpio 412	(1968)

Albums

Pre-Creedence: The Golliwogs	-Fantasy 9474	(1975)

The Blue Ridge Rangers (Singing and Playing by John Fogerty)-

Singles

Blue Ridge Mountain Blues/Have Thine Own Way	-Fantasy 683	(1972)
Jambalaya(On the Bayou)/Workin' on a Building	-Fantasy 689	(1972)
Hearts of Stone/Somewhere Listening	-Fantasy 700	(1973)
Back in the Hills/You Don't Owe Me a Thing	-Fantasy 710	(1973)

Albums

Blue Ridge Rangers	-Fantasy 4502	(1972)
Blue Ridge Rangers (CD)	(R)-Fantasy 4502	(1985)

John Fogerty-
(Lead singer of Creedence Clearwater Revival)

Singles

Coming Down the Road/Comin' Down the Road	-Fantasy 717	(1973)
Rockin' All Over the World/The Wall	-Asylum 45274	(1975)
Almost Saturday Night/Sea Cruise	-Asylum 45291	(1975)
You Got the Magic/Evil Thing	-Asylum 45309	(1976)
Old Man Down the Road	-Warner Bros 2234	(1984)
Rock 'n' Roll Girls	-Warner Bros 2267	(1985)
I Can't Help Myself	-Warner Bros 2337	(1985)
Vanz Kant Danz	-Warner Bros 2362	(1985)
Vanz Kant Danz (Edited version)	(R)-Warner Bros 2363	(1985)
Eye of the Zombie	-Warner Bros 2514	(1986)

Albums

John Fogerty	(R)-Asylum 5E-1046	(1975)
Centerfield (CD)	-Warner Bros 25203	(1985)
Eye of the Zombie (CD)	-Warner Bros 25449	(1985)
John Fogerty (CD)	-Asylum 5E-1046	(1986)

Tom Fogerty-

Singles

Goodbye, Media Man/Goodbye, Media Man	-Fantasy 661	(1971)

-Tom Fogerty Cont'd-

Goodly Media Man/Goodly Media Man Part II	-Fantasy 661	(1971)
Lady of Fatima/Cast the First Stone	-Fantasy 680	(1972)
Faces Places People	-Fantasy 691	(1972)
Joyful Resurrection/Heartbeat	-Fantasy 702	(1973)
Mystic Isleavalon	-Fantasy 715	(1973)
Sweet Things to Come	-Fantasy 737	(1975)
	-Fantasy	(1971-82)

Albums

Tom Fogerty	-Fantasy 9407	(1972)
Excalibur	-Fantasy 9414	(1972)
Zephyr National	-Fantasy 9448	(1974)
Myopia	-Fantasy 9469	(1974)
Deal It Out	-Fantasy 9611	(1981)

Tommy Fogerty & The Blue Velvets-

Singles

Come On Baby/Oh! My Love	-Orchestra 617	(1961)
Have You Ever Been Lonely?/Bonita	-Orchestra 1010	(1961)
Yes, You Did/Now You're Not Mine	-Orchestra	(1962)

Don Harrison Band-
(Members of Creedence: Doug Clifford, Stu Cook, Don Harrison)

Singles

Sixteen Tons	-Atlantic 3323	(1976)
Helter Skelter	-Mercury 73948	(1977)

Mac Curtis-

Singles

Sunshine Man	-Epic BN-26419	(1968)
You're the One	-Dot 16315	(1969)
When the Hurt Moves In	-GRT 26	(1970)
I'd Run a Mile	-GRT 41	(1971)
Early in the Morning	-GRT 026	(1971)
Early in the Morning	(R)-GRT 20002	(1971)
Dance Her by Me	-Le Cam 954	(197?)
Ruffabilly	-Rollin' Rock 002	(1976)
Good Rockin' Tomorrow	-Rollin' Rock 007	(1976)
Rock Me!	-Rollin' Rock 016	(1977)

Bobby Darin(and the Jaybirds-and the Ding Dongs-and the Rinky Dinks)-

Singles

Rock Island Line/Timber	-Decca 29833	(1956)
Silly Willy/Blue-eyed Mermaid	-Decca29922	(1956)
Hear Them Bells/The Greatest Builder	-Decca 30031	(1956)
Dealer in Dreams/Help Me	-Decca 30225	(1957)
Silly Willy/Dealer in Dreams	(R)-Decca 30737	(1957)
I Found a Million Dollar Baby/Talk To Me	-Atco 6092	(1957)
Don't Call My Name/Pretty Baby	-Atco 6103	(1957)
Just in Case You Change Your Mind/So Mean	-Atco 6128	(1958)
Splish Splash/Judy, Don't Be Moody	-Atco 6116	(1958)
Early in the Morning/Now We're One	-Atco 6121	(1958)
Queen of the Hop/Lost Love	-Atco 6127	(1958)
Mighty Mighty Man/You're Mine	-Atco 6128	(1958)
Plain Jane/While I'm Gone	-Atco 6133	(1959)
Dream Lover/Bullmoose	-Atco 6140	(1959)

(Further records were pop and later folk)

Albums

For Teenagers Only	-Atco SP-1001	(1960)
The Bobby Darin Story	-Atco	(1961)
The Ultimate Bobby Darin (CD)	-WSP 27606	(198?)
The Bobby Darin Story (CD)	(R)-Atco 33131	(198?)
Splish Splash--The Best of Bobby Darin, Vol. 1	-Atco 91794	(1991)

(Other albums were Folk or Pop)

Extended Play Mini Albums

EP Hear Them Bells	-Decca ED-2676	(1957)
EP Bobby Darin	-Atco 4502	(1959)
EP For Teenagers Only	-Atco 4513	(1960)

Frankie Dee(With The Carter Rays)-

Singles

After Graduation/Shake It Up, Baby	-RCA 7276	(1958)

Jimmy Dee(and the Offbeats)-

Singles

	-Inner-Glo	
Henrietta/Don't Cry No More	-TNT 148	(1957)
Henrietta/Don't Cry No More	(R)-Dot 1664	(1957)
You're Late Miss Kate	-TNT 159	(1958)
You're Late Miss Kate/Here I Come	(R)-Dot 15721	(1958)

-Jimmy Dee Cont'd-

I Feel Like Rockin'/Rock Tick Tock	-TNT 161	(1958)
	-Taper	(1959)
	-Scope	(1959)
Wanda	-Ace 627	(196?)
You Say You Beat Me to the Punch/I've Got a Secret	-Cutie 1400	(1963)
	-Hear Me	

Johnny Dee(John D. Loudermilk)-

Singles

	-Bullet	(1953)
Sittin' in the Balcony/A-Plus in Love	-Colonial 430	(1957)
Teenage Queen/It's Gotta Be You	-Colonial 433	(1957)
Somebody Sweet/They Were Right	-Dot 15699	(1957)

Lonnie Donegan(and His Skiffle Group)-

Singles

Rock Island Line/John Henry	(Imp)	-Decca 10647	(1955)
Rock Island Line/John Henry		-London 1650	(1956)
Bury My Body/Diggin' My Potatoes	(Imp)	-Decca	(1956)
On a Christmas Day/Take My Hand Precious Lord	(Imp)	-Columbia 3850	(1956)
Midnight Special/When the Sun Goes Down	(Imp)	-Pye-Nixa 2006	(1956)
Lost John/Stewball	(Imp)	-Pye-Nixa 15036	(1956)
Lost John/Stewball		-Mercury 70872	(1956)
Bring a Little Water, Sylvie/Dead or Alive	(Imp)	-Pye-Nixa 15071	(1956)
Bring a Little Water, Sylvie/Dead or Alive		-Mercury 709491	(1956)
Cumberland Gap/Wabash Cannonball		-Mercury 7109	(1956)
Don't You Rock Me Daddy-o/I'm Alabamy Bound	(Imp)	-Pye-Nixa 15080	(1957)
Cumberland Gap/Love Is Strange	(Imp)	-Pye-Nixa 15087	(1957)
I'm Just a Rolling Stone/My Dixie Darling	(Imp)	-Pye-Nixa 15108	(1957)
Ham 'N' Eggs/Jack O'Diamonds	(Imp)	-Pye-Nixa 15116	(1957)
Nobody Loves an Irishman/The Grand Cooley Dam	(Imp)	-Pye-Nixa 15129	(1958)
Betty Betty Betty/Sally Don't You Grieve	(Imp)	-Pye-Nixa 15148	(1958)
Lonesome Traveller/Times Are Getting Hard	(Imp)	-Pye-Nixa 15158	(1958)
Lonnie's Skiffle, Part 1/Lonnie's Skiffle, Part 2	(Imp)	-Pye-Nixa 15165	(1958)
Rock of My Soul/Tom Dooley	(Imp)	-Pye-Nixa 15172	(1958)
Aunt Rhody/ Does Your Chewing Gum Loose Its Flavor	(Imp)	-Pye-Nixa 15181	(1959)
Darling Cory/The Battle of New Orleans	(Imp)	-Pye-Nixa 15206	(1959)
Does Your Chewing Gum Lose Its Flavor/Aunt Rhody		(R)-Dot 15911	(1961)
Fort Worth Jail/Whoa Buck	(Imp)	-Pye-Nixa 15198	(1959)
Fort Worth Jail/Whoa Buck		-Dot 15953	(1959)
Keven Barry/My Lagan Love	(Imp)	-Pye-Nixa 15219	(1959)
Sal's Got a Sugar Lip/Chesapeake Bay	(Imp)	-Pye-Nixa 15223	(1959)
San Miguel/Talking Guitar Blues	(Imp)	-Pye-Nixa 15237	(1959)

-Lonnie Donegan Cont'd-

My Old Man's a Dustman/The Golden Vanity	(Imp)	-Pye-Nixa 15256	(1960)
My Old Man's a Dustman/The Golden Vanity		-Atlantic 2058	(1960)
Take This Hammer/Nobody Understands Me		-Atlantic 2063	(1960)
I Wanna Go Home/Jimmie Brown, the News Boy	(Imp)	-Pye-Nixa 15267	(1960)
In All My Wildest Dreams/Lorelei	(Imp)	-Pye-Nixa 15275	(1960)
Junco Partner/Lorelei		-Atlantic 2081	(1960)
Black Cat/Lively	(Imp)	-Pye-Nixa 15312	(1960)
Beyond The Sunset/Virgin Mary	(Imp)	-Pye-Nixa 15315	(1960)
Have a Drink on Me/Beyond the Sunset		-Atlantic 2108	(1960)
The Willow/Leave My Woman Alone	(Imp)	-Pye-Nixa 15330	(1960)
Rock Island Line/John Henry		(R)-Felsted 8630	(1961)
Wreck of the John B./Sorry, But I'm Gonna Pass		-Atlantic 2123	(1961)
Have a Drink on Me/Seven Daffodils	(Imp)	-Pye-Nixa 15354	(1961)
Light from the Lighthouse/Whoa Back, Buck		-Dot 16263	(1961)
Lumbered/Michael Row the Boat Ashore (Imp)		-Pye-Nixa 15371	(1961)
The Commancheros/Ramblin' Round	(Imp)	-Pye-Nixa 15410	(1962)
Over the Rainbow/The Party's Over	(Imp)	-Pye-Nixa 15424	(1962)
I'll Never Fall in Love Again/Keep on the Sunnyside	(Imp)	-Pye-Nixa 15446	(1962)
Marketsong/Titbits	(Imp)	-Pye-Nixa 15493	(1962)
Losing By a Hair/Trumpet Sounds	(Imp)	-Pye-Nixa 15514	(1962)
Ramblin' Round/Pick a Bale O' Cotton		-Apt 25067	(1962)
Lemon Tree/Very Good Year		-Hickory 1247	(1964)
Fisherman"s Luck/There's a Big Wheel		-Hickory 1267	(1965)
Bad News/Interstate 40		-Hickory 1274	(1965)
		-ABC	(1976)
		-MCA	(1976)

(As you can see, most releases were available on direct import, as well)

Albums

New Orleans		-Decca LF1198	(1955)
Tops with Lonnie	(Imp)	-Pye-Nixa 18034	(1956)
Lonnie Donegan	(Imp)	-Pye-Nixa 19012	(1956)
Traditional Jazz at the Royal Festival Hall		-Decca LP4088	(1957)
An Englishman Sings American Folk Songs		-Mercury 20299	(1957)
Lonnie	(Imp)	-Pye-Nixa 84000	(1957)
Lonnie Donegan		(R)-Dot DLP-3159	(1960)
Lonnie Donegan		(R)-Dot DLP-3394	(1961)
Skiffle Folk Music		-Atlantic 8038	(1960)
Sing Hallelujah		-ABC/Paramont 433	(1963)
The Golden Age of Donegan, Vol. 1		-Golden Guana 0135	(197?)
The Golden Age of Denegan, Vol. 2		-Golden Guana 0170	(197?)
Donegan File Series	(Imp)	-Pye FILD 011	(197?)

Ral Donner(Ralph Donner)-

Singles

Tell Me Why/That's All Right with Me	-Scottie 1310	(1959)

-Ral Donner Cont'd-

Girl of My Best Friend/It's Been a Long Time	-Gone 5102	(1960)
You Don't Know What You've Got/ So Close to Heaven	-Gone 5108	(1961)
Please Don't Go/I Didn't Figure on Him	-Gone 5114	(1961)
School of Heartbreakers/Because We're Young	-Gone 5119	(1961)
She's Everything/Because We're Young	(R)-Gone 5121	(1961)
She's Everything/Will You Love Me in Heaven	(R)-Gone 5121	(1961)
(Flip side is actually a girl group)		
To Love Someone/Will You Love Me in Heaven	-Gone 5125	(1961)
Loveless Life/Bells of Love	-Gone 5129	(1962)
To Love/Sweetheart	-Gone 5133	(1962)
You Don't Know What You've Got/She's Everything	-End GG-19	(1963)
Loneliness of a Star/And Then	-Tau 105	(1963)
Christmas Day/Second Miracle	-Reprise 20135	(1962)
I Got Burned/A Tear in My Eye	-Reprise 20141	(1962)
I Wish This Night Would Never End/Don't Put Your		
Heart in His Hand	-Reprise 20176	(1963)
Run Little Linda/Beyond the Heartbreak	-Reprise 20192	(1963)
Poison Ivy League/You Finally Said Somethg Good	-Fontana 1502	(1964)
Poison Ivy League/Tear in My Eye	-Fontana 1502	(1964)
Good Lovin'/Other Side of Me	-Fontana 1515	(1965)
Good Lovin'/Other Side of Me	(R)-Smash 34774	(1965)
Love Isn't Like That/It Will Only Make You Love Me More	-Red Bird10-051	(1966)
Love Isn't Like That/It Will Only Make You Love Me More	(R)-Red Bird10-057	(1968)
If I Promise/Just a Little Sunshine in the Rain	-Rising Sun 714	(1968)
	-Roulette	(1971)
(All of a Sudden)My Heart Sings/Lovin' Place	-M.J. 222	(1972)
Wait a Minute/Don't Let It Slip Away	-Sunlight 1006	(1972)
	-ABC	(1973)
The Wedding Song/Godfather Per Me	-Chicago Fire 7402	(1974)
(If I Had My)Life to Live Over/Lost	-Mid-Eagle 101	(1974)
So Much Love/Lovin'	-Mid-Eagle 275	(1968-76)
The Day the Beat Stopped/Rock on Me	-Thunder 7801	(1978)
Christmas Day	-Starfire 103	(1978)
Rip It Up/Don't Leave Me Now	-Starfire 114	(1979)
Rip It Up/Don't Leave Me Now (Picture Disc)	-Starfire 114	(1979)

Albums

Takin' Care of Business	-Gone LP5012	(1961)
Elvis Scrapbook	-Gone LP5033	(1962)
Ral Donner,Ray Smith and Bobby Dale	-Crown CLP-5335	(1963)
	-Gypsy	(1979)
	-Audio Research	(1980)
	-Starfire	(1982)
	-Murray Hill	(1988)

Joe Dowell-

Singles		
Wooden Heart/Little Bo Peep	-Smash 1708	(1961)
The Bridge Of Love/Just Love Me	-Smash 1717	(1961)
(I Wonder) Who's Spending Christmas With You/		
A Kiss For Christmas	-Smash 1728	(1961)
Sound Of Sadness/Thorn on the Rose	-Smash 1730	(1962)
Little Red Rented Rowboat/One I Left For You	-Smash 1759	(1962)
Poor Little Cupid/No Secrets	-Smash 1786	(1962)
Our School Days/Bringa-Branga-Brought	-Smash 1799	(1963)
Bobby Blue Loves Linda Lou/My DarlingWears White Today	-Smash 1816	(1963)
Albums		
Wooden Heart	-Smash 27000	(1961)
German American Hits	-Smash 27011	(1962)

Jimmy Edwards(Jimmie Edwards)-

Singles		
Love Bug Crawl/Honey Lovin'	-Mercury 71209	(1957)
	-Mercury	(1957-58)
Just As Long As You Love	-RCA 6631	(1955)
Money	-RCA 6823	(1956)
Getten' Used To Being...	-RCA 6918	(1957)
Live and Let Live	-RCA 7717	(1959)
Draggin' Main Street	-Fabor 118	(1963)

Narvel Felts-

Singles		
Kiss-A-Me Baby/Foolish Thoughts	-Mercury 71140	(1957)
Cry Baby Cry/Lonesome Feeling	-Mercury 71190	(1957)
Dream World/Rocket Ride	-Mercury 71249	(1957)
Dream World/Rocket Ride Stroll	(R)-Mercury 71275	(1957)
Cutie Baby/Three Thousand Miles	-Pink 701	(1959)
Honey Love/Genavee	-Pink 702	(1960)
All That Heaven Sent/Four Seasons of Life	-Era 203	(196?)
Mountain of Love/End of My World	-Groove 0029	(1963)
Dee-Dee	-Hi 2137	(1967)
Don't Let Me Cross Over	-Hi 2126	(1967)
This Time	-Hi 2305	(1969)
A Little Bit of Soap/You're Out of My Reach	-Hi Country 8002	(1972)
Butterfly	-Hi Country 8003	(1972)
	-Hi	(1967-76)
Hey There Johnny	-Reprise 0882	(1971)

-Narvel Felts Cont'd-

Drift Away	-Cinnamon 763	(1972)
All In The Name of Love	-Cinnamon 771	(1973)
Fraulein/When Your Good Love	-Cinnamon 779	(1974)
Someone To Give My Love To/Untl the End of Time	-Cinnamon 793	(1974)
I Want To Stay	-Cinnamon 798	(1974)
Raindrops	-Cinnamon 809	(1975)
Reconsider Me	-ABC/Dot 17549	(1975)
Funny How the Time Slips Away/No One Knows	-ABC/Dot 17569	(1975)
Somebody Hold Me(Until She Passes By)	-ABC/Dot 17598	(1975)
Reconsider Me/Funny How the Time Slips Away	(R)-ABC/Dot 2768	(1975)
Lonely Teardrops/I Remember You	-ABC/Dot 17620	(1976)
My Prayer	-ABC/Dot 17634	(1976)
My Good Thing's Gone	-ABC/Dot 17664	(1976)
The Feelings Right	-ABC/Dot 17680	(1976)
To Love Somebody	-ABC/Dot 17715	(1977)
Runaway	-ABC/Dot 12338	(1977)
One For the Roses	-ABC/Dot 12414	(1978)
Please	-ABC/Dot 17731	(1978)
	-Collage	(1979)
Drift Away/When Your Good Love Was Mine	(R)-MCA 2748	(1979)
Reconsider Me/Lonely Teardrops	(R)-MCA 2795	(1979)
Moment By Moment	-MCA 41011	(1979)
Tower of Strength	-MCA 41055	(1970)
	-Kari	(1980)
	-GMC	(1981)
Roll Over Beethoven	-Lobo 11	(1982)
I'd Love You To Want Me	-Lobo 111	(1982)
	-Compleat	(1982-83)
	-Evergreen	(1982-87)
Welcome Home Mr. Blues	-Celebrity Circ6903	(198?)

Albums

Drift Away	-Cinnamon 5000	(1973)
Narvel Felts 'Live'	-Power Pak PO-237	(1974)
Narvel Felts	-ABC/Dot 2025	(1975)
Greatest Hits, Vol. 1	-ABC/Dot 2036	(1976)
Greatest Hits, Vol. 1	(R)-MCA 636	(1976)
Narvel the Marvel	-ABC/Dot 2033	(1976)
Narvel the Marvel	(R)-MCA 633	(1976)
Doin' What I Feel	-ABC/Dot 2065	(1976)
This Time	-Hi 32098	(1976)
Narvel	-ABC/Dot 2095	(1977)
Narvel	(R)-MCA 635	(1977)
Touch of Felts	-ABC/Dot 2070	(1977)
Touch of Felts	(R)-MCA 634	(1977)
Inside Love	-ABC AY-1080	(1978)
Inside Love	(R)-MCA 699	(1978)
One Run for the Roses	-ABC AY-1115	(1978)

-Narvel Felts Cont'd-

One Run for the Roses	(R)-MCA 799	(1978)
The Very Best of Narvel Felts	-Gusto GTV9-118	(198?)
The Very Best of Narvel Felts (CD)	(R)-DeLuxe 7833	(198?)

The Fendermen-
   (Group consisted of Jim Sundquist, 11/26/37, and Phil Humphrey, 11/26/37)

Singles

	-Cuca	(1960)
Mule Skinner Blues/Torture	(R)-Soma 1137	(1960)
Don't You Just Know It/Beach Party	-Soma 1142	(1960)
Can't You Wait?/Heart Breakin' Special	-Soma 1155	(1961)
Rain Drop/"Fas-nacht-kuechel"	-Dab 102	(1962)
	-Era	(1972)
Mule Skinner Blues	(R)-Eric 121	(198?)
Mule Skinner Blues	(R)-Collectables	(198?)

Albums

Mule Skinner Blues	-Soma MG-1240	(1960)

Mickey Gilly-

Singles

Tell Me Why/Ooh Wee Baby	-Minor 106	(1957)
Call Me Shorty	-Dot 15706	(1958)
Grapevine/That's How It's Got To Be	-Rex 1007	(1958)
Drive-In Movie/Give Me a Chance	-Khoury 712	(1959)
No Greater Love/Is It Wrong?	-Potomac 901	(1960)
Everything Turned To Love/Your Selfish Pride	-Lynn 503	(1960)
Turn Around/My Baby's Been Cheating Again	-Lynn 508	(1960)
My Baby's Been Cheating Again/Lonely Lonely Night	-Lynn 508	(1960)
Slippin' and Slidin'/(It's The)End of the Line	-Lynn 512	(1961)
My Babe	-Lynn 515	(1961)
Valley of Tears/I Need Your Love	-Sabra 518	(1961)
Now That I Have You	-Supreme 101	(1962)
Everything Turned To Love	(R)-Supreme 102	(1962)
You First Time/Drive-In Movie	(R)-Princess 4004	(1962)
Wild Side of Life/Caught in the Middle	-Princess 4006	(1962)
I'll Keep On Dreaming/I'll Keep Searching	-Princess 4011	(1962)
World Of My Own/I Still Care	-Princess 4015	(1962)
I'm To Blame/I Ain't No Bo Diddley	-San 1513	(1963)
What Have I Done/Three's a Crowd	-Daryl 101	(1963)
I Ain't Going Home/No Greater Love	(R)-Goldband	(1964)
Whole Lot Of Twistin' Going On	-Eric 7021	(1964)
The Surf Siders Chug-A-Lug Charlie/I Want To Love You	-Astro 101	(1964)
Lonely Wine/Down the Line	-Astro 102	(1964)

-Mickey Gilly Cont'd-

Night After Night/Susie Q	-Astro 104	(1964)
Lotta Lovin'/I Miss You So	-Astro 106	(1964)
If I Didn't Have a Dime/A Certain Smile	-Astro 110	(1965)
If I Didn't Have a Dime/Little Egypt	-Astro 110	(1965)
When Two Worlds Collide/Let's Hurt Together	-Tcg Hall 126	(1965)
Say No to You/Make Me Believe	-Act-1 101	(1966)
Say No to You/Make Me Believe	(R)-Paula 256	(1966)
World Of My Own/I'm Gonna Put My Love in the Want Ads	(R)-Paula 269	(1967)
Blame It on the Moon/Sounds Like Trouble	-Paula 280	(1967)
That Heart Belongs to Me/A New Way To Live	-Paula 301	(1968)
Now I Can Love Again/Without You	-Paula 1200	(1968)
She's Still Got a Hold On You/There's No One Like You	-Paula 1208	(1969)
Watching The Way/It's Just a Matter of Making Up My Mind	-Paula 1215	(1969)
I'm Nobody Today/She's Not Yours Anymore	-GRT 27	(1970)
Time To Tell Another Lie/Because I Love You	-GRT 45	(1971)
Everything Is Yours That Once Was Mine/		
Don't Throw a Good Love Away	-Astro 5002	(1971)
A Toast to Mary Ann/You Touched My Life	-Astro 5003	(1971)
Room Full of Roses/She Called Me Baby	-Astro 10003	(1973)
A Toast to Mary Ann/You Touched My Life	(R)-Resco 617	(1974)
Quiting Time/She Gives Me Love	-Resco 622	(1974)
Room Full of Roses/She Called Me Baby	(2) -Astro 10003	(1974)
Night After Night/I'm to Blame	-Paula 402	(1974)
Room Full of Roses/She Called Me Baby	(R)-Playboy 5056	(1974)
I Overlooked An Orchid/Swinging Doors	-Playboy 6004	(1974)
City Lights/Fraulein	-Playboy 6015	(1974)
I'm Movin' On/The Window Up Above	-Playboy 6031	(1975)
Bouquet of Roses	-Playboy 6041	(1975)
Roll Like a Wheel/Let's Sing a Song	-Playboy 6045	(1975)
She Gives Me Love	-Resco 662	(1975)
I'll Sail My Ship Alone/Overnight Sensation	-Playboy 6055	(1975)
Don't The Girls All Get Prettier At Closng Time	-Playboy 6063	(1976)
Bring It On Home To Me/How's My X Treating You	-Playboy 6075	(1976)
Lawdy Miss Clawdy	-Playboy 6089	(1976)
Lonely Christmas Call/Pretty Paper	-Playboy 6095	(1977)
She's Pulling Me Back Again	-Playboy 6100	(1977)
Honky Tonk Memories/Five Foot Two Eyes of Blue	-Playboy 5807	(1977)
Chains of Love/No. 1 Rock 'N' Roll Man	-Playboy 5818	(1977)
Power of Positive Drinkin'	-Playboy 5826	(1977)
Here Comes the Hurt Again	-Epic 15-2363	(1978)
Here Comes the Hurt Again	(R)-Epic 8-50580	(1978)
Bouquet of Roses/The Window Up Above	(R)-Epic 15-2374	(1978)
The Song We Made Love To/Memphis Memories	-Epic 8-50631	(1978)
Just Long Enough To Say Goodbye/Tonight I'll Help		
You Say Goodbye Again	-Epic 8-50672	(1978)
Don't the Girls All Get Prettier At Closng Time	-Epic 15-2375	(1978)

-Mickey Gilly Cont'd-

Room Full of Ross/She's Pulling Me Back Again	(R)-Epic 15-2376	(1978)
My Silver Lining	-Epic 8-50740	(1979)
A Little Gettin' Used To	-Epic 9-50801	(1979)
True Love Ways/The More I Turn the Bottle Up	-Epic 9-50876	(1980)
That's All That Matters	-Epic 9-50940	(1980)
That's All That Matters/True Love Ways	(R)-Epic 15-02161	(1980)
A Headache Tomorrow(Or a Heartache Tonight)/		
Million Dollar Memories	-Epic 9-50973	(1980)
Mamas Don't Let Your Babies Grow Up To Be Cowboys/		
Bayou City Beats Cotton Eyed Joe	-Epic 9-51003	(1980)
Stand By Me	(R)-Elektra 45115	(1980)
Orange Blossom Special	-Asylum 46639	(1980)
Stand By Me	(R)-Asylum 46640	(1980)
Orange Blossom Special	(R)-Asylum 47033	(1981)
Honky Tonk Memories	-Full Moon 02102	(1981)
Christmas Medley	-Epic AE7-1356	(1981)
You Don't Know Me	(R)-Epic 14-02172	(1981)
Lonely Nights	(R)-Epic 14-02578	(1981)
Tears of the Lonely	-Epic 14-02774	(1982)
Put Your Dreams Away	-Epic 14-03055	(1982)
Talk to Me	-Epic 34-03326	(1982)
	-Airborne	(1988)

Albums

Lonely Wine	-Astro 1001	(1964)
Mickey at Gilley's	-Astro 1005	(1965)
Welcom to Gilley's	-Astro 1007	(1966)
Down the Line	-Paula 2195	(1967)
	(R)-Astro	(1973-78)
Mickey Gilley At His Best	-Paula 2224	(1974)
Room Full of Roses	-Playboy 401	(1974)
Room Full of Roses	(R)-Playboy 128	(1974)
City Lights	-Playboy 403	(1974)
Mickey's Movin' On	-Playboy 405	(1975)
Overnight Sensation	-Playboy 408	(1975)
Mickey Gilly Greatest Hits, Vol.1	-Playboy 409	(1976)
Gilley's Smokin'	-Playboy 415	(1976)
First Class	-Playboy 418	(1976)
Room Full of Roses	(R)-Epic 34736	(1977)
City Lights	(R)-Playboy 34737	(1977)
Mickey Gilly Greatest Hits, Vol.1	(R)-Playboy 34743	(1977)
Gilley's Smokin'	(R)-Playboy 34749	(1977)
First Class	-Playboy 34776	(1977)
Mickey Gilly Greatest Hits, Vol.2	-Playboy 34881	(1977)
Flyin' High	-Playboy 35099	(1978)
Wild Side of Life	(R)-Pickwick JS-6180	(1976)
Mickey Gilley	-Paula 2234	(1978)
Mickey Gilley	(R)-Epic 36201	(1979)

-Mickey Gilly Cont'd-

Encore	-Epic 36851	(1979)
The Songs We Made Love To	-Epic 35714	(1979)
Wild Side of Life	(R)-51 West Q-16012	(1979)
Urban Cowboy Soundtrack	-Asylum 90002	(1979)
Mickey Gilley	-Epic 36201	(1980)
That's All That Matters	-Epic 36492	(1980)
Encore	-Epic 36851	(1980)
Urban Cowboy II: More Music From the Original Soundtrck	-Epic 36921	(1980)
You Don't Know me	-Epic 37416	(1981)
Tough Enough Soundtrack	-Liberty 51141	(1981)
Norwegian Wood	-Album Globe 8127	(1981)
Texas Dynamite	-Plantation 48	(1981)
Mickey Gilley at His Best, Vol. 1	-Paula 37500	(1981)
Mickey Gilley at His Best, Vol. 2	-Paula 37501	(1981)
Christmas at Gilley's	-Epic 37595	(1981)
Put Your Dreams Away	-Epic 38082	(1982)
Biggest Hits - Mickey Gilly	-Epic 38320	(1982)
Fool for Your Love	-Epic 38583	(1982)
Mickey Gilley	-Country Fidelty204	(1982)
All My Best	-CSP 16198	(1982)
You've Really Got a Hold On Me	-Epic 39000	(1983)
Mickey Gilley and Charly McClain-It Takes Believers	-Epic 39292	(1984)
Too Good To Stop Now	(CD)	-Epic 39324	(1984)
Ten Years of Hits	(2 CD)	-Epic 39867	(1984)
Live at Gilley's	(CD)	-Epic 39900	(1985)
Mickey Gilley['s Greatest Hits	(Tape)	-CSP 17736	(198?)
Mickey at Gilley's	(CD)	(R)-Gilley 1005	(198?)
Welcome to Gilley's	(CD)	(R)-Gilley 1007	(198?)
Why Me Lord?	(CD)	-Gilley 1078	(198?)
Christmas at Gilley's	(CD)	(R)-Columbia 37595	(198?)
Biggest Hits - Mickey Gilly	(CD)	(R)-Columbia 38320	(198?)
Mickey Gilley's Greatest Hits, Vol. 1	(CD)	-Epic 34743	(1987)
Mickey Gilley's Greatest Hits, Vol. 2	(CD)	(R)-Playboy 34881	(1987)
With Love From Pasadena, Texas	(CD)	-Intermedia 5024	(199?)
Make It Like The First Time	(CD)	-Branson 9306	(1993)

Charlie Gracie-

Singles

	-Cadillac	(1954)
Butterfly/Fabulous	-Abko 4012	(1957)
Butterfly/Ninety-Nine Ways	(R)-Cameo 105	(1957)
Fabulous/Just Lookin'	-Cameo 107	(1957)
I Love You So Much It Hurts/Wanderin' Eyes	-Cameo 111	(1957)
Cool Baby/You've Got a Heart Like a Rock	-Cameo 118	(1958)
Crazy Girl/Dressin' Up	-Cameo 127	(1958)

-Charlie Gracie Cont'd-

Love Bird/Trying	-Cameo 141	(1959)
Doodlebug/Hurry Up Buttercup	-Coral 62073	(1959)
Angel of Love/I'm a Fool, That's Why	-Coral 62115	(1959)
Oh-Well-A/Because I Love You So	-Coral 62141	(1959)
The Race/I Look For You	-Roulette 4255	(1959)
Sorry for You/Scenery	-Roulette 4312	(1961)
W-Wow/Makin' Whoopie	-Felsted 8629	(1961)
Night and Day U.S.A./Pretty Baby	-President 825	(1962)
My Baby Loves Me/Head Home, Honey	-20th Century 5033	(1965)
He'll Never Love You Like I Do/Keep My Love		
Next to Your Heart	-Diamond 178	(1965)
	-Abkco	(1975)

Roy Hall(and His Jumping Cats-Roy Hall's Alley Cats)-

Singles

Whole Lotta Shakin'/All By Myself	-Decca 29697	(1955)
See You Later, Alligator/Don't Stop Now	-Decca 29786	(1955)
You Ruined My Blue Suede Shoes/Luscious	-Decca 29880	(1956)
Three Alley Cats/Diggin' the Boogie	-Decca 30060	(1956)
Goin' Down the Road Feelin' Bad	-Fortune	(195?)
Three Alley Cats	-Hi-Q 5045	(196?)
Go Go Little Queenie	-Hi-Q 5050	(196?)
One Monkey Can't Stop the Show	-Pierce	(196?)

George Hamilton IV-

Singles

A Rose and a Baby Ruth /If You Don't Know	-Colonial 420	(1956)
A Rose and a Baby Ruth /If You Don't Know	(R)-ABC/P 9765	(1957)
Only One Love/If I Possessed a Printing Press	-ABC/P 9782	(1957)
High School Dance/Everybody's Body	-ABC/P 9838	(1958)
Why Don't They Understand/Even Tho	-ABC/P 9862	(1958)
Now And For Always/One Heart	-ABC/P 9898	(1959)
I Know Where I'm Going'/Who's Takin' You To The Prom?	-ABC/P 9924	(1959)
When Will I Know?/Your Cheatin' Heart	-ABC/P 9946	(1959)
The Two of Us/Lucy, Lucy	-ABC/P 9966	(1960)
Steady Game/Can You Blame Us?	-ABC/P10009	(1960)
Gee, I Know/Your Sweetheart	-ABC/P10028	(1960)
Little Tom/One Little Acre	-ABC/P10059	(1961)
A Rose and a Baby Ruth /If You Don't Know Him	(R)-Roulette 143	
Even Tho'/Why Don't They Understand?	(R)-Roulette 144	
A Rose and a Baby Ruth/Why Don't They Understand	(R)-Goldies 1459	

(Later songs were country)

-George Hamilton IV Cont'd-
Albums

George Hamilton IV on Campus	-ABC/P 220	(1957)
Sing Me a Sad Song	-ABC/P 251	(1958)
Big 15	-ABC/P 461	(1963)
By George	-ABC/P 535	(1966)
16 Greatest Hits	-ABC/P 750	(1972)
The ABC Collection	-ABC/P30032	(1976)

Extended Play Mini Albums

EP George Hamilton IV on Campus	-ABC/P A220	(1957)

Dale Hawkins-

Singles

See You Soon Baboon/Four Letter Word	-Checker 843	(1956)
Susie-Q/Don't Treat Me This Way	-Checker 863	(1957)
Baby Baby/Mrs. Merguitory's Daughter	-Checker 876	(1957)
Tornado/Little Pig	-Checker 892	(1958)
La-Do-Da-Da/Crossties	-Checker 900	(1958)
A House, a Car And a Wedding Ring/My Babe	-Checker 906	(1958)
Take My Heart/Someday, One Day	-Checker 913	(1959)
Class Cutter(Yeah Yeah)/Lonely Nights	-Checker 916	(1959)
Ain't That Lovin' You Baby/My Dream	-Checker 923	(1959)
Our Turn/Lifeguard Man	-Checker 929	(1959)
Back to School Blues/Liza Jane	-Checker 934	(1959)
Hot Dog/Don't Break Your Promise to Me	-Checker 940	(1960)
Poor Little Rhode Island/Every Little Girl	-Checker 949	(1960)
Linda/Who	-Checker 962	(1960)
I Want to Love You/Grandma's House	-Checker 970	(1961)
Peaches/Gotta Dance	-Atlantic 1002	(1961)
Stay at Home Lulu/I Can't Erase You (Out of My Heart)	-Atlantic 2126	(1962)
With a Feeling/Women-That's What's Happening	-Atlantic 2150	(1962)
The Same Old Way/Money Honey	-Tilt 781	(1962)
Wish I Hadn't Called Home/Forbidden Love	-Tilt 783	(1962)
Gotta Dance	-Zonk 1002	(1962)
Baby We Had It/Johnny Be Good	-Lincoln 002	(1963)
The La La Song/I'll Fly High	-ABC/P 10668	(1965)
Little Rain Cloud/Back Street	-Bell 807	(1969)
Joe	-Bell 827	(1969)
What I Keep Saying Is a Lie	-Warner Bros 8104	(1975)
La De Da Da/Susie Q	(R)-Chess 9034	(1976)

Albums

Dale Hawkins	-Chess 703	(1957)
Suzie-Q	-Chess 1429	(1958)
Let's All Twist at the Miami Peppermint Lounge	-Roulette SR-25175	(1962)
L.A., Memphis and Tyler Texas	-Bell 6036	(1969)

Jimmie Heap-

Singles

Release Me	-Capitol ??	
Butternut	-Capitol F3333	(1956)
Gismo	-Dart 119	(1960)

Bobby Helms-

Singles

Tennessee Rock and Roll/I Don't Owe You Anything	-Decca 29947	(1956)
Fraulein/Heartsick Feeling	-Decca 30194	(1956)
My Special Angel/Standing at the End of My World	-Decca 30423	(1957)
Jingle Bell Rock/Captain Santa Claus	-Decca 30513	(1957)
Just a Little Lonesome/Love My Lady	-Decca 30557	(1957)
Jacqueline/Living in the Shadow of the Past	-Decca 30619	(1958)
Borrowed Dreams/Schoolboy Crush	-Decca 30682	(1958)
The Fool and the Angel/Hundred Hearts	-Decca 30749	(1958)
New River Train/Miss Memory	-Decca 30831	(1959)
I Guess I'll Miss the Prom/Soon It Can Be Told	-Decca 30886	(1959)
No Other Baby/You're No Longer Mine	-Decca 30928	(1959)
My Lucky Day/Hurry Baby	-Decca 30976	(1960)
Someone Was Already There/To My Sorrow	-Decca 31041	(1960)
Let Me Be the One/I Want To Be with You	-Decca 31103	(1960)
Guess We Thought the World Would End/		
The Lonely River Rhine	-Decca 31148	(1960)
Sad-Eyed Baby/You're the One	-Decca 31230	(1961)
My Greatest Weakness/How Can You Divide A Little Child?	-Decca 31287	(1961)
One Deep Love/Once in a Lifetime	-Decca 31356	(1961)
Yesterday's Champagne/Then Came You	-Decca 31403	(1962)
It's a Girl	-Columbia 43031	(1964)
The Bell That Couldn't Jingle/Jingle Bell Rock	-Kapp 85	(1965)
Those Snowy Glowy Blowy Days of Winter	-Kapp 732	(1966)
My Special Angel/Freulein	(R)-MCA 60026	(1969)
The Bell That Couldn't Jingle/Jingle Bell Rock	(R)-MCA 65029	(1969)
So Long	-Lil Darlin' 00	(1967)
Mary Goes Round	-Lil Darlin'	(1968)
He Thought He'd Die Laughing	-Lil Darlin' 30	(1969)
The Day You Stopped Loving Me/ You Can Tell the World	-Lil Darlin' 34	(1970)
Jingle Bell Rock	(2) -Lil Darlin' 38	(1970)
I Feel You, I Love You	-Lil Darlin' 44	(1970)
	-Little Darlin'	(1967-79)
Mary Goes Round/Cold Winds Blow on Me	(R)-Certron 10002	(1970)
Jingle Bell Rock/The Old Year Is Gone	(R)-Certron 10021	(1970)
(Decca ReReleases)	(R)-MCA	(1969-74)
	-Capitol	(1970)
Hand in Hand With Love	-Am Nat Sound 102	(1971)

-Bobby Helms Cont'd-

It's The Little Things	-Million 5	(1972)
It's Started To Rain Again	-Million 22	(1972)
Hand in Hand with Love	(R)-Amer Nat 0102	(1973)
Fraulein/My Special Angel	(R)-Gusto 2046	(1974)
Jingle Bell Rock	(R)-Misstltoe 802	(1974)
Baby(If I Could Make It Better)	-Larrick	(1975)
Every Man Must Have a Dream	-Golden Angel 187	(1976)
You	-Golden Angel 342	(1976)
	-Black rose	(1983-84)

Albums

Sings to My Special Angel	-Decca 8638	(1957)
The Best of Bobby Helms	-Columbia CS-8860	(1963)
Bobby Helms	-Vocalion Vl7-3743	(1965)
I'm the Man	-Kapp KS-3463	(1966)
Sorry My Name Isn't Fred	-Kapp KS-3505	(1966)
Bobby Helms Sings Freulein	-Harmony 11209	(1967)
All New Just For You	-Little Darlin'8008	(1968)
My Special Angel	(R)-Vocalion Vl7-3874	(1969)
Greatest Performance	-Certron CS-7003	(1970)
Jingle Bell Rock	-Mistletoe 1206	(1974)
Bobby Helms Sings His Greatest Hits	-Power Pak PO-283	(1975)
My Special Angel	(R)-MCA Vl7-3874	
Pop-A-Billy	-MCA 1557	(1983)
Somebody Wrong is Loving You (CD)	-Lauri 1007	(198?)
Bobby Helms Country (CD)	-Playback 72708	(1989)

Extended Play Mini Albums

EP Bobby Helms Sings to My Special Angel	-Decca 2555	(1957)
EP Tonight's the Night	-Decca 2586	(1958)
EP Bobby Helms With Anita Kerr Singers	-Decca 1629	(1959)

Wanda Jackson-   (One of the few women associated with rockabilly)

Singles

(Basically country songs on Decca)	-Decca	(1954-55)
I Gotta Know/Half as Good a Girl	-Capitol 3485	(1956)
Hot Dog! That Made Him Mad/		
Silver Threads and Golden Needles	-Capitol 3575	(1957)
Baby Loves Him/Cryin' Thru the Night	-Capitol 3637	(1957)
Let Me Explain/Don'a Wan'a	-Capitol 3683	(1957)
Cool Love/Did You Miss Me?	-Capitol 3764	(1958)
Fujiyama Mama/No Wedding Bells for Joe	-Capitol 3843	(1958)
Honey Bop/Just a Queen for a Day	-Capitol 3941	(1959)
Mean Mean Man/Every Time They Play Our Song	-Capitol 4026	(1959)
Rock Your Baby/Sinful Heart	-Capitol 4081	(1959)
Savin' My Love/I Wanna Waltz	-Capitol 4142	(1960)
Please Call Today	-Capitol 4354	(1960)

-Wanda Jackson Cont'd-

Let's Have a Party/Cool Love	-Capitol 4397	(1960)
Happy Happy Birthday Baby/Mean, Mean Man	-Capitol 4469	(1961)
Riot In Cell Block #9/Little Charm Bracelet	-Capitol 4520	(1961)
Right or Wrong/Funncl of Love	-Capitol 4553	(1961)
In the Middle of a Heartache/I'd Be Ashamed	-Capitol 4635	(1961)
A Little Bitty Tear/I Don't Wanta Go	-Capitol 4681	(1961)
If I Cried Every Time You Hurt Me/Let My Love Walk In	-Capitol 4723	(1962)
(Later songs basically country)		
	-Myrrh	(1973-75)
	-ABC	(1975)

Albums

Wanda Jackson	-Capitol ST-1041	(1958)
Rockin' With Wanda	-Capitol ST-1384	(1960)
There's a Party Goin' On	-Capitol ST-1511	(1961)
Right or Wrong	-Capitol ST-1546	(1961)
Wonderful Wanda	-Capitol ST-1776	(1962)
Rockin' With Wanda Gold Starline Label	(R)-Capitol ST-1384	(1962)
Lovin' Country Style	-Decca DL-4224	(1962)
Love Me Forever	-Capitol ST-1911	(1963)
Two Sides of Wanda Jacksn	-Capitol ST-2030	(1964)
Blues in My Heart	-Capitol ST-2306	(1964)
Rock 'n' Roll Away Your Blues	-Varrick VR-025	(1987)
Rockin' in the Country: The Best of Wanda Jackson (CD)	-Rhino 70990	(1990)
Greatest Hits (CD)	-Curb/CEMA 77398	(1990)
(Recorded and manufactured in Sweeden in 1984)		

Extended Play Mini Albums

EP Wanda Jackson	-Capitol 1-1041	(1958)
(Songs after this, and before this on Decca tended to be straight country)		

Sonny James(James Loden)-

Singles

Young Love	-Groove 001	(1956)
For Rent/My Stolen Love	-Capitol 3357	(1956)
All Mixed Up	-Capitol 3441	(1956)
Downfall of Me	-Capitol 3475	(1956)
The Cat Came Back	-Capitol 3542	(1957)
Reach Out Your Hand and Touch Me	-Capitol 3564	(1957)
Young Love/You're the Reason I'm in Love	(R)-Capitol 3602	(1957)
Young Love/You're the Reason I'm in Love	(R)-Capitol 6041	(1957)
Heaven on Earth	-Capitol 3653	(1957)
First Date, First Kiss, First Love/Speak to Me	-Capitol 3674	(1957)
Lovesick Blues	-Capitol 3734	(1957)
What Am I Living For?/Surprise Surprise	-Capitol 3779	(1957)
Love Conquered	-Capitol 3792	(1957)
Uh-Huh-Mm/Why Can't They Remember	-Capitol 3840	(1957)

-Sonny James Cont'd-

You Got That Touch/I Can See It in Your Eyes	-Capitol 4020	(1957)
Let Me Be the One to Love You	-Capitol 4066	(1957)
Big Dream	-Capitol 4127	(1958)
Talk of the School/The Table	-Capitol 4178	(1958)
Pure Love/This Love of Mine	-Capitol 4229	(1958)
Red Mug	-Capitol 4268	(1958)
I Forgot More Than You'll Ever Know/Til Tomorrow	-Capitol 4307	(1958)
Jenny Lou/Passin' Through	-NRC 050	(1960)
Young Love	(R)-Groove	(1961)
Apache/Magnetism	-RCA 37-7858	(1962)
	-Dot	(1962)
The Minute You're Gone/Gold and Silver	-Capitol 4969	(1962)
My Love/Blue for You	-Capitol 4993	(1962)
Hey Little Ducky/Innocent Angel	-RCA 37-7919	(1962)
Going Through the Motions	-Capitol 5057	(1963)
Baltimore	-Capitol 5129	(1964)
Ask Marie/Sugar Lump	-Capitol 5197	(1964)
You're the Only World I Know	-Capitol 5280	(1964)
I'll Keep Holding On(Just to Your Love)	-Capitol 5375	(1965)
Behind the Tear	-Capitol 5454	(1965)
True Love's a Blessing	-Capitol 5536	(1965)
I'll Keep Holding On/I'll Never Find Another You	-Capitol 5375	(1965)

(These two songs were unintentionally pressed back to back)

'Till the Last Leaf Shall Fall	-Capitol	(1965)
Behind the Tear/Runnin'	(R)-Capitol 6116	(1965)
True Love's a Blessing	(R)-Capitol	(1966)
Take Good Care of Her/On The Fingers of One Hand	-Capitol 5612	(1966)
Room in Your Heart	-Capitol 5690	(1966)
Barerfoot Santa Claus/My Christmas Dream	-Capitol 5733	(1966)
Need You	-Capitol 5833	(1967)
I'll Never Find Another You/Goodbye Maggie	-Capitol 5914	(1967)
It's the Little Things/Don't Cut Timber On a Windy Day	-Capitol 5987	(1967)
A World of Our Own	-Capitol 2067	(1967)
Only a Fool/Endless	-Capitol 2074	(1967)
Heaven Says Hello	-Capitol 2155	(1968)
Born To Be with You	-Capitol 2271	(1968)
Only the Lonely/The Journey	-Capitol 2370	(1969)
Running Bear	-Capitol 2486	(1969)
Since I Met You Baby	-Capitol 2595	(1969)
Only the Lonely/Running Bear	(R)-Capitol 6145	(1970)
My Love/Blue for You	-Capitol 2782	(1970)
It's Just a Matter of Time	-Capitol 2700	(1970)
Don't Keep Me Hanging On	-Capitol 2834	(1970)
Don't Keep Me Hanging On/Since I Met You Baby	(R)-Capitol 6176	(1970)
Endlessly	-Capitol 2914	(1970)
I Forgot To Remember Santa	-Capitol 2958	(1970)
Empty Arms	-Capitol 3015	(1971)

-Sonny James Cont'd-

Bright Lights, Big City	-Capitol 3112	(1971)
The Last Leaf Shall Fall	-Capitol 3163	(1971)
Here Comes Honey Again	-Capitol 3174	(1971)
Let's Go Bunny Huggin'	-Capitol 3198	(1971)
Only Love Can Break a Heart	-Capitol 3232	(1971)
Pigtails and Ribbons	-Capitol 3281	(1972)
That's Why I Love You Like I Do/ Still Waters Run Deep	-Capitol 3322	(1972)
For Rent	-Capitol 3357	(1972)
Traces	-Capitol 3398	(1972)
When The Snow Is on the Roses	-Columbia 45644	(1972)
White Silver Sands	-Columbia 45706	(1972)
I Love You More and More Everyday	-Columbia 45770	(1972)
If She Just Helps Me Get Over You	-Columbia 45871	(1973)
Is It Wrong?/Suddenly There's a Valley	-Columbia 46003	(1973)
A Mi Esposa Con Amor	-Columbia 10001	(1974)
Just a Little Bit South of Saskatoon	-Columbia 10072	(1975)
A Little Band of Gold	-Columbia 10121	(1975)
Maria Elena	-Columbia 10139	(1975)
What in the World's Come Over You	-Columbia 10184	(1975)
(Eres Tu)Touch the Wind	-Columbia 10249	(1975)
Back in the Saddle Again/The Prisoners Song	-Columbia 10276	(1976)
Big Silver Bird/When Something Is Wrong With My Baby	-Columbia 10335	(1976)
Come on In	-Columbia 10392	(1976)
You're the Only World I Know/You're Free To Go	-Columbia 10466	(1977)
In the Jailhouse Now	-Columbia 10551	(1977)
Pistol Packin' Mama/Abilene	-Columbia 10628	(1977)
This Is the Love	-Columbia 10703	(1978)
Caribbean	-Columbia 10764	(1978)
Building Memories	-Columbia 10852	(1978)
Lorelei	-Monument 288	(1979)
Innocent Lies	-Dimension 1026	(1982)
	-Dimension	(1976-82)

Albums

Young Love	-Capitol ST-71196	(1957)
This Is Sonny James	-Capitol ST-1178	(1958)
The Sonny Side	-Capitol T-1178	(1958)
Young Love	-Dot DLP-3462	(1962)
The Minute You're Gone	-Capitol ST-2017	(1964)
The Southern Gentleman	-Guest Star GS-1487	(1964)
You're the Only World I Know	-Capitol ST-2209	(1965)
Young Love	(R)-Hamilton 12160	(1965)
I'll Keep Holding On	-Capitol ST-2317	(1965)
Behind the Tear	-Capitol ST-2415	(1965)
True Love's a Blessing	-Capitol ST-2500	(1966)
Till the Last Leaf Shall Fall	-Capitol ST-2561	(1966)
My Christmas Dream	-Capitol ST-2589	(1966)
The Best of Sonny James	-Capitol ST-2615	(1966)

-Sonny James Cont'd-

Need You	-Capitol ST-2703	(1967)
Sonny James Sings Young Love	-Camden CAS-2140	(1967)
I'll Never Find Another You	-Capitol ST-2788	(1967)
Country Style	-Crown 328	(196?)
A World of Our Own	-Capitol ST-2884	(1968)
Heaven Says Hello	-Capitol ST-2937	(1968)
Born To Be With You	-Capitol ST-111	(1968)
* Number One Hits of Sonny James	(DJ)-Capitol SkAO-112	(1969)
Only the Lonely	-Capitol ST-193	(1969)
Close Up - Sonny James	-Capitol SWBB-258	(1969)
The Astrodome Presents In Person Sonny James	-Capitol ST-320	(1969)
The Best of Sonny James, Vol.2	-Capitol SKAO-144	(1969)
Invisible Tears	-Pickwick JS6067	(1969)
Love Letters in the Sand	-Pickwick JS6129	(1969)
Roses are Red	-Pickwick JS6100	(1969)
Sonny James	-Crown CST-499	(1969)
Timberline	-PickwickSPC-3650	(1969)
It's Just a Matter of Time	-Capitol ST-432	(1970)
My Love/Don't Keep Me Hangin' On	-Capitol ST-478	(1970)
You're The Only World I Know (2 LP)	-Capitol STBB-535	(1970)
I'll Never Find Another You	-Capitol ST-2788	(1970)
Number One(Biggest Hits)	-Capitol ST-629	(1970)
Empty Arms	-Capitol ST-734	(1971)
The Southern Gentleman	-Capitol ST-779	(1971)
Honey	-Capitol ST-988	(1971)
The Sensational Sonny James	-Capitol ST-804	(1971)
Here Comes Honey Again	-Capitol ST-849	(1971)
Sonny	-Capitol ST-867	(1971)
Traces	-Capitol ST-11108	(1972)
The Hit Sounds of Sonny James	-Capitol SL-6689	(1972)
Biggest Hits of Sonny James, Vol.3	-Capitol ST-11013	(1972)
That's why I Love You Like I Do	-Capitol ST-11067	(1972)
Sonny James	-Columbia KC31091	(1973)
When the Snow Is on the Roses	-Columbia KC31646	(1973)
Sings the Greatest Country Hits of 1972	-Columbia KC32028	(1973)
Gentleman from the South	-Capitol ST-11144	(1973)
Young Love	-Capitol ST-11196	(1973)
If She Just Helps Me Get Over You	-Columbia KC32291	(1973)
Is It Wrong?	-Columbia KC32805	(1974)
A Mi Esposa Con Amor	-Columbia KC33056	(1974)
The Biggest Hits of Sonny James	-Capitol ST-11013	(1975)
A Little Bit South of Saskatoon	-Columbia KC33428	(1975)
The Guitars of Sonny James	-Columbia KC33477	(1975)
Sonny James (2 LP) TV item	-TVP TVP-1014	(1975)
Greatest of Sonny James (2 LP)	-Brookville 6898	(1975)
Country Male Artist of the Decade	-Columbia KC33836	(1975)
When the Snow Is on The Roses/If She Helps Me (2 LP)	(R)-Columbia CG33627	(1975)

-Sonny James Cont'd-

200 Years of Country Music	-Columbia KC34035	(1975)
Traces	-Pickwick SPC-3650	(1976)
Sonny James Sings When Something Is Wrong With My Baby	-Columbia KC34309	(1976)
You're Free To Go	-Columbia KC34472	(1976)
Sonny James: In Prison, In Person	-Columbia KC34708	(1977)
The ABC Collection	-ABC AC-30027	(1977)
This Is the Love	-Columbia KC35379	(1978)
(Re-package of Young Love on Dot)	(R)-ABC	(1977)
Greatest Hits of Sonny James	-Columbia KC35626	(1978)
Sonny's Side of the Street	-Monument MG-763	(1979)
Sonny James Favorites	-Capitol SL-8125	(1979)
I'm Looking Over the Rainbow	-Dimension 5005	(1982)
American Originals(1972-77)	-Columbia CK45066	(1989)
The Best of Sonny James	-Capitol C21K91630	(1989)
Sonny James Greatest Hits, Vol. 1 (CD)	-Capitol/C 77359	(1990)
The Best of Sonny James (CD)	(R)-Curb/CEMA 77460	(1991)
Young Love (CD)	-Pair 1310	(1992)

Extended Play Mini Albums

EP First Date, First Kiss, First Love	-Capitol EAP-1-861	(1957)
EP Honey (3 records)	-Capitol EAP-988	(1958)
EP Sonny (3 records)	-Capitol EAP-867	(1957)
EP The Southern Gentleman (3 records)	-Capitol EAP-779	(1957)
EP Young Love	-Capitol EAP-1-827	(1957)
EP Honey (3 records)	-Capitol EAP-988	(1958)
EP Sensational Sonny James (Jukebox)	-Capitol 804	(1971)

Legendary Stardust Cowboy-

Singles

Who's Knocking on My Door?/Paralyzed	-Psycho Suave 1033	(1968)
Paralyzed	(R)-Mercury 72862	(1968)
I Took a Trip on a Gemini Spaceship/ Down in the Wrecking Yard	-Mercury 72891	(1969)
Everything's Getting Bigger But Our Love/Kiss and Run	-Mercury 72912	(1969)

Bob Luman-

Singles

All Night Long/Red Cadilac and a Red Moustache	-Imperial 8311	(1957)
Red Hot/Whenever You're Ready	-Imperial 8313	(1957)
Your Love/Make Up Your Mind Baby	-Imperial 8315	(1957)
Svengali/Precious	-Capitol 4059	(1958)
Class of '59/My Baby Walks All Over Me	-Warner Bros 5081	(1959)
Buttercup/Dreamy Doll	-Warner Bros 5105	(1959)
Let's Think About Living/You've Got Everything	-Warner Bros 5172	(1960)

-Bob Luman Cont'd-

Oh, Lonesome Me/Why, Bye, Bye	-Warner Bros 5184	(1960)
Let's Think About Living	(R)-Warner Bros 60	(1960)
The Great Snowman/The Pig Latin Song	-Warner Bros 5204	(1961)
Private Eye/You've Turned Down the Light	-Warner Bros 5233	(1961)
Louisiana Man/Rocks of Reno	-Warner Bros 5255	(1961)
Big River Rose/Belonging to You	-Warner Bros 5272	(1962)
Hey Joe/Fool	-Warner Bros 5299	(1962)
You're Everything/Envy	-Warner Bros 5321	(1962)
Boston Rocker	-Warner Bros 5506	(1963)
Let's Think About Living	(Rx)-Warner Bros 83	(196?)
	-Interstate Forty	(196?)
	-Hickory 1201	(1963)
Can't Take the Country from the Boy	-Hickory 1219	(1963)
I Like Your Kind of Love	-Hickory 1221	(1963)
The File	-Hickory 1238	(1964)
(Empty Walls) A Lonely Room	-Hickory 1266	(1964)
Fire Engine Red	-Hickory 1277	(1965)
Go On Home Boy	-Hickory 1307	(1965)
Love Worked a Miracle	-Hickory 1333	(1965)
Five Miles from Home	-Hickory 1355	(1966)
Poor Boy Blues/Off My Mind	-Hickory 1382	(1966)
Come on and Sing	-Hickory 1410	(1966)
Hardly Anymore	-Hickory 1430	(1967)
If You Don't Love Me/Throwin' Kisses	-Hickory 1460	(1967)
The Best Years of My Wife/Running Scared	-Hickory 1481	(1967)
Ain't Got Time To Be Unhappy	-Epic 5-10312	(1968)
I Like Trains	-Epic 5-10381	(1968)
Woman Without Love	-Epic 5-10416	(1968)
Come on Home and Sing the Blues To Daddy	-Epic 5-10439	(1969)
Everyday I Have To Cry Some	-Epic 5-10480	(1969)
The Gun	-Epic 5-10535	(1969)
It's All Over(But the Shouting)	-Hickory 1536	(1969)
Still Loving You/Meet Mr. Mud	(1)-Hickory 1564	(1970)
Gettin' Back to Norma/Maybellene	-Epic 5-10581	(1970)
Honky Tonk Man	-Epic 5-10631	(1970)
What About the Hurt?	-Epic 5-10667	(1970)
Is It Any Wonder That I Love You?	-Epic 5-10699	(1971)
I Got a Woman	-Epic 5-10755	(1971)
A Chain Don't Take to Me	-Epic 5-10786	(1971)
When You Say Love	-Epic 5-10823	(1972)
It Takes You/Let's Think About Living	(2)-Epic 5-10869	(1972)
Lonely Women Make Good Lovers/Love Ought To Be Happy	-Epic 5-10905	(1972)
Let's Think About Living/Memphis	(R)-Epic 15-2271	(1972)
Come On Home and Sing the Blues to Daddy/The Gun	(R)-Epic 15-2287	(1972)
Neither One of Us	-Epic 5-10943	(1972)
A Good Love Is Like a Good Song	-Epic 5-10994	(1973)
Still Loving You	(2)-Epic 5-11039	(1973)

-Bob Luman Cont'd-

Lonely Women Make Good Lovers/When You Say Love	-Epic 15-2325(R)	(1973)
Just Enough To Make Me Stay	-Epic 5-11087	(1974)
A Good Love Is Like a Good Song/Still Loving You	(R)-Epic 15-2338	(1974)
Let Me Make the Bright Lights Shine for You/		
The Closest Thing to Heaven	-Epic 5-11138	(1974)
Proud of You Baby	-Epic 8-50065	(1975)
Cleanin' Up the Streets of Memphis/A Satisfied Mind	-Epic 8-50183	(1975)
The Man from Bowling Green	-Epic 8-50216	(1976)
How Do You Start Over?	-Epic 8-50247	(1976)
Labor of Love	-Epic 8-50297	(1976)
He's Got a Way With Women	-Epic 8-50323	(1976)
	-Rollin Rock	(1977)
The Pay Phone	-Polydor 14431	(1977)
A Christmas Tribute	-Polydor 14444	(1977)
Let Me Love Him Out Of You	-Polydor 14454	(1978)

Albums

Let's Think About Livin'	-Warner Bros 1396	(1960)
Livin' Lovin Sounds	-Hickory 124	(1965)
Ain't Got Time To Be Unhappy	-Epic BN-26393	(1968)
Come on Home and Sing the Blues to Daddy	-Epic BM-26463	(1969)
Gettin' Back to Norma	-Epic BN-26541	(1970)
Is It Any Wonder That I Love You?	-Epic E-30617	(1971)
A Chain Don't Take to Me	-Epic E-30923	(1971)
When You Say Love	-Epic KE-31375	(1972)
Lonely Women Make Good Lovers	-Epic KE-31746	(1972)
Bob Luman	-Harmony KH32006	(1972)
Neither One of Us	-Epic KE-32192	(1973)
Bob Luman's Greatest Hits	-Epic KE-32759	(1974)
Still Loving You	-Hickory 4508	(1974)
Red Cadillac & Black Mustache	-Epic KE-33177	(1974)
Lonely Women/When You Say Lv	-Epic BG-33755	(1975)
A Satisfied Mind	-Epic KE-33942	(1976)
Bob Luman Alive and Well	-Epic KE-34445	(1977)
Bob Luman	-Polydor PD1-6135	(1978)
American Originals(1970 - 73) (CD)	-Columbia CK45078(1989)	

Extended Play Mini Album

EP Let's Think About Livin'	-Warner Bros E-1396(1960)
EP Bob Luman	-Warner Bros E-5506(1960)
EP Bob Luman(That's All Right)	-Rollin' Rock 034 (1977)

Bill Mack-

Singles

Play My Boogie	-Imperial 8177	(1956)
That's The Way I Like You	-Imperial 8212	(1956)

-Bill Mack Cont'd-

That's How I Feel	-Imperial 8222	(1956)
Sue-Suzie Boogie	-Imperial 8278	(1957)
Kitty Kat	-Starday 231	(195?)
Cat Just Got in Town	-Starday 252	(195?)
It's Saturday Night	-Starday 280	(195?)
Cheatin' on Your Mind	-Starday 313	(195?)
Long Long Train	-Starday 418	(195?)

Clint Miller-

Singles

Bertha Lou/Doggone It Baby, I'm In Love	-ABC/P 9878	(1958)
A Lover's Prayer/No Never My Love	-ABC/P 9979	(1958)
Teenage Dance	-ABC/P 9938	(1958)
	-Big Top	(1959)
	-Headline	(1960-61)
Forget-Me-Nots	-Lenox 5557	(1962)

Ned Miller-

Singles

From a Jack to a King/Parade of Broken Hearts	-Dot 15601	(1957)
Lights in the Street	-Dot 15651	(1957)
Ring the Bell for Johnny	-Jackpot 48020	(1959)
Cold Gray Blues	-Capitol 4607	(1961)
Dark Moon/Go on Back You Fool	-Capitol 4652	(1961)
From a Jack to a King/Parade of Broken Hearts	-Fabor 114 (R)	(1962)
(Leased to Dot in 1957,later released by Fabor)		
One Among the Many	-Fabor 116	(1963)
Another Fool Like Me	-Fabor 121	(1963)
Big Love/Sunday Morning Texas	-Fabor 125	(1963)
Invisible Tears/Old Restless One	-Fabor 128	(1964)
Do What You Do Do Well/Dusty Guitar	-Fabor 137	(1963)
Just Before Dawn	-Fabor 139	(1965)
Roll O Rollin' Stone	-Fabor 143	(1965)
Whistle Walkin'	-Capitol 5431	(1965)
Summer Roses/Right Behind These Lips	-Capitol 5661	(1966)
Teardrop Lane	-Capitol 5742	(1966)
The Hobo	-Capitol 5868	(1967)
From a Jack to a King/Do What You Do Do Well	(R)-Capitol 6092	(196?)
Only a Fool/Endless	-Capitol 2074	(1968)
	-Republic	(1969-70)

Albums

From a Jack to a King	-Fabor FLP-1001	(1963)
Teardrop Lane	-Capitol 2586	(1966)
In the Name of Love	-Capitol 2914	(1968)

Guy Mitchell-

      Contrary to what it may seem Guy Mitchell was not really rockabilly music.

NRBQ-

      (Original members include:Terry Adams, Steve Ferguson,)
        (Frank Gadler, Joey Spampinato, and Tom Staley)

Singles

Boppin' the Blues(with Carl Perkins)	-Columbia CS-9981	(1969)

      (Other records by NRBQ are blues)

Paul Peek-

Singles

Sweet Skinny Jenny/The Rock-A-Round	-NRC 001	(1958)
Olds-Mo-William/I'm Not Your Fool, Anymore	-NRC 008	(1958)
Gee But I Miss That Girl/Waikiki Beach	-NRC 033	(1959)
Hurtin' Inside/Walkin' the Floor Over You	-NRC 048	(1960)
I'm a Happy Man/Where There's a Will	-NRC 059	(1960)
Brother-in-Law(He's a Moocher)/Through the Teenage Years	-Fairlane 702	(1961)
Watermelon	-Fairlane 21005	(1962)
	-Mercury	(1962-63)
Pin The Tail on the Donkey/Rockin' Pneumonia and the Boogie Woogie Flu	-Columbia 43527	(1966)
The Shadow Knows/I'm Moving Uptown	-Columbia 43771	(1966)
Sweet Lorraine/Out Went the Lights	-1-2-3 1714	(1969)

Johnny Preston-

Singles

Running Bear/My Heart Knows	-Mercury 71474*	(1959)
Cradle of Love/City of Tears	-Mercury 71528	(1960)
Cradle of Love/Running Bear	(R)-Mercury 30089	(1960)
Cradle of Love/City of Tears	(S)-Mercury 10027	(1960)
Feel So Fine/I'm Starting to Go Steady	-Mercury 71651	(1960)
Up in the Air/Charming Billy	-Mercury 71591	(1960)
(I Want a)Rock and Roll Guitar/New Baby for Christmas	-Mercury 71728	(1960)
Leave My Kitten Alone/Token of Love	-Mercury 71761	(1961)
I Feel Good/Willy Walk	-Mercury 71803	(1961)
Let Them Talk/She Once Belonged to Me	-Mercury 71865	(1961)
Kissin' Tree/Free Me	-Mercury 71903	(1961)
Broken Hearts Anonymous/Let's Leave It That Way	-Mercury 71951	(1962)
Let the Big Boss Man/The Day After Forever	-Mercury 72049	(1962)
This Little Bear/The Day the World Stood Stll	-Imperial 5924	(1963)
All Around the World/Just Plain Hurt	-Hallway 1201	(1964)

-Johnny Preston Cont'd-

Willie and the Hand Jive/I've Got My Eyes on You	-Hallway 1204	(1965)
Running Bear '65/Dedicated to the One I Love	-TCF Hall 101	(1965)
Good Good Lovin'/I'm Asking Forgiveness	-TCF Hall 120	(1965)
I'm Only Human/There's Only One Like You	-ABC 11085	(1968)
Kick the Can/I've Just Been Wasting My Time	-ABC 11187	(1968)
	-ABC	(1968-73)

*J.P. Richardson and George Jones on backup vocals

Albums

Running Bear	-Mercury MG20592	(1960)
Come Rock With Me	-Mercury MG20609	(1961)
Running Bear	-Wing SRW-16246	(1963)
	-Chicago "Skyline"	(1981)

Extended Play Mini Albums

EP Johnny Preston (Running Bear)	-Mercury EP-3397	(1960)

Marvin Rainwater-

Singles

Albino Stallion	-MGM 12071	(1955)
Tennessee Hound Dog Yodel	-MGM 12096	(1955)
Dem Low Down Blues	-MGM 12152	(1955)
Hot and Cold	-MGM 12240	(1956)
Why Do You Have To Go and Leave Me?	-MGM 12313	(1956)
Get Off the Stool	-MGM 12370	(1956)
Gonna Find Me a Bluebird/So You Think You've Got Trbles	-MGM 12412	(1957)
My Brand of Blues/My Love Is Real	-MGM 12511	(1957)
Majesty of Love/You My Darlin You(with Connie Francis)	-MGM 12555	(1957)
Look for Me/Lucky Star	-MGM 12586	(1958)
Baby, Don't Go/Whole Lotta' Woman	-MGM 12609	(1958)
Gamblin' Man	-MGM 12653	(1958)
I Dig You Baby/Moanin' The Blues	-MGM 12665	(1959)
Nothin' Needs Nothin'	-MGM 12701	(1959)
Lonely Island	-MGM 12739	(1959)
That's When I'll Stop Loving You	-MGM 12773	(1959)
Half Breed/A Song of Love	-MGM 12803	(1960)
The Valley of the Moon	-MGM 12829	(1960)
Wayward Angel	-MGM 12865	(1960)
Hard Luck Blues	-MGM 12891	(1960)
Yesterday's Kisses	-MGM 12938	(1961)
Boo-Hoo	-Warwick 666	(1961)
Tough Cat	-Warwick 674	(1961)
	-Brave	(1963-67)
It Wasn't Enough	-UA 837	(1965)
Black Sheep	-UA 917	(1965)
Sorrow Brings a Good Man Down	-UA 50023	(1966)
	-Warner Brs	(1970)

-Marvin Rainwater Cont'd-

Mama's Girl/Talk to Me	-Wesco 2105	(1971)
(I Don't Need No) Enemies	-Wesco 7201	(1971)
The Haircut	-Nu Trayl 902	(1976)
Goodnight Darling	-Casino ? ?	(197?)
Hearts Hall of Fame	-ESP For Frnds	(197?)
Hey Good Lookin'	-Star Dale 337	(197?)
Henryetta Oklahoma	(R)-Star Dale 1957	(197?)
Especially for Friends	-Mr 1	(197?)
I Don't Care About Tomorrow	-Kajac 501	(197?)
I Gotta Go Get My Baby	-Coral 9-61342	(197?)
It Wasn't Enough	-Brave 7001	(197?)
Parttime Lover	-Brave 1001	(197?)
Love's Prison	-Brave 1003	(197?)
Sad Girl	-Brave 1004	(197?)
The Old Gang's Gone	-Brave 1017	(197?)
Henryetta Oklahoma	-Hornet 5	(1982)

Albums

Songs by Marvin Rainwater	-MGM E-3534	(1957)
Marvin Rainwater Sings With a Heart	-MGM E-3721	(1958)
Gonna Find Me a Bluebird	-MGM E-4046	(1962)
Marvin Rainwater	-Crown CST-307	(196?)
Country's Favorite Country Singer	-Mount Vernon 146	(196?)
Golden Country Hits of Marvin Rainwater	-Spinorama 109	(196?)

Extended Play Mini Albums

EP Songs by Marvin Rainwater	-MGM 1464-1466	(1957)

Wayne Raney(and The Raney Family)-

Singles

Why Don't You Haul Off and Love Me	-King 791	(1949)
Shake Baby Shake	-Decca 30212	(1956)

Albums

Songs from the Hills	-King 588	(1958)
Wayne Raney and the Raney Family	-Starday 124	(1960)
Harmonica Blues	-Starday 133	(1960)
Don't Try To Be What You Ain't	-Starday 279	(1962)
We Love To Live	-King 1469	(196?)
Tear Down the Mountains	-King 1480	(196?)
Gathering in the Sky	-Rimrock 492	(196?)
Best of Wayne Raney	-Memory 001	(196?)
Wayne Raney and the Raney Family	(R)-Nashville 2002	(197?)
We Need a Lot More of Jesus	-Rimrock 2002	(197?)
Early Country Favorites	-Old Homestead 305	(197?)
We Need A Lot More Of Jesus	-Old Homestead 308	(197?)
Songs of the Hills (CD)	-King 588	(198?)

Extended Play Mini Albums

-Wayne Raney Cont'd-

EP Wayne Raney and His Talking Harmonica	-Starday SEP-126	(1960)
EP Wayne Raney and The Raney Family	-Starday SEP-126	(1960)

Jerry Reed-

Singles

Here I Am	-Capitol 3294	(1954)
Honey Chile	-Capitol 3381	(1954)
Just a Romeo	-Capitol 3504	(1954)
Too Busy	-Capitol 3592	(1954)
Bessie Baby	-Capitol 3882	(1955)
Soldier's Joy	-NRC 5008	(1959)
Love Is the Cause of It All	-Columbia 42047	(1961)
Hit and Run	-Columbia 42183	(1961)
Goodnight Irene/I'm Movin' On	-Columbia 42417	(1961)
Hully Gully Guitars/Twist-A-Roo	-Columbia 42533	(1962)
Overlooked and Underloved/Too Old To Cut the Mustard	-Columbia 42639	(1962)
If I Don't Live It Up	-RCA 47-8565	(1965)
Ain't That Just Like A Fool	-RCA 47-8667	(1965)
Fighting for the USA	-RCA 47-8730	(1966)
Woman Shy	-RCA 47-8957	(1966)
Guitar Man	-RCA 47-9152	(1967)
Tupelo Mississippi Flash/Wabash Cannonball	-RCA 47-9334	(1967)
Remembering	-RCA 47-9493	(1968)
Alabama Wild Man	(1) -RCA 47-9623	(1968)
Oh What A Woman	-RCA 47-9701	(1969)
There's Better Things in Life/Blues Land	-RCA 74-0124	(1969)
Are You From Dixie/ A Worried Man	-RCA 74-0211	(1969)
Alabama Jubilee/Talk About the Good Times	-RCA 47-9804	(1970)
Georgia Sunshine	-RCA 47-9870	(1970)
Amos Moses	-RCA 47-9904	(1970)
When You're Hot, You're Hot	-RCA 47-9976	(1970)
Amos Moses/When You're Hot, You're Hot	(R)-RCA 447-0896	(1970)
Koko Joe	-RCA 48-1011	(1971)
Another Puff	-RCA 74-0613	(1972)
Smell the Flowers	-RCA 74-0667	(1972)
Nashtown Ville	-RCA 74-0775	(1972)
You Took All the Ramblin' Out of Me	-RCA 74-0857	(1972)
Lord Mister Ford	-RCA 74-0960	(1973)
Alabama Wild Man/Smell the Flowers	(R)-RCA 447-0949	(1973)
Uptown Poker Club	-RCA APBO-0194	(1973)
Lightning Rod	-RCA PB-10013	(1974)
Boogie Woogie Rock and Roll	-RCA PB-10063	(1974)
Crude Oil Blues	-RCA APBO-0224	(1974)
A Good Woman's Love	-RCA APBO-0273	(1974)
Let's Sing Our Song	-RCA PB-10132	(1975)

-Jerry Reed Cont'd-

Mind Your Love	-RCA PB-10247	(1975)
???	-RCA PB-10389	(1975)
Gator	-RCA PB-10717	(1976)
Semolita	-RCA PB-10893	(1977)
East Bound and Down/Redneck in a Rock and Roll Bar	-RCA PB-11056	(1977)
You Know What	-RCA PB-11164	(1977)
East Bound and Down/Redneck in a Rock and Roll Bar	(R)-RCA GB-11986	(1977)
Alabama Wild Man	(2) -RCA 74-0738	(197?)
Sweet Love Feelings	-RCA PB-11232	(1977)
Stars and Stripes Forever	-RCA PB-11370	(1979)
Second-Hand Satin Lady(and a Bargain Basment Boy)	-RCA PB-11472	(1979)
(Who Was the Man Who Put)The Line in Gasoline	-RCA PB-11638	(1979)
Hot Stuff	-RCA PB-11698	(1979)
Sugar Foot Rag	-RCA PB-11764	(1979)
Workin' at the Carwash Blues/Age	-RCA PB-11944	(1980)
The Friendly Family Inn	-RCA PB-12034	(1980)
Texas Bound and Flying	-RCA PB-12083	(1980)
Patches	-RCA PB-12318	(1981)
The Man with the Golden Thumb	-RCA PB-13081	(1982)
She Got the Goldmine(I Got the Shaft)	-RCA PB-13268	(1982)
Bessie Baby	-RCA PB-13355	(1982)
Down on the Corner	-RCA PB-13442	(1982)
She's Ready For Someone	-RCA PB-13527	(1982)

Albums

	-Columbia	(1961)
The Unbelievable Guitar & Voice of Jerry Reed	-RCA LSP-3756	(1967)
Nashville Underground	-RCA LSP-3978	(1968)
Alabama Wild Man	-RCA LSP-4069	(1968)
Better Things in Life	-RCA LSP-4147	(1969)
Jerry Reed Explores Guitar Country	-RCA LSP-4204	(1969)
Cookin'	-RCA LSP-4293	(1970)
Georgia Sunshine	-RCA LSP-4391	(1970)
Me and Jerry (with Chet Atkins)	-RCA AHL1-4396	(1970)
I'm Movin' On	-Harmony 30547	(1971)
When You're Hot, You're Hot	-RCA ANL1-1345	(1971)
Ko-Ko Joe	-RCA LSP-4596	(1971)
Smell the Flowers	-RCA LSP-4660	(1972)
Me And Chet (with Chet Atkins)	(R)-RCA LSP-4707	(1972)
The Best of Jerry Reed	-RCA LSP-4729	(1972)
Oh What a Woman	-CAMDEN 2585	(1972)
Jerry Reed	-RCA LSP-4750	(1972)
Hot A' Mighty	-RCA LSP-4838	(1973)
Just To Satisfy You	-RCA DRL1-0056	(1973)
Lord, Mr. Ford	-RCA APL1-0238	(1973)
The Uptown Poker Club	-RCA APL1-0356	(1973)
A Good Woman's Love	-RCA APL1-0544	(1974)
Tupelo Mississippi Flash	-Camden ACL10331	(1974)

-Jerry Reed Cont'd-

Mind Your Love	-RCA APL1-0787	(1975)
Jerry Reed in Concert	-RCA APL1-1014	(1975)
Paper Roses	-Camden ACL10533	(1975)
Red Hot Picker	-RCA APL1-1226	(1975)
When You're Hot You're Hot	(R)-RCA ANL1-1345	(1976)
Alabama Wild Man	(R)-Camden ACL17024	(1976)
Both Barrels	-RCA APL1-1861	(1976)
Me and Chet (with Chet Atkins)	(R)-RCA ANL1-2167	(1977)
Jerry Reed Rides Again	-RCA APL1-2346	(1977)
East Bound and Down	-RCA APL1-2516	(1977)
Sweet Love Feelings	-RCA APL1-2764	(1978)
Half Singin' and Half Pickin'	-RCA AFL1-3359	(1979)
Jerry Reed Live!	-RCA AHL1-3453	(1979)
I'm a Lover, Not a Fighter	(R)-Pickwick JS-6127	(197?)
(Reissues of Camden)	-Pickwick/Hilltop	(197?)
Jerry Reed Sings Jim Croce	-RCA AHL1-3604	(1980)
East Bound and Down	(R)-RCA AYL1-3677	(1980)
Texas Bound and Flying	-RCA AHL1-3771	(1980)
Dixie Dreams	-RCA AHL1-4021	(1981)
The Best of Jerry Reed	(R)-RCA AYL1-4109	(1981)
Jerry Reed Live	(R)-RCA AYL1-4167	(1981)
Man with the Golden Thumb	-RCA AHL1-4315	(1982)
Texas Bound and Flying	(R)-RCA AYL1-4394	(1982)
The Bird	-RCA APL1-1861	(1983)
Ready	-RCA AHL1-4692	(1983)
Jerry Reed's Greatest Hits	-RCA AHL1-5176	(1984)
Collector's Series	-RCA AHL1-5472	(1985)
Lookin' At You	-Capitol ST-12492	(1986)
The Bird	(R)-RCA AUK1-9525	(1987)
The Best of Jerry Reed (CD)	(R)-RCA 54109	(1988)
East Bound and Down (CD)	(R)-RCA 58450	(199?)

Glenn Reeves(and His Rock-Billy - and His Town & Country Playboys)-

Singles

Drinkin' Wine Spo-Dee-O-Dee	-Atco 6080	
Betty Bounce	-Decca 30589	(1957)
Tarzan	-Decca 30780	(1957)
I'm Johnny on the Spot	-TNT 120	(195?)
I Ain't Got Room to Rock	-TNT 129	(195?)

Johnny Restivo-

Singles

The Shape I'm In/Ya Ya	-RCA 7559	(1959)

The Shape I'm In/Ya Ya	(S) -RCA 61-7759	(1959)
Two Crazy Kids	-RCA 7818	(1960)
I Like Girls	-RCA 7601	(1959)
The Magic Age Is Seventeen/Doctor Love	-20th Cen Fox 279	(1961)
	-Epic	(1962)

Jody Reynolds-

Singles

Endless Sleep/Tight Capris	-Demon 1507	(1958)
Fire of Love/Daisy Mae	-Demon 1509	(1958)
Closin' In/Elope with Me	-Demon 1511	(1958)
Golden Idol/Beauleah Lee	-Demon 1515	(1959)
Please Remeber/The Storm	-Demon 1519	(1959)
The Whipping Post /I Wanna Be with You Tonite	-Demon 1523	(1959)
Stone Cold/(The Girl with the)Raven Hair	-Demon 1524	(1959)
Thunder/Tarantula	-Indigo 127	(1961)
Raggedy Ann/The Girl from King Marie	-Brent 7042	(1963)
Don't Jump/Stormy	-Smash 1810	(1963)
Endless Sleep	(R)-Era 026	(196?)
	-Pulsar	
	-ABC	(1973)
Endless Sleep	(Rx)-Collectables 3040	(198?)
Endless Sleep	(Rx)-Titan 1801	(198?)
Endless Sleep	(Rx)-Original Gold 509	(198?)
Endless Sleep/Tight Capris	(Rx)-Goldies 2455	(198?)

Jimmy Richards-

Singles

Strollin' and Boppin'/Cool As a Moose	-Columbia 4-41083	(195?)

Johnny Rive-s:

(While he was influenced by the rockabilly sound, most of his music was rock and a go go)

The Rockin' Saints-

Singles

Alright, Baby/The Saints Rock	-Decca 30990	(1959)
Cheat on Me Baby/Half and Half	-Decca 31144	(1960)

Jack Scott(Jack Scafone)-

Singles

Baby She's Gone/You Can Bet Your Bottom Dollar	-ABC/P 9818	(1957)
Two Timin' Woman/I Need Your Love	-ABC/P 9860	(1957)
Before the Bird Flies/Insane	-ABC/P 10843	(1957)
My True Love/Leroy	-Carlton 462	(1958)
With Your Love/Geraldine	-Carlton 483	(1958)
Goodbye Baby/Save My Soul	-Carlton 493	(1958)
I Never Felt Like This/Bella	-Carlton 504	(1959)
The Way I Walk/Midgie	-Carlton 514	(1959)
There Comes a Time/Baby Marie	-Carlton 519	(1959)
What Am I Living For?/Indiana Waltz	-Guaranteed 209	(1960)
Go Wild, Little Sadie/No One Will Ever Know	-uaranteed 211	(1960)
What in the World's Come Over You/Baby, Baby	-Top Rank 2028	(1960)
Burning Bridges/Oh Little One	-Top Rand 2041	(1960)
It Only Happened Yesterday/Cool Water	-Top Rank 2055	(1960)
Patsy/Old Time Religion	-Top Rank 2075	(1961)
Is There Something On Your Mind?/ Found a Woman	-Top Rank 2093	(1961)
A Little Feeling Called Love/Now That	-Capitol 4554	(1961)
My Dream Come True/Strange Desire	-Capitol 4597	(1961)
Steps 1 and 2/One of These Days	-Capitol 4637	(1961)
Cry, Cry, Cry/Grizzly Bear	-Capitol 4689	(1962)
The Part Where I Cry/You Only See What You Want To See	-Capitol 4738	(1962)
Sad Story/I Can't Hold Your Letters	-Capitol 4796	(1962)
If Only/Green, Green Valley	-Capitol 4855	(1963)
Strangers/Laugh and the World Laughs With You	-Capitol 4903	(1963)
All I See Is Blue/Me-O My-O	-Capitol 4955	(1963)
There's Trouble Brewing/Jingle Bell Slide	-Groove 0027	(1963)
I Knew You First/Blue Skies	-Groove 0031	(1964)
Wiggle on Out/What a Wonderful Night Out	-Groove 0037	(1964)
Thou Shalt Not Steal/I Prayed for an Angel	-Groove 0042	(1964)
Tall Tales/Flakey John	-Groove 0049	(1964)
I Don't Believe in Tea Leaves/Separation's Now Granted	-RCA 8505	(1965)
Looking For Linda/I Hope, I Think, I Wish	-RCA 8685	(1965)
Don't Hush the Laughter/Let's Learn To Live and Love Again	-RCA 8724	(1965)
Burning Bridges/Goodbye Baby	(2) -Gusto 2088	(196?)
Before the Bird Flies/Insane	(R)-ABC/P	(1966)
My Special Angel/I Keep Changing My Mind	-Jubilee 5606	(1967)
Burning Bridges/What I Would	(R)-Capitol 6077	(196?)
Billy Jack/Mary Marry Me	-GRT 35	(1970)
May You Never Be Alone/Face To The Wall	-Dot 17475	(1973)
You're Just Getting Better/Walk Throu My Mind	-Dot 17504	(1974)
Spirit of '76	-Ponie 4104-30	(197?)
	-Eric	(198?)
My True Love	(R)-Oldies 89	(198?)
My True Love	(R)-Collectables 3021	(198?)

-Jack Scott Cont'd-
Albums

Jack Scott		-Carlton ST-LP 107	(1958)
What Am I Living For?		-Carlton ST-LP 122	(1960)
I Remember Hank Williams		-Top Rank RS-319	(1960)
What in the Worlds Come Over You		-Top Rank RS-326	(1961)
The Spirit Moves Me		-Top Rank RS-348	(1961)
Burning Bridges		-Capitol ST-2035	(1964)
Great Scott		-Jade 33-202	(196?)
Soul Stirring		-Sesac 4201	(196?)
		-Ponie	(1974-77)
Burning Bridges & Other Hits	(CD)	-CESP 9775	(198?)
The Greatest Hits of Jack Scott	(CD)	-Curb/CEMA 77255	(1990)
Jack Scott (Collector's Series)	(CD)	-Capitol/C 93192	(1990)

Extended Play Mini Albums

EP Presenting Jack Scott	-Carlton EP1070-71	(1958)
EP Jack Scott Sings	-Carlton EP1072	(1959)
EP Starring Jack Scott	-Carlton EP1073	(1959)
EP Jack Scott (What in the World's Come Over You)	-Top Rnk REK1001	(1960)

Ronnie Self-

Singles

Pretty Bad Blues/Three Hearts Later	-ABC/P 9714	(1955)
Sweet Love	-ABC/P 9768	(1956)
Big Fool	-Columbia 40875	(1956)
Ain't I'm a Dog/Rocky Road Blues	-Columbia 40989	(1957)
Bop-A-Lena/I Ain't Goin' Nowhere	-Columbia 41101	(1957)
Big Blon' Baby/Date Bait	-Columbia 41166	(1957)
Petrified/You're So Right for Me	-Columbia 41241	(1958)
This Must Be the Place/Big Town	-Decca 30958	(1959)
I've Been There/So High	-Decca 31131	(1960)
Some Things You Can't Change/Instant Man	-Decca 31351	(1960)
Oh Me, Oh My/Past,Present, and Future	-Decca 31431	(1961)
Bless My Broken Heart/Houdine	-Kapp 546	(1963)

Albums
Extended Play Mini Albums

EP Ronnie Self Sings Ain't I'm a Dog	-Columbia EP-2149	(1957)

Charles Senns-

Singles

Gee Whiz Liz/Dig Me a Crazy Record	-OJ Inc 1047	(1959)

Chuck Sims-

Singles

Little Pigeon/Life Isn't Long Enough	-Trend 30-000	(1958)

Clyde Stacy-(& The Nightcaps)

Singles

Baby Shame/Nobody's Darlin'	(R)-Bullseye 1004	(1958)
Sure Do Love You Baby	-Bullseye 1006	(1958)
Sure Do Love You Baby	(R)-Bullseye 1008	(1958)
You Want Love/Once In A While	-Bullseye 1014	(1958)
So Young/Hoy Hoy	(R)-Argyle 1001	(1959)
Tutti Fruitti	-White Rock	(1960)
	-Len	(1961)

Terry Stafford-

Singles

Suspicion/Judy	-Lana 139	(1964)
Suspicion/Judy	(R)-Crusader 101	(1964)
I'll Touch a Star/Playing with Fire	-Crusader 105	(1964)
Follow the Rainbow/Are You a Fool Like Me?	-Crusaer 109	(1964)
A Little Bit Better/Hoping	-Crusader 110	(1964)
The Joke's on Me/A Step or Two Behind	-Sidewalk 914	(1965)
	-Mercury	(1966)
Big in Dallas	-Warner Bros 7286	(1969)
Mean Woman Blues/Candy Man	-MGM 14232	(1971)
It Sure Is Bad To Love Her	(2) -Casablanka 1291	(1973)
Say Has Anybody Seen My Sweet Gypsy Rose	-Atlantic 4006	(1973)
Captured/It Sure Is Bad To Love Her	-Atlantic 4015	(1973-74)
	-Melodyland	(1975)
	-Eric	
I'll Touch a Star/Suspicion	(Rx)-Collectables 1291	(198?)
I'll Touch a Star/Suspicion	(Rx)-Oldies 45 198	(198?)

Albums

Suspicion	-Crusader CLP-1001	(1964)

Ray Stanley-

Singles

Pushin'/Market Place	-Zephyr 011	(1956)
My Lovin' Baby/I Love Charms	-Zephyr 012	(1956)
Over a Coke	-Argo 5280	(195?)
My Lovin' Baby/Love Charms	-Zephyr 012	(1956)

Stray Cats-
(Brian Setzer, lead guitar; Lee Rocker (Leon Drucker, String Bass; Slim Jim Phantom (Jim McDonell), drums)

Singles

Stray Cat Strut	-EMI/A	(1982)
(She's) Sexy + 17	-EMI/A 8132	(1983)
I Won't Stand In Your Way	-EMI/A 8185	(1983)
Look At That Cadillac	-EMI/A 8194	(1984)
Rock Therapy	-EMI/A	(1986)
Blast Off	-EMI/A	(1989)
Rock This Town	-EMI/A	(1990)

Albums

Gonna Ball	-Arista/Stray 2	(1981)
Built For Speed	-EMI/A 17070	(1982)
Rant N' Rave with the Stray Cats	-EMI/A 17102	(1983)
Rock Therapy	-EMI/A 17226	(1986)
Blast Off	-EMI/A 91401	(1989)
Rock This Town	-EMI/A 94975	(1990)
Stray Cat Strut	-EMI/A 9538	
The Stray Cats' Greatest Hits	-EMI/A 77592	(1992)
Choo Choo Hot Fish	-JRS 35812	(1992)

Phantom, Rocker & Slick-
(Jim Phantom, Lee Rocker, Earl Slick)
Singles

	-EMI/A	(1985-86)

Albums

	-EMI/A	(1985-86)

Brian Setzer-

Singles

	-EMI/A	(1985-88)

Albums

The knife Feels Like Justice	-EMI/A 17178	(1986)
Live Nude Guitars	-EMI/A 46963	(1988)
	-EMI/A	(1985-88)

Sylva-Tones-

Singles

Roses are Blooming/That's All I Want From You	-Argo 5281	(1957)
Weepin' and Wailin'/That's All I Want From You	-Monarch	(1957)

Mitchell Torok(and The Louisiana Heyride Band-and The Matches)-

Singles

Nacogdoches County Line	-FBC 102	(1952)
Piney Woods Boogie	-FBC 115	(1952)
Caribbean/Weep Away	(1) -Abbott 140	(1953)
Little Hoo Wee/Judalina	-Abbott 146	(1953)
Living On Love/Edgar the Eager Easter Bunny	-Abbott 156	(1954)
Dancerette	-Abbott 162	(1955)
Roulette	-Decca 9-29326	(1957)
A Pleasant Guitar	-Decca 9-29408	(1957)
Too Late Now	-Decca 9-29576	(1957)
Wish I Was A Bit Younger	-Decca 9-29986	(1957)
Pledge of Love/What's Behind That Strange Door	-Decca 9-30230	(1957)
Sweet Revenge	-Decca 9-30661	(1958)
Go Ahead and Be a Fool	-Decca 9-30859	(1958)
Caribbean/Hootchy Kootchy Henry	(2) -Guyden 2018	(1959)
Guadian Angel/I Want to Know Ev'rything	-Guyden 2032	(1960)
Pink Chiffon/What You Don't Know	-Guyden 2034	(1960)
	-Mercury	(1961)
	-Capitol	(1962-63)
	-Inette	(1963)
Sober Up	-Imperial 8224	(1956)
The Man With the Golden Hand	-RCA	(1965)
Instant Love	-Reprise 541	(1966)
	-Reprise	(1966-67)
Caribbean	(3) -Parjo 1005	(196?)

Trashmen-

Singles

Surfin' Bird/King of the Surf	-Garrett 4002	(1963)
Bird Dance Beat/A-bone	-Garrett 4003	(1963)
Bad News/On the Move	-Garrett 4005	(1963)
Peppermint Man/New Generation	-Garrett 4010	(1964)
Whoa, Dad/Walkin' My Baby	-Garrett 4012	(1964)
Dancing with Santa	-Garrett 4013	(1966)
Surfin' Bird/Bird Dance	(R)-Teriffic 5003	(1965)
	-Argo	(1966)
	-Bear	(1966)
Same Lines/Hangin' on Me	-Tribe 8315d	(1966)
Green, Green Backs of Home/Address Enclosed	-Metromedia 7927	(1966)
	-Era	(1972)
	-Eric	(198?)
Surfin' Bird/King of the Surf	(Rx)-Lana 136	(1968)
Surfin' Bird/(B Side by The Castaways)	-Soma 1469	(196?)

-Trashmen Cont'd-
Albums

Surfin' Bird	-Garrett GA-200	(1964)

Jesse Lee Turner-
Singles

Little Space Girl/Shake Baby Shake	-Carlton 496	(1959)
Baby Please Don't Tease/Thinkin'	-Carlton 509	(1959)
Teen-Age Misery/That's My Girl	-Fraternity 855	(1959)
Do I Worry?(Yes, I Do)/All Right, Be That Way	-Top Rank 2064	(1960)
The Little Space Girl's Father/Valley of Lost Soldiers	-Imperial 5649	(1960)
The Elopers/Together	-Sudden 105	(1961)
All You Gotta Do/The Voice Changing Song	-GNP 184 (1962)	(1962)
Ballad of Billie Sol Estes/Shotgun Boogie	-GNP 188 (1962)	(1962)
All You Gotta Do/The Voice Changing Song	(R)-GNP/Crescendo 184 (1963)	
Ballad of Billie Sol Estes/Shotgun Boogie	(R)-GNP/Crescendo 188 (1963)	

Thomas Wayne(Thomas Wayne Perkins,brother of Luther and Carl)-
Singles

Your the One That Done It/This Time	-Fernwood 106	(1958)
This Time/You're the One That Done It	(R)-Mercury 71287	(1958)
Tragedy/Saturday Date	-Fernwood 109	(1958)
This Time/You're the One That Done It	(Rx)-Mercury 71454	(1959)
Boppin' the Blues	-Mercury N/A	(1959)
Eternally/Scandalizing My Name	-Fernwood 111	(1959)
Gonna Be Waitin'/Just Beyond	-Fernwood 113	(1959)
Guilty of Love/Poncho Villa	-Fernwood 120	(1959)
Girl Next Door/Because of You	-Fernwood 122	(1960)
No More, No More/Tragedy	(2) -Capehart 5009	(1961)
Stop the River/Eighth Wonder of the World	-Santo 9053	(1962)
I Got It Made	-Phillips Int 3577	(1962)
	-Pacer	(1965)
	-Chalet	(1969)
Tragedy	(R)-Gusto 2075	(198?)
Tragedy	(Rx)-Eric	(198?)
Tragedy	(Rx)-Orig Gold	(198?)
Tragedy	(Rx)-Oldies 45	(1964)
Tragedy	(Rx)-Collectables 3035	(198?)

Rod Willis-
Singles

Old Man Mose/Somebody's Been Rocking My Baby	-Chic 1010	(1959)

Andy Wilson-

Singles

Too Much of Not Enough	-Back Beat 518	(1958)
Teenage Martha	-Bullseye 1012	(1958)
Worry Worry	-Bullseye 1020	(1958)
Little Boy Blue	-Bullseye 1023	(1959)
Hillbilly Boogie	-Dot 1127	(1959)
Little Mama/Tonite Tonite	-Athens 700	(196?)

Donny Young (Johnny Paycheck)-

Singles

Shakin' The Blues	-Decca 31077	(1960)
The Girl They Talk About	-Decca	(1960)

The following codes and classifications are used in the discography.

CMF	Country Music Foundation
Smithsonian	Smithsonian collection of recordings
Sony	Sony Music Special Products

Most CD listings are available on tape with similar numbers
Most LP Records are no longer available

The Assorted Artists Collections

Most Are Available On Cd And Tape
(These listings are in alphabetical order due to their availability)

The All-Time Greatest Hits of Rock 'N' Roll	-Curb/CEMA 77323	(1990)
The Best of Ace Rockabilly	-Ace 45	
The Best Of Sun Rockabilly No.1	-Charly CD-16	
The Best Of Sun Rockabilly No. 2	-Charly CD-36	
Billboard Top Rock 'N' Roll Hits, 1955	-Rhino 70598	(1988)
Billboard Top Rock 'N' Roll Hits, 1956	-Rhino 70599	(1988)
Billboard Top Rock 'N' Roll Hits, 1957	-Rhino 70618	(1988)
Billboard Top Rock 'N' Roll Hits, 1958	-Rhino 70619	(1988)
Billboard Top Rock 'N' Roll Hits, 1959	-Rhino 70620	(1988)
Billboard Top Rock 'N' Roll Hits, 1960	-Rhino 70621	(1988)
Billboard Top Rock 'N' Roll Hits, 1961	-Rhino 70622	(1988)
Bo Diddley Beats	-Rhino 70291	(1992)
Class Of '55: Jerry Lee Lewis, Roy Orbison, Carl Perkins, And Johnny Cash Live	-Smash 830002	(1986)
Columbia Country Classics, Volume 1: The Golden Age	-Columbia 46029	(1991)
Country Music Classics, Volume 1 (1950's)	-K-tel 335	(1991)
The Cruisin' Years	-Increase 1000	
The Cruisin' Years: AM Radio Rock Hits, 1956-67	-Rykodisc 40032	(1986)
(Also contains commercials, jingles, and DJ patter of the time)		
Eddie Cochran & Gene Vincent: Their Finest Years (1958 & 1956)	-Capitol 12454	(1985)
Get Hot Or Go Home: Vintage RCA Rockabilly '56-'59	-CMF 014	
Jukebox Classics Vol 1	-Rhino 75893	(1987)
Jukebox Classics Vol 2	-Rhino 75894	(1987)
Legends of Rock Guitar: The '50's, Volume 1	-Rhino 70719	(1990)
Legends of Rock Guitar: The '50's, Volume 2	-Rhino 70561	(1991)
Legends of Rock Guitar: The '60's, Volume 2	-Rhino 70562	(1991)
Let's Have A Party: The Rockabilly Influence	-Capitol 12455	(1985)
Memphis Ramble: Sun Country Collection, Vol. 1	-Rhino 70963	(1990)
Memphis Rocks: Rockabilly in Memphis 1954-1068	-Smithonian 051	(1992)
Rock 'N' Roll And Rhythm Review	-Polydor 834536	(1988)
Rock & Roll: The Early Days	-RCA 5463	(1985)
Rock & Roll Show	-Deluxe CD-1019	
Rock This Town: Rockabilly Hits, Volume 1	-Rhino 70741	(1991)
Rock This Town: Rockabilly Hits, Volume 2	-Rhino 70742	(1991)
Rockabilly Classics (1956-61)..20 Recordings	-MCAD-5935	(1987)
Rockabilly Classics Vol 1	-MCA 25088	(1987)
Rockabilly Classics Vol 2	-MCA 25089	(1987)
Rockabilly Memories	-Intersound 5005	(1992)
Rockabilly Psychosis & The Garage Disease	-Big Beat WIK18	
Rockabilly Shakeout No.1	-Ace CHC-191	(1987)
Rockabilly Stars, Vol. 1	-Sony 37618	
Rockabilly Stars, Vol. 2	-Sony 37621	
Rockin' Rebels	-K-tel 3062	(1992)

Sun's Greatest Hits	(Picture Disc)	-Rhino RNDF-256	
Sun Rockabilly: The Classic Recordings		-Rounder 37	
The Sun Story 28 Recordings	(2 CD)	-Rhino 71103	(1986)
Twenty Great Rockabilly Hits Of The 50's Vl1		-Cascade Drop 1003	
Twenty Great Rockabilly Hits Of The 50's Vl2		-Cascade Drop 1009	

Bibliography

Belz, Carl. (1972). *The Story of Rock.* New York: Harper & Row

Cooper, Bettie, ed. *Retailer's Buying Guide: Fall/Winter 1993.* Baltimore: JEK Enterprises.

Docks, L. R. (1982). 1915-1965 *American Premium Record Guide: 78's, 45's & LPs.* Florence, AL: Books Americana

Gillitt, Charlie. (1983). *The Sound of the City.* New York: Pantheon Books, Random House.

Given, Dave. (1980). *The Dave Given Rock 'N' Roll Stars Handbook.* Smithtown, NY: Exposition Press.

Hudgeons, Thomas E., III, ed. (1985). *The Official Price Guide to Records.* New York: House of Collectables Division, Random House.

Malone, Bill C. (1985). *Country Music U.S.A.* (2nd ed.). Austin: University of Texas Press.

_____ and McCulloh, Judith, eds. (1975) *Stars of Country Music.* Chicago: University of Illinois Press.

Marcus, Greil. (1982). *Mystery Train: Images of America in Rock 'N' Roll Music.* New York: E. P. Dutton.

Marsh, Dave, and Swenson, John, eds. (1983) *New Rolling Stone Record Guide.* New York: Rolling Stone Press, Random House.

Mawhinneg, Paul C. (1983) *Music Master: The 45 RPM Record Directory 1947-1982.* Pittsburgh: Record - Rama Sound Archives.

Miller, Jim, ed. (1976). *The Illustrated History of Rock & Roll.* New York: Rolling Stone Press, Random House.

Nite, Norm N. (1977). *Rock On: The Illustrated Encyclopedia of Rock and Roll.* New York: Popular Library.

Osborne, Jerry. (1976). *Record Collector's 1st Edition Price Guide.* Phoenix: O'Sullivan Woodside & Co.

_____ (1982). *Record Collector's Record Albums Price Guide.* Phoenix: O'Sullivan Woodside & Co.

_____ (1984). *Country Music Reference Book and Price Guide.* Tempe, AZ: Osborne Enterprises.

_____ (1990). *The Official Price Guide to Records.* New York: House of Collectables Division, Random House.

_____ (1993). *The Official Price Guide to Records (10th ed.).* New York: House of Collectables Division, Random House.

Pareles, Jon, and Romanowski, eds. (1983). *The Rolling Stone Encyclopedia of Rock 'N' Roll.* New York: Rolling Stone Press.

Prakel, David. (1987). Rock 'n' Roll On Compact Disc. New York: Crown Publishers, Inc.

Propes, Steve. (1975). *Golden Goodies.* Radnor, PA: Chilton.

Rogers, David. (1982). *Rock 'N' Roll.* Boston: Routledge & Kegan, Paul.

Roxon, Lillian. (1969). *Rock Encyclopedia.* New York: Workman.

Stambler Irwin. (1977). *Encyclopedia of Pop, Rock and Soul* (2nd ed.). New York: St Martins Press.

_____ and Landon., Grellun. (1971). *Golden Guitars.* New York: Four Winds Press.

_____ and _____ (1983). *Encyclopedia of Folk, Country, and Western Music* (2nd ed.). New York: St. Martin's Press.

Wren, Christopher S. (1971). *Winners Got Scars, Too.* New York: The Dual Press.

Tobler, John. (1983). *The Buddy Holly Story.* New York: Plexus Publishing-Blanfor Books.

Tosches, Nick. (1985). *Country-Living Legends and Dying Metaphors in America's Biggest Music.* New York: Charles Scribner's Sons.

Schwann Spectrum -- Vol. 5 No. 1, Winter 1993/94. Santa Fe, NM: Stereophile, Inc.

Umphred, Neal. (1993). *Goldmine's Price Guide to Collectible Record Albums 1949-1989 (3rd ed.).* Iola, WI: Krause Publications.

Umphred, Neal. (1993). *Goldmine's Rock 'n' Roll 45 RPM Record Price Guide 1949-1989 (3rd ed.).* Iola, WI: Krause Publications.

Ward, Ed, and Stokes, Geoffrey, and Tucker, Ken. (1986). *Rock of Ages: The Rolling Stone History of Rock & Roll.* New York: Rolling Stone Press.

Index

"Claudette" 115
Clement, Jack 47, 109, 118, 126
Clifford, Buzz 199, 233, 234
Club Bandstand 159
Club Hollywood 196
"C'mon Everybody" 172
Cochran Brothers 172, 183
Cochran, Eddie 169, 171, 172, 173,
   176, 182-183, 209, 210
Cochran, Hank 172
Cochran, Jackie Lee 234
Cole, Nat King 40, 199
Colorado. 103
Colt, Arkansas 113
Columbia Records 2, 3, 74, 104,
   107, 169, 170, 200
Commander Cody and His Lost
   Planet Airmen 234, 235
Como, Perry 2, 110
Como, Perry Hour 107
Copper Creek 8
Coral Records 71, 72, 75, 169
Cosmopolitan Club 158
Cotton Club 117
Cotton, James 47
country and western 3, 170, 171,
   197, 205, 206, 209
country music 5, 73, 111, 178, 180,
   202, 205, 207
Country Music Association 179
Country Music Hall of Fame 16, 20
country-and-western 16, 17
County Music Hall of Fame 13
Craddoc, Gene Vincent 192
"Crazy Arms" 109
Crazy Beat Of Gene Vincent, The
   177
"Crazy Man Crazy" 43
Crazy Tennesseans 11

Creedence Clearwater Revival 235,
   236
Crest Records 172
Crickets 75, 76, 86-87, 90, 169
Crown Electric Company 48, 71, 72
"Cry, Cry, Cry!" 103
"Cryin'" 115
"Crying, Waiting, Hoping" 76
Curtis, Mac 238
Curtis, Sonny 74, 88-89
"Cut Across Shorty" 173

D

"Daddy Sang Bass" 104
"Daddy What If?" 200
Dandelion Records 177
Dandelion/Reprise Records 178
Danko, Rick 93, 95
Darin, Bobby 76, 239
Darin, Bobby, and the Rinky Dinks
   76
Daryl Records 198
David, Houston 47
Davis, Sammy, Jr. 196
Decator, Georgia 46
Decca Records 2, 3, 43, 73, 74, 75,
   76, 77, 79, 80, 107, 169, 178
Dee, Frankie 239
Dee, Jimmy 239, 240
Dee, Johnny 172, 240
DeKalb, Texas 80
Del Rio, Texas 10
Delaney and Bonnie, Bramlett 73
Delaware 107
Delta Rhythm Ramblers 101
Demon Records 198
Denson, Lee 184
"Detroit City" 200

Natchez, Louisiana 198
Naylor, Jerry 86, 89, 90
Nelson, Rick 73, 79, 96-99, 169,
     201
Nelson, Willie 17, 105
New Mexico 102, 159
"New San Antonio Rose, The" 15
New York 6, 8, 10, 72, 75, 76, 80,
     107, 110, 159, 196, 197
Newbury, Mickey 200
Newhall, California 178
Newport, Arkansas 100
"Next in Line" 103
"Next in Line" 178
"Nice and Easy" 114
Nickelsville, Virginia 8
Norfolk, Virginia 174
North Carolina 202
"Now And For Always" 202
"Now We're One" 76
NRBQ 261

O

"Oh Boy" 76
"Oh, Pretty Woman" 116
"Oh Susie Q." 201
Ohio 199
Oklahoma 113, 171
"One Minute Past Eternity"\ 112
"Only One Love" 202
"Only The Lonely" 115
"Ooby Dooby" 75, 100, 115
Orbison, Roy 46, 47, 49, 75, 100,
     113, 115, 137, 177
Owens, Buck 80
Ozzie and Harriet Show, The 79

P

Paducah, Kentucky 196
Palomino Club 73
Paramount Theater 110, 159
Parker, Colonel Tom 49
Parsons, Bill 200
"Party Doll" 75, 196
Paula Records 198
Paycheck, Johnny 73, 274
Payne, Rufus 18
Peek, Paul 261
Peer, Ralph 6, 9
"Peggy Sue" 75
"Peggy Sue Got Married" 76
Pendarvis, Tracey 137
Penner, Dick 138
Perkins, Carl 46, 47, 49, 100, 104,
     106, 107, 109, 110, 138-140,
     176, 210
Perkins, Carl, Johnny Cash, Jerry
     Lee Lewis 140
Perkins, Carl /Sonny Burgess 140
Perkins, Carl, Johnny Cash, Jerry Lee
     Lewis & Roy 140
Perkins, Luther 102
Perkins, Thomas Wayne 199, 273
Peterson, Earl 141
Petty, Norman 75, 76, 197
Petty, Norman Trio 90
Phantom, Rocker & Sllick 271
Philadelphia 198
Phillips County Ramblers 178
Phillips Records 199, 210
Phillips, Sam 45, 46, 48, 72, 100,
     103, 106, 110, 115, 117, 199
Phonogram Records 210
Pierce, Webb 19
Pink Records 204

Order Form

Send To:

> Box Car Publishing
> P O Box 53
> Worcester, Ma. 01603-0053

Here is the chance to make a hit with your friends
and loved ones, by sending them a copy of this book.

Retail		**$15.95**
Retail Canada		**$21.95**
Shipping & Handling	1	**$ 2.00**
	2+	**$ 1.00 ea addtnl**
discount on 6 or more		**10%**

Payment form   ☐Check   ☐Money Order

Massachusetts residents must ad 5% sales tax.
Canadian Residents add $1.00 each for shipping

ORDER FORM
What It Was Was Rockabilly

Name: _____

Address: _____

City: _____

State: _____ **Zip:** _____ **Tel.No.** _____

Number of Copies: _____
Cost Per Book   _____
Shipping   _____
Sales Tax: _____
Total Included: _____

We will drop ship to your list for $2.00 ea for freight.